STECK-VAUGHN

Achieve It!®

Reading and Language Arts

Teacher's Edition

Harcourt Achieve

Rigby • Saxon • Steck-Vaughn

www.HarcourtAchieve.com

1.800.531.5015

Photography Acknowledgments:

P.iv ©Gabe Palmer/CORBIS

Additional photography by Comstock Royalty Free.

ISBN 0-7398-8409-3

Printed in China.

2 3 4 5 6 7 8 9 985 07 06 05

Contents

Blackline Masters

Welcome to

STECK-VAUGHN
Achieve It!

Targeted Instruction for Test Success

Achievement on high-stakes tests is something you and your students can anticipate with *Achieve It!*

The easy-to-use and flexible program ensures that every learner receives exactly the instruction and practice needed to learn key skills and to perform well on standardized tests. This research-based program provides differentiated instruction, helping each student maximize his or her growth potential.

easy-to-use

- Has everything you and your students need for test success

- Provides a clear path for differentiated instruction to meet the needs of every student

- Includes easy-to-follow lesson plans that allow ongoing assessment to drive instruction

flexible

- Offers both group and individual activities
- Presents curriculum and assessment standards for easy decision-making
- Adapts to a full year, short-term, after-school, or summer school schedule

Achieve It! will help your students perform well by offering

- a complete system that will save you and your students time
- standards-based instruction and ongoing assessment
- learning logs to encourage student self-monitoring and reflection

differentiated instruction

- Diagnoses test readiness and prescribes individual practice
- Accommodates different kinds of learners: tactile, visual, auditory, kinesthetic, and ELL
- Targets specific skills
- Emphasizes specific strategies to solve problems

Research Base

Differentiated Instruction

Achieve It! supports teaching and learning through different modalities.

"Best practice means that teachers need to acknowledge learner needs and interests and take advantage of them."

D.L. Spiegel

Instruction and Assessment

Achieve It! supports diagnostic and prescriptive instruction.

"In a differentiated classroom, assessment is ongoing and diagnostic. Its goal is to provide teachers day-to-day data on students' readiness for particular ideas and skills, their interests, and their learning profiles."

C.A. Tomlinson

Prior Knowledge

Achieve It! lessons build on background knowledge and personal experience.

"Thoughtful readers use existing knowledge to make sense of text. While reading, thoughtful readers use prior knowledge constantly to evaluate the adequacy of the model of reading they have developed. This is true for readers of all ages or levels of sophistication."

P. D. Pearson, L. R. Roehler, J. A. Dole, and G. G. Duffy

English Language Learners

Achieve It! provides intervention support for English language learners.

"In examining the ways schools work to meet the needs of children who are learning English as a second language, it is vital to keep in mind that such programs need to help childern become competent users of English, but more importantly, become successful learners."

G.E. Garcia

Research-Based Strategies

Achieve It! uses guided instruction and the QAR reading strategy.

"...children can be taught about the existence and use of reading strategies through informed, direct instructions in their regular classrooms."

S. G. Paris, D. R. Cross, and M. Y. Lipson

Program Features

1 Diagnose

Use the pretest to determine whole class and individual needs.

2 Instruct

Teach critical content skills and appropriate test-taking strategies.

3 Prescribe

Prescribe additional practice plans based upon ongoing assessment.

6 Achieve

Use the post test to document progress.

5 Reteach

Reteach those skills still needing remediation.

4 Develop

Develop self-monitoring skills, motivation, and reflection through personalized learning logs.

Program Options

Option 1
Full Year
30 minute lessons

Help students

- develop skills incrementally
- master specific skills
- focus attention on their individual needs
- apply their learning preferences
- gain confidence in their knowledge and abilities

Option 2
Short Term
1 hour lessons

Help students

- review important skills across all of the assessment strands
- overcome specific skill deficiencies
- become familiar with assessment question formats
- apply problem-solving strategies for success
- acquire test-taking confidence
- be better prepared

Option 3

Extended Day

30 minute lessons

Help students

- review what they learn in class
- master fundamental skills
- improve their ability to solve problems
- work at their own pace
- communicate with others to solve problems
- gain greater confidence in the regular classroom

Option 4

Summer School

1$\frac{1}{2}$ hour lessons

Help students

- maintain their skills
- extend their learning
- eliminate skill deficiencies
- accelerate their understanding
- prepare for a new, successful year

Program at a Glance

Achieve It! makes it easy to access the specific content and skills to match your students' needs.

Teacher's Edition

Direct instruction makes it easy for you to guide your students toward test success. The lessons contain

- clear objectives
- step-by-step instructional guidance
- definitions for critical vocabulary
- questions and statements for focused instruction
- activity suggestions for meeting students' individual needs
- annotated reduced student pages for easy reference and scoring
- correlations to standards

Student Edition

Each *Student Edition* contains

- *Practice Tests* that allow you to determine students' skill level and document their growth
- easy-to-follow lessons with a focus on critical skill development
- step-by-step guided instruction, allowing both independent and interactive learning
- specific test-taking strategies to enhance test success
- end-of-unit skills checks to monitor personal progress
- skill-specific links to extra practice for skill mastery

Teacher Answers for Practice Cards

Contains
- easily-accessed answers
- simple explanations for you to share with students
- all of the answers you need to help your students

Practice Cards Answer Book

Contains
- easy-to-understand answers
- instant performance feedback
- the key to independence

Learning Log

Unique to *Achieve It!*

Students can
- make learning personal
- track their *Practice Card* assignments
- reflect upon what they already know and what they learned
- set personal learning goals
- pick up *Tips* for greater test success

Practice Cards

Students can
- focus on critical skills
- work independently
- sharpen skills and overcome deficiencies
- build on existing skills
- receive instant feedback
- accelerate their learning

Student Edition

Whether working independently or as part of a class, your students will find the *Student Edition* to be their key to test success. Each unit in the *Student Edition* is built to keep the learning process accessible, allowing students to master critical skills quickly and confidently.

The *Student Edition* is organized in a progression of instructional units that focus on critical skill strands. Each unit has:

An engaging *Unit Opener* that links learning to the real world

Step-by-step Lessons that guide students toward incremental skill development

Valuable test-taking *Tips*

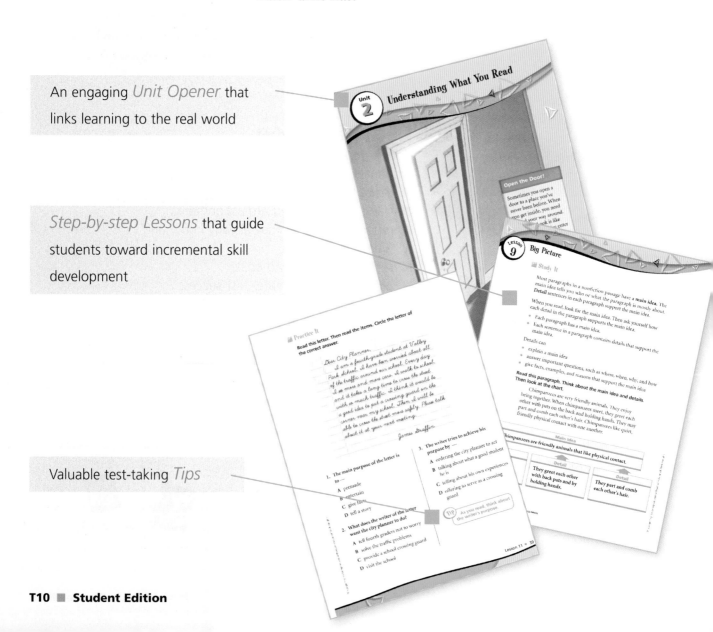

An end-of-unit *Test-Taking Strategy* that students can apply in a variety of test-taking situations to answer test items successfully

Put It to the Test, a unit skills check in a simulated test format that assesses students' mastery of specific skills

Unit 2
Test-Taking Strategy

Strategy: Find the Main Idea
In this unit you learned that paragraphs and passages have a main idea that is supported by detail sentences. The main idea is what the paragraph is mostly about. Sometimes it is not stated directly. Use this strategy to help you find the main idea of a paragraph.

• Read the entire paragraph. Ask yourself, *Who or what is this paragraph mostly about?* Circle any sentences that answer this question.
• Then look for details that support the main idea. Remember to ask when, where, how, and why to find the details. Underline sentences that answer these questions.

Try It Out
Read this passage. Then read the question. Circle the letter of the correct answer.

Earth has seasons because it is tilted. In July the Northern Hemisphere is tilted toward the sun. That makes it summer in the United States. Six months later Earth has circled half way around the sun. The Northern Hemisphere then tilts away from the sun. That makes it winter in the United States.

What is the main idea of this passage?

A Earth has seasons because it is tilted.

B Winter is cold in the United States.

C Summer is hot in the United States.

D The United States is in the Northern Hemisphere.

The main idea is stated in the first sentence. The rest of the paragraph gives you details about how seasons happen. **A** is the correct answer.

44 • Unit 2

Unit 3 • Putting Ideas Together   Name _____
Put It to the Test

This test will check what you have learned in this unit.
DIRECTIONS: Read these passages. Then read the items. Circle the letters of the correct answers.

Flags
Flags have been used since ancient times. Flags are usually made of cloth. They are usually rectangles. Flags are most often used to identify a country or a group. For example, flags can be used in a parade to name the group marching behind the flag. Flags are also used as signals. In car races, flags tell drivers when to go fast or slow. At sea, flags are used to send messages from one ship to another. Sometimes flags are given as rewards for good work. Flags are often put on poles so that people can see them easily.

Jason's Project
Jason was working at the table. He was drawing on a piece of paper.
"That looks nice. What is it?" his father asked.
"My friends and I are going to ride our bikes in the parade. I'm making a flag for us. It's fun to make things."
"How will you carry the flag?"
"I have a pole for it. Can you help me put the _____
done drawing this?" said Jason.
"Sure, and I can't wait to se_____

1. Why would flags usually be made _____
the same way?

A Flag makers are lazy.

B There are not enough flag makers
to make different flags.

C It makes flags easy to use in many
different places.

D It is the law.

3. Flags are used in races—

A to add color

B to show history

C for safety

D as prizes for winners

4. Why would flags be used to send
messages at sea?

A Ships do not have telephones.

B There is no mail service.

C Ships do not have computers.

D They can be seen easily across
distances.

5. What inference can you make
about Jason?

A He has a new bike.

B He likes art projects.

C He is worried about the parade.

D He needs to plan his flag better.

6. Which detail supports the conclusion
that Jason's father is helpful?

A He wants to see the parade.

B He likes Jason's work.

C He will help Jason put the flag on
the bike.

D He asks many questions.

7. Jason and his friends are using
the flag—

A to identify their group

B to win a prize

C to show that they can go fast

D to send a message to another group

8. How is Jason's flag different from
most of the flags mentioned in the
first passage?

A It will be in a parade.

B It is being made at home.

C It will be on a pole.

D It is made out of paper.

9. How is the passage on Jason's project
different from the passage on flags?

A It tells how to make a flag.

B It tells how flags are used to
identify groups.

C It explains that flags are
usually carried.

D It tells about two characters,
Jason and his father.

GO ON →

Achieve It! Practice Cards

70 • Unit 3

Unit Opener

With its large, attractive photograph, the Unit Opener introduces each unit, sparking student interest and conversation.

The *Achieve It!* Unit Opener

- provides a visual link between learning and the real world

- ignites individual imagination

- promotes independent analysis and questioning

- prompts class discussion

- gives a purpose for learning

Unit **2** Understanding What You Read

Open the Door!

Sometimes you open a door to a place you've never been before. When you get inside, you need to find your way around. Opening a book is like opening a door. You enter a place where you can learn something new or find something to enjoy. First, you need to be sure you can "find your way around" as you read.

In this unit you will learn skills to help you find your way around, or understand, what you read.

17

Lessons are easy-to-follow and concise. Their consistent
format helps students work comfortably and confidently.

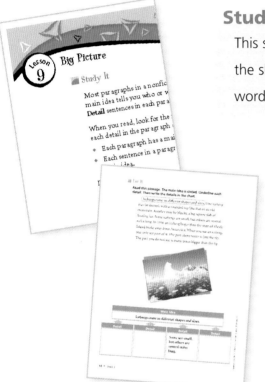

Study It

This section presents an important concept or skill. It breaks
the skill into clear, easy-to-follow steps. Important vocabulary
words are highlighted and defined in context.

Use It

This section offers models to help students
apply the skill they're mastering. Processes are
guided step-by-step to ensure success.

Practice It

This section provides students with immediate practice of
what they've learned. As students gain confidence, their
test-taking anxiety decreases.

Tip

Tips are helpful hints, shortcuts, or reminders
that can help boost students' test-taking skills.

Test-Taking Strategy

Students who are familiar with test-taking strategies approach tests with greater confidence. *Achieve It!* introduces students to useful strategies that help prepare them for the challenging testing situations they face throughout the year.

Each *Test-Taking Strategy* in *Achieve It!* identifies an important test-taking strategy.

Students are guided through the process, helping them understand how the strategy works.

Students are asked to *Try It Out* by applying the strategy to an actual test item.

Explanations let students know how successfully they have applied the strategy to the question.

Unit 2
Test-Taking Strategy

Strategy: Find the Main Idea

In this unit you learned that paragraphs and passages have a main idea that is supported by detail sentences. The main idea is what the paragraph is mostly about. Sometimes it is not stated directly. Use this strategy to help you find the main idea of a paragraph.

* Read the entire paragraph. Ask yourself, *Who or what is this paragraph mostly about?* Circle any sentences that answer this question.
* Then look for details that support the main idea. Remember to ask when, where, how, and why to find the details. Underline sentences that answer these questions.

Try It Out

Read this passage. Then read the question. Circle the letter of the correct answer.

> Earth has seasons because it is tilted. In July the Northern Hemisphere is tilted toward the sun. That makes it summer in the United States. Six months later Earth has circled half way around the sun. The Northern Hemisphere then tilts away from the sun. That makes it winter in the United States.

What is the main idea of this passage?

A   Earth has seasons because it is tilted.

B   Winter is cold in the United States.

C   Summer is hot in the United States.

D   The United States is in the Northern Hemisphere.

The main idea is stated in the first sentence. The rest of the paragraph gives you details about how seasons happen. **A** is the correct answer.

44 ● Unit 2

Put It to the Test

At the conclusion of each unit, students answer questions
that are carefully constructed to test what students know, and
to determine which skills require additional practice.

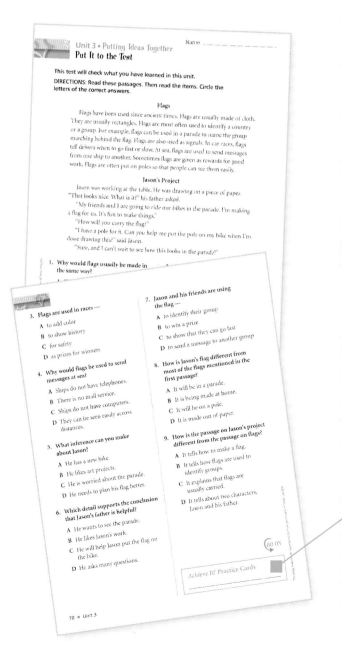

Each question in *Put It to the Test* is tied
directly to a skill covered in its unit.
Consequently, when students answer an item
correctly, both you and they can be assured
that they have mastered that skill.

An incorrect answer lets you and your students
know which skills require more practice. And
that practice is available in the *Achieve It!
Practice Cards*.

Connect the Test to the Cards

Beneath each *Put It to the Test* page in the
Teacher's Edition is *Connect the Test to the
Cards*, an easy-to-read chart identifying the
correct answer to each test item and a
complete list of related *Practice Cards*.

Use the chart to determine the cards each
student should complete for further skill
practice. Then write the cards you wish to
assign on the student's test.

Learning Log

Individual *Learning Logs* help students
- evaluate their learning
- reflect upon their performance
- keep track of their progress
- set future goals

Research shows that students who are challenged to think about and summarize their learning substantially improve their learning (Schorow, 1990). Having students note and analyze important personal achievements helps motivate them to take responsibility for their own progress as learners. It also helps bring closure to lessons and "lock in" learning.

Using their *Learning Logs,* students can

- make notes, draw sketches, and paste clippings from newspapers or magazines to personalize their learning

- keep track of their *Practice Card* assignments and scores in a *Log It In* chart

- track their progress, set goals, and reflect upon their learning

- read *Tips* that remind them of valuable skills or strategies they can use to improve their performance on high-stakes assessments

Practice Cards

Skill-specific *Practice Cards* are unique tools that prepare students for high-stakes tests. These cards deliver targeted instruction that matches the needs of individual students and propels them toward greater test success.

Each *Achieve It!* kit includes 200 practice cards designed to meet your students' diverse needs. Students use only the specific cards they need to master critical skills.

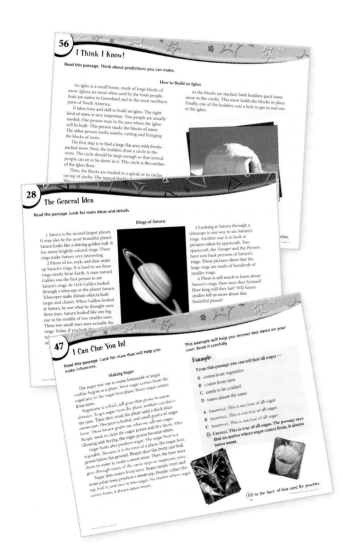

Achieve It! Practice Cards make it possible for you to

prescribe specific instruction for individual students based on their performance on each unit's *Put It to the Test*

create flexible learning environments, where students can work independently, in small groups, or as a class

be sure students are getting the practice they need to master skills necessary for success on standardized tests

Practice Cards in Focus

Practice Cards help students focus on the skills they need—one skill at a time. This allows targeted practice that leads toward overall skill mastery.

Every *Practice Card* begins with an example, containing a sample item and complete explanation for the item's correct solution. This all-in-one instructional element allows students to work entirely independently.

Although *Practice Cards* are designed to help your students master important skills, you can also assign cards to help students

■ maintain and build skill competence

■ review skills fundamental to new skill development

■ boost their test-taking confidence

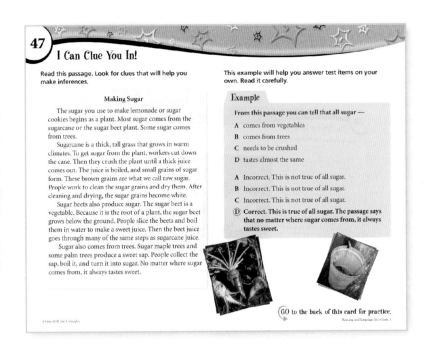

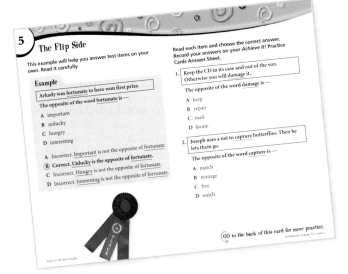

Additional Practice Cards

Not all of the *Practice Cards* have a direct link to lessons within the Student Edition. These cards are intended as bonus cards that can help students

- extend or accelerate their learning
- apply strategies they learn in *Achieve It!* to answer questions they may find on standardized tests
- gain more test-taking experience and competence

Practice Cards Answer Book

Answer keys are provided for students to check their work and foster independence. *Practice Cards Answer Book* make it easy for individual students to take responsibility for their learning and monitor their own progress.

Teacher Answers for Practice Cards

*Teacher Answers for Practice Cards takes the time and worry out of reteaching. Complete explanations for each answer make it easy for you to resolve difficulties individual students may have with any skill.

Teacher's Edition

Here is your tool for delivering efficient and effective instruction. Everything your students need to improve their performance on standardized tests is contained in one easy-to-use guide.

A complete list of *Skills* lets you know at a glance which standards-based skills your students will learn, practice, and master in each unit.

Everything you need to teach is in your hands, but if you think your students would benefit from additional instruction, we've suggested a list of common, easy-to-find *Materials* to accompany our suggestions for *Differentiated Instruction*.

Motivate your students to put their skills to work by *Introducing the Unit*. Each unit opener ties student learning to real-world circumstances, and spurs thinking from the start.

Achieve It! is founded upon solid research principles. Examples are cited at point of use so that you can put research into practical classroom action.

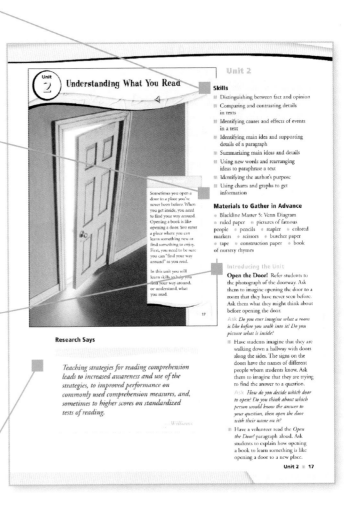

Each Lesson opens with a clearly stated *Lesson Objective.* To be sure your students are familiar with important *Words to Know*, many lessons include concise, student-friendly definitions.

Each lesson is supported by a *Curriculum and Assessment Standard.*

Suggestions for *Differentiated Instruction* offer the different kinds of learners in your classroom—visual, auditory, kinesthetic, tactile, and ELL—an opportunity to master skills in the way they learn best.

Guided strategy instruction makes it easy for you to give your students the edge they need to improve their test-taking skills.

The *Connect the Test to the Practice Cards* chart makes it easy for you to assign specific *Practice Cards*, giving you the ability to individualize instruction for your students.

Reading Strategies

Empower your students by teaching them reading strategies that work. The strategies outlined in *Achieve It! Reading and Language Arts* follow the QAR (Question-Answer Relationships) method developed by well-known educators Dr. Taffy Raphael and Dr. Kathryn Au. Their research proves that once students understand the two main ways to approach reading and language arts questions— "in the book" or "in my head"—they not only improve their reading comprehension skills, they perform better on tests.

QAR Strategies

The Different Kinds of Question-Answer Relationships

"In the Book"

"In my head"

Right There
Student can point to the answer in the text.

On My Own
Student has the whole answer in his or her head.

Think and Search
Student can find the answer in many places throughout the text.

Author and Me
Student can connect what he or she already knows with what the author says.

QAR strengthens students reading comprehension.

- The *Right There* strategy helps students with literal comprehension questions.
- The *Think and Search* strategy helps students synthesize information from several parts of a text to answer higher-level comprehension questions such as making inferences.
- The *On My Own* strategy helps students with personal response questions , such as "What would you do if you were lost in the woods like the character in the story?"
- The *Author and Me* strategy helps students combine prior knowledge with information in a text to answer higher level comprehension questions such as drawing conclusions.

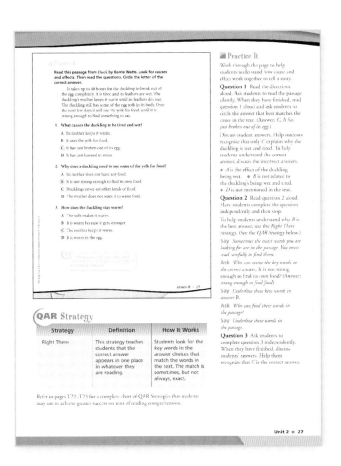

QAR Strategies on *Practice It!* pages help you guide students to use the right strategy for the skill.

Classroom Management

Blackline Masters

Monitor Student Progress

Distribute the *Achieve It! Practice Test Answer Sheet* for your students to record their answers to *Practice Test* items. Then record your students' scores on the *Achieve It! Class Progress Sheet*. Keep the master as a snapshot of your students' learning by noting each student's pre- and post-test performance.

Provide Individual Instruction

Use the *Achieve It! Practice Cards Student Record* to maintain an individualized instructional plan for each of your students. Record a student's *Put It to the Test* scores, assign specific *Practice Cards* the student needs to achieve skill mastery, and then note when the student achieves the goals you set.

Save Time

Encourage student independence by keeping a supply of the *Achieve It! Practice Card Answer Sheet* on hand for your students to use whenever they're engaged in skills practice.

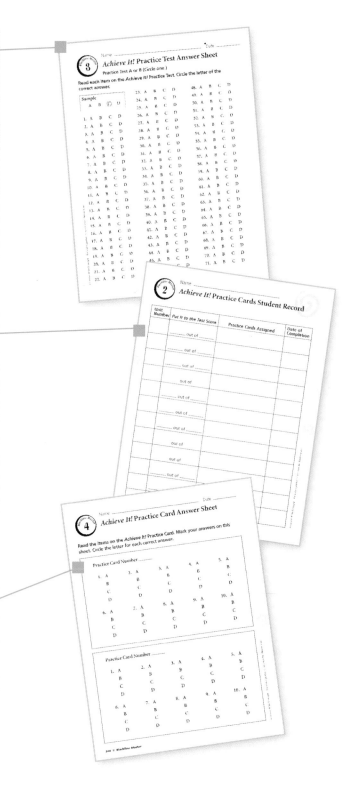

Achieve It! offers *Differentiated Instruction* activities in every unit, helping you help your students learn in the way they learn best. Activities offer easy-to-follow suggestions for effective ways to engage English language learners, as well as students who learn best when they see, hear, touch, or move.

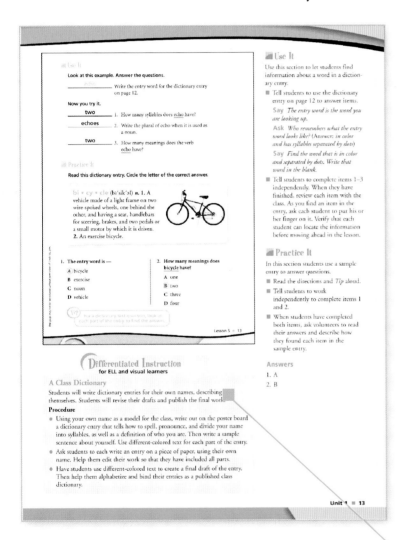

Tailor your instructional program to meet the needs of the diverse students in your classroom by offering *Differentiated Instruction*.

Assessment Tools

Whether it is diagnostic, prescriptive, evaluative, formal, or informal, assessment is an important part of every instructional program.

Collectively, daily observations, anecdotal records, and students' performance results help describe your students' skill deficiencies, skill readiness, and skill mastery. *Achieve It!* includes the following assessment tools to help you collect the information you need to propel your students toward test success.

Pretest: *Practice Test A*

Use *Practice Test A* to assess each student's skill performance, identify skill deficiencies, and prescribe instruction. Used as a diagnostic tool, *Practice Test A* establishes a baseline from which to measure student progress.

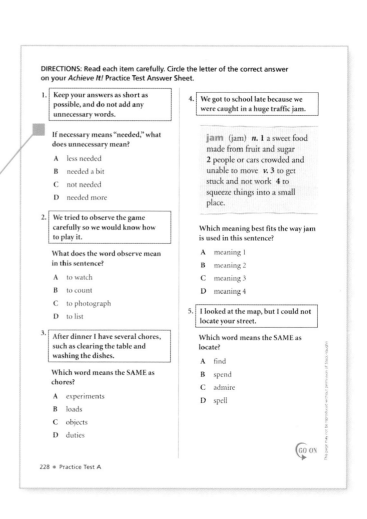

DIRECTIONS: Read each item carefully. Circle the letter of the correct answer on your *Achieve It!* Practice Test Answer Sheet.

1. Keep your answers as short as possible, and do not add any unnecessary words.

   If necessary means "needed," what does unnecessary mean?

   A   less needed

   B   needed a bit

   C   not needed

   D   needed more

2. We tried to observe the game carefully so we would know how to play it.

   What does the word observe mean in this sentence?

   A   to watch

   B   to count

   C   to photograph

   D   to list

3. After dinner I have several chores, such as clearing the table and washing the dishes.

   Which word means the SAME as chores?

   A   experiments

   B   loads

   C   objects

   D   duties

4. We got to school late because we were caught in a huge traffic jam.

   jam (jam) *n.* **1** a sweet food made from fruit and sugar **2** people or cars crowded and unable to move *v.* **3** to get stuck and not work **4** to squeeze things into a small place.

   Which meaning best fits the way jam is used in this sentence?

   A   meaning 1

   B   meaning 2

   C   meaning 3

   D   meaning 4

5. I looked at the map, but I could not locate your street.

   Which word means the SAME as locate?

   A   find

   B   spend

   C   admire

   D   spell

   GO ON

228 ● Practice Test A

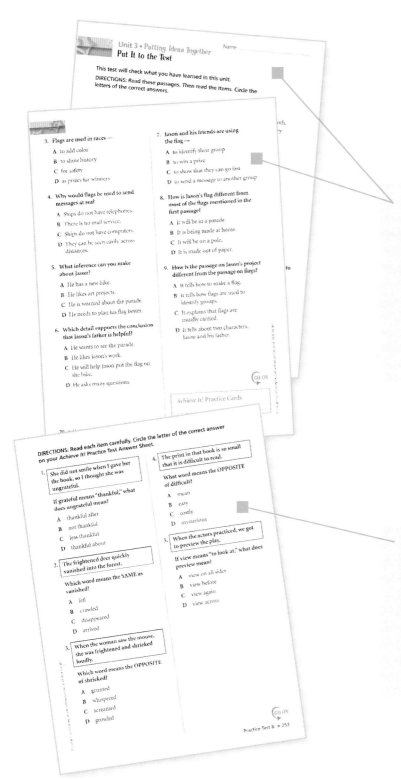

Progress Monitoring: *Put It to the Test*

At the end of each unit in the *Student Edition*, students are asked to *Put It to the Test*. The results of these regular skills checks serve as snapshots of each students' progress. Use these snapshots to adjust instruction to meet the needs of individual learners.

Post Test: *Practice Test B*

Assign *Practice Test B* at the conclusion of *Achieve It!* Then compare performance results to the baseline scores established by *Practice Test A* to document student progress and to determine new instructional goals for each student.

Scope and Sequence

Content Area	Specific Skill	Grade 3	Grade 4	Grade 5
Vocabulary	• Synonyms	■		
	• Antonyms	■		
	• Base words		■	■
	• Greek and Latin roots			■
	• Multi-meaning words	■	■	■
	• Prefixes		■	■
	• Suffixes		■	■
	• Context clues	■	■	■
	• Dictionary	■	■	
	• Thesaurus		■	
Comprehension Skills	• Fact and opinion	■	■	■
	• Comparison and contrast		■	
	• Cause and effect	■	■	■
	• Main idea and supporting details	■	■	■
	• Order of events	■		
	• Summarize		■	■
	• Paraphrase	■	■	■
	• Interpret graphics	■	■	■
	Charts	■	■	■
	Maps	■	■	■
	Diagrams	■	■	■
	Pictures	■	■	■
	Graphs	■	■	■
	Time lines			■
	• Author's purpose	■	■	■
	• Audience	■	■	■
	• Inferences	■	■	■
	• Conclusions	■	■	■
	• Generalizations			■
	• Predictions	■	■	
	• Support from text	■	■	■
	• Connections (paired passages)		■	■
Text Structure	• Sequence and Chronology		■	■
	• Text organization			■
	• Table of contents	■	■	■
	• Title page	■	■	
	• Index		■	■
	• Headings	■	■	■
	• Typeface	■	■	■

Content Area	Specific Skill	Grade 3	Grade 4	Grade 5
Types of Texts	• Fiction	■	■	■
	• Nonfiction	■	■	■
	• Biographies	■	■	■
	• Autobiographies	■	■	■
	• Informational texts	■	■	■
	• Fantasy	■	■	
	• Fables		■	
	• Fairy tales		■	
	• Myths	■	■	
	• Legends	■	■	
	• Narratives			■
	• Historical fiction	■		■
	• Plays	■	■	■
	• Poetry	■	■	■
Literary Analysis	• Character	■	■	■
	• Narrator	■	■	■
	• Plot	■	■	■
	• Theme	■	■	■
	• Setting	■	■	■
	• Mood	■	■	■
	• Figurative language		■	■
	Simile		■	■
	Metaphor		■	■
	Personification		■	■
	Hyperbole		■	■
	• Poetic language		■	■
	Sensory words		■	■
	Rhyme		■	■
	Rhythm	■	■	■
	Alliteration		■	■
	Assonance		■	■
	Imagery			■
	Meter			■
	Free verse			■
	Symbols			■
	• Cultural characteristics		■	
	• Historical attitudes and values		■	
	• Literary terms			■
	• Support from text			■

Scope and Sequence

Content Area	Specific Skill	Grade 3	Grade 4	Grade 5
Research and Information	• Plan a research report	■	■	■
	• Narrow a topic	■	■	■
	• Encyclopedia	■	■	
	• Atlas and maps	■		
	• Identify and locate sources		■	■
	• Dictionary	■		
	• Thesaurus	■		■
	• Take notes	■	■	■
	• Summarize		■	■
	• Paraphrase			■
	• Outline		■	■
	• Bibliography		■	■
	• Synthesize information from sources			■
Writing Skills	• Audience	■	■	■
	• Purpose	■	■	■
	• Introduction (beginning)	■	■	
	• Body (middle)	■	■	
	• Conclusion (end)	■	■	
	• Main idea and supporting details	■	■	■
	• Topic sentence	■	■	■
	• Coherence	■	■	■
	• Point of view			■
	• Voice			■
	• Tone			■
	• Word choice	■		
	• Sentence variety			■
	• Literary devices			■
Kinds of Writing	• Narrative writing	■	■	■
	• Personal narrative		■	■
	• Point of view			■
	• Descriptive writing	■		
	• Expository writing	■	■	■
	Directions	■	■	
	Explanations			■
	Compare and contrast	■	■	■
	• Formal letters	■		
	• Informal letters	■		
	• Response to literature		■	■
	• Poems			■
	• Persuasive writing		■	■

Content Area	Specific Skill	Grade 3	Grade 4	Grade 5
Language Conventions	• Parts of speech	■	■	■
	Nouns	■	■	■
	Pronouns	■	■	■
	Verbs	■	■	■
	Regular and irregular verbs		■	
	Linking verbs			■
	Verb tense	■	■	■
	Adjectives	■	■	■
	Comparative and superlative			■
	Adverbs	■	■	■
	Conjunctions	■		■
	Prepositions		■	■
	Interjections			■
	• Subject-verb agreement	■	■	■
	• Simple sentences		■	■
	• Compound sentences		■	■
	• Complex sentences		■	■
	• Independent clauses		■	■
	• Dependent clauses		■	■
	• Sentence fragments			■
	• Commas	■	■	■
	• Apostrophes	■	■	■
	• Quotation marks	■	■	■
	• Colons			■
	• Capitalization	■	■	■
Spelling	• Similar sounds	■		
	• Final *e*	■	■	
	• Doubling final consonant	■	■	■
	• Plurals	■	■	■
	• Changing *y* to *i*	■	■	■
	• *i* before *e*	■		
	• Contractions	■		
	• Adding prefixes and suffixes			■
	• Homographs	■		
	• Homophones	■		
	• High-frequency words		■	■
	• Syllabic rules		■	

Skills and Practice Tests Correlation

Vocabulary

Skill	Practice Test A Item	Practice Test B Item
Vocabulary		
Structural analysis	1, 9	1,5
Synonyms/antonyms	3, 5 ,7	2, 3, 4
Multi-meaning words	4, 6	6, 10
Context clues	2, 8, 10	7, 8, 9

Comprehension

Skill	Practice Test A Item	Practice Test B Item
Understanding What You Read		
Fact and opinion	30, 49	34, 50
Compare and contrast	12, 26, 35	17, 46, 53
Sequence	13, 27, 32	14, 23, 45
Cause and effect	19, 33, 41	11, 16, 27
Main idea and supporting details	39, 44, 50	36, 41, 49
Paraphrase and summary	34, 51	37, 47
Author's purpose/point of view	28, 40, 53	20, 24, 52
Graphics	36, 37	32, 33
Putting Ideas Together		
Inferences	15, 24, 42	13, 26, 43
Conclusions	23	51
Support from text	31, 43, 138	12, 28, 35
Connections (paired passages)	54, 55	54, 55
Understanding Parts of a Story		
Character	11, 25, 48	15, 19, 38
Plot	14, 21, 22, 47	21, 22, 25, 42
Theme	16, 46	39, 40
Setting	17, 29, 45	18, 29, 44
Figurative/poetic language	18, 20	30, 31
Cultural values and historical attitudes	52	48

Language

Skill	Practice Test A Item	Practice Test B Item
Writing Skills		
Audience and purpose	58, 72	60, 65
Introduction, body, and conclusion	65	59
Main idea and supporting details	56, 64	66, 68
Coherence	57	57
Language Rules		
Subject-verb agreement	69, 71	62, 63
Parts of speech	61, 68	61, 70
Punctuation	59, 67	64, 71
Capitalization	62, 70	56, 67
Spelling		
Structural analysis	63, 66	58, 72
High frequency words	60	69

Bibliography

Resources Cited in Support of Achieve It!

Armbruster, B., Leht, R. & Osborn, J. (2001). *Put Reading First: The Research Building Blocks for Teaching Children to Read.* Washington: National Institute for Literacy/U.S. Department of Education.

Dahl, K. L., & Farnan, N. (1998). *Children's Writing: Perspectives from Research.* Newark, DE: International Reading Association.

Devine, T. G. (1991). Studying: Skills, strategies, and systems. In J. Flood, J.M. Jensen, D. Lapp, & J.R. Squire (Eds.) *Handbook of Research on Teaching the English Language Arts* (pp. 743-753). New York: Macmillan Publishing Company.

Duke, N. K., & Pearson, P. D. (2002). Effective practices for developing reading comprehension. In. A. E. Farstrup & S. J. Samuels (Eds.). *What Research Has to Say About Reading Instruction* (pp. 205-243.) Newark: DE: International Reading Association.

Garcia, G. E. (2003). Comprehension development and instruction of English-language learners. In A. P. Sweet, & C.E. Snow (Eds.). *Rethinking Reading Comprehension* (pp. 30-50). New York: The Guilford Press.

Moss, B. (2003). *Exploring the Literature of Fact: Children's Nonfiction Trade books in the Elementary Classroom.* New York: The Guilford Press.

National Institute of Child Health and Human Development. (2000). Report of the National Reading Panel. *Teaching Children to Read: An Evidence-Based Assessment of the Scientific Research Literature on Reading and Its Implications for Reading Instruction* (NIH Publication No. 00-4769). Washington, DC: U.S. Government Printing Office.

Noyce, R. M. & Christie, J. F. (1983). Effects of an integrated approach to grammar instruction on third graders' reading and writing. Cited in G.E Tompkins,.(1995), *Language Arts: Content and Teaching Strategies* . (p. 513). Upper Saddle River, NJ: Merrill, an imprint of Prentice Hall

Paris, S. G., Cross, D. R., & Lipson, M. Y. (1984). Informed strategies for learning: A program to improve children's reading awareness and comprehension. *Journal of Educational Psychology,* 76, (6), 1239–1252.

Pearson, P. D., Roehler, L. R., Dole, J. A., & Duffy, G. G.(1992). Developing expertise in reading comprehension. In S. J. Samuels, & A.E. Farstrup (Eds.). *What Research Has to Say About Reading Instruction* (pp. 145-199). Newark, DE: International Reading Association.

Pressley, Michael (2000). Comprehension Instruction. In M.L Kamil., P.B Mosenthal,. P.D. Pearson, & R. Barr (Eds.). *Handbook of Reading Research, Volume III.* Mahwah , N.J.: Eribaum.

Spiegel, D. L. (1999). Meeting each child's literacy needs. In L. B. Gambrell, L. M. Morrow, S. B. Neuman, & M. Pressley. *Best Practices in Literacy Instruction* (pp. 245-257). New York: The Guilford Press.

Templeton, S. (1991). *Teaching the Integrated Language Arts.* Boston: Houghton Mifflin Company.

Tomlinson, C.A. (1999). *The Differentiated Classroom: Responding to the Needs of All Learners.* Alexandria, VA: Association for Supervision and Curriculum Development.

Williams, J. P. (2002). Reading comprehension strategies and teacher preparation. In A. E. Farstrup, & S. J. Samuels (Eds.). *What Research Has to Say About Reading Instruction* (pp. 243-260). Newark, DE: International Reading Association.

Unit 1 Vocabulary

Language Stew

English is like language stew. English has words, spellings, and sounds from many different languages.

In this unit you will learn more about the words of the English language and how to recognize what they mean.

Research Says

Students learn vocabulary directly when they are explicitly taught both individual words and word-learning strategies.

—*Armburster, Lehr, and Osborn*

Skills

- Using base words to determine the meanings of words
- Identifying word parts, such as prefix, suffix, and base word
- Using context clues to find word meanings
- Learning new words with multiple meanings and distinguishing between definitions and uses
- Using a dictionary or thesaurus entry to find information about a word

Materials to Gather in Advance

- green and brown construction paper
- scissors • tape or glue stick • blank index cards • crayons, markers, or colored pencils • paper • poster board

Introducing the Unit

Language Stew Refer students to the photograph of the stew. Ask students to think about a stew and how it has many different items cooked together. Explain that the different food items, no matter how small, work together to make a special food. Invite students to think about how the different parts of a word might mix together like a stew. Each part of a word, no matter how small, works together with the main part of a word to make a new meaning.

Ask *What do you do when you see an unfamiliar word? Do you try to find out what it means?*

Say *In the lessons in this unit, you will see that words do not always have just one meaning. Sometimes words are made up of several smaller meanings.*

Read the *Language Stew* paragraph aloud. Tell students that in this unit they will learn to recognize the different parts of a word, which will help them understand and use new and different words.

Lesson 1

Objective

Students will use base words to understand the meanings of other words.

Words to Know

Base—the main part of a word without prefixes or suffixes

◢ Study It

Review the concept of *base* words with students, and have them look at the examples in the chart.

Ask *What do you do when you read a word that you do not know? Do you ever try to guess its meaning by thinking of another word it looks like?*

Say *Good readers guess what a word means by thinking about other words it looks like.*

■ Write the word *believable* on the board.

Ask *Do you know what this word means? What base word is in this word?* (Answer: *believe*) Underline the word *believe.*

Say *If you do not know what the word* believable *means, you can see that it is has the word* believe *as a base word. You can use the base word to figure out the meaning.*

■ Explain to students that knowing what the base word means will help them understand what the whole word means.

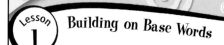
Building on Base Words

▨ Study It

How do words become part of our language? English words come from many languages. New words are added to name new things or new ideas. The word Internet, for example, has been a part of our language for only a short time. Sometimes English words are built from words we already have.

Look at these words.

Base Word	Word That Comes from the Base
electric	electricity
real	realistic

How can knowing a word's **base,** or origin, help you understand the word's meaning?

- You can use the base to help determine a word's meaning.
- You can recognize words that have similar base words.
- Knowing the base can help you remember a word's meaning.

Look at the second column in the chart. If you do not know what the word electricity means, you can see that it is similar to the word electric, a word that you do know. Can you think of other words that come from the base word electric?

Look at the last word in the first column. You may know that one meaning of the word real is "occurring in fact or something that is true." Realistic may be an unfamiliar word, but it has the same base as real, so you may reason that the meaning of realistic is "something that has the qualities of being true." Knowing the base word can give you an important clue to a word's meaning.

Curriculum and Assessment Standard

Word origins

Use It

The following words come from base words. Write the base word for the underlined word in the blank.

roll — 1. We rode the <u>roller</u> coaster.

phone — 2. The singer used a <u>microphone</u>.

Now you try it.

live — 1. The <u>lively</u> child danced across the floor.

gym — 2. <u>Gymnastics</u> is a sport.

Practice It

Look at the underlined word. Think about its base word. Circle the letter of the correct answer.

1. The attic door made a <u>dreadful</u> creaking sound when she opened it.

   The base word for <u>dreadful</u> is *dread*. **Dreadful** means —

   (A) terrible

   B noisy

   C squeaky

   D loud

2. The <u>government</u> will build a new highway around the city.

   The base word for <u>government</u> is *govern*. **Government** means —

   (A) rulers

   B truck drivers

   C cement suppliers

   D people

   Tip Look for the base word to help you understand a word's meaning.

Lesson 1 ● 3

This page may not be reproduced without permission of Steck-Vaughn

---

Differentiated Instruction
for ELL, visual, kinesthetic, and tactile learners

Word Tree
Students use definitions of words, base words, prefixes, and suffixes to make a word tree.

Procedure

- Have students cut two pieces of green paper in the shape of leaves. Then have them cut two pieces of brown paper in the shape of rectangles.
- Give each student a list of two words with prefixes and suffixes. Then ask them to write their words and their definitions on the green pieces of paper.
- Then have each student find the base word for his or her two words. Students will write their base words on the brown pieces of paper.
- Let students place their base words in the shape of a tree trunk and attach their original words as leaves to the top of the tree.

Use It

Use this activity to have students identify base words.

- Write the words *roller* and *microphone* on the board.

   Ask *What would you guess that a roller is?* (Answer: *something that turns around in circles; something that rolls*)

   Ask *Who can tell me the base word for roller?* (Answer: *roll*)

   Ask *Can you use this word to figure out the meaning of the word* roller? (Possible answer: *Something that rolls.*)

   Say *Now look at microphone.*

   Ask *Do you recognize the base word in this word?* (Answer: *phone*)

Read the *Use It* directions aloud. Have students complete the section independently. Ask volunteers to share their answers.

Practice It

In this section students use base words and sentence context to choose correct word meanings.

- Read the directions and *Tip* aloud.
- Have students complete items 1 and 2 independently.
- When students have finished, review answers with the class. Ask students whether the base-word meanings helped them choose the correct answers.

Answers
1. A
2. A

Unit 1 ■ 3

Lesson 2

Objective

Students will use prefixes, suffixes, and base words to form new words.

Words to Know

Prefix—a word part added to the beginning of a word that changes its meaning

Suffix—a word part added to the end of a word that changes its meaning

Study It

Review the definitions of *prefix* and *suffix*. Write the following words on the board as column headings: *Prefix or Suffix, Base Word, New Word.*

■ Direct students to the chart. As you read the word parts, ask students to help you use these word parts to create new words.

Ask *What is the base word of prepay?* (Answer: *pay*)

Say *The part that is left over at the beginning of the base word is the prefix. What is the prefix of prepay?* (Answer: *pre-*)

■ As the students help you break down the word *hopeful,* write the parts of the word under the appropriate column headings on the board. Then review the meanings of the word parts.

Ask *What does the base word* hope *mean?* (Answer: *to wish for and expect*)

Say *Now look for the suffix -ful in the chart. Put the two meanings together.*

Ask *What does the word* hopeful *mean?* (Answer: *filled with hope*)

Lesson 2 — Covering the Bases

Study It

Sometimes a word part is added to a base word. A **prefix** is added at the beginning of a word. A **suffix** is added at the end of a word. Prefixes and suffixes change the meanings of the base words.

Some examples of prefixes are *dis-*, meaning "not" or "away"; *pre-*, meaning "before"; and *un-*, meaning "not."

Some examples of suffixes are *-ful*, meaning "filled with"; *-less*, meaning "without"; and *-ment*, meaning "the state of."

If you know the meaning of the base word and the meaning of its prefix or suffix, you can determine what a word means.

Look at how these words were formed. Then look at their meanings.

Prefix or Suffix	Base Word	New Word
pre- means "before"	pay means "to give money for"	prepay means "to pay or give money for in advance"
-ful means "filled with"	hope means "to wish for and expect"	hopeful means "filled with hope"

What are the differences between the columns above?

- The first column has only word parts, or prefixes and suffixes.
- The second column has base words. Prefixes and suffixes can be added to base words to make new words.
- The third column includes the base word combined with the prefix or suffix to form a new word. The words in this column have meanings that combine the meaning of the base word and the meaning of its prefix or suffix.

4 ● Unit 1   Structural analysis

This page may not be reproduced without permission of Steck-Vaughn.

Curriculum and Assessment Standard

Structural analysis

Look at this sentence. Think about the underlined word.

Jason tried to disappear after his last class of the day.

The base word appear means "to be in sight." The word appear has the prefix dis- added to it. The prefix dis- means "not," so disappear means "not to be in sight."

Look at this chart. Notice how the new words were formed.

Prefix or Suffix	Base Word	New Word
-less means "without"	life means "being alive"	lifeless means "without life"
-hood means "the condition of"	child means "a young person"	childhood means "the condition of being a young person"
-ly means "like"	friend means "one attached by affection"	friendly means "like one attached by affection"
-ist means "doer or believer"	art means "skill of creating"	artist means "one who does something very well" or "one who uses a skill to create"
-able means "can or able to"	trace means "to follow a path"	traceable means "able to be followed"
re- means "again"	new means "made fresh or made recently"	renew means "to make fresh again"
-er means "one who"	drive means "to operate a car"	driver means "one who drives"

Think about other words that combine base words with prefixes and suffixes. How would you figure out the meaning of these words?

- Look for the base word to see whether you know its meaning.
- Look for a prefix or a suffix and think about what it means.
- Combine the meaning of the base word with the meaning of the prefix or suffix to see whether the meaning of the new word makes sense in the sentence.

Lesson 2 • 5

- Direct students to the chart. Repeat the process of combining the meanings of base words with the meanings of prefixes and suffixes, and then review the meanings of the new words.

  Ask *What does the word* life *mean?* (Answer: *being alive*)

  Ask *When you add the suffix* -less, *how does it change the meaning? What does* lifeless *mean?* (Answer: *It now means without life.*)

- Go over the chart with students, and then have them read the bulleted list at the bottom of the page.

Remind students that they should first find the base word and its meaning, and then find how the other parts can change the meaning. Give students an opportunity to ask questions about prefixes, suffixes, and base words.

Differentiated Instruction
for ELL, tactile, and visual learners

Building Words

Students mix and match word parts to make words.

Procedure

- Give each student five note cards and seven smaller cards.
- Have students think of five verbs and write each one on a separate note card.
- Write the prefixes *re-, pre-, dis-,* and *mis-* and the suffixes *-able* and *-er* on the board. Ask students to copy the prefixes and the suffixes onto the smaller cards.
- Give students five minutes to mix and match their verbs with the affixes and write down the words they create. Tell them that they may have to correct the spelling of the new words they have formed.
- When they have finished, ask students to share their words with the class, and ask them to explain what each new word means.

Use It

Use this section to help students practice adding prefixes and suffixes to base words.

■ Have students look at example item 1.

  Ask *Would you add a prefix or a suffix to* quiet *to complete the sentence?* (Answer: *a suffix, -ly*)

  Ask *Does the suffix attach to the beginning or the end of* quiet? (Answer: *the end*)

  Ask *What do you call a word part that attaches to the beginning of a word?* (Answer: *a prefix*)

■ Direct students to example item 2.

  Ask *What is being added to the word* teach? *Is it a prefix or a suffix?* (Answer: *the suffix -er*)

  Say *Put together the meaning of the base word and the suffix. Then tell the meaning of the word* teacher.

Read the *Use It* directions aloud. Have students complete the page independently. Ask volunteers to share their answers.

Use It

Add a prefix or a suffix to the base word underlined in the sentence to make a word that fits in the sentence. Write the new word in the blank. Check the spelling of the new word.

_____quietly_____ 1. We quiet ly finished our homework.

_____teacher_____ 2. The teach er read to the students.

Now you try it.

_____scientist_____ 1. The science ___ finished the experiment.

_____easily_____ 2. Can you ease ___ complete your homework tonight?

_____noticeable_____ 3. The change in the weather was notice ___ when the wind blew harder.

_____dishonest_____ 4. John got in trouble for being ___ honest.

_____unfinished_____ 5. The ___ finished work needs to be completed.

_____organist_____ 6. The organ ___ played the song beautifully.

_____retry_____ 7. You need to ___ try that phone number if you did not get an answer.

_____replace_____ 8. Please ___ place the book when you are finished with it.

_____worthless_____ 9. We put the worth ___ chair out with the trash.

_____pitcher_____ 10. We watched the pitch ___ throw the ball.

Practice It

Read these sentences. Circle the letter of the correct answer.

1. | Mrs. Brown rewound the kite string. |

   The prefix *re-* in rewound means —

   (A) again
   B before
   C away
   D not

2. | The shoeless man waded into the water. |

   The suffix *-less* in shoeless means —

   A filled with
   (B) without
   C able to
   D condition of

3. | The artist painted several excellent pictures. |

   The suffix *-ist* in artist means —

   A like
   B filled with
   (C) one who does
   D condition of

4. | The neighborhood children played a game. |

   The suffix *-hood* in neighborhood means —

   A without
   (B) condition of being
   C doer or believer
   D like

> **Tip** Look for base words, prefixes, and suffixes to understand unfamiliar words.

Lesson 2 • 7

This page may not be reproduced without permission of Steck-Vaughn.

Practice It

In this section students use base words, suffixes, and prefixes to define words.

■ Read the directions and the *Tip* aloud. Then direct students to item 1.

Say *First, read the sentence inside the box. Then, read the item that follows.*

Ask *What does the question ask you to define?* (Answer: *the prefix re- in rewound*)

Ask *What is the base word of* rewound? (Answer: *wound*)

Ask *What does* wound *mean?* (Answer: *twisted or rolled around something*)

Say *Now reread the sentence in the box. What do you think the prefix means? Look through the answer choices and find the one that best matches the meaning.* (Answer: *re- means again*)

■ Repeat the process above for items 2–4. When students have finished, ask for volunteers to answer each question.

Answers

1. A
2. B
3. C
4. B

Lesson 3

Objective

Students will use context clues to find word meanings.

◢ Study It

Tell students that good readers are like detectives because they use clues to find information. Explain that good readers use other words in a sentence as clues to find the meaning of a word they do not understand.

■ Write on the board: *In order to make an omelet, you have to break a few eggs.* Underline the word *omelet.* Read the sentence aloud.

Say *To find out what* omelet *means, you can ask questions to find clues. Then you might be able to guess the meaning of* omelet.

Ask *What are some clues in the sentence?* (Answer: *make, break, eggs*)

Ask *If an* omelet *is something that you have to break eggs in order to make, what could it be?* (Answer: *a food made out of eggs*)

■ Ask students to write a definition for the word *omelet.* Ask volunteers to read their definitions aloud.

Direct students to the examples in the student book, and use the explanations to help them learn to look for context clues.

◢ Find the Clues

◢ Study It

What can you do if you do not understand a word in a sentence? Sometimes you can use the words or sentences near the word to help you determine a word's meaning.

Look at this sentence. Notice the underlined word.

The students watched the play in the auditorium. They had seats near the stage.

What clues can help you find the meaning of auditorium?

● The sentence says that the students watched a play in the auditorium. So an auditorium must be a place, such as a room.

● The next sentence says that students had seats near the stage. Now you know that an auditorium has seats and a stage. So an auditorium must be a room with seats and a stage.

Look at this sentence. Notice the underlined word.

The airplane reached a high altitude.

The words airplane and high suggest the meaning of altitude, or the height at which the plane is flying.

What should you do when you read a word that you do not understand?

● Look at the words near the word to see what they suggest.

● Look at the other sentences near the word. Do they suggest what the word's meaning might be?

8 ● Unit 1   Context clues

Curriculum and Assessment Standard

Context clues

Use It

In the sentences below, circle clue words that you can use to figure out the meaning of the underlined word. Then write the meaning for the underlined word in the blank. Look at the examples.

_____cold_____ 1. George put on a (sweater) because he was chilly.

_____surprised_____ 2. When Darcy walked up (behind) Matt, she startled him.

Now you try it.

_____kept her from seeing_____ 1. The (sun's reflection) blinded Marie.

_____taught_____ 2. Mrs. Lee instructed several (students.)

Practice It

Look for clues about the meaning of the underlined word. Circle the letter of the correct answer.

1. After she ran three miles, Andrea was exhausted.

   (A) tired

   B placed

   C tiny

   D cool

2. The raven flew onto the tree branch and squawked.

   A mouse

   (B) bird

   C squirrel

   D cat

Tip
Use words you know in a sentence to help you figure out the meaning of unfamiliar words.

Lesson 3 • 9

(sidebar, vertical text) This page may not be reproduced without permission of Steck-Vaughn.

Use It

Use this section to provide students with practice using context clues to guess the meanings of words.

■ Write the first example sentence on the board. Underline the word *chilly.*

Say *Use the clues in this sentence to find the meaning of the word* chilly. *Look at the words near it.*

Ask *What does* chilly *describe?* (Answer: *how George felt*)

Ask *What does George put on when he is chilly?* (Answer: *a sweater*)

■ Invite a volunteer to circle the word *sweater.*

Ask *If chilly is another word for the way George felt when he needed a sweater, what is a word that means the same as chilly?* (Answer: *cold*)

■ Read the *Use It* directions aloud. Have students look at the second example and then complete the section independently. Review answers with the class.

Practice It

In this section students use clues to choose the correct meaning of words.

■ Read the directions and *Tip* aloud.

■ Direct students to complete items 1 and 2 independently.

■ Ask a student to answer each question. If they do not have the correct answer, ask if anyone else has another answer.

Answers

1. A
2. B

Differentiated Instruction
for auditory, tactile, and kinesthetic learners

Guess What Is in the Box

Students use context clues to guess the contents of a box.

Procedure

● Have students draw a picture of a box on a sheet of paper. On the back of the paper, have them write a secret word for something that they would put in the box. Then have them write three sentences that tell about their secret word. (Example: For the word *soap,* students could write *Soap is something that you use to wash your hands.*)

● Then have students draw a line through the secret word in each sentence and write the word *blank* above it.

● Have each student hold the picture of the box so that the class can see it, and read his or her sentences to the class, using *blank* in place of the secret word.

● Let the rest of the class guess the secret word in the box.

Unit 1 ■ 9

Lesson 4

Objective

Students will learn words with multiple meanings and distinguish between definitions and uses.

Study It

Use the first sentence in the student book to introduce the idea of multiple meanings. Then write the word *favor* on the board.

- Have students read the two definitions of *favor* in the first paragraph, and ask the following questions.

  Ask *When I say the word* favor, *what do you think of first? What is the other definition here for* favor? *When would you use this definition?*

- Ask students to write two sentences, one for each definition of *favor.*

- Direct students to the word *loaf* in the chart, and write it on the board.

  Ask *What kind of* loaf *do you eat?* (Answer: *the shaped mass of bread*)

  Ask *If I told you that I did not want you to* loaf, *which definition would I be using?*

- Read the sample sentence with the word *gorge* aloud.

  Ask *What are the two definitions of* gorge? (Answer: *to eat greedily; a deep, narrow passage*)

- Have each student write a sentence using the meaning of *gorge* as a way of eating.

Lesson 4 · More Than One Meaning

Study It

This sentence might seem confusing at first. Lisa did Alex a favor when she brought the party favors. We know that favor is "a helpful act." Favor also can mean "an item used as a party gift."

Look at these words. Each word has more than one meaning.

Word	One Meaning	Second Meaning
loaf	to spend time lazily	a shaped mass of bread or meat
gorge	to eat greedily	a deep, narrow passage

- If a sentence is confusing, find any words in the sentence that may have more than one meaning.
- Reread the sentence, using another of the word's meanings.

Read this sentence. Think about the word loaf.

During my vacation, I plan to loaf for a whole day.

If you read the word loaf as "to spend time lazily," the sentence makes sense. If you use the other meaning of loaf, it does not.

Another way to find the correct meaning is to look at the word's part of speech. If the word is a noun, look for a meaning as a noun. If it is a verb, use an action meaning.

Read this sentence. Look at the word gorge.

They followed the gorge through the mountains.

"To eat greedily" does not make sense in the sentence because it expresses an action. "A deep narrow passage" does make sense because the word is used as a noun.

10 · Unit 1   Multi-meaning words

Curriculum and Assessment Standard

Multi-meaning words

10 ■ Unit 1

Use It

Each word below has one meaning. Write another meaning for the word on the blank line.

a young student 1. pupil: a part of the eye that responds to light

a collection of information 2. file: a steel tool with a rough edge

Now you try it.

speedy 1. fast: to go without food

swift in motion; quick 2. fleet: a group of ships

Practice It

Choose the word that fits in both sentences. Circle the letter of the correct answer.

1. We must _____ our own lunches for the field trip.
   We bought a table and chairs to _____ the dining room.

   (A) furnish
   B make
   C buy
   D bring

2. The school will _____ Jennifer to the art class.
   I will _____ that I am wrong when you show me proof.

   A say
   B take
   (C) admit
   D confess

Tip Choose the word that makes sense in the sentence.

Lesson 4 • 11

Use It

Use this activity to give students practice using and defining words with multiple meanings.

- Direct students to the first example. Ask a student to read the definition for *pupil.*

  Say Pupil *has another definition. For example, you could say,* Felipe was a polite and respectful pupil.

- Write the sentence on the board.

  Ask *What definition of* pupil *fits this sentence?* (Answer: *a student*)

- Read the next example aloud.

  Say *Can you think of another definition for this word?* (Answer: *a collection of information*)

- Ask students for definitions, and then write volunteers' answers on the board.

Direct students to complete the section independently. Ask volunteers to read their definitions aloud. Remind students that they can use example sentences to check whether their words or definitions make sense.

Practice It

In this section students select one word with multiple meanings to complete two sentences.

- Read the directions and *Tip* aloud.
- Direct students to complete items 1 and 2 independently and then stop.
- Ask volunteers to read their answers to the class. Remind students that the correct answer must fit in both sentences.

Answers

1. A
2. C

Differentiated Instruction
for ELL and visual learners

Double Meaning Cards

Students make picture flash cards for words with multiple meanings.

Procedure

- On the board, write a list of words with multiple meanings from Lesson 4.
- Tell students to choose a word. Then have them draw a picture that shows one meaning of the word on each side of a note card.
- If some students finish quickly, ask them to draw a second word.
- Organize students into pairs or groups of three.
- Ask students to exchange cards with partners and to use the drawings to guess the words' meanings.

Lesson 5

Objective

Students will use a dictionary or thesaurus entry to find information about a word.

Words to Know

Dictionary—a book that lists words in alphabetical order and shows the meanings of words

Thesaurus—a book that tells you synonyms and antonyms for words

Study It

Review the definitions of a *dictionary* and a *thesaurus* with students.

- Direct students to look at the sample dictionary entry.

- Review the entry, giving students a chance to locate each part as you discuss it.

  Say *First, find the entry word.*

  Ask *How is this word different than other words in the entry?* (Answer: *It is in color and has the syllables separated by dots.*)

  Say *In many dictionaries the entry word will be boldface.*

  Ask *How do you know how to say the word?* (Answer: *The dictionary gives the pronunciation of the word.*)

  Ask *What part of speech is* echo? (Answer: *It can be a noun or a verb.*)

  Ask *How can you tell when a word has more than one meaning?* (Answer: *The meanings are numbered.*)

- Direct students to the sample thesaurus entry. Ask them to find two synonyms and an antonym for the word *happy,* as well as each word's part of speech.

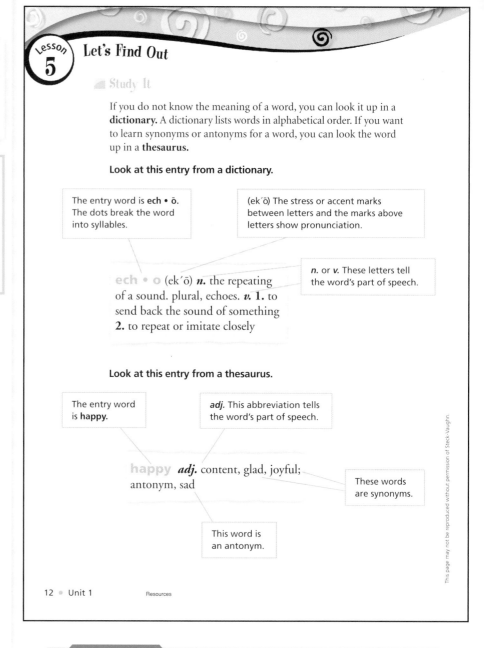

Lesson 5 Let's Find Out

Study It

If you do not know the meaning of a word, you can look it up in a **dictionary**. A dictionary lists words in alphabetical order. If you want to learn synonyms or antonyms for a word, you can look the word up in a **thesaurus**.

Look at this entry from a dictionary.

The entry word is **ech • ō.** The dots break the word into syllables.

(ek´ō) The stress or accent marks between letters and the marks above letters show pronunciation.

ech • o (ek´ō) *n.* the repeating of a sound. plural, echoes. *v.* **1.** to send back the sound of something **2.** to repeat or imitate closely

n. or *v.* These letters tell the word's part of speech.

Look at this entry from a thesaurus.

The entry word is **happy.**

adj. This abbreviation tells the word's part of speech.

happy *adj.* content, glad, joyful; antonym, sad

These words are synonyms.

This word is an antonym.

12 • Unit 1   Resources

Curriculum and Assessment Standard

Resources

Use It

Look at this example. Answer the questions.

echo _____ Write the entry word for the dictionary entry on page 12.

Now you try it.

___two___ 1. How many syllables does <u>echo</u> have?

___echoes___ 2. Write the plural of <u>echo</u> when it is used as a noun.

___two___ 3. How many meanings does the verb <u>echo</u> have?

Practice It

Read this dictionary entry. Circle the letter of the correct answer.

bi • cy • cle (bīʹsikʹəl) _n._ **1.** A vehicle made of a light frame on two wire-spoked wheels, one behind the other, and having a seat, handlebars for steering, brakes, and two pedals or a small motor by which it is driven. **2.** An exercise bicycle.

1. **The entry word is —**
   (A) bicycle
   B exercise
   C noun
   D vehicle

2. **How many meanings does bicycle have?**
   A one
   (B) two
   C three
   D four

Tip For a dictionary test question, look at each part of the entry to find the answer.

Lesson 5 • 13

Use It

Use this section to let students find information about a word in a dictionary entry.

■ Tell students to use the dictionary entry on page 12 to answer items.

  Say _The entry word is the word you are looking up._

  Ask _Who remembers what the entry word looks like?_ (Answer: _in color and has syllables separated by dots_)

  Say _Find the word that is in color and separated by dots. Write that word in the blank._

■ Tell students to complete items 1–3 independently. When they have finished, review each item with the class. As you find an item in the entry, ask each student to put his or her finger on it. Verify that each student can locate the information before moving ahead in the lesson.

Practice It

In this section students use a sample entry to answer questions.

■ Read the directions and _Tip_ aloud.

■ Tell students to work independently to complete items 1 and 2.

■ When students have completed both items, ask volunteers to read their answers and describe how they found each item in the sample entry.

Answers
1. A
2. B

Differentiated Instruction
for ELL and visual learners

A Class Dictionary

Students will write dictionary entries for their own names, describing themselves. Students will revise their drafts and publish the final work.

Procedure

● Using your own name as a model for the class, write out on the poster board a dictionary entry that tells how to spell, pronounce, and divide your name into syllables, as well as a definition of who you are. Then write a sample sentence about yourself. Use different-colored text for each part of the entry.

● Ask students to each write an entry on a piece of paper, using their own name. Help them edit their work so that they have included all parts.

● Have students use different-colored text to create a final draft of the entry. Then help them alphabetize and bind their entries as a published class dictionary.

Teach the Strategy

Write on the board: *Elena loved to watch the seagull fly. It would land on the rocks and hunt for food.* Underline *seagull*.

Tell students that you want to know what a *seagull* is, but you do not have a dictionary.

Ask *Both an airplane and a bird can fly, but which one lands on rocks and hunts for food?* (Answer: *a bird*)

Say *Next, look at the word itself.*

Ask *Do you see any other words you know that are a part of this word?* (Answer: *sea*)

Say *Think of a definition that would make sense in this sentence. Read the sentence with your definition in place of the word, and see if it fits.*

Find Clues Strategy

Tell students that you were just using the *Find Clues Strategy* to figure out the meaning of the word *seagull*.

- Write these answer choices under the sentence on the board.

  A   small airplane

  B   striped fish

  C   bird that lives near the sea

  D   person that hunts for food

- Ask students to use the clues you found in the sentence to find the correct answer. (Answer: *C, bird that lives near the sea*)

Try It Out

Read the directions aloud, and tell students to complete the item independently. Ask them to use the *Find Clues Strategy* to find answers.

Ask *How did the* Find Clues Strategy *help you find the answer?*

Ask *Which other words helped you the most?*

Discuss the explanation that follows the item in the student book.

Test-Taking Strategy

Strategy: Find Clues

In this unit you learned how to take a closer look at words. You discovered that you can learn the meaning of an unfamiliar word by looking at the words and sentences around the word. Looking for clues outside the word can help you answer questions about the meaning of a word.

- Read the sentence. Can you guess the meaning of the underlined word? Use the words around it as clues. Also look for clues in the sentences before and after the word.

- Compare your answer to each answer choice. Which is the closest match?

Try It Out

Choose the word that means about the same as the underlined word. Fill in the circle next to the correct answer.

> Marie drove with her dad to the train station to wait for a parcel. When the train arrived, Marie watched with excitement. Porters unloaded suitcases and freight packages. There it was! Her father signed for the parcel. Then they both picked up the box and carried it out to the car.

In this paragraph the word parcel means —

A   a suitcase

B   a train station

Ⓒ   a package

D   a car

Marie and her father wait for the parcel to arrive by train. The words porters and unloaded tell you that people took things out of the train. Marie and her father lift the box and carry it to their car. A parcel is a package of some kind. So, the correct answer is **C**.

Put It to the Test

Name _____

This test will check what you have learned in this unit.

DIRECTIONS: Circle the letter of the correct answer.

1. | Hannah has just learned to swim. She practices in the shallow end of the pool. |

   The opposite of shallow is —

   A narrow
   Ⓑ deep
   C full
   D low

2. | You may need a wrench to do bike repairs. |

   The word wrench means a type of —

   A book
   Ⓑ tool
   C light
   D box

3. | Turn down that ____ coming from the radio.
   Hold your ____ like this to hit the ball. |

   The word that fits both sentences is —

   A noise
   B bat
   C music
   Ⓓ racket

4. | Our host was at the front door to greet all the guests. |

   The word greet means —

   A address
   Ⓑ welcome
   C hear
   D search

5. | Who won the 30-yard ____ ?
   Sprinkle a ____ of salt on your popcorn. |

   The word that fits both sentences is —

   A teaspoon
   B race
   Ⓒ dash
   D handful

6. | The cat eyed the dog cautiously. |

   The word cautiously means —

   A quickly
   B happily
   C peacefully
   Ⓓ carefully

GO ON

Achieve It! Practice Cards

_____

Put It to the Test • 15

Connect the Test to the Practice Cards (page 15)

Correct Answers	Related Practice Cards	Skill
1. B	5, 12	Antonyms, Dictionary & thesaurus
2. B	4, 8, 9, 12	Synonyms, Context clues, Dictionary & thesaurus
3. D	6, 7	Multi-meaning words
4. B	8, 9	Context clues
5. C	6, 7	Multi-meaning words
6. D	4, 8, 9, 12	Synonyms, Context clues, Dictionary & thesaurus

Put It to the Test

Students will:

- demonstrate what they have learned
- identify skills that require more practice before students achieve proficiency*

* Refer to pages T17–T19 for a complete explanation and directions for using *Achieve It!* Practice Cards.

Administer the Test

Explain that students will now practice the skills from this unit by taking a short test. Tell students that the test has items like those they will find on standardized tests. Explain that you will read the directions aloud. Remind students to pay close attention and follow your directions exactly.

Say *Open your books to page 15. I will read the directions aloud.* Read the directions to students. Then continue.

Say *You will have 10 minutes to finish this test. Read each item and the answer choices carefully. Circle the letter of the correct answer. When you reach the words* GO ON *at the bottom of a page, turn the page and continue working. When you reach the word* STOP *at the bottom of a page, stop working and put down your pencil. Are there any questions?*

If students have no questions,

Say *You may begin.*

At the end of 10 minutes,

Say *Stop. Check to be sure that you have circled the letter of the correct answer choice. Erase any stray pencil marks. Then put down your pencil.*

Assign Practice Cards

After scoring a student's test, note which items the student missed. Match each incorrectly answered item to the related *Achieve It!* Practice Cards listed in the chart on this page.

In the *Achieve It!* Practice Cards space in each student's book, write all of the Practice Cards you want the student to complete.

Additional Practice Cards

The following cards cover additional skills for

Unit 1: Vocabulary

Card	Topic
10	Idioms
11	Figurative language

You may want to assign these cards as practice for students who have done well on the unit test or as extended practice for all students.

---

7. | The gardener whistled a cheerful tune as she mowed the grass. |

The base word for cheerful is *cheer*. Cheerful means —

(A) full of joy

B full of confusion

C full of anger

D full of sadness

8. | Rita divided the pizza equally among 16 guests. |

The ending -*ly* in the word equally is called a —

A simile

B prefix

(C) suffix

D base word

9. | There was an uneasy quiet in the room after Todd broke the picture. |

The prefix *un*- means —

(A) not

B on

C in

D very

pres • i • dent (prez´i dənt)
n. the chief officer of a country, a company, a club, or another organization

10. What part of speech is the word president?

A adjective

B verb

(C) noun

D adverb

11. Which syllable in president is pronounced the most strongly?

(A) first

B second

C third

D all are equal

STOP

Achieve It! Practice Cards

_____

Connect the Test to the Practice Cards (page 16)

Correct Answers	Related Practice Cards	Skill
7. **A**	1	Word origins
8. **C**	2, 3	Structural analysis
9. **A**	2, 3	Structural analysis
10. **C**	12	Dictionary & thesaurus
11. **A**	12	Dictionary & thesaurus

Unit 2
Understanding What You Read

Open the Door!

Sometimes you open a door to a place you've never been before. When you get inside, you need to find your way around. Opening a book is like opening a door. You enter a place where you can learn something new or find something to enjoy. First, you need to be sure you can "find your way around" as you read.

In this unit you will learn skills to help you find your way around, or understand, what you read.

17

Research Says

Teaching strategies for reading comprehension leads to increased awareness and use of the strategies, to improved performance on commonly used comprehension measures, and, sometimes to higher scores on standardized tests of reading.

—*Williams*

Skills

- Distinguishing between fact and opinion
- Comparing and contrasting details in texts
- Identifying causes and effects of events in a text
- Identifying main idea and supporting details of a paragraph
- Summarizing main ideas and details
- Using new words and rearranging ideas to paraphrase a text
- Identifying the author's purpose
- Using charts and graphs to get information

Materials to Gather in Advance

- Blackline Master 5: Venn Diagram
- ruled paper • pictures of famous people • pencils • stapler • colored markers • scissors • butcher paper • tape • construction paper • book of nursery rhymes

Introducing the Unit

Open the Door! Refer students to the photograph of the doorway. Ask them to imagine opening the door to a room that they have never seen before. Ask them what they might think about before opening the door.

Ask Do you ever imagine what a room is like before you walk into it? Do you picture what is inside?

- Have students imagine that they are walking down a hallway with doors along the sides. The signs on the doors have the names of different people whom students know. Ask them to imagine that they are trying to find the answer to a question.

  Ask How do you decide which door to open? Do you think about which person would know the answer to your question, then open the door with their name on it?

- Have a volunteer read the *Open the Door!* paragraph aloud. Ask students to explain how opening a book to learn something is like opening a door to a new place.

Lesson 6

Objective

Students will learn to distinguish between fact and opinion.

Words to Know

Fact—something that can be proven

Opinion—a statement of feeling or belief

Study It

Review the definitions of *fact* and *opinion* with students.

- Write on the board: *Bicycles have two wheels.* Ask a volunteer to read the sentence aloud.

  Ask *Can I prove that a bicycle has two wheels?* (Answer: *yes*)

  Ask *If I had a bicycle right here, how could I prove that it has two wheels?* (Answer: *You could look at it and count the wheels.*)

  Ask *If I can prove that this sentence is true, is it a fact or an opinion?* (Answer: *fact*)

- Write the words *best, worst, should, feel, think,* and *believe* on the board. Explain to students that opinions often use these words.

  Say Kittens are the best pets *is an example of an opinion.*

  Ask *Can anyone think of an example of an opinion about a bicycle?*

- Ask students to write sentences that express opinions on the board. Then review the sentences with the class.

- Ask a student to read the directions for the chart. Have students take turns reading sentences and answering questions about the sentences. Help students understand that if the information in a sentence can be proven, it is a fact; otherwise, it is an opinion.

Prove It!

Study It

A **fact** is a statement or sentence that you can prove. You can look up a fact in a book. You can prove facts by using your senses: sight, hearing, touch, taste, and smell. Different people agree that the same facts are true. The sentence *Bicycles have two wheels* is a fact that can be proved. You can look at a bicycle and see that it has two wheels.

An **opinion** is a sentence or statement that tells a belief or feeling. You cannot prove an opinion. Different people have different opinions. The sentence *Kittens are the best pets* is an opinion because some people might think dogs or birds are the best pets.

Sometimes there are clues that help you find an opinion. Words like best, worst, should, feel, think, and believe can tell you that a sentence is an opinion.

Read this chart. It shows examples of facts and opinions.

Sentence	Can It Be Proved?	Fact or Opinion?
A banana is a fruit.	Yes	Fact
I think red is the prettiest color.	No	Opinion
John Glenn was the first U.S. astronaut to orbit the earth.	Yes	Fact
Bears should live in the zoo.	No	Opinion
George Washington was the first president of the United States.	Yes	Fact
I believe that our school band is the best in the state.	No	Opinion

Fact/opinion

This page may not be reproduced without permission of Steck-Vaughn.

Curriculum and Assessment Standard

Fact/opinion

Use It

In the blanks before each sentence, write the word <u>fact</u> or <u>opinion</u>. Look at these examples.

1. _____opinion_____ Dogs are wonderful pets.

2. _____fact_____ Texas is part of the United States.

Now you try it.

1. _____opinion_____ I think oranges are delicious.

2. _____opinion_____ Mr. Riley is the best teacher in the school.

3. _____fact_____ Polar bears are white.

4. _____fact_____ Pine trees grow in North America.

Practice It

Read each question. Circle the letter of the correct answer.

1. **Which sentence is a FACT?**

   A People should ride bikes more often.

   B Abraham Lincoln was a United States president.

   C Our team has the best players.

   D That movie was awful.

2. **Which sentence is an OPINION?**

   A Bears eat meat and plants.

   B Sacramento is the capital of California.

   C I think we should go swimming today.

   D The law in our state says that you must wear a seatbelt.

Tip In a report try to use only facts.

Lesson 6 • 19

This page may not be reproduced without permission of Steck-Vaughn

Differentiated Instruction
for ELL, visual, and auditory learners

What You Think and What You Know

Students will write facts and opinions about a famous person.

Procedure

- Place the class in two groups, *Group 1* and *Group 2.* Show a picture of a famous person, and then pass it around. Explain that Group 1 will write facts that can be proven by looking at the picture. Group 2 will write opinions that express how they feel about the person in the picture.

- Have each student write one sentence, labeling it *fact* or *opinion.* Ask students to read each sentence aloud. Encourage them to explain why they believe they have written a fact or opinion.

- Show a second picture of a famous person, and ask Group 1 to write opinions and Group 2 to write facts. After each student writes and labels a sentence, share answers again.

Use It

Use this section to have students demonstrate their understanding of the differences between fact and opinion.

- Write the two example sentences on the board. Then ask a student to read the first sentence aloud.

   Ask *Can I prove that dogs are wonderful, or is this sentence an expression of someone's feelings?* (Answer: *an expression of feelings*)

   Ask *If the sentence expresses feelings or beliefs, is it a fact or an opinion?* (Answer: *an opinion*)

- Write *O* on the board next to the first example sentence. Then ask a student to read the second example sentence aloud.

   Ask *Can I prove that Texas is part of the United States, or is this sentence an expression of someone's feelings?* (Answer: *You can prove that Texas is part of the United States.*)

   Ask *If it can be proven, is it a fact or an opinion?* (Answer: *fact*) Write *F* on the board next to the sentence.

- Have students complete the section independently. When they have finished, ask students to share their answers with the class. Encourage students to explain why each sentence is a fact or an opinion.

Practice It

In this section students decide which answers are facts and which are opinions.

- Read the directions aloud.

- Read the *Tip* aloud.

- Have students complete items 1 and 2 independently. When they have finished, ask students to share their answers with the class. If students have trouble finding the correct answers, remind them that a sentence is only a fact if it can be proven.

Answers

1. B

2. C

Unit 2 ■ 19

Lesson 7

Objective

Students will compare and contrast details in a passage.

Words to Know

Compare—to show how two or more things are alike

Contrast—to show how two or more things are different

◢ Study It

Review the definitions of *compare* and *contrast* with students, as well as the key words associated with each.

■ Write the headings *Me, My Brother,* and *Both of Us* on the board. Then ask a student to read the directions for the passage. Ask a volunteer to read the passage aloud.

■ Ask students to underline details that tell how the narrator and the narrator's brother are alike. Ask them to circle details that tell how the two subjects are different. Give students a few minutes to work independently.

Ask *How is the narrator like his or her brother?* (Answer: *Both like bikes and have the same kind of bike; the two look alike with both having red hair and green eyes.*) Write student responses on the board under *Both of Us.*

Ask *How are the two bikes different?* (Answer: *One has a bell; the other does not.*)

Ask *What is different about how the two characters look?* (Answer: *Both have a different haircut.*)

Write responses on the board under *Me* and *My Brother.*

Say *Sometimes an author will compare two things in one paragraph and contrast them in the next paragraph.*

Lesson 7 — Same but Different

◢ Study It

Think about your brother or sister or your friend. How are you and that person alike? To answer this question, you need to **compare** yourself to that person.

How are you and your brother, sister, or friend different? To answer this question, you need to **contrast** yourself with that person.

When you compare, you look for ways that things are alike. When you contrast, you look for ways that things are different.

When you compare, you might use these words.

| alike | same | both | as | just as | similar to |

When you contrast, you might use these words.

| different | but | however | in contrast | unlike |

Read the passage below. Look at the underlined words that show comparison and contrast.

> Both my brother and I love to ride our bikes. We have the same kind of bike, but my brother's bike has a bell. When we ride our bikes, it is hard to tell us apart because we look a lot alike. We both have red hair and green eyes, but our haircuts are different, and my brother is the one ringing the bell on his bike!

In the passage above, the author uses the words both, same, and alike to compare. The words different and but show contrast.

Sometimes an author compares and contrasts things in the same paragraph, as the author did above. At other times, an author may compare in one paragraph and contrast in the next paragraph.

20 ● Unit 2   Compare and contrast

This page may not be reproduced without permission of Steck-Vaughn.

Curriculum and Assessment Standard

Compare and contrast

Read the passage. Look at the <u>underlined</u> words that compare and contrast.

Rabbits and hares are <u>alike</u> in many ways. <u>Both</u> have long ears, big eyes, and short, fluffy tails. <u>Both</u> rabbits and hares have excellent hearing and can run very fast.

In other ways they are <u>different</u>. Hares live alone in open fields. <u>However</u>, rabbits like to live in groups. Rabbits are usually smaller than hares.

rabbit

In the passage above, the author compares the two animals in the first paragraph and contrasts them in the second paragraph

Look at the Venn diagram below. It shows how you can compare and contrast hares and rabbits.

Hares	Both	Rabbits
Live alone	Long ears	Live in groups
Larger than rabbits	Big eyes	Smaller than hares
Live in open fields	Short, fluffy tails	
	Good hearing	
	Fast runners	

hare

Using a Venn diagram can help you understand how things are alike and how they are different.

Lesson 7 ● 21

- Ask a student to read aloud the directions for the passage about rabbits and hares. Ask another volunteer to read aloud the first paragraph of the passage.

  Ask *Does this paragraph compare or contrast hares and rabbits?* (Answer: *It compares them.*)

  Ask *How are hares and rabbits alike?* (Answer: *They have long ears, big eyes, short tails, fluffy tails, good hearing, and can run fast* .) Ask a volunteer to read the second paragraph aloud.

  Ask *Does this paragraph compare or contrast hares and rabbits?* (Answer: *It contrasts them.*)

  Ask *How are hares and rabbits different?* (Answer: *Hares live alone; rabbits are smaller.*)

- Direct students to the Venn diagram at the bottom of the page.

  Say *A Venn diagram can help you compare and contrast. In this example, one circle tells you facts about hares, and one circle tells you facts about rabbits. The place where the circles overlap tells facts about both groups.*

- Draw two overlapping circles on the board. Label one circle *Hares* and the other circle *Rabbits*.

  Ask *What facts are in the circle about hares? What facts are in the circle about rabbits? What facts are in the space where the circles overlap?*

- Write students' responses in the circles on the board. When you have finished, lightly shade the overlapping area. Tell students that the shaded area compares the animals. The unshaded area of each circle contrasts them.

⌒Differentiated Instruction
for ELL, visual, and tactile learners

How We Are Alike and Different

Students work in pairs to compare and contrast each other.

Procedure

- Ask each student to write his or her name at the top of a sheet of paper.
- Write a series of questions on the board for students to answer on the paper. These questions might include: *Where do you go to school? Where do you live? What are your hobbies? How many brothers and sisters do you have?*
- Pair students to share their answers. Give students a copy of Blackline Master 5: Venn Diagram. Have each student write his or her name as the heading for one of the circles and the word *Both* as a heading for the overlapping area. Ask partners to place answers they have in common in the *Both* section and the other information under the appropriate name. Have pairs share their diagrams with the class.

Unit 2 ■ 21

Use It

Use this section to help students practice comparing and contrasting with Venn diagrams.

■ Write on the board: *Juliette and Alex both like ice cream, but Juliette likes vanilla and Alex likes strawberry.* Underline the words *both* and *but.* Draw two overlapping circles on the board. Label one circle *Alex* and the other *Juliette.*

Ask *What do both Juliette and Alex like?* (Answer: *ice cream*) Ask a volunteer to write *ice cream* in the overlapping area.

Ask *What flavor does Juliette like?* (Answer: *vanilla*) Ask a volunteer to write *vanilla* in the area labeled *Juliette.*

Ask *What flavor does Alex like?* (Answer: *strawberry*) Ask a student to write *strawberry* in the area labeled *Alex.*

■ Read the *Use It* directions aloud. Have students follow along as you read the passage aloud.

■ Direct students to the Venn diagram below the passage. Read the directions for completing the diagram.

Say *A small screen is one example of how a television is different from a movie theater.*

Ask *Where can you eat popcorn: at home or at a theater?* (Answer: *both places*)

Have students work independently to fill in the diagram. Then discuss students' answers. To help students see the correct answers, copy the entire diagram on the board and write in the correct answers as you discuss them.

Use It

Read the passage. Underline the words that tell you that things are being compared or contrasted.

Today you can watch movies on television, or you can see them in a movie theater. You can often see the same movie in both places. You can even eat popcorn in both places. But watching a movie at the theater is different from watching it on television. The theater has a bigger screen, and the sound is better than it is on a television set at home. You may see scenes from upcoming movies, or previews, in a theater. Television movies are usually interrupted for commercials, but movies at a movie theater are not. Finally, there are usually more people watching the movie in the theater.

Read the Venn diagram below. Then fill in the blanks.

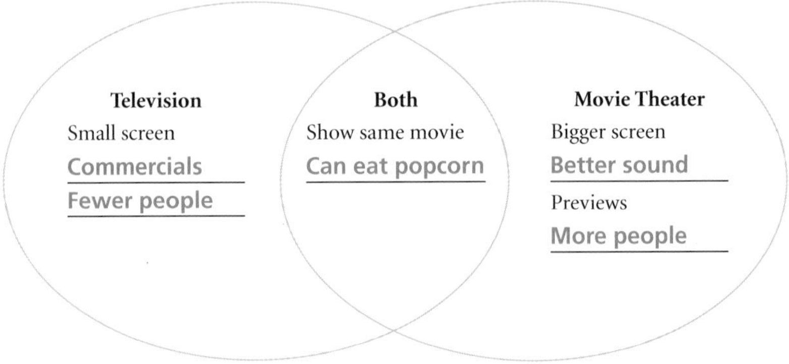

Television	Both	Movie Theater
Small screen	Show same movie	Bigger screen
Commercials	Can eat popcorn	Better sound
Fewer people		Previews
		More people

Read this passage. Then read the questions. Circle the letter of the correct answer.

Snowboarding and skiing are both popular winter sports. These sports are alike in many ways. Find a snowy mountain, and you will find skiers and snowboarders. Skiers and snowboarders use many of the same movements as they swish down a mountain.

Unlike skiers, snowboarders use one board strapped to both of their feet. Skiers have two boards, one strapped to each foot. Skiers also use poles to help them balance. But snowboarders balance without help and even do tricks with their boards. Although snow skiing has been around for a long time, more people every year are taking up snowboarding.

1. **How are snowboarding and skiing ALIKE?**

   A Both sports use poles.

   (B) Both sports take place in snow.

   C Both sports use one board.

   D Both sports use two boards.

2. **How are snowboarders DIFFERENT from skiers?**

   A Snowboarders need snow.

   B Snowboarders use poles.

   C Snowboarders use mountain runs.

   (D) Snowboarders use one board.

3. **Which statement about the passage is TRUE?**

   A The first paragraph tells how the sports are different.

   (B) The second paragraph tells how the sports are different.

   C The first paragraph is only about skiing.

   D The second paragraph is only about snowboarding.

> **Tip**
> Remember that comparing shows how things are alike and contrasting shows how they are different.

Lesson 7 ● 23

◀ Practice It

Work through the page to help students understand how to find details that compare and contrast.

Read the directions aloud. Then have students read the passage silently and stop when they have finished.

Question 1 Read the question aloud. Ask students to find details in the passage that tell how snowboarding and snow skiing are alike. Then ask them to find the correct answer to question 1. (Answer: *B, Both sports take place in snow.*)

Discuss student answers. Help students recognize that *B* is the only detail from the passage that tells how snowboarding and snow skiing are alike. To help students understand the correct answer, explain why the other answers are incorrect.

● *A* is incorrect because only skiing uses poles.   ● *C* is incorrect because only snowboarding uses one board.
● *D* is incorrect because only skiing uses two boards.

Questions 2 and 3 Ask students to complete questions 2 and 3 independently. When they have finished, discuss students' answers.

Help students recognize that *D* is a detail about how the two sports are different. This is the correct answer to question 2. Explain the incorrect answers.

● *A* and *C* are incorrect because they state how the sports are similar.
● *B* is incorrect because the passage states that skiers use poles.

Help students recognize that *B* is a true statement about the text and is the correct answer to question 3.

Lesson 8

Objective

Students will identify the cause and effect of actions in a text.

Words to Know

Cause—tells why something happened

Effect—what happens as a result of a cause

◢ Study It

Review the definitions of *cause* and *effect* with students.

■ Write on the board: *When Mr. Okami walked into his office, his papers were all over the floor.* Ask a volunteer to read the sentence aloud.

Say *We don't know why the papers were all over the floor. Good readers will read the text carefully and look for the reason why, or the cause.*

Ask *If you were the author, what cause might you invent to explain why the papers were on the floor?* (Possible answers: *The wind blew through an open window; a burglar broke in.*) Write student responses on the board.

■ Write the headings *Cause* and *Effect* on the board. Direct students to the sentence about turtles, and ask a student to read it aloud.

Ask *What two things happen in this sentence?* (Answer: *Turtles come out; weather gets warm.*)

Ask *Do you think that the weather gets warm because the turtles come out?* (Answer: *no*)

Ask *Do you think that the turtles come out of their winter homes because the weather is warm? Does that make more sense?* (Answer: *yes*)

Say *If the weather makes the turtles come out, the weather is the cause. The turtles coming out is the effect.*

Lesson 8 — What Happened and Why?

◢ Study It

One way writers explain something is by using **cause** and **effect** sentences. You can find a cause and an effect by asking the right questions and looking for signal words.

Cause	Effect
Ask, *Why did it happen?*	Ask, *What happened?*
A **cause** tells <u>why</u> something happened.	An **effect** explains <u>what</u> happened.

Look for word clues in a passage to find causes and effects. Signal words such as <u>because</u>, <u>since</u>, <u>after</u>, <u>before</u>, and <u>as a result</u> are often used in cause and effect sentences.

Writers sometimes tell you about an effect before they tell you the cause. You will need to ask the right questions and look for signal words to find the cause and the effect.

Read this sentence. Then look at the chart.

Turtles come out of their winter homes when the weather gets warm.

Cause (Why Did It Happen?)	Effect (What Happened?)
The weather gets warm.	Turtles come out of their winter homes.

In this sentence the cause is the warm weather. The effect is that turtles come out of their winter homes.

When you look for cause and effect, remember the following.

- Cause and effect help readers answer the questions <u>why</u> and <u>what</u>.
- Cause and effect can usually be found by looking for signal words.

Curriculum and Assessment Standard

Cause and effect

Sometimes a paragraph can have more than one cause and effect. In some paragraphs you may find two causes and two effects. In other paragraphs you may find several effects from one cause.

Read this passage. Look for more than one cause and effect.

The Final Baseball Game

The Hampton Hawks were finally playing in the championship game, but the score was tied. Then Joe Malik came up to bat for the Hawks. On the first pitch, he swung hard and hit a home run. The tie was broken! As a result the Hawks became the league champions.

Look at the chart that shows the causes and effects in the passage.

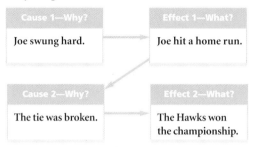

Cause 1—Why?	Effect 1—What?
Joe swung hard.	Joe hit a home run.

Cause 2—Why?	Effect 2—What?
The tie was broken.	The Hawks won the championship.

You can use a chart like this one to help you find more than one cause and effect in a passage. Remember to ask *Why did something happen?* and *What happened?* when you read.

Lesson 8 • 25

- Explain to students that sometimes there can be more than one cause and effect in a text. Direct students to "The Final Baseball Game." Ask a volunteer to read the passage aloud. Have students underline each cause and effect.

  Ask *What does Joe Malik do that is important in this story?* (Answer: *He hits a home run.*)

  Ask *Does the story tell you why he hits a home run?* (Answer: *because he swings hard*)

  Say *So the home run is the effect of Joe Malik's swinging hard.*

- Write the cause *swing hard* and the effect *home run* under the appropriate headings on the board.

  Ask *Does the home run cause anything to happen?* (Answer: *It breaks the tie.*)

  Say *So the home run is also a cause.*

- Write the cause *home run* and the effect *break tie* under the appropriate headings on the board.

  Ask *Does breaking the tie cause anything else to happen?* (Answer: *The Hawks become league champions.*)

  Say *So becoming champions is the effect of the tie being broken.*

- Write the cause *break tie* and the effect *become champions* under the appropriate headings on the board.

Help students understand that a single event can be both a cause of one action and the effect of another action.

Differentiated Instruction
for ELL, visual, and auditory learners

Matching Causes and Effects

Students practice identifying cause and effect relationships.

Procedure

- Divide the class into two equal groups. Name one group the *Causes* and give each member a yellow strip of paper. Name the other group the *Effects* and give each member a pink strip of paper.
- Ask the Effects group to write on their strips one sentence each about something that happened recently. Tape the pink strips to the board and number each one. Write the word *BECAUSE* in big letters after the strips.
- Assign one of the effects sentences to each student in the Causes group, and ask him or her to invent a sentence that explains why that effect happened.
- Collect the yellow strips from the Causes and read them aloud in random order. Ask the class to match each cause with its effect. As you go, tape the yellow strip to the right of the *BECAUSE,* next to its effect.

Use It

Use this section to help students practice finding cause and effect.

■ Write the headings *Cause* and *Effect* on the board. Then direct students to the passage "The Strange Effect," and read the directions aloud. Have students follow along as you read the passage aloud. Remind them to underline any signal words they find.

Ask *Which words in the passage tell you that there is a cause and an effect?* (Answer: *because, as a result, after*)

Say *Look at the word* because *and the words around it. Underline the whole sentence.*

Ask *What cause-and-effect relationship does the word* because *signal?*

■ Write the following sentence on the board under the heading *Effect: Dr. Jacobs threw the jar in the trash.*

Ask *Why did Dr. Jacobs throw the jar in the trash? What is the cause of her actions?* (Answer: *Slime started to ooze from the jar.*)

Have the students complete the *Use It* section independently. When they have finished, discuss their answers. Ask students to identify the signal words that go with each cause and effect. Help students understand that sometimes they must use their background knowledge to determine which action is the cause and which is the effect.

Use It

Read this passage. Look for causes and effects. Underline the signal words that show cause and effect.

The Strange Effect

Dr. Jacobs was in her secret lab working on a special project. She quickly threw a jar into the trash <u>because</u> slime started to ooze from it. The slime had already covered her hands. <u>As a result</u>, her hands began to glow. <u>After</u> she got home, her family said she looked like a space alien.

Look at the chart. Fill in the empty box in each chart.

Cause (Why Did It Happen?)	Effect (What Happened?)
Slime oozed from a jar.	Dr. Jacobs threw the jar in the trash.

Now you try it.

Cause (Why Did It Happen?)	Effect (What Happened?)
Dr. Jacobs got slime on her hands.	Her hands started to glow.

Cause (Why Did It Happen?)	Effect (What Happened?)
Dr. Jacobs's hands were glowing.	Her family said she looked like a space alien.

Read this passage from *Duck* by Barrie Watts. Look for causes and effects. Then read the questions. Circle the letter of the correct answer.

It takes up to 48 hours for the duckling to break out of the egg completely. It is tired and its feathers are wet. The duckling's mother keeps it warm until its feathers dry out. The duckling still has some of the egg yolk in its body. Over the next few days it will use the yolk for food, until it is strong enough to find something to eat.

1. **What causes the duckling to be tired and wet?**

   A Its mother keeps it warm.

   B It uses the yolk for food.

   C It has just broken out of its egg.

   D It has just learned to swim.

2. **Why does a duckling need to use some of the yolk for food?**

   A Its mother does not have any food.

   B It is not strong enough to find its own food.

   C Ducklings never eat other kinds of food.

   D The mother does not want it to waste food.

3. **How does the duckling stay warm?**

   A The yolk makes it warm.

   B It is warm because it gets stronger.

   C The mother keeps it warm.

   D It is warm in the egg.

Tip When you read, use cause and effect charts to help you understand why things happen.

Practice It

Work through the page to help students understand how cause and effect work together to tell a story.

Question 1 Read the directions aloud. Ask students to read the passage silently. When they have finished, read question 1 aloud and ask students to circle the answer that best matches the cause in the text. (Answer: *C, It has just broken out of its egg.*)

Discuss student answers. Help students recognize that only *C* explains why the duckling is wet and tired. To help students understand the correct answer, discuss the incorrect answers.

- *A* is the effect of the duckling being wet. ● *B* is not related to the duckling's being wet and tired.
- *D* is not mentioned in the text.

Question 2 Read question 2 aloud. Have students complete the question independently and then stop.

To help students understand why *B* is the best answer, use the *Right There Strategy*. (See the *QAR Strategy* below.)

Say *Sometimes the exact words you are looking for are in the passage. You must read carefully to find them.*

Ask *Who can name the key words in the correct answer,* It is not strong enough to find its own food*? (Answer: strong enough to find food)*

Say *Underline these keys words in answer* B.

Ask *Who can find these words in the passage?*

Say *Underline these words in the passage.*

Question 3 Ask students to complete question 3 independently. When they have finished, discuss students' answers. Help them recognize that *C* is the correct answer.

QAR Strategy

Strategy	Definition	How It Works
Right There	This strategy teaches students that the correct answer appears in one place in whatever they are reading.	Students look for the *key words* in the answer choices that match the words in the text. The match is sometimes, but not always, exact.

Refer to pages T22–T23 for a complete chart of QAR Strategies that students may use to achieve greater success on tests of reading comprehension.

Lesson 9

Objective

Students will identify the main idea and supporting details of a paragraph.

Words to Know

Main Idea—what a passage is about

Details—support for the main idea

Study It

Review the definition of *main idea* and *details* with students. Explain that details often answer questions about the main idea.

- Direct students to the passage about chimpanzees. Ask students to follow along as you read the passage aloud. Ask students to draw a line under the sentence that best explains the main idea of the paragraph.

  Ask *Who can tell me what the main idea of this paragraph is?* (Answer: *Chimpanzees are friendly.*)

  Ask *Which sentence best states the main idea?* (Answer: *the first sentence*)

- Write the main idea on the board and underline it. Draw three lines extending from the main idea, and then draw a large circle at the end of each line.

  Ask *What details does the writer use to tell us how chimpanzees show that they are friendly?*

  Say *The middle three sentences give the most details.*

- Write one of the three details in each of the circles on the board. Point out that the last sentence is a way of restating the main idea in a different way.

Big Picture

Study It

Most paragraphs in a nonfiction passage have a **main idea**. The main idea tells you who or what the paragraph is mostly about. **Detail** sentences in each paragraph support the main idea.

When you read, look for the main idea. Then ask yourself how each detail in the paragraph supports the main idea.

- Each paragraph has a main idea.
- Each sentence in a paragraph contains details that support the main idea.

Details can

- explain a main idea
- answer important questions, such as <u>where</u>, <u>when</u>, <u>why</u>, and <u>how</u>
- give facts, examples, and reasons that support the main idea

Read this paragraph. Think about the main idea and details. Then look at the chart.

> Chimpanzees are very friendly animals. They enjoy being together. When chimpanzees meet, they greet each other with pats on the back and holding hands. They may part and comb each other's hair. Chimpanzees like quiet, friendly physical contact with one another.

Main Idea
Chimpanzees are friendly animals that like physical contact.

Detail	Detail	Detail
They enjoy being together.	They greet each other with back pats and by holding hands.	They part and comb each other's hair.

Curriculum and Assessment Standard

Main idea/supporting details

Read this paragraph. Think about the main idea and details. Then look at the chart.

Roald Dahl became interested in writing books for children when he made up bedtime stories for his own children. Some of Roald Dahl's best-known books are *James and the Giant Peach* and *Charlie and the Chocolate Factory*. His books are found in many libraries and bookstores. Roald Dahl is one of today's most popular children's writers.

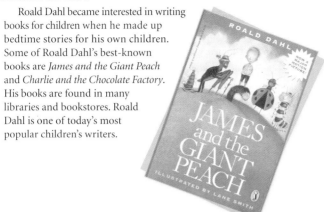

Main Idea
Roald Dahl is one of today's most popular children's writers.

Detail	Detail	Detail
He has written many well-known books.	His books are found in libraries and bookstores.	Dahl's books include *James and the Giant Peach* and *Charlie and the Chocolate Factory*.

Remember, the main idea is who or what the paragraph is about. The detail sentences tell when, where, why, and how something happens.

Lesson 9 • 29

- Direct students to the paragraph about Roald Dahl. Ask a volunteer to read the paragraph aloud.

  Say *The main idea is not always the first sentence in a paragraph.* Then have students look at the chart below the passage.

  Ask *According to this chart, what is the main idea?* (Answer: *Roald Dahl is one of today's most popular children's writers.*)

  Ask *Who can find the place in the paragraph where this sentence appears?* (Answer: *at the end of the paragraph*)

  Say *Sometimes the first sentence will not state the main idea of a paragraph. The main idea may be stated at the end of the paragraph.*

- Read the first detail in the chart aloud. Then model a question that this detail could answer.

  Say *This detail can answer the question "Why is Roald Dahl popular?"*

  Ask *What questions about Roald Dahl do the other details in this passage answer?*

- Give students a few minutes to invent questions for each of the remaining details. Then ask volunteers to share their questions with the class. Write student responses on the board. Help students understand that details should always relate to the main idea.

Differentiated Instruction
for ELL, visual, tactile, and auditory learners

My Favorite Animal

Students will practice identifying main ideas and details by describing an animal.

Procedure

- Have students fold a sheet of paper in half crosswise, and then fold it crosswise again. When they open the page, have students label the top section *Main Idea* and each of the next three sections *Detail 1, Detail 2,* and *Detail 3.*

- Tell students that they will be writing about an animal, such as a pet or an animal that interests them. Have students write three facts about the animal in the *Details* sections. Suggest that students tell about how the animal acts and looks or where it lives.

- Have students take turns reading their details to the class. Ask the class to tell the student what the selected animal is like. Then have students use the class's ideas to write the main idea.

◢ Use It

Use this section to help students practice finding the main idea and details in a passage.

- Write the heading *Main Idea* on the board. Then extend four lines from the heading and draw a box at the end of each line.

- Direct students to the passage about icebergs, and read aloud the directions. Have students follow along as you read the passage aloud. Tell them to underline at least four details.

  Ask *What are some of the details about icebergs that you found in this passage?*

- Write the details in the boxes on the board. (Use the chart as a guide to the important details.)

  Ask *What questions do these details answer about icebergs?*

Have students work independently to complete the chart. When they have finished, discuss their answers. Ask students to point to the sentence in the paragraph that best expresses the main idea (the first sentence). Check to be sure that students can locate this sentence in the text. Help students understand that in this paragraph, all of the details answer the questions *"What are the different sizes and shapes that icebergs come in?"*

Read this passage. The main idea is circled. Underline each detail. Then write the details in the chart.

Icebergs come in different shapes and sizes. One iceberg may be domed, with a rounded top like that of an old mountain. Another may be blocky, a big square slab of floating ice. Some icebergs are small, but others are several miles long. In 1996 an iceberg larger than the state of Rhode Island broke away from Antarctica. When you see an iceberg, you only see part of it. The part above water is just the tip. The part you do not see is many times bigger than the tip.

Main Idea			
Icebergs come in different shapes and sizes.			

Detail	Detail	Detail	Detail
An iceberg can be domed.	An iceberg can be a square slab of floating ice.	Some are small, but others are several miles long.	One iceberg was bigger than the state of Rhode Island.

Work through the page to help students understand how main ideas and details go together to explain an idea.

Question 1 Read the directions aloud. Then read question 1 aloud. Have students read the passage silently. Then review with them the main idea and details in the chart.

To help students understand why *C* is the best answer, use the *Right There Strategy*. (See the *QAR Strategy* below.) Explain that the strategy uses key words to find the correct answer to a question.

Say *The correct answer has important words called* key words. *Sometimes the same key words are also in the passage. At other times, the key words in a correct answer mean the same thing as key words in the paragraph.*

Ask *Who can name the key words in the correct answer,* "Cats make faces to communicate." (Answer: *make faces*)

Say *Underline these keys words in answer* C.

Ask *Who can find these words in the passage?*

Say *Underline these words in the passage.*

Say *You have used the* Right There Strategy *to find the correct answer to question 1. The answer you needed was* "right there."

Discuss the incorrect answers with students.

● *A* and *B* are not mentioned in the text. ● *D* is the main idea.

Practice It

Read the passage and look at the chart. Then read the question. Circle the letter of the correct answer.

Cats have many ways to communicate, or share information, with each other. Sometimes they use their bodies, and sometimes they make sounds. One way that cats let other cats know that they are angry or afraid is to make faces. Cats also move their tails to communicate. They may hold their tails straight up to say, "I feel friendly." If they are unhappy, they may move their tails back and forth. Cats make sounds like meowing, hissing, or growling. Some sounds can mean "hello," while other sounds can mean "leave me alone."

Main Idea
Cats have many ways to communicate with each other.

Detail	Detail	Detail
Cats make faces to communicate.	Cats use their bodies to communicate.	Cats make sounds to communicate.

1. **Which is the BEST detail to fill in the empty box?**

   A Cats hunt and catch birds.

   B Cats chase one another.

   C Cats make faces to communicate.

   D Cats communicate.

Tip To find the main idea, ask yourself who or what the paragraph is MOSTLY about.

Lesson 9 ● 31

◯ QAR Strategy

Strategy	Definition	How It Works
Right There	This strategy teaches students that the correct answer appears in one place in whatever they are reading.	Students look for the *key words* in the answer choices that match the words in the text. The match is sometimes, but not always, exact.

Refer to pages T22–T23 for a complete chart of QAR Strategies that students may use to achieve greater success on tests of reading comprehension.

Lesson 10

Objective

Students will summarize main ideas and details and use their own words to paraphrase texts.

Words to Know

Summary—statement of the main idea and details in as few words as possible

Paraphrase—to restate a writer's work in one's own words

◢ Study It

Discuss the concepts of *summarizing* and *paraphrasing* with students.

■ Direct students to the passage. Ask students to follow along as you read the passage aloud.

Say *When you read a passage with many details, it is sometimes difficult to remember all of the ideas in the passage. Writing a summary is one way to help you better understand and remember what you have read.*

■ Write the headings *Main Idea, Details,* and *Summary* on the board. Then direct students to the chart beneath the passage. Explain that the chart shows the important parts of a summary.

Ask *What is the main idea of this passage?* (Answer: *The colonists wanted a new life.*) Write the answer under the heading *Main Idea.*

Ask *Who can tell me some of the most important details in the passage?* (See chart for answers.)

■ Write the answers under the heading *Details.* Discuss with students how the main idea and details contribute to the summary.

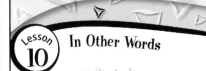

Lesson 10 — In Other Words

◢ Study It

When you read, it is a good idea to put the author's ideas into your own words. Using your own words helps you understand the information and remember what you have read.

There are two ways to put ideas into your own words. You can write a **summary,** or you can **paraphrase** a passage.

When you write a summary, write down only the main ideas and most important details of a passage. A summary is shorter than the original passage.

To write a summary, you should

- look for main ideas and important details
- write in your own words
- be sure that the information is correct and written clearly

Read this passage. Then look at the chart.

In the early 1600s, people came from England to North America. In North America they set up colonies. These colonists wanted a new life. North America was a beautiful and mostly unexplored continent. Many people dreamed of owning their own land there. In England some colonists had not owned their own land. Some people also came to America so that they could be free to practice their religion.

Summary Chart	
Main Idea: The colonists wanted a new life.	**Summary:**
Detail: came to North America from England **Detail:** came in early 1600s **Detail:** wanted to own land **Detail:** wanted to practice their own religion	Colonists came to North America from England in the early 1600s. They came so they could own land and have religious freedom.

Paraphrase/summarize

Curriculum and Assessment Standard

Paraphrase/summarize

Paraphrasing can help you understand difficult passages. When you paraphrase, you are rewriting a passage without changing its meaning.

When you paraphrase, look up difficult words and replace them with synonyms. You can also put the words in a different order. Finally, make sure the paraphrase is about the same length as the original passage.

A paraphrase is useful for taking notes for a report, but you would not paraphrase a whole book.

Read this passage.

"My country 'tis of thee,
Sweet land of liberty,
Of thee I sing.
Land where my fathers died!
Land of the Pilgrim's pride!
From every mountain side,
Let freedom ring!"

Use a dictionary to look up words that you do not understand.

father means "forefather or ancestor"

liberty means "freedom from control"

Pilgrim means "any of the group of English Puritans who founded Plymouth Colony in 1620"

'tis is a contraction of it is

Now read this paraphrase of the passage above.

I am singing about my country, a land of freedom.
My ancestors died here.
The Pilgrims were proud of this land.
Let the sound of freedom ring out from every mountain.

Lesson 10 • 33

- Direct students' attention to the passage in the text, and ask a volunteer to read it aloud. Ask students to underline any words that they don't know.

  Ask *What are the words that you don't understand in this passage?*

- List the difficult words from the passage. Then have students use the definitions below the passage to come up with synonyms for the difficult words. Cross out difficult words on the board and replace them with synonyms.

  Say *Sometimes it helps to put words and ideas in a new order when you paraphrase.*

  Ask *How can I rearrange the first sentences to put the ideas in a simpler order?*

- Direct students to the chart to see how the sentences have been rearranged.

- Write on the board: *In order to get a better view, Jonah dragged a chair from the dining room to the fence in the backyard and then climbed up onto the chair.* Ask a volunteer to read this sentence aloud.

  Ask *How can I paraphrase this sentence?*

- Give students a few minutes to write a simpler version of the sentence. Encourage them to use as few words as possible to express the main idea of the sentence. (Possible answer: *Jonah stood on a chair to see over the fence.*)

 **Differentiated Instruction**
for visual and auditory learners

Abridged Nursery Rhymes

Students will rewrite nursery rhymes in their own words.

Procedure

- Write the first verse of "Mary Had a Little Lamb" on the board, and then read it aloud. Model the process of paraphrasing by writing the following sentence on the board: *Mary's white lamb followed her everywhere.* Discuss the difference between the information in the verse and that in the sentence.

- Post other nursery rhymes around the classroom, and have a different student read each one aloud. Then ask students to select one of the rhymes to paraphrase. Have students write one or two sentences in their own words.

- Ask students to read their sentence(s) in front of the class. Ask the class to guess which nursery rhyme is being paraphrased. Discuss which important details were included and which were left out.

Use It

Use this section to help students paraphrase complex ideas.

■ Direct students to the passage about corals. Have students take turns reading sentences 1 through 10. After each sentence,

Ask *Are there any difficult words in this sentence?*

■ Have students underline the difficult words. When they have finished, copy sentence 1 onto the board and read it aloud.

Ask *How can I paraphrase sentence 1?* (Answer: *Corals live in saltwater.*)

■ Write the paraphrased sentence on the board next to the original sentence.

■ Direct students to the first question below the passage. Have a student read the question and then read sentence 2 from the passage aloud.

Ask *What synonyms can I use to replace the words* shallow *and* temperate? (Answer: *not deep; warm*)

■ If students are not familiar with the words *shallow* and *temperate,* ask a volunteer to find the words in the dictionary and read the definitions aloud. Then give students a few minutes to rewrite Sentence 2 in their own words. When they have finished, discuss student answers.

■ Repeat the process with questions 2 and 3.

Use It

Read the passage. Underline any difficult words. Then write the answers to the questions.

(1) Corals are saltwater animals. (2) They grow where the ocean is shallow and temperate. (3) After many years the little corals build huge reefs. (4) A coral reef is similar to a vibrant, submerged garden.

(5) Plants and animals live in the coral reef. (6) The reef has many holes where animals can live. (7) Lobsters and octopuses can live in a coral reef. (8) Brightly colored sponges grow on the rocks. (9) Snails, sea stars, and many fish come to the reef to consume the sponges. (10) Butterfly fish and grouper are just a few of the kinds of fish found there.

1. How would you paraphrase sentence 2?
   Corals grow where the ocean water is warm and not very deep.

2. How would you paraphrase sentence 4?
   A coral reef looks like a colorful, underwater garden.

3. How would you paraphrase sentence 9?
   Many forms of sea life such as snails, sea stars, and fish eat sponges on the reef.

Practice It

Read the passage and look at the chart. Then read the questions. Circle the letter of the correct answer.

(1) Native Americans in the Pacific Northwest used to make totem poles. (2) Each totem pole told a story. (3) The decorative poles were enhanced with animals and faces. (4) Some were painted. (5) Totem poles passed on family histories and legends and marked the places where families lived. (6) The totem poles were often placed along riverbanks so that people in canoes could see them.

Summary Chart

Main Idea:	Summary:
Detail: told stories **Detail:** told family histories and legends **Detail:** marked where a family lived	Native Americans in the Pacific Northwest used totem poles to record stories, legends, and family histories. A totem pole also marked where a family lived.

1. **What main idea should be placed in the chart?**

   A Totem poles had animals and faces carved on them.

   B Native Americans lived in the Pacific Northwest.

   C Native Americans had family villages.

   (D) Native Americans in the Pacific Northwest used to make totem poles.

2. **Which sentence is the best paraphrase of sentence 3?**

   A The poles were made out of animals.

   B Animals made the poles with pictures of faces.

   (C) The poles had animals and faces carved on them.

   D Animals used their faces to make the poles.

> **Tip**
> When you paraphrase, put all the ideas from a passage into your own words.

Lesson 10 • 35

This page may not be reproduced without permission of Steck-Vaughn.

Practice It

Work through the page to help students understand that summaries focus on the main idea of a text.

Question 1 Read the directions aloud. Then read question 1 aloud. Have students read the passage silently and then read over the details in the chart. Ask them to choose the main idea of the passage and circle the best answer.

To help students understand why *D* is the correct answer, talk through the steps of finding the main idea.

Ask *If you had to think of a title of only two words for this passage, what would it be?* (Answer: *Totem Poles*)

Say *This passage is mostly about totem poles. Which answers can you cross out because they don't mention totem poles?* (Answer: *B* and *C*)

Say *Now look at answers* A *and* D, *and decide which is a better main idea. Answer* A *is more of a detail, so* D *is the main idea.*

Question 2 Read the *Tip* aloud, and have students complete question 2 independently. Discuss students' answers.

To help students understand why *C* is the best answer, use the *Think and Search Strategy.* (See the *QAR Strategy* below.) Explain that with this strategy, it is important to think about the questions and reread the sentence to find the best answer.

Say *First reread Sentence 3. Think of a way to simplify this sentence.*

Say *Then read all of the possible answers, and cross out any answers that do not match the text.*

Ask *When you reread the sentence and the answers, which answer best matches Sentence 3?* (Answer: *C*)

QAR Strategy

Strategy	Definition	How It Works
Think and Search	This strategy teaches students to use knowledge that they already have and relate it to the sentence as they choose the correct answer.	Students think about the answer they are looking for as they reread the text. They remember that they may need to draw conclusions about what they are reading.

Refer to pages T22–T23 for a complete chart of QAR Strategies that students may use to achieve greater success on tests of reading comprehension.

Unit 2 ■ 35

Lesson 11

Objective

Students will identify the author's purpose in a written text.

Words to Know

Purpose—a reason for doing something

Study It

Review the definition of *author's purpose,* and discuss the four reasons for writing: to entertain, to persuade, to inform, and to express feelings. Write these four purposes on the board.

■ Direct students to the list of questions to ask about a text.

   Ask *What kind of writing do you find in a newspaper?* (Answer: *news articles, informative writing*)

   Ask *Why do you read the newspaper?* (Answer: *to get news and information*)

   Ask *What do you think is the author's main purpose in a news article?* (Answer: *to inform*)

■ Write *newspaper article* on the board under the heading *To Inform.* Then ask students to think of other texts they would read to get information. Write student responses on the board. (Possible answers: *magazines, dictionaries, reference books, textbooks*)

■ Repeat the same questions, this time using *nursery rhymes* as an example. Ask students to think of nursery rhymes that they know. Help them understand that the author's main purpose in writing a nursery rhyme is to entertain.

Lesson 11 — What's the Point?

Study It

An author always has a **purpose,** or reason, for writing. Usually the author does not tell you directly what the purpose is. Instead, you need to look for hints.

Look at the chart. It shows different reasons why authors write.

Author's Purpose
to persuade, or get you to agree with an idea or to do something
to express feelings
to entertain
to inform or tell about something

When you read something, ask yourself some questions.

- Who is the audience?
- What kind of writing is it? Is it a poem? Is it a story? Is it an article? Is it a play? Is it journal writing?
- What is the topic or subject?

Then ask yourself these questions to learn the author's purpose.

- Does the writing mostly show personal feelings?
- Does the writing try to entertain the reader?
- Does the writing give information or explain something?
- Does the writing try to get me to agree with an idea?

36 ● Unit 2   Author's purpose

Curriculum and Assessment Standard

Author's purpose

Read the letter. Suppose that Goldilocks is a real person and that she wrote this letter after she visited the house of the three bears. Think about her purpose.

> Dear Mother,
>   You should feel sorry for me. I was hungry after skipping through the woods. Then I saw a house with the door wide open, and there was soup on the table. It smelled delicious. I didn't want the soup to get cold, so I ate it.
>   After I ate, I was sleepy. So I climbed into the smallest bed and fell asleep.
>   When the owners came home, they screamed at me. I was really afraid. I jumped up and ran home. I didn't do anything wrong.
>   Love,
>   Goldilocks

Who is the audience?	Goldilocks is writing to her mother.
What kind of writing is it?	It is a letter.
What is the writing about?	Goldilocks's visit to the house of the three bears.
What is the purpose of the letter?	Goldilocks wants to persuade her mother that she did not do anything wrong.

Goldilocks wrote the letter to persuade her mother.

She did not write to entertain her mother. If that had been her purpose, she would have written a different letter. She might have told how funny things were.

She did not write to give information about the three bears' house. A letter with that purpose would have told what all the rooms were like and what the food tasted like.

She did not write just to say how afraid she was either. If that were her purpose, she probably would have written a lot about her feelings.

Lesson 11 ● 37

- Direct students to the letter written by Goldilocks. Ask students to follow along as you read it aloud.

- Direct students to the chart below the letter. Copy on the board the questions from the left-hand column of the chart. Have a student read the first question aloud.

  Ask *Who will read this text?* (Answer: *Goldilocks's mother*)

- Write the answer on the board next to the question. Then ask a student to read the second question aloud.

  Ask *What do you call a text when someone addresses it directly to another person?* (Answer: *a letter*)

- Write the answer on the board next to the question. Then ask a student to read the third question aloud.

  Ask *What is Goldilocks describing in the letter?* (Answer: *what she did in the three bears' house*)

- Write the answer on the board next to the question. Then ask a student to read the fourth question aloud.

  Say *Let's read the first sentence again: "You should feel sorry for me." Goldilocks is trying to make her mother feel a certain way. What is the purpose when an author wants to make the reader feel the same way he or she feels?* (Answer: *to persuade*)

Review the text below the chart with students. Help students understand that although a text can sometimes have more than one purpose, there is usually only one main purpose.

Differentiated Instruction
for ELL, visual, and auditory learners

Mapping Author's Purpose

Students make word webs to match author's purpose to types of texts.

Procedure

- Review the four purposes for writing: *to entertain, to express, to inform,* and *to persuade.*

- Model a word web on the board by writing one purpose with a circle around it and drawing lines out from the circle. Have students brainstorm the kinds of writing that have that purpose. Suggest different texts (magazines, letters, stories, reports, and so on) and ask whether these items match this purpose.

- Organize students in pairs or small groups and have them make their own word webs with one of the remaining purposes and its matching texts.

- On the board, compile lists of the different types of texts that students suggest for each purpose. Point out texts that may have more than one purpose.

Use It

Use this section to help students demonstrate what they know about author's purpose.

- Direct students to the passage about bike helmets. Ask a volunteer to read the passage aloud. Then read the question aloud.

  Say *Think about questions to ask when you are reading a text.*

  Ask *What kind of text is this? Is it a poem? A letter? An essay? A story?* (Answer: *essay*)

  Ask *Where do you think you would find a text like this?* (Answer: *in a newspaper, book, or magazine*)

  Ask *What is the author telling the reader? What is the main idea?* (Answer: *why it is important to wear a helmet*)

  Ask *What do you think is the author's purpose for writing this?* (Answer: *to persuade*)

  Ask *What idea is the author trying to get the reader to agree with?* (Answer: *that all states should have a helmet law*)

Read the *Use It* directions aloud. Have students read the next passage silently and decide what the author's purpose is. When they have finished, discuss their answers.

Use It

Read this passage. Look for hints about the author's purpose. Then answer the question.

It is important to wear a helmet while riding a bicycle. There are as many as 45,000 head injuries to children each year. The laws of many states say that anyone under the age of sixteen who rides a bike must wear a helmet. But some states still do not have a helmet law. All states need to have laws about bike helmets. It would make bicycling safer for all children.

What is the author's purpose?

to persuade

Now you try it.

Read this poem. Then read the question. Write your answer on the line.

The Library

I choose a book and on its pages
I enter a world of knights and sages.
The dragon is winning—no, now the knight!
I think I know who'll win this fight.
In another book we're making bread
the same way as my Uncle Ted!
(Let it rise, push it down,
bake until the top is brown.)
Now I follow one small bear
through the forest, to his favorite chair.
There are so many worlds inside these books
no matter on which shelf I look.

1. What is the author's purpose?
   to entertain

Practice It

Read this letter. Then read the items. Circle the letter of the correct answer.

Dear City Planner,

I am a fourth-grade student at Valley Park School. I have been worried about all of the traffic around our school. Every day I see more and more cars. I walk to school, and it takes a long time to cross the street with so much traffic. I think it would be a good idea to put a crossing guard on the corner near my school. Then I will be able to cross the street more safely. Please talk about it at your next meeting.

James Graffin

1. The main purpose of the letter is to —

(A) persuade

B entertain

C give facts

D tell a story

2. What does the writer of the letter want the city planner to do?

A tell fourth graders not to worry

B solve the traffic problems

(C) provide a school crossing guard

D visit the school

3. The writer tries to achieve his purpose by —

A ordering the city planner to act

B talking about what a good student he is

(C) telling about his own experiences

D offering to serve as a crossing guard

Tip — As you read, think about the writer's purpose.

Lesson 11 • 39

Practice It

Read the directions aloud. Then have students read the passage silently and stop when they have finished.

Question 1 Read the question aloud. Ask students to circle the answer that best matches the author's purpose. (Answer: *A, persuade*)

Discuss student answers. Help students recognize that only *A* can be the author's purpose for writing the letter. To help students understand the correct answer, explain the incorrect answers.

● *B* is incorrect because the author would have described funny or interesting experiences. ● *C* is not a purpose. ● *D* is incorrect because the text is a letter.

Question 2 Read the question aloud. Ask students to circle the answer that tells what the writer wants (Answer: *C, provide a school crossing guard*)

Discuss student answers. Help students recognize that only *C* offers the correct solution to a problem. To help students understand the correct answer, explain the incorrect answers.

● *A* is incorrect because the writer does not talk about others being worried. ● *B* is incorrect because James is not solving traffic problems. ● *D* is incorrect because James says nothing about visiting the school.

Question 3 Read the question aloud. Ask students to circle the answer that best describes the way the writer tried to persuade the reader. (Answer: *C, telling about his own experiences*)

Discuss student answers. Help students recognize that only *C* is a technique that the author uses. To help students understand the correct answer, explain the incorrect answers.

● *A* is incorrect because the author does not order anyone to act. ● *B* and *D* are not what the author does in this text.

Unit 2 ■ 39

Lesson 12

Objective

Students will read graphics to get information about a topic.

Words to Know

Graphics—a way of showing information with images and labels instead of with words

Chart—a graphic that arranges information in a certain order, often using columns and rows or a circle

Map—a graphic that shows where different places are in relation to one another

Diagram—a graphic that shows how parts of an object or steps in a process fit together

Graph—a graphic that compares information

Picture—a drawing or photograph of a person or an object

◢ Study It

Introduce students to various kinds of graphics.

- Explain that it is often easier to present information in a format that does not include having everything written out in a paragraph. For example, a chart can use fewer words to display the same information as a paragraph.

- Read aloud the bulleted list for understanding graphics. Discuss each point with students.

  Ask *What is the first step you should take when you see a graphic, such as a chart or graph?* (Answer: *Read the title.*)

  Ask *What else should you do when you see a graphic?* (Answer: *Read all the labels, words, map symbols, and numbers.*)

Review the definitions of the different types of graphics with students.

Lesson 12 — Picture This!

◢ Study It

Graphics are **charts, maps, diagrams, graphs,** or **pictures** that show information. Writers sometimes use graphics when there are too many facts and numbers to include in a paragraph. Graphics arrange information so that it is easy to understand.

Graphics show information in different ways.

- Charts put information in a certain order.
- Maps show where places are.
- Diagrams show steps for doing something, how parts of things fit together, or how a process works.
- Graphs compare information.
- Pictures can be drawings or photographs. They show what something looks like.

Here are some helpful hints for understanding graphics.

- Read the title. It tells you the topic of the graphic.
- Read the labels on the side and the bottom of graphs. These labels tell you what each bar, mark, or figure means.
- Read all the words. They will tell you more about the graphic.
- If you are looking at a map, look at the map key to understand what the symbols, or marks, mean.
- Look at all the numbers if there are any. Are they percents? Are they dollars? Are they in tens or hundreds?
- Look at the highest, or greatest, number if the chart or graph has numbers. Then look for the lowest, or least, number.

Curriculum and Assessment Standard

Graphics

Look at this chart.

Student	Days of the Week					Total
	Mon.	Tue.	Wed.	Thurs.	Fri.	
Catherine	6	7	0	0	1	14
Kaya	0	2	1	2	2	7
Raymond	3	2	1	0	3	9
Raphael	0	2	1	1	0	4

Table title: Pages Read by Students During the Week

Here is what this chart tells you.

- The title tells you that the chart is about the number of pages read by students during a week.
- The labels for each column tell you what kind of information is in each column. For example, the first column lists students' names, and the next five columns list the days of the week. The last column lists the total number of pages read by each student for the week.
- The rows tell you how many pages each student read each day and the total number of pages that each student read in five days.

Now you can answer these questions.

Which student read the most pages during the week?	Catherine
Which student read the fewest pages during the week?	Raphael
Who did not read any pages on Friday?	Raphael
How many pages did Kaya read in the week?	7 pages
What is the title of the chart?	"Pages Read by Students During the Week"

Lesson 12 • 41

Differentiated Instruction
for ELL, visual, tactile, and kinesthetic learners

Life-Sized Bar Graph
Students will create life-sized charts.

Procedure

- Place a length of butcher paper on the floor, and ask a volunteer to lie on the paper with his or her feet against the paper's bottom edge. Draw a line across the paper at the point where the top of the student's head meets the paper. Have the student use that sheet of paper to draw a life-sized, full-length self-portrait while you continue the process with the other students.
- When students have finished their drawings, help them measure the length of each drawing in centimeters. Record the height of each student.
- Tape student drawings along a wall so that the bottom edges are flush.
- Using more butcher paper, help students create a graph of their heights. The x-axis will show each student's name, and the y-axis will measure from 0 centimeters to the height of the tallest student.

- Direct students to the chart.

  Ask *What is the title of this chart?* (Answer: *Pages Read by Students During the Week*)

  Ask *What heading do you see in the top left corner of the chart?* (Answer: *Student*)

- Point out the location of headings and labels as you go.

  Ask *What information do you see below this heading?* (Answer: *the name of each student*)

  Ask *What heading do you see at the top of the chart?* (Answer: *Days of the Week*)

  Ask *What do the numbers in the chart tell you?* (Answer: *how many pages each student read on each day*)

- Copy the questions from below the chart on the board. Ask a volunteer to read the first question aloud.

  Say *To answer this question, first find the column that tells you the total number of pages that each student read. Then find the number that shows the most pages read.*

  Ask *What is the greatest number?* (Answer: *14*)

  Say *Now move your finger to the left until you find the name of the student who read 14 pages.*

  Ask *Who read 14 pages during the week?* (Answer: *Catherine*)

- Ask for a volunteer to read the next question on the board.

  Say *Now find the number that shows the fewest pages read.*

  Ask *What is the smallest number?* (Answer: *4*)

  Say *Move your finger to the left until you find the name of the student who read 4 pages.*

  Ask *Who read only 4 pages during the week?* (Answer: *Raphael*)

- Ask a volunteer to read the next question on the board. Repeat the process, helping students locate the correct headings and numbers for each question.

Unit 2 ■ **41**

◢ Use It

Use this section to help students get information from a chart.

■ Read the *Use It* directions aloud. Then direct students to the chart, and read aloud the names of the cities and the high and low temperatures recorded for each. Then copy the example questions on the board, and have a student read the first question aloud.

Ask *Where is the title on this chart?* (Answer: *at the top*)

■ Ask students to point to the location of the title. Make sure that all students can locate it. Then ask a student to read the title aloud. Write the title on the board next to the first example question.

■ Read the second example question aloud.

Ask *What heading will you look for first after reading this question,* High *or* Low? (Answer: *Low*)

Say *Find* Low *on the chart.*

Ask *What is the lowest number in the* Low *column?* (Answer: *47°*)

Say *Now move your finger over to find the city that goes with the number 47.*

Ask *What city goes with the number 47?* (Answer: *Anchorage*)

■ Write *Anchorage* on the board next to the question.

Have the students complete the remaining items independently. When they have finished, discuss their answers. As students answer the questions, have them point to the place on the chart where each answer can be found. Make sure that all students can locate the correct answers on the chart.

◢ Use It

Look at this chart. Then answer the questions.

Average High and Low Temperatures in June		
City	High	Low
Anchorage	62°	47°
Denver	81°	52°
New York	79°	63°
Phoenix	104°	73°
Pittsburgh	79°	57°
Seattle	70°	52°

Look at these examples.

1. What is the title of the chart?
   Average High and Low Temperatures in June

2. Which city has the lowest average temperature in June?
   Anchorage

Now you try it.

1. What cities are listed on the chart?
   Anchorage, Denver, New York, Phoenix, Pittsburgh, Seattle

2. Which city has the highest average temperature?
   Phoenix

3. Which city has a high average temperature of 81°?
   Denver

4. Which city has a low average temperature of 57°?
   Pittsburgh

A **circle graph** is another kind of graphic. It is sometimes called a **pie chart** because each part of the circle looks like a slice of pie.

Look at the circle graph. Then read the items. Circle the letter of the correct answer.

Daily Activities

Sleep
9 hours

School
6 hours

Playing
4 hours

Eating
3 hours

Homework
2 hours

1. **What activity takes up the MOST amount of time in a day?**

   (A) sleeping

   B playing

   C eating

   D school

2. **This circle graph tells you that —**

   A doing homework takes up more time than sleeping

   B most of a day is spent eating

   (C) more time is spent at school than playing

   D eating takes up less time than doing homework

3. **Which activity takes up the LEAST amount of time in a day?**

   A eating

   (B) homework

   C school

   D playing

Tip

Read the titles and labels carefully when you look at a graphic.

Lesson 12 ■ 43

This page may not be reproduced without permission of Steck-Vaughn

Work through the page to help students understand how to use a circle graph to find information.

Read the directions aloud. Give students time to look at the information on the circle chart.

Question 1 Read the question aloud. Have students circle the answer that matches the activity that takes the most time.

Say *A circle graph makes it easy to find the largest and smallest numbers. Just look for the largest or smallest piece of the pie.*

Ask *To answer this question, do you want to find the largest or smallest piece of the pie?* (Answer: *largest*)

Ask *What color is the largest piece of the pie?* (Answer: *blue*)

Ask *What is the activity label on the blue section?* (Answer: *Sleep*)

Ask *Which answer best corresponds to the activity label?* (Answer: *A, sleeping*)

Question 2 Read the question aloud. Ask students to circle the answer that is a true statement about the chart. (Answer: *C, more time is spent at school than playing*)

Discuss student answers. Help students recognize that only *C* is a true statement. To help students understand the correct answer, explain the incorrect answers.

● *A* is incorrect because the Homework section is smaller than the Sleep section. ● *B* is incorrect because the Eating section is not larger than all the other sections. ● *D* is incorrect because the Eating section is larger than the Homework section.

Question 3 Read the question aloud. Have students circle the answer that matches the activity that takes the least amount of time. (Answer: *B, homework*)

Discuss the answers. Help students understand that the smallest section corresponds to the least amount of time.

Unit 2 ■ 43

Teach the Strategy

Write on the board: *Rob likes to grow many different plants. Yesterday he planted flowers in his yard. He is growing three tomato plants in pots on the porch. He has a cactus in his window.*

Ask *Which of these sentences tells you who or what the paragraph is about?* (Answer: *the first sentence*) Circle the first sentence.

Ask *Which of these sentences are details that tell you when, where, how, and why?* (Answer: *the next three sentences*) Underline the sentences.

Say *Read the passage again. The underlined sentences should answer questions about the circled sentence.*

Find the Main Idea Strategy

Explain to students that looking for the sentences that answer such questions as *when, where, how* and *why* is a test-taking strategy called the *Find the Main Idea Strategy.*

- Write these answer choices below the paragraph on the board:
  - A Rob's favorite trees
  - B where a cactus can grow
  - C the plants Rob grows
  - D what tomato plants look like
- Ask students to use the *Find the Main Idea Strategy* to find the correct answer. (Answer: *C*)
- Read aloud and discuss the Strategy section.

Try It Out

Read the directions aloud, and have students complete this section independently.

Ask *How did the strategy help you find the correct answer?*

Ask *Which details in the paragraph answer questions about the main idea? What questions do the details answer?*

Discuss the explanation that follows the question in the student book.

Test-Taking Strategy

Strategy: Find the Main Idea

In this unit you learned that paragraphs and passages have a main idea that is supported by detail sentences. The main idea is what the paragraph is mostly about. Sometimes it is not stated directly. Use this strategy to help you find the main idea of a paragraph.

- Read the entire paragraph. Ask yourself, *Who or what is this paragraph mostly about?* Circle any sentences that answer this question.
- Then look for details that support the main idea. Remember to ask <u>when</u>, <u>where</u>, <u>how</u>, and <u>why</u> to find the details. Underline sentences that answer these questions.

Try It Out

Read this passage. Then read the question. Circle the letter of the correct answer.

> Earth has seasons because it is tilted. In July the Northern Hemisphere is tilted toward the sun. That makes it summer in the United States. Six months later Earth has circled half way around the sun. The Northern Hemisphere then tilts away from the sun. That makes it winter in the United States.

What is the main idea of this passage?

(A) Earth has seasons because it is tilted.

B Winter is cold in the United States.

C Summer is hot in the United States.

D The United States is in the Northern Hemisphere.

The main idea is stated in the first sentence. The rest of the paragraph gives you details about how seasons happen. **A** is the correct answer.

Put It to the Test

Name _____

This test will check what you have learned in this unit.

DIRECTIONS: Read the passage. Then read each item. Circle the letter of the correct answer.

Spaceship Earth

1 Even as you are sitting still, Earth is moving. You can't feel it, but Earth travels in two different ways. It spins around like a top. At the same time, Earth moves around the sun. The way Earth spins is unlike the way it moves around the sun. It is amazing that Earth does both of these things at once.

2 How does Earth's spinning cause day and night? Day changes into night and back again because Earth spins. When sunlight shines on part of Earth, it is daytime there. As that part of Earth moves away from the sun, that part gets darker. Finally, when that part of Earth is no longer getting any sunlight, it is nighttime there. On one side of the planet, it is daytime, while on the opposite side it is night. Each day is 24 hours long because that is how long it takes for Earth to spin around completely.

1. **Which of these sentences is an OPINION from the passage?**

   A A day is 24 hours long.

   B Earth moves around the sun.

   C Sunlight causes daytime.

   D It is amazing that Earth does both of these things at once.

GO ON

Achieve It! Practice Cards

_____

Put It to the Test • 45

Connect the Test to the Practice Cards (page 45)

Correct Answers	Related Practice Cards	Skill
1. D	13, 14	Fact/opinion

Put It to the Test

Students will:

- demonstrate what they have learned
- identify skills that require more practice before students achieve proficiency*

* Refer to pages T17–T19 for a complete explanation and directions for using *Achieve It!* Practice Cards.

Administer the Test

Explain that students will now practice the skills from this unit by taking a short test. Tell students that the test has items like those they will find on standardized tests. Explain that you will read the directions aloud. Remind students to pay close attention and to follow your directions exactly.

Say *Open your books to page 45. I will read the directions aloud.* Read the directions to students. Then continue.

Say *You will have 20 minutes to finish this test. Read each item and the answer choices carefully. Circle the letter of the correct answer. When you reach the words* GO ON *at the bottom of a page, turn the page and continue working. When you reach the word* STOP *at the bottom of a page, stop working and put down your pencil. Are there any questions?*

If students have no questions,

Say *You may begin.*

At the end of 20 minutes,

Say *Stop. Check to be sure that you have circled the letter of the correct answer. Erase any stray pencil marks. Then put down your pencil.*

Assign Practice Cards

After scoring a student's test, note which items the student missed. Match each incorrectly answered item to the related *Achieve It!* Practice Cards listed in the chart on this page.

In the *Achieve It!* Practice Cards space in each student's book, write all of the Practice Cards you want the student to complete.

2. **Which statement is a FACT from the passage?**

   A You cannot see the moon from Earth.

   Ⓑ It takes 24 hours for Earth to spin around completely.

   C Earth spins around the moon.

   D You can feel Earth spinning.

3. **In this passage Earth is compared to —**

   Ⓐ a top

   B the moon

   C the sun

   D a light

4. **The main purpose of this passage is to —**

   A entertain

   B persuade

   Ⓒ inform or explain

   D express feelings

5. **What is paragraph 2 MOSTLY about?**

   Ⓐ how Earth's spinning causes day and night

   B how many hours there are in a day

   C when it is daytime in the United States

   D how Earth moves around the sun

6. | The way Earth spins is unlike the way it moves around the sun. |

   What key word in this sentence does the author use to show contrast?

   A moves

   B around

   Ⓒ unlike

   D spins

7. | Earth spins. That is why we have day and night. A day is 24 hours long. It takes 24 hours for Earth to spin around completely. |

   Which of these sentences could you add to this summary of paragraph 2?

   A Earth spins like a top.

   B Even as you are sitting still, Earth is moving.

   C It is amazing that Earth does both of these things at once.

   Ⓓ As one part of Earth spins away from the sun, day changes into night there.

Achieve It! Practice Cards

Connect the Test to the Practice Cards (page 46)

Correct Answers	Related Practice Cards	Skill
2. B	13, 14	Fact/opinion
3. A	15, 16	Compare and contrast
4. C	35, 36	Author purpose
5. A	25, 26, 27, 28, 29	Main idea/supporting details
6. C	15, 16	Compare and contrast
7. D	32, 33, 34	Summarize

8. | I think students should have a say in the design of this new school playground. If you vote for me for class president, I will make sure that your ideas are heard. |

In the passage above, the author's purpose is —

A to entertain

(B) to persuade

C to tell information

D to express feelings

9. When an author writes about a cause and effect, he or she is telling you —

A why you should agree with his or her opinion

(B) why something happened and what happened

C how two things are the same and different

D how to make something

10. When you write a summary, you should —

(A) write the main ideas and details of a passage in your own words

B include the author's name

C include every detail in the passage

D write the same number of words as the passage

11. A FACT is —

A what someone thinks

(B) something that can be proved to be true

C a belief about something

D not always true

12. What should you do when you paraphrase?

A copy every word from the passage

B read the passage out loud

C skip over the hard words in the passage

(D) look up hard words and rewrite the passage in your own words

13. The details in a passage give facts about —

A the introduction

B the title

C the conclusion

(D) the main idea

GO ON

Achieve It! Practice Cards
_____

Put It to the Test ● 47

Connect the Test to the Practice Cards (page 47)

Correct Answers	Related Practice Cards	Skill
8. **B**	35, 36	Author purpose
9. **B**	35, 36	Author purpose
10. **A**	32, 33, 34	Summarize
11. **B**	13, 14	Fact/opinion
12. **D**	30, 31	Paraphrase
13. **D**	25, 26, 27, 28, 29	Main idea/supporting details

Additional Practice Cards

The following cards cover additional skills for

Unit 2: Understanding What You Read

Card	Topic
17, 18	Sequence
19, 20, 21, 22, 23	Cause and effect
24	Persuasion
37	Author's point of view

You may want to assign these cards as practice for students who have done well on the unit test or as extended practice for all students.

Look at the chart. Circle the letter of the correct answer.

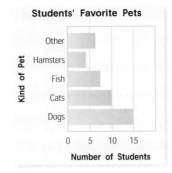

Students' Favorite Pets

Kind of Pet: Other, Hamsters, Fish, Cats, Dogs

Number of Students: 0, 5, 10, 15

14. **The graph shows that these students —**

   A like fish more than cats

   B like fish more than dogs

   (C) like cats more than fish

   D like hamsters more than fish

15. **The graph shows that —**

   A most students do not like pets

   B students like hamsters the most

   C students like fish and cats the same

   (D) dogs are the most popular pet

16. **How many students said that cats were their favorite pet?**

   (A) 10

   B 15

   C 8

   D 6

Look at the chart. Circle the letter of the correct answer.

Student	Score on First Test	Score on Second Test
Marla	96	100
Scott	76	97
Isa	87	35
Kim	68	69

17. **This chart shows —**

   A which student did best on the homework

   (B) which student did best on the first test

   C which student is oldest

   D which student is new in the class

Achieve It! Practice Cards

Connect the Test to the Practice Cards (page 48)

Correct Answers	Related Practice Cards	Skill
14. C	38, 39, 40, 41, 42	Interpret information from maps, charts, graphics, and other media
15. D	38, 39, 40, 41, 42	Interpret information from maps, charts, graphics, and other media
16. A	38, 39, 40, 41, 42	Interpret information from maps, charts, graphics, and other media
17. B	38, 39, 40, 41, 42	Interpret information from maps, charts, graphics, and other media

Unit 3 Putting Ideas Together

Connect the Details!

When you build a project with Legos®, you need all of the correct pieces to finish it. When all the pieces are snapped together, the project is strong and complete. Reading a book is like this, too.

In this unit you will learn to connect facts and details to get the complete message in a reading passage.

49

Research Says

As they read, good readers frequently make predictions about what is to come. . . . Thoughtful readers synthesize information when they read.

—*Duke and Pearson*

Unit 3

Skills

- Using background knowledge to make inferences about information in texts
- Using facts and details to draw conclusions about a text
- Using clues to make predictions about a text
- Finding facts and details in a text to support conclusions
- Comparing and contrasting information in two texts that discuss the same topic

Materials to Gather in Advance

- Blackline Master 6: Support from text
- paper • pencils • scissors
- construction paper • paste

Introducing the Unit

Connect the Details! Refer students to the photograph of the Legos®. Ask them to think about how attaching the individual pieces together creates a new structure that uses all of the pieces. Explain that when students find pieces of information in a passage, they connect them to pieces of information that they already know to create a complete understanding from the passage.

Ask *What happens when you read a text with new information?*

Ask *How do you connect the new information with information you already know to expand your ideas?*

- Read the *Connect the Details* paragraph aloud. Help students understand that, when they read, they are connecting the information they read in the text with information they already know.

Lesson 13

Objective

Students will use background knowledge to make inferences about information in texts.

Words to Know

Inference—combining prior knowledge or background information with information in the text

Study It

Review the concept of an *inference* with students.

- Write on the board: *John looked at the clock and ran out of the house.*

  Ask *What are the two things that John did?* (Answer: *looked at the clock and ran out of the house*)

- Invite a volunteer to underline the answers on the board.

  Ask *Why do you look at a clock?* (Answer: *to see what time it is*)

- Write the answer on the board, followed by a plus sign (+).

  Ask *What is a reason for running somewhere?* (Answer: *to get there quickly*)

- Write this answer after the plus sign.

  Ask *If you add these ideas together, what can you guess about John?* (Answer: *He is in a hurry.*)

- Explain to students that they have just used what they already know to make an inference about John's actions. Ask a volunteer to explain the inference in his or her own words. (Possible answer: *John saw the clock and knew that he was late; to get where he was going in a hurry, he ran.*)

Using Clues

Study It

As a student you often read to learn new information. You learn new things directly from the facts and details in a passage. However, you can often learn new information even when it is "hidden," or not directly written in a passage. The facts and details in a passage are like clues. You use these clues and what you already know to find hidden information. This is called making an **inference.** The inference is the hidden information you find.

Read this sentence. Pay attention to the underlined words.

John looked at the clock and ran out of the house.

Use this chart to make an inference.

Question: What inference can I make about John from this sentence?		
Clues from Sentence • John looked at the clock. • John ran out of the house.	**+** **What I Know** • Clocks show the time. • People run when they are in a hurry.	**=** **Inference** • John is late and needs to get somewhere in a hurry.

First, read the clues from the sentence. The sentence says that John looked at the clock and then ran out of the house.

Then, add what you know to the clues from the sentence. You know that

- clocks show the time
- people run when they are in a hurry

The clues from the sentence plus what you already know help you make the inference that John is late and needs to get somewhere in a hurry.

Make inferences

Curriculum and Assessment Standard

Make inferences

Inferences are ideas that are based on the passage but do not actually appear in the passage. Inferences can help you figure out

- the main idea of a passage
- what characters in a story think or feel
- the reason why something happened

Read this passage. Some clues are <u>underlined</u>.

Subways are underground trains in big cities. Boston and New York have subways. <u>Subways move many people very quickly.</u> They are crowded between 7:00 A.M. and 9:00 A.M. They are also <u>crowded from 4:00 P.M. to 6:30 P.M.</u>

Now look at this chart. It shows an inference you can make from the clues and what you already know.

Question: What inference can I make about subways from this passage?		
Clues from Passage • Subways move people quickly. • Subways are crowded at certain hours.	**What I Know** • People travel between home and school or work at these times.	**Inference** • People use subways to get to work and school.

(Clues from Passage) **+** (What I Know) **=** (Inference)

Lesson 13 • 51

- Write on the board: *The girl took a sip of water. She put down the glass and frowned. "This tastes like soap,"* she said. Underline *water, frown,* and *tastes like soap.* Then ask a volunteer to read the sentence aloud.

   Say *You can make several inferences from the information in these sentences. You already know things that are not written in the text.*

   Ask *What does* frown *mean? What feelings does it express?* (Answer: *A frown is a facial expression that shows when a person is unhappy or does not like something.*)

- Write *makes a face showing that she doesn't like something* on the board, followed by a plus sign (+).

   Ask *Do most people like the taste of soap? Should water taste like soap?* (Answer: *no; no*)

- After the plus sign, write *water tastes like soap,* followed by an equal sign (=).

   Ask *Why did the girl frown? What inference can you make?* (Answer: *The girl frowned because she did not like the taste of the water.*)

- After the equal sign, write *The girl does not like the taste of the water.*

- Refer students to the passage about subways. Have students use the underlined phrases to help make an inference about why people use subways.

⌒Differentiated Instruction
for auditory and kinesthetic learners

How Am I Feeling?

Students describe an emotion or a feeling, and other students infer what that emotion or feeling is.

Procedure

- Have students think of emotions or sensations that they have experienced recently (such as hunger, excitement, confusion, and so on) and recall what they did when they felt that way.
- Then have students write several sentences describing how they acted at that moment, including what they did and what they said. Emphasize that they should not name the emotion or sensation being described.
- Have students read their sentences aloud, and ask other students in the class to infer what feeling is being described.

Use It

Use this activity to help students make inferences.

- Write on the board: *Plants can grow quickly if you take care of them. Make sure the dirt is moist, and keep the plant near a window with lots of light.* Ask a student to read these sentences aloud.

  Ask *What do you need to make dirt moist?* (Answer: *water*)

  Ask *What kind of light would come through a window but not from inside the house?* (Answer: *sunlight*)

  Ask *What two things can you infer may be needed to make plants grow?* (Answer: *water and sunlight*)

Read the *Use It* directions aloud. Have students read the passage silently. When they have finished, help them fill in the chart.

Ask *What do you think is happening in this passage?* (Answer: *The family is deciding where to go on a trip.*)

Ask *What are some clues in the passage that tell you what is going on?*

- Ask students to fill in the first box on the chart with at least two clues. Have students share clues with the class.

- Invite a student to read each item in the *What I Know* box aloud.

  Ask *If you combine the clues with the information you already know, what inference can you make about the pieces of paper in the hat?* (Answer: *The pieces of paper have names of places that the family might visit.*)

- Ask students to fill in the last box on their own. Then have students share their inferences with the class.

◢ Use It

Read this passage from *The Mystery in San Francisco* by Gertrude Chandler Warner. <u>Underline</u> clues about what the Alden family is doing.

First thing in the morning, Aunt Jane said, "Andy, here's your cap." <u>She handed him the baseball cap containing the four slips of paper.</u>

"Hurry, Uncle Andy!" Benny said.

The Aldens watched as <u>Uncle Andy reached into the hat. He drew out a piece of paper</u> and looked at it.

"What does it say?" Violet asked.

<u>Uncle Andy smiled. "I think I'll keep it a surprise," he said, and put the paper in his pocket.</u>

At first the Aldens were disappointed. <u>They didn't want to wait another minute to find out where they were going.</u>

Then Jessie said, "That's a good idea, Uncle Andy."

Look at this chart. Fill in the empty spaces.

Question: What can you infer about this family from the passage?		
Clues from Passage	**What I Know**	**Inference**
• Uncle Andy picked a piece of paper out of a hat. • The Aldens want to know where they are going.	**+** • People pick pieces of paper out of hats to help them make decisions. • Trips can be surprises.	**=** • The piece of paper has a place written on it that the Aldens will visit together.

Practice It

Read this passage. Then read the questions. Circle the letter of the correct answer.

Cowhands use special clothes and supplies. From their ten-gallon hats to the spurs on their boots, each item has a purpose. The wide edge of their hats keeps out the sun and the rain. A triangle of cloth, called a bandana, keeps dust out of their mouths. The heels on their boots keep their feet from slipping out of the stirrups on their saddles. Their ropes are useful, too, for any calves that stray.

1. **A ten-gallon hat is useful in places that are —**

   A dusty

   B shady

   C cool

   D rainy

2. **Complete this chart.**

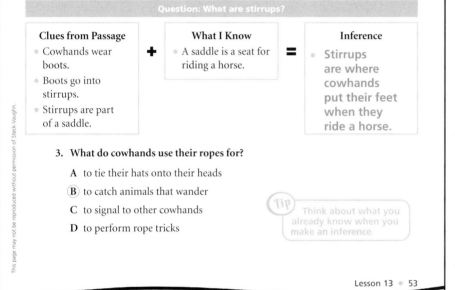

3. **What do cowhands use their ropes for?**

   A to tie their hats onto their heads

   B to catch animals that wander

   C to signal to other cowhands

   D to perform rope tricks

Tip Think about what you already know when you make an inference.

Lesson 13 • 53

Practice It

Work through the page to help students understand that making inferences can help them answer questions about a text.

Question 1 Read the directions aloud. Have students complete the question independently and then stop.

To help students understand why *D* is the correct answer, use the *Right There Strategy*. (See the *QAR Strategy* below.)

Say *A correct answer has important words called* key words. *Sometimes the same key words are also in the passage. At other times, the key words in a correct answer are closely related to the key words in the passage.*

Ask *Who can find the key words in the question that match words in the paragraph?* (Answer: *ten-gallon hat*)

Ask *Now, who can find the key word in the text that matches the correct answer?* (Answer: *rain*)

Say *You have used the* Right There Strategy *to find the correct answer to question 1. The answer you needed was "right there."*

Question 2 Read the directions and the question aloud. Then read the *Tip* aloud. Ask students to work independently to complete the chart by filling in the inference. Help students understand how to reach the inference.

Question 3 Read the question aloud. Then have students circle the correct answer independently. Encourage students to use the *Right There Strategy* again to find the correct answer.

Help students understand that *animals that wander* are the key words in the correct answer. These have the same meaning as those words in the paragraph: *calves that stray.*

QAR Strategy

Strategy	Definition	How It Works
Right There	This strategy teaches students that the correct answer appears in one place in whatever they are reading.	Students look for the *key words* in the answer choices that match the words in the text. The match is sometimes, but not always, exact.

Refer to pages T22–T23 for a complete chart of QAR Strategies that students may use to achieve greater success on tests of reading comprehension.

Lesson 14

Objective

Students will use facts and details to draw conclusions about a text.

Words to Know

Conclusion—an idea about a given text, based on information from that text

◢ Study It

Tell students that they must review details before drawing a conclusion.

■ Ask a volunteer to read the passage. Then direct students to the chart below the passage. As students answer questions about details, list their responses on the board.

Ask *What details tell you that Josie is looking for something?* (Answer: *She looked in the refrigerator and in the cupboards.*)

Ask *What do you already know about cupboards and refrigerators?* (Answer: *People keep food in them.*)

Ask *What do the details tell you that Josie grabbed?* (Answer: *She grabbed an apple.*)

Say *Based on the details so far, you can draw the conclusion that Josie is looking for food.*

■ Ask a volunteer to write the conclusion on the board: *Josie is looking for food.* Then ask a student to read the last sentence in the passage again.

Ask *What does the detail tell you?* (Answer: *It's long after lunchtime.*)

Say *Now look at the first conclusion again. If you know that Josie is looking for food and that it has been a long time since lunch, you can draw another conclusion about why Josie is looking for food.*

■ Ask a volunteer to draw a conclusion about why Josie is looking for food. (Examples: *Josie wants to eat.*)

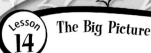

The Big Picture

◢ Study It

All kinds of writing have facts or details. Stories have details about the characters, the action, and the setting. Other kinds of passages have facts about a topic. The facts and details in a story or passage are like clues. You can put the clues together to draw a **conclusion**. When you draw a conclusion, you see what the clues from the passage are telling you.

Read this passage.

> Josie looked in the refrigerator. She looked in the cupboards. She grabbed an apple from a bowl on the counter. She said, "It's been so long since lunchtime!"

Look at this chart. It shows a conclusion you can draw.

Detail	Detail	Detail	Detail
Josie looked in the refrigerator.	Josie looked in the cupboards.	Josie grabbed an apple.	Josie said, "It's been so long since lunchtime!"

Conclusion
Josie is hungry.

Josie's actions and her statement are details that help you draw the conclusion that Josie is hungry.

A conclusion is a statement you can make from the facts and details in a passage.

- It comes directly from information in a passage.
- It helps you find the main ideas in a passage.

Drawing conclusions

Curriculum and Assessment Standard

Draw conclusions

You can draw good conclusions if you
- look for facts and details as you read
- use the facts and details to draw conclusions

Read this passage from *Where Land Meets Sea* by Allan Fowler.

Some seashores are marshes, thick with tall reeds and other plants growing in the salty sea water. Great numbers of fish live in these salt marshes. Certain trees, such as mangroves, can grow in salt water. There are muddy seashores, too. People dig for clams in mud flats or sandy beaches. Not all beaches have fine sand . . . the sand that feels so nice and soft under your feet when you run on it. There are pebbly and stony beaches. You wouldn't want to run barefoot on one of those.

Look at this chart. Think about the facts you read. The chart shows a conclusion you can draw about seashores.

Fact	Fact	Fact	Fact
Some seashores are marshes.	Some seashores are muddy.	Some seashores have fine sand.	Some seashores are pebbly and stony.

Conclusion
There are many different kinds of seashores.

The passage tells facts about different kinds of seashores. You can use the facts to draw the conclusion that there are many different kinds of seashores.

Lesson 14 ● 55

■ Direct students to the passage. Ask students to follow along as you read the passage aloud. Then give them a few minutes to look over the passage again and to write down any details that they think are important.

Ask *What are some of the details that you noticed about seashores?* (Answer: *Some have plants and trees and mud. Not all beaches are soft and sandy.*)

■ Have students write details on the board as they respond.

Ask *What conclusion can you draw about seashores? Are all seashores the same?* (Answer: *There are many different kinds of seashores.*)

Ask students whether these details helped them draw any other conclusions about the text.

Differentiated Instruction
for ELL, auditory, and visual learners

Debate

Students will work in groups to suggest ideas that support a conclusion.

Procedure

- Organize the class in two groups.
- Write a question on the board that presents a simple two-sided debate, such as *Which weekend day is better, Saturday or Sunday?*
- Have students supply ideas that support their side of the debate. (For example, *Saturday is better because you don't have to go to school the next day.*)
- Have groups take turns sharing their ideas with the class. Write the responses in two columns on the board.
- When students have shared all of their ideas, compare the two lists. Help students draw a conclusion about which side wins the debate.

◢ Use It

Use this section to help students find details and draw conclusions.

■ Read the *Use It* directions aloud. Then ask volunteers to read one sentence each from the passage about beads.

Say *This text has many details. Focus on the details that will help you draw a conclusion about beads and where they are found.*

■ Direct students to the chart below the passage, and read the first column aloud.

Ask *What other facts can you find about where beads are used?* (Answer: *In Europe glass beads were used in jewelry.*)

■ Give students a few minutes to fill in the next two columns. Then encourage volunteers to share their answers.

Ask *What conclusion can you draw about which ancient peoples used beads?* (Answer: *Ancient people in many countries used beads.*)

■ On the board, write the conclusion *Ancient people in many countries used beads.*

Ask *What conclusion can you draw about how people used beads? Add* in jewelry and on clothes *to the end of the first conclusion.*

Help students understand that they use details to draw many conclusions about a text. Explain that when taking a test, it is important to read the question carefully to understand the details from which conclusions can be drawn.

◢ Use It

Read this passage. What conclusion can you draw about beads?

Scientists who look for objects from the past sometimes find very old beads. Ancient Egyptians wore necklaces that looked like big collars. The necklaces were made of glass beads. In Europe glass beads and pearls were used in jewelry. They were also used to decorate clothes. Native Americans and Africans also added beads to clothes.

Look at this chart. Fill in the missing facts. Then write a conclusion.

Fact	Fact	Fact
Ancient Egyptians wore necklaces made of glass beads.	Glass beads and pearls were worn in Europe.	Native Americans and Africans used beads on clothes.

Conclusion
Ancient people in many countries used beads in jewelry and on clothes.

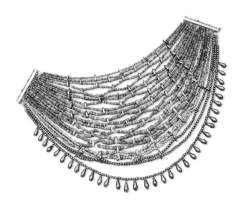

56 ● Unit 3

Read this passage. Then read the questions. Circle the letter of the correct answer.

Tina and Carole moved their beds into the center of the room. Then they helped their mother paint the walls. Tina said, "Can we paint our bookcase to match the walls?"

"Yes, we should have enough paint to do that," said their mother. "And maybe I can sew some curtains, too."

"This room is going to look great," said Carole.

1. **Which room is being painted?**

   A a kitchen

   (B) a bedroom

   C a library

   D a sewing room

> **Tip** The best conclusion will come from the details and facts in a passage.

2. **Look at this chart.**

Fact	Fact	Fact
Tina and Carole moved the beds in their bedroom.	Tina and Carole helped their mother paint the walls.	Tina asked to paint the bookcase.

Conclusion
Tina and Carole work well together.

What is the BEST conclusion to write in the chart? Circle the letter of the correct answer.

A Tina and Carole have painted the hallway.

B Tina and Carole read a lot of books.

C Tina and Carole are going to sew curtains.

(D) Tina and Carole work well together.

Lesson 14 ● 57

QAR Strategy

Strategy	Definition	How It Works
Think and Search	This strategy requires students to put together different parts of the text to find the correct answer.	Students look for *key words* throughout the text to help them draw conclusions about what they are reading.

Refer to pages T22–T23 for a complete chart of QAR Strategies that students may use to achieve greater success on tests of reading comprehension.

Practice It

Work through the page to help students understand that facts and details in a text can help them draw conclusions about the text.

Question 1 Read the directions aloud. Ask students to work independently to find the correct answer and then stop.

Discuss students' answers. Ask them what clues helped them find the correct answer. To help students understand that *B* is the correct answer, review the incorrect answers.

Say *Read answers* A, C, *and* D.

Ask *Does anything in the text make you think that the girls' beds would be in the kitchen, the library, or the sewing room?* (Answer: *no*)

Question 2 Read the directions and the *Tip* aloud. Ask students to work independently to find the answer that best completes the chart.

To help students understand why *D* is the best answer, use the *Think and Search Strategy*. (See the *QAR Strategy* below.)

Say *First, read the facts in the chart. Then, read the possible answers.*

Ask *Is* A *a possible conclusion? Explain your answer.* (Answer: *No, the facts say nothing about the hallway.*)

Ask *Is* B *a possible conclusion? Explain your answer.* (Answer: *No, the facts say nothing about how many books the girls read.*)

Ask *Is* C *a possible conclusion? Explain your answer.* (Answer: *No, the facts in the chart say nothing about sewing curtains.*)

Say *When you find clues in several places as you search for information in the text, you are using the* Think and Search Strategy.

Lesson 15

Objective

Students will use clues to make predictions about text.

Words to Know

Predicting—using clues such as titles, pictures, and prior knowledge to guess what a story is about or what will happen next

◢ Study It

Explain and discuss the process of making predictions.

■ Write the title "Amelia Goes to Camp" on the board. Explain to students that they can make predictions about a story after reading the title.

Ask *What do you think this story is about?* (Answer: *a girl going to camp*)

Ask *What do you know about camps? Where do people usually go when they camp?* (Answers will vary.)

■ Have students brainstorm, and write their ideas about camps on the board. Then read the first prediction aloud.

Ask *Is it a logical prediction that Amelia will go to camp in the woods?*

■ Ask a volunteer to read the beginning of the story. Explain to students that they can change their predictions as they read.

Ask *Do these sentences change or add to your predictions about what Amelia's camp will be like? How?* (Answers will vary.)

Discuss students' answers, and encourage each student to make a prediction about this story.

What's Next?

◢ Study It

When a friend tells you a story, sometimes you can guess what will happen next. You do the same thing when you read. Guessing what will happen next is called **making a prediction.**

As you read, you make predictions. Some of your predictions will be correct. Other predictions will not happen the way you thought they would. You can change your predictions as you read and get more information. You can begin predicting with the title of a story or passage.

Think about the title "Amelia Goes to Camp." What do you think this story is about?

Prediction	Clues
It is about a girl who goes to camp in the woods.	Amelia is going to camp. Camps are usually in the woods.

Remember that you can change your prediction as you read.

Read the beginning of "Amelia Goes to Camp."

Amelia packed her uniform and her basketball. She was excited about learning new moves.

The beginning of the story shows that the first prediction was incorrect. You can make a new prediction from what you have just learned.

New Prediction	Clues
This story is about a girl who goes to basketball camp.	Amelia is packing her uniform and a basketball. She is excited about learning new moves.

58 ● Unit 3   Making predictions

Curriculum and Assessment Standard

Make predictions

Use It

Read this passage.

> Jackie walked down the block. She saw her best friend Jillian. Jillian was looking for her lost dog.

What will Jackie do now? Write your prediction in this chart. Then write another clue.

Prediction	Clues
Jackie will help Jillian find her dog.	Jillian's dog is lost. Jackie and Jillian are friends.

Practice It

Read this passage. Then make predictions. Circle the letter of the correct answer.

> Liam sat at the table. He was staring at his science book. "What's the problem?" his brother Sean asked. "We have a test tomorrow. I don't understand this," Liam said. "Let me take a look. I always liked fourth-grade science," Sean said.

1. **What will happen next?**

   A Liam will get a snack.

   B Liam will close the book.

   C Sean will leave the room.

   D Sean will help Liam study.

   Tip: Use clues from the story and what you know to make predictions.

2. **What is Liam probably thinking?**

   A "My poor big brother."

   B "I want to ride my bike."

   C "I'm lucky Sean is willing to help me."

   D "I need to call my friends."

Lesson 15 • 59

Differentiated Instruction
for ELL, auditory, tactile, and kinesthetic learners

What Do I Do Next?

Students write about a daily routine and predict one another's last actions of the day.

Procedure

- Ask each student to make a list of four or five sentences on a sheet of paper, explaining something that he or she does every day.

- When students have finished, tell each one to cut the last sentence from his or her paper and fold it in half.

- Ask a volunteer to give you the piece of paper containing his or her last sentence. Then have the student read the rest of his or her sentences to the class.

- Encourage the class to make predictions about what the volunteer's last action of the day is. Allow students to make several predictions.

Use It

Use this activity to help students make predictions.

- Write on the board: *Janissa slipped the key in the lock and unlocked the door. Then she turned the handle.* Ask a student to read the text aloud.

  Ask *What do you think will happen next? What do you predict Janissa will do next?* (Answer: *open the door*)

  Ask *What are some clues in the text that support your prediction?* (Answer: *unlocked the door, turned the handle*)

- Direct students to the passage in the student book. Ask students to follow along as you read the passage aloud.

  Ask *What logical prediction can you make about what Jackie will do next?*

- Have students fill in the first box in the chart. Then have them share their predictions with the class.

- Ask students to tell you which clues in the text helped them make their predictions. Tell them to underline the clues in the text, and then fill in the chart with the missing clues. Review students' answers.

Practice It

In this section students will use their background knowledge to make predictions about a passage that they have read.

- Read the directions and the *Tip* aloud.

- Have students complete items 1 and 2 independently.

- Ask a student to answer each question. Ask students to explain which clues in the text helped them find the correct answers.

Answers

1. D

2. C

Lesson 16

Objective

Students will find facts and details in a text to support conclusions.

Words to Know

Supporting Information—the facts and details in the text and the reader's prior knowledge that support a conclusion

Study It

Review the terms *conclusion* and *supporting information* with the class.

- Write the headings *Conclusion* and *Supporting Information* on the board. Then direct students to the passage. Ask students to follow along as you read the passage aloud.

  Ask *If you didn't know anything else about Jamal and Marcus, what conclusion would you draw about the two boys?* (Answer: *They are friends.*)

- Write several student responses under *Conclusion*.

  Say *Now look at each of these conclusions to figure out which details support them.*

- Ask students to find supporting facts and details in the text for each conclusion. Encourage students to include facts that they already know from personal experience.

  Ask *Can you draw this conclusion with the facts you have, or do you need more supporting information to draw this conclusion?*

Prove It!

Study It

When you draw a conclusion or make an inference about a story or passage, you are thinking about what you have read. You use the details and facts in the passage to draw conclusions. You can also use the details and facts, along with information you already know, to make inferences. The details and facts plus your own knowledge are the **supporting information** for your conclusions and inferences.

To draw a conclusion, put together the details or facts in a passage. Ask yourself, *What do the details or facts in this passage tell me?*

Read this passage. Then look at the chart. It shows supporting information for a conclusion you can draw.

> Marcus and Jamal were walking to school one morning. They carried their book bags and lunches. Marcus said, "I'm always sad to leave summer vacation behind."
> Jamal said, "Me, too. But think about seeing the friends we haven't seen in a while. There may be new kids and teachers to meet, too."

Conclusion	Supporting Information
Marcus and Jamal are good friends.	Details from the passage: The boys are walking to school together. They are talking about their feelings. Jamal is offering Marcus encouragement.

Good friends like to spend time together. They often share their feelings with each other and offer encouragement. You can conclude that Marcus and Jamal are good friends.

These steps will help you draw a conclusion.

1	2	3	4
Underline important facts and details.	Think about what the facts and details tell you.	Put together the facts and details to draw a conclusion.	Check your conclusion against the passage.

Support from text

Curriculum and Assessment Standard

Support from text

Using the clues in a passage and your own knowledge helps you make inferences and find missing information. An inference answers the question, *What information is missing from this passage?*

Read this passage. Then look at the chart. It shows the supporting information for an inference you can make.

Vera and Kristin were blowing up balloons in the kitchen. Kristin was trying to tie a balloon full of air. She accidentally let go of the balloon. The girls started to laugh. "Did you see that?" Vera asked.

Conclusion	Supporting Information
Kristin's balloon flew around the kitchen.	Detail from the passage: Kristin accidentally let go of the balloon. What I know: Balloons fly around when they release air.

Kristin is blowing up a balloon when she accidentally lets it go. You know that balloons fly around when they release air. You can make the inference that Kristin's balloon flew around the kitchen.

These steps will help you use supporting information to make an inference.

As you read, underline important facts and details in the passage.	Then think about what you already know about the topic of the passage.	Use all of this information to make an inference.	Check to be sure that the facts and details in the passage support your inference.

Lesson 16 • 61

■ Review the necessary steps for making inferences. Then ask volunteers to read the passage aloud. Guide students through the steps as shown below, listing each task on the board as you go.

Step 1—Have students underline important facts and details in the passage.

Step 2—Encourage students to think about what they know about the topic.

Step 3—Ask students to use the details and their own knowledge to make inferences.

Step 4—Have students reread the passage to make sure that the facts and details support their inferences.

Ask *What inferences did you draw about Kristin and Vera?* Ask volunteers to write inferences on the board.

Ask *Which details support your inference?* Write supporting information next to the inference.

Ask *Did anyone make an inference about why Kristin and Vera were laughing or about what they saw?*

■ Review the inference and details in the student book, and discuss how close they come to any of the student inferences.

Differentiated Instruction
for ELL, tactile, and visual learners

House of Details

Students will use supporting details to make a paper house.

Procedure

● Explain to students that just as a roof depends on support, so does a conclusion.

● Give each student a copy of Blackline Master 6: Support from Text.

● In the *Conclusion* section, have each student write a sentence that states an opinion about his or her house or another familiar building. Then in the *Details* section, have student write at least three sentences explaining why the opinions are true.

● When students have finished, have them cut apart the sections. Tell them to paste the supporting details to a piece of construction paper in the shape of walls and to paste the conclusion on as the roof.

Use It

Use this section to help students demonstrate what they know about conclusions and supporting details.

■ Direct students to the passage from *Pluto.* Have students follow along as you read the passage aloud.

■ Give students a moment to read the passage independently. Have them underline any important facts and details.

Say *As you read a passage like this, think about what you know about the topic. Then you can use all of your information to draw conclusions and make inferences.*

■ On the board, write the conclusion: *The temperature of stars affects their color.*

Say *Read this conclusion.*

Ask *What information can you find in the text to support this conclusion?* (Answer: *The hottest stars are blue-white; the red stars are "coolest."*)

■ Write the supporting details on the board, and have students fill in the chart. Then ask a volunteer to read aloud the supporting information in the second chart.

Ask *What inference does this information help you draw?* (Answer: *Light and heat are connected.*)

■ Have students work in pairs to decide on an inference. Then have students share inferences with the class. If students' inferences cannot be supported by the details in the chart, ask them whether other information in the text might support their inference, and have them identify that information.

Use It

Read this passage from *Pluto* by Dennis Brindell Fradin. Look for clues that help you draw conclusions and make inferences.

Have you ever looked at the sky on a clear night? If so, you have seen many twinkling points of light. They are called stars.

The nighttime stars look like points of light because they are so very far away from us. In fact, stars are giant balls of hot, glowing gas. The hottest stars are blue-white. Their surfaces are at a temperature of over 55,000°F. If our world were that hot, it would soon burn up. The red stars are the "coolest." Their surfaces are at a temperature of about 5,500°F, which is still plenty hot.

Look at this chart. Add supporting information for the conclusion.

Conclusion	Supporting Information
The temperature of stars affects their color.	Details from the passage: **The hottest stars are blue-white.** **The red stars are the coolest.**

Now, complete this chart by adding the inference.

Inferences	Supporting Information
Light and heat are connected.	Details from the passage: Twinkling points of light are called stars. Stars are giant balls of hot, glowing gas. What I Know: The blue flame on a gas stove is very hot.

◢ Practice It

Read this passage.

Mr. Lampton led his class to a stream. "Fossils show us what things used to look like. Maybe a leaf fell in the mud. The mud turned into a rock. The leaf washed away. But the mark of the leaf stayed. Let's see what we can find here." The children started turning over rocks.

Junie called out, "Mr. Lampton, could a fossil look like a bug carved into a rock?"

"Let me see. You have good eyes, Junie!"

1. **Look at this chart. What is the BEST conclusion to write? Circle the letter of the correct answer.**

Conclusion	Supporting Information
The students are looking for fossils.	Details from the passage: Fossils are made from mud and leaves, animals, and insects that have turned into rock.
	The children are turning over rocks.

A The students are looking for a stream.

B The students are looking for rocks.

C The students are looking for bugs.

D The students are looking for fossils.

 Tip Check the passage again to see whether the facts and details support your inference or conclusion.

2. **Look at this chart. What is the BEST supporting information to write? Circle the letter of the correct answer.**

Inference	Supporting Information
Junie found a fossil.	Details from the passage: Junie described a rock, and Mr. Lampton praised her.

A Junie was near a stream and found a rock.

B Junie described a rock, and Mr. Lampton praised her.

C Mr. Lampton described how a fossil is made.

D Mr. Lampton's example included a leaf.

Lesson 16 • 63

This page may not be reproduced without permission of Steck-Vaughn.

◖QAR Strategy

Strategy	Definition	How It Works
Think and Search	This strategy requires students to put together different parts of the text to find the correct answer.	Students look for *key words* throughout the text to help them draw conclusions about what they are reading.

Refer to pages T22–T23 for a complete chart of QAR Strategies that students may use to achieve greater success on tests of reading comprehension.

◢ Practice It

Work through the page to help students understand that details and facts are necessary to draw logical conclusions and inferences.

Question 1 Read the directions and the *Tip* aloud. Ask students to read the passage and work independently to find the conclusion that best completes the chart.

To help students understand why *D* is the best answer, use the *Think and Search Strategy*. (See the *QAR Strategy* below.)

Say *First read the supporting information in the chart. Then read the possible answers.*

Ask *If you use what you already know about how to draw conclusions, how can you eliminate some of the incorrect answers from the text?*

Ask *Is A a possible conclusion? Explain.* (Answer: *No. The supporting information does not mention a stream.*)

Say *Read answers* B, C, *and* D.

Ask *Do the details in the chart make you think that the students are looking for bugs or rocks? Are fossils a more logical conclusion?* (Answer: *Fossils are a more logical conclusion.*)

Say *When you think about the answers as you search for information in the text, you are using the* Think and Search Strategy.

Question 2 Read the directions for question 2 aloud. Ask students to identify the missing detail and circle the correct answer. (Answer: *B, Junie described a rock, and Mr. Lampton praised her.*)

Discuss students' answers. Explain to students that they must sometimes use their background knowledge to find the correct answers. Their experience should tell them that if the task is to find a fossil and the teacher praises Junie, these facts support the conclusion that Junie found a fossil.

Lesson 17

Objective

Students will compare and contrast information in two texts about the same topic.

Words to Know

Sources—books, articles, or other documents used for gathering information

Study It

Review the process of looking for information, and list on the board the sources students might use when gathering information.

- Direct students to Passage 1. Ask a volunteer to read the passage aloud.

  Ask *What kind of writing is this?* (Answer: *a story*)

  Ask *What is the story about?* (Answer: *a girl looking at pictures she has taken*) Ask students to underline any important details about the story. Then have students follow along as another volunteer reads Passage 2 aloud.

  Ask *What kind of writing is this? Where might you find it?* (Answer: *in nonfiction/informational writing; in a book or an article*) Ask students to underline any important details about this text.

  Say *Now think about what these two texts have in common. Circle any details that you find in both texts.*

- Copy the column headings from the chart onto the board. Have students share the details that they underlined and circled, and write their responses on the board. Point out the middle column, and discuss how the two sources are connected.

Lesson 17 — Making Connections

Study It

Different reading materials, or **sources**, offer different information about a subject. For example, in school you might read a social studies book about the election process. At home you might read a newspaper article about someone who is running for president. In the park you might read a story about a girl who wants to be the president of the United States when she grows up.

When you read about a subject in two or more sources, you should compare and contrast the sources. Ask yourself these questions.

- What is the same about these sources?
- What is different about them?

Read these passages. Then look at the chart that shows what is the same and what is different about the passages.

Passage 1

Sally looked at the pictures she had taken. She was disappointed with them. "Why does this picture look so dark? I can barely see the decorations we worked so hard on!"

Passage 2

Photographs are pictures taken with cameras. Photographs record how light falls on an object. If an object is too dark, it will not reflect light. The picture will turn out dark. If there is too much light, the opposite might happen. The picture will have too much light.

Passage 1	Both Passages	Passage 2
• story about Sally • one character • talks about feelings	• topic is photographs • talk about the darkness of photographs	• explains how light affects photographs • no characters • no feelings

Curriculum and Assessment Standard

Connections (paired passages)

Read the first passage from *Mei Li* by Thomas Handforth and the second passage from *Chinese New Year* by Catherine Chambers. Notice what is the same and what is different about them.

Passage 1

Inside the house on the morning before New Year's Day, everyone was very busy. Mei Li, a little girl with a candle-top pigtail, was scrubbing and sweeping and dusting. Her mother, Mrs. Wang, was baking and frying and chopping. Her brother, San Yu, was fixing and tasting and mixing. A fine feast was being prepared for the Kitchen God, who would come out at midnight to every family in China to tell them what they must do during the coming year.

Passage 2

Not many people go to bed on New Year's Eve. The streets buzz with happy people, young and old alike. Temples are full of worshipers. Families gather from far and wide to eat a special meal together.

Now look at this chart. It shows how you can compare the passages.

Passage 1	Both Passages	Passage 2
• story about Chinese family • three characters • set in the morning	• talk about Chinese New Year's celebration • talk about the special meal	• true description • characters are general people • set at night

When you make connections between passages,

- read each passage carefully
- notice what is different between the passages
- notice what is the same about the passages
- compare the organization and style of writing
- compare the characters, the setting, and the action

■ Direct students to the two passages. Have students work independently to read the passages and underline the details. As they do, talk them through the important steps.

Step 1—Have students read the first passage and underline important details.

Step 2—Have students read the second passage and underline important details.

Step 3—Ask students to think about what the two passages have in common and to circle those details.

■ Use the same column headings as the ones in the chart to sort out details in these two passages. Include details about the text, such as what kind of writing it is and what its characteristics are.

Ask *What kind of writing is this? Is it a story or an informational text? Are there characters? What happens in this text? When does it happen?*

Discuss the details that the passages have in common. Help students understand that reports they write will be stronger if they use details that they find in more than one source.

Differentiated Instruction
for ELL and auditory learners

Comparing Histories

Students will conduct interviews and compare results with other students.

Procedure

- Select a topic to which all students can relate, such as the history of their town or region. As homework, have each student ask a friend or relative to tell what he or she knows about the topic. Ask students to write down what the person tells them.

- In class have students work in pairs to compare their interviews. Have them look for facts that are different from each interview and facts that are the same.

- Ask groups to share with the class what they have learned about the topic, explaining which facts they were able to get from more than one source.

- Write important facts on the board so that students can comment if they have similar details.

Use It

Use this section to help students compare and contrast texts.

■ Write the following sentences on the board: 1) *When she walks on the beach, Lorraine likes to collect shells.* 2) *Ocean waves can wash many things onto a beach, including rocks, shells, wood, and seaweed.* Ask volunteers to read the sentences aloud.

Ask *What is the same about these two sentences?* (Answer: *They are both about the beach.*)

■ Underline key words in both sentences, such as *beach* and *shells.*

Ask *What is different about the kind of writing in these two sentences? Which one has a character? Which one gives information about beaches?*

■ Discuss how the two sentences are different and what sources they might represent.

Read the *Use It* directions aloud. Ask students to read the passages independently and fill in the chart with the missing details. Remind students of the important steps for underlining details and then finding the common details. When they have finished, discuss students' answers, listing student responses on the board in appropriate columns. Help students understand that both passages are sources of information about immigrants who see the Statue of Liberty when they come to New York City.

Use It

Read these passages. Notice what is the same and what is different about them.

Passage 1

The sun was setting behind the statue. Agnes caught her breath. The statue was the most beautiful thing she had ever seen. She had read about the statue. She had no idea how she would feel when she finally saw it. Some people said it was green and ugly. All Agnes saw was the beautiful torch and the statue's crown. She knew her long journey was almost over. She would be in New York soon. She would be in the United States.

Passage 2

The Statue of Liberty is a large statue. The statue is of a woman wearing a crown and carrying a torch. It stands on an island in Upper New York Bay. The statue was a gift to the United States from France in the 1800s. When people arrive in New York by boat, the statue is one of the first things that they see.

Now look at this chart. Fill in the empty spaces to show how the passages are the same and different.

Passage 1	Both Passages	Passage 2
• story about Agnes • one character • **talks about thoughts and feelings** • uses many adjectives	• **talk about the Statue of Liberty** • immigrants see statue when they arrive in New York City • **set in New York City**	• **true information** • no characters • no thought or feelings • **gives facts**

Tip When you compare two passages, look at all the parts of each passage.

66 ● Unit 3

Practice It

Read these passages. Then look at the chart. Read the question. Circle the letter of the correct answer.

Passage 1

Amanda loved Uncle Fred. She thought he was amazing because he played the fiddle so well. When he came to visit, she could not wait until he opened the old black case. He let her put the rosin, a chalky powder, on the bow. Then he tuned the fiddle. Finally, he tapped his foot and played the fiddle as Amanda sang.

Passage 2

Fiddles are stringed instruments. They are played with a bow. They are sometimes called violins. Fiddles are used to play anything from very formal music to simple country songs. It takes years to learn to play the fiddle well. Fiddles are easily carried, so music can be made anywhere.

Passage 1	Both Passages	Passage 2
• story about Amanda and Uncle Fred • fiddle is played • **talks about one character's feelings and thoughts**	• topic is fiddles • talk about fiddle bows	• gives facts about fiddles • describes a fiddle • **talks about types of fiddle music**

1. **Which item belongs in the Passage 1 box?**

   A characters talk to each other

   Ⓑ talks about one character's feelings and thoughts

   C three characters

   D describes how characters look

2. **Which item belongs in the Passage 2 box?**

   A talks about types of fiddles

   B talks about types of fiddle bows

   Ⓒ talks about types of fiddle music

   D talks about types of fiddle players

Practice It

Guide students through this activity to help them understand how the details in these two passages differ.

Read the directions and the *Tip* aloud. Then ask students to read the two passages independently and underline the important details.

Question 1 Read the question aloud. Tell students to read the details in the chart, and then read the answers. Ask them to select the answer that matches a detail in Passage 1 that does not appear in the chart.

Discuss students' answers. To help students understand why only *B* identifies a detail that is not already in the chart, explain the incorrect answers.

● *A* is incorrect because there is no dialogue in the passage. ● *C* is incorrect because there are only two characters, Amanda and Uncle Fred. ● *D* is incorrect because the characters are not described.

Question 2 Read question 2 aloud. Tell students to read the details in the chart, and then read the answers. Ask them to select the answer that matches a detail in Passage 2 that does not appear in the chart.

Discuss student answers. Help students understand that only *C* identifies a detail that is in Passage 2. Ask a volunteer to read the sentence in the passage that corresponds to the detail in *C*. (Answer: *Fiddles are used to play anything from very formal music to simple country songs.*)

Teach the Strategy

Write the following paragraph on the board: *Jacob said, "I want to sit in the front!" Then he turned to his brother and said, "I forgot my glasses, so I need to sit in a row close to the screen."*

Ask a volunteer to read the passage aloud.

Ask *Where does Jacob want to sit?* (Answer: *in the front row*)

Ask *Why does Jacob want to sit in the front?* (Answer: *so he can see the screen*)

Ask *What inference can you make about where Jacob and his brother are?* (Answer: *at the movies, or in a movie theater*)

Use Details Strategy

Explain that rereading the passage to decide which answer fits best is a test-taking strategy.

■ Write these answer choices under the sentence on the board:

A   in a car

B   at the movies

C   in a boat

D   on a horse

■ Ask students to go back and look at the details in the sentences and decide which answers do not fit. Point out that a *screen* or a *row* would not be in a car, in a boat, or on a horse. Then have students reread the text to make sure that the answer makes sense. (Answer: *B*)

■ Read aloud and discuss the Strategy section.

Try It Out

Read the directions aloud, and have students complete this section independently. Encourage them to use the *Use Details Strategy* to choose the correct answer.

Ask *Which words in the paragraph are clues that help you rule out some of the answers?*

Discuss the explanation that follows the question in the student book.

Test-Taking Strategy

Strategy: Use Details

In this unit you learned how to draw conclusions, make inferences, support your conclusions and inferences, and compare and contrast two passages. On tests you will see questions that ask you to use these skills.

Read the question and each answer choice carefully. If you cannot decide between two answer choices, go back to the passage. Look for the choice that agrees with the passage.

Try It Out

Read this passage. Choose the answer that is the BEST inference for the passage. Circle the letter of the correct answer.

> Bess and her mother prepared for their trip. They packed a picnic lunch, swimsuits, and towels. "Don't forget your sandals. The sand might be really hot!" Bess's mother said.

Bess and her mother are probably going to the —

A   swimming pool

B   desert

C   mountains

(D)   beach

You can rule out answers by looking at the details in the passage. Bess's mother says that the sand might be hot. There is not usually sand at a swimming pool, so **A** is not a good answer. You do not swim in the desert, so **B** is not a good answer. Sand is not usually a problem in the mountains, so **C** is not a good answer. All of the items Bess and her mother pack can be used at the beach, so **D** is the best answer.

Name _____

This test will check what you have learned in this unit.

DIRECTIONS: Read these passages. Then read the items. Circle the letters of the correct answers.

Flags

Flags have been used since ancient times. Flags are usually made of cloth. They are usually rectangles. Flags are most often used to identify a country or a group. For example, flags can be used in a parade to name the group marching behind the flag. Flags are also used as signals. In car races, flags tell drivers when to go fast or slow. At sea, flags are used to send messages from one ship to another. Sometimes flags are given as rewards for good work. Flags are often put on poles so that people can see them easily.

Jason's Project

Jason was working at the table. He was drawing on a piece of paper. "That looks nice. What is it?" his father asked.

"My friends and I are going to ride our bikes in the parade. I'm making a flag for us. It's fun to make things."

"How will you carry the flag?"

"I have a pole for it. Can you help me put the pole on my bike when I'm done drawing this?" said Jason.

"Sure, and I can't wait to see how this looks in the parade!"

1. Why would flags usually be made in the same way?

A Flag makers are lazy.

B There are not enough flag makers to make different flags.

C It makes flags easy to use in many different places.

D It is the law.

2. Why would flags be a popular way to identify a country or group?

A They are large and easily seen.

B Many people make flags.

C They are colorful and beautiful.

D They are easy to put on poles.

GO ON

Achieve It! Practice Cards

_____

Put It to the Test • 69

Connect the Test to the Practice Cards (page 69)

Correct Answers	Related Practice Cards	Skill
1. C	46, 47, 48, 49	Make inferences
2. A	46, 47, 48, 49	Make inferences

Put It to the Test

Students will:

- demonstrate what they have learned
- identify skills that require more practice before students achieve proficiency*

* Refer to pages T17–T19 for a complete explanation and directions for using *Achieve It!* Practice Cards.

Administer the Test

Explain that students will now practice the skills from this unit by taking a short test. Tell students that the test has items like those they will find on standardized tests. Explain that you will read the directions aloud. Remind students to pay close attention and to follow your directions exactly.

Say *Open your books to page 69. I will read the directions aloud.* Read the directions to students. Then continue.

Say *You will have 20 minutes to finish this test. Read each item and the answer choices carefully. Circle the letter of the correct answer. When you reach the words* GO ON *at the bottom of a page, turn the page and continue working. When you reach the word* STOP *at the bottom of a page, stop working and put down your pencil. Are there any questions?*

If students have no questions,

Say *You may begin.*

At the end of 20 minutes,

Say *Stop. Check to be sure that you have circled the letter of the correct answer choice. Erase any stray pencil marks. Then put down your pencil.*

Assign Practice Cards

After scoring a student's test, note which items the student missed. Match each incorrectly answered item to the related *Achieve It!* Practice Cards listed in the chart on this page.

In the *Achieve It!* Practice Cards space in each student's book, write all of the Practice Cards you want the student to complete.

3. Flags are used in races —

   A to add color

   B to show history

   Ⓒ for safety

   D as prizes for winners

4. Why would flags be used to send messages at sea?

   A Ships do not have telephones.

   B There is no mail service.

   C Ships do not have computers.

   Ⓓ They can be seen easily across distances.

5. What inference can you make about Jason?

   A He has a new bike.

   Ⓑ He likes art projects.

   C He is worried about the parade.

   D He needs to plan his flag better.

6. Which detail supports the conclusion that Jason's father is helpful?

   A He wants to see the parade.

   B He likes Jason's work.

   Ⓒ He will help Jason put the flag on the bike.

   D He asks many questions.

7. Jason and his friends are using the flag —

   Ⓐ to identify their group

   B to win a prize

   C to show that they can go fast

   D to send a message to another group

8. How is Jason's flag different from most of the flags mentioned in the first passage?

   A It will be in a parade.

   B It is being made at home.

   C It will be on a pole.

   Ⓓ It is made out of paper.

9. How is the passage on Jason's project different from the passage on flags?

   A It tells how to make a flag.

   B It tells how flags are used to identify groups.

   C It explains that flags are usually carried.

   Ⓓ It tells about two characters, Jason and his father.

Achieve It! Practice Cards

_____

Connect the Test to the Practice Cards (page 70)

Correct Answers	Related Practice Cards	Skill
3. C	46, 47, 48, 49	Make inferences
4. D	53, 54, 55	Draw conclusions
5. B	46, 47, 48, 49	Make inferences
6. C	53, 54, 55	Draw conclusions
7. A	46, 47, 48, 49	Make inferences
8. D	59, 60, 61	Find support/evidence from text
9. D	62, 63, 64	Find similarities and differences across texts

Window Gardens

Even if you do not have much space outdoors, you can still grow a small garden. You can make a window garden. Window gardens are grown in boxes. The boxes are made of wood or plastic. They are attached beneath a window. Most window gardens contain flowers. To pick plants for a window garden, think about how much sunlight the plants will get. Then ask someone at a garden store to help you choose plants. In no time your window will be alive with growth!

Delia's Surprise

Delia wanted to make a surprise for her father. He liked pepper plants, so she decided to make him a window garden. She and her brother worked to make a wooden box. They found dirt to put in it. With her mother's help, Delia picked out and planted some seeds. Delia and her brother watered the seeds and watched them grow. Just in time for Father's Day, the first small pepper appeared. When Delia gave her father the box, he was excited. He said, "Where can we put this great garden? How about next to the kitchen window? Then we can harvest our dinner without even going outside!"

10. The author of "Window Gardens" thinks that window gardens are —

A troublesome

B expensive

C useful

D enjoyable

11. What is one of the MOST important things to consider when making a window garden?

A finding space in a garden

B choosing plants for it

C finding dirt for it

D picking a shape for it

Achieve It! Practice Cards

Connect the Test to the Practice Cards (page 71)

Correct Answers	Related Practice Cards	Skill
10. D	53, 54, 55	Draw conclusions
11. B	59, 60, 61	Find support/evidence from text

Additional Practice Cards

The following cards cover additional skills for

Unit 3: Putting Ideas Together

Card	Topic
43, 44, 45	Make generalizations
50, 51, 52	Judge consistency and logic
56, 57, 58	Make and confirm predictions

You may want to assign these cards as practice for students who have done well on the unit test or as extended practice for all students.

12. **Why do most window gardens contain flowers?**

   A Flowers attract bees and other insects.

   B Flowers are often eaten in salads and other dishes.

   C Flowers can be cut and given away as gifts.

   (D) Flowers are small, smell good, and are pretty to look at.

13. **Which of these BEST describes the gift for Delia's father?**

   (A) a family project

   B an indoor present

   C an expensive present

   D a beautiful sight

14. **What will Delia's family do with the peppers?**

   (A) eat them

   B give them to neighbors

   C sell them at a stand

   D save them for the winter

15. **Delia's window garden is different because it —**

   A was next to a kitchen

   B needed lots of water

   (C) contained pepper plants

   D was made of wood

16. **Delia's choice of plants for her father's window garden shows that she is —**

   (A) thoughtful

   B rude

   C forgetful

   D funny

17. **Delia's father is excited when he gets his gift because —**

   A he does not like the gift

   (B) he likes the gift

   C he plans to return the gift

   D he plans to give Delia a gift

18. **Delia's window box is made of wood. She could also have used a box made of —**

   A foil

   B rock

   (C) plastic

   D paper

19. **The passage on window gardens and the passage on Delia's surprise both tell about —**

   (A) fun ways to enjoy plants

   B the price of window boxes

   C a Father's Day celebration

   D people and their feelings

Achieve It! Practice Cards

Connect the Test to the Practice Cards (page 72)

Correct Answers	Related Practice Cards	Skill
12. D	53, 54, 55	Draw conclusions
13. A	53, 54, 55	Draw conclusions
14. A	53, 54, 55	Draw conclusions
15. C	59, 60, 61	Find support/evidence from text
16. A	59, 60, 61	Find support/evidence from text
17. B	59, 60, 61	Find support/evidence from text
18. C	62, 63, 64	Find similarities and differences across texts
19. A	62, 63, 64	Find similarities and differences across texts

Unit
4 Parts and Patterns

It All Fits Together

Have you ever seen something that is in pieces, and then watched someone put it together? At first, it looks like a mess. But soon you begin to understand the way the parts match up.

In this unit you will learn how writers gather their ideas into neat patterns and then group those ideas into sections to make a book. You will also learn about sections in a book that tell you how a book is arranged.

73

Research Says

Good readers typically look over the text before they read, noting such things as the structure of the text and text sections that might be most relevant to their reading goals.

—*Duke and Pearson*

Skills

- Identifying sequence or pattern of ideas
- Using the title page and table of contents to find and organize information in a book
- Using headings and subheadings to locate information in a passage
- Finding information in the index of a book

Materials to Gather in Advance

- cartoon strips ● textbook ● library or other books ● pencils ● paper ● newspapers ● articles or pages from a children's magazine ● large sheets of paper or posterboard ● colored pencils, markers, or crayons

Introducing the Unit

It All Fits Together Refer students to the photograph of nuts, bolts, and springs. Ask students to think of a time when they followed instructions to put something together that was in pieces. Ask what strategies they used to make sense of all the pieces. Tell them that they probably used information from the instructions and information that they already knew. Help students recognize that this strategy also works when looking for information in a book.

- Read aloud the *It All Fits Together* paragraph.

   Ask *Did you ever try to put something together without the instructions? What strategies did you use?*

- Explain that some parts of a book tell you how the information in the book is organized. Using these parts of the book to find information is like using instructions to put something together.

Lesson 18

Objective

Students will identify the sequence of events or steps in passages.

Words to Know

Sequence—the order in which events occur

Signal words—words such as *first, second,* and *third* that help a reader understand the order in which events happen

Study It

- Copy the sequence chart from the lesson to the board. Leave space in each box for text.

- Ask a volunteer to describe how to make a bowl of cereal. Write the steps in the chart on the board, guiding the volunteer to use signal words such as *first, next,* and *then.*

- Read the definition of signal words under the chart on the student page. Then direct students' attention back to the board.

  Ask *Which signal words let you know when to do each step?* (Answer: *first, next, then,* and *so on*)

- Review the examples on the student page.

First, Next, and Finally

Study It

Writers use patterns to make their ideas clear to the reader. One pattern that writers often use is **sequence**. Sequence, or time order, is the order in which events happen or the order in which steps in a process are explained.

If you are making a sandwich, think about what you do first. What do you do next? Putting ideas or steps in proper order helps you understand the sequence.

```
Event 1
   ↓
Event 2
   ↓
Event 3
   ↓
Event 4
```

Signal words can tell you the order in which things happen. For sequence, look for time-order words such as <u>later</u>, <u>before</u>, <u>first</u>, <u>second</u>, <u>next</u>, <u>last</u>, <u>finally</u>, <u>after</u>, <u>then</u>, and <u>now</u>.

First, Sandra wrote a shopping list. Then, she went to the store.

The words <u>first</u> and <u>Then</u> show you when each event happened.

Some signal words, such as <u>yesterday</u>, <u>noon</u>, <u>tomorrow</u>, <u>last month</u>, <u>in June</u>, or <u>in 1942</u>, are more exact.

Carl wrote a three-page paper <u>last Thursday</u>.

The words <u>last Thursday</u> show exactly when the event happened.

Sometimes writers do not use signal words when they tell a story or explain a process. You will need to use what you already know to follow the sequence of events if time-order words are not used.

Curriculum and Assessment Standard

Sequence/chronology

Read these directions for making a treat. Look at the boxes to follow the order of the steps in the directions. Notice how the signal words first, then, now, and next are used in the passage.

It is easy to make a great, healthful treat. First, wash your hands well. Then, get out cornflakes, two bananas, and a small container of yogurt. Put the cornflakes into a plastic bag and crush them with a rolling pin. Now, put the crushed cereal into a pie tin. Next, peel the bananas. Dip each whole banana in the yogurt. Roll the bananas in the cereal until they are completely coated. Place the coated bananas on a tray lined with waxed paper. Put the bananas in the freezer. Wait three hours, and then enjoy your treat!

1	Wash your hands.
2	Get out the food items you will use.
3	Crush the cornflakes.
4	Peel the bananas.
5	Dip the bananas in yogurt.
6	Roll the bananas in the cereal.
7	Put the bananas in the freezer.
8	Wait three hours, and enjoy your treat.

Lesson 18 • 75

- Read the directions at the top of this page.
- Have a volunteer read the passage aloud.
- Invite volunteers to link sentences from the passage with the steps in the chart.

Ask *Which signal words let you know when to do each step?* (Answers will vary with the sentence or step.)

Ask *What else in the passage helps you follow the sequence of steps?* (Answer: *The steps are written in the order in which they are to be done.*)

Say *Sometimes the sequence of events or steps is not written in the correct order. You must pay careful attention to signal words to follow the sequence.*

(D)ifferentiated Instruction
for ELL, tactile, and visual learners

Putting the Cartoon Back Together

Students will use cartoon strips to identify sequence of events.

Procedure

- Have students work in pairs. Give each pair a copy of a cartoon strip with the boxes cut apart.
- Ask each pair to study the images and determine a logical sequence for them. If no text accompanies the images, encourage students to write their own.
- Have each pair show the completed cartoon strip to another pair of students. Students should discuss the clues they used to sequence the cartoons. Encourage students to point out signal words in the accompanying text.

◢ Use It

In this section students identify signal words in two passages.

Ask *Who here has asked someone for directions? Let's suppose that you want to go to the cafeteria from this classroom. What's the best way to get there?*

■ Have a volunteer give the directions. Write the directions on the board.

    Ask *What are the signal words?* (Possible answers: *first, then, next, after that,* and *so on*)

■ Write the answers on the board.

Read the *Use It* directions aloud. Have students complete the page independently. Ask volunteers to share their answers. Help students understand how signal words indicate sequence in the passage.

◢ Use It

Read the passage and underline the signal words. Then read the questions and write your answers on the lines. Look at these examples.

> To get to Marcela's house from school, first make a left turn on Worthington Avenue. After that, go two blocks. Then, make a second left onto Smithfield Avenue. When you come to the third stoplight, you are at Essex Road. Turn right. Marcela lives at 1980 Essex Road.

1. What are the signal words in the paragraph? ___ first, ___
   ___ After that, Then ___

2. What pattern is the writer using? ___ sequence, or ___
   ___ time order ___

Now you try it.

> Starting in May or June, most classes stop for summer vacation. When the final bell rings at around three o'clock on the last day of school, you can feel how excited the children are. Now they are ready for a well-earned holiday. In September, they will return to start learning again.

3. What are the signal words in the paragraph? ___ in May or ___
   ___ June, three o'clock, Now, In September ___

4. What pattern is the writer using? ___ sequence, or time ___
   ___ order ___

Practice It

Read this passage. Then read the items. Circle the letter of the correct answer.

The year was 1608. By now strangers lived by the river. When my mother sent me to gather berries, I didn't mean to go near the people.

I didn't notice the girl come near until it was too late. Suddenly we were face to face. We stared at each other. Finally she smiled, and I smiled back. Then I gave her some berries. She handed me a ribbon.

"Sarah, where are you?" a man called as he came up the hill.

The girl put a finger to her lips, turned around, and walked slowly toward the man. At last, I slipped away through the brush.

1. **What happened first?**

   A The child telling the story was sent to get berries.

   (B) Strangers built homes near the river.

   C The child telling the story walked many miles to the river.

   D A strange girl was holding a ribbon.

2. **What signal words tell you that the author used sequence in the second paragraph?**

   (A) Finally, Then

   B back, up

   C stared, smiled

   D Suddenly, near

Tip Signal words help you recognize the order of steps and events.

Lesson 18 ● 77

This page may not be reproduced without permission of Steck-Vaughn.

Practice It

Students use signal words in the passage to identify the sequence of events. First, students will read the passage about friendship. Then they will answer the questions about what they have read. Have students answer the questions independently, and then review the answers.

Question 1 Read the directions aloud. Ask students to complete the question independently and then stop. To help students reach an understanding of why *B* is the correct answer, use the *Right There Strategy*. (See the *QAR Strategy* below.)

Say *To answer this question correctly, you must be able to find the answer in one place in the passage. First, read the story and put all events in the right order.*

Ask *What signal words in this passage helped you decide the answer to question 1?* (Answer: *The words* By now *indicate that the people moved to the area before the time that the writer went to the river.*)

Question 2 Read the directions and question aloud. Remind students to look for signal words that indicate sequence.

Ask *Which words tell you something about time or sequence?* (Answer: *Finally, Then*)

Discuss students' answers. Help students recognize that only *A* includes signal words. Explain the incorrect answers.

● *B* These words indicate direction, not time order. ● *C* These words are verbs that tell what the people did. They do not tell when the actions took place. ● *D* These words tell how the actions took place, but not when.

QAR Strategy

Strategy	Definition	How It Works
Right There	This strategy requires students to find information in one place from the passage.	Students look for important information in the text to answer the question.

Refer to pages T22–T23 for a complete chart of QAR Strategies that students may use to achieve greater success on tests of reading comprehension.

Unit 4 ■ 77

Lesson 19

Objective

Students will learn to use the title page and table of contents of a book to find information.

Words to Know

■ Use a book from the classroom to illustrate the meaning of the following terms as you read the definitions aloud.

Title page—usually the first page inside the book cover

Title—name of the book

Author—name of the person who wrote the book

Illustrator—name of the person who drew the pictures in the book

Publisher—company that printed the book

City—the place where the book was published

Table of contents—shows sections into which books are divided

Chapters—sections of books

Study It

This section will introduce students to the title page and table of contents. Ask questions about the various features, such as:

Ask *Where can you find the title page and table of contents in a book?* (Answer: *at the front of the book*)

Ask *Who is the illustrator of the book?* (Answer: *Ed McWest*)

Ask *Who wrote the book?* (Answer: *Alice Brown*)

Ask *How many chapters does the book have?* (Answer: *four*)

Ask *Where is information about materials to make your own instruments?* (Answer: *Chapter 1*)

Ask *On which page does Chapter 3 begin?* (Answer: *page 37*)

Before You Read

Study It

Knowing the parts of a book will help you locate information quickly and easily. The first page you are likely to see is the **title page.**

The title page tells you important information. It shows you the book **title** and the **author,** or the person who wrote the book. It also names the **illustrator,** or the person who did the art for the book. The **publisher,** or the company that printed the book, and the **city** where the book was published are also on the title page.

The next part you see is called the **table of contents.** This part lists the **chapters,** or main topics, in the book. If the book is a collection of stories, the table of contents tells you the names of the stories. It also lists the page numbers on which the chapters or stories begin. Most important, it gives the order of the contents in the book.

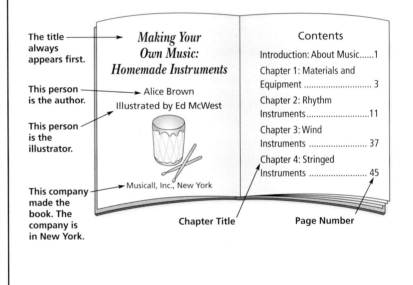

The title always appears first.

This person is the author.

This person is the illustrator.

This company made the book. The company is in New York.

Making Your Own Music: Homemade Instruments

Alice Brown
Illustrated by Ed McWest

Musicall, Inc., New York

Contents

Introduction: About Music......1
Chapter 1: Materials and Equipment 3
Chapter 2: Rhythm Instruments.........................11
Chapter 3: Wind Instruments 37
Chapter 4: Stringed Instruments 45

Chapter Title   Page Number

Curriculum and Assessment Standard

Table of contents and title page

Use It

Use the title page and table of contents on page 78 to answer the questions. Write your answers on the lines. Look at these examples.

1. Who is the author of the book? _____Alice Brown_____

2. Where could you MOST LIKELY find information on how to make a drum? _____Chapter 2: Rhythm Instruments_____

Now you try it.

1. What is the title of the book? ___Making Your Own Music: Homemade Instruments___

2. Which chapter would probably tell you what supplies you need to make strings for a guitar? ___Chapter 1: Materials and Equipment___

Practice It

Read the title page and table of contents on page 78. Then read the items. Circle the letter of the correct answer.

1. **Who is the publisher of the book?**

   A Ed McWest

   (B) Musicall, Inc.

   C New York

   D Alice Brown

2. **Where are you likely to find directions for making a flute?**

   A Chapter 1

   B Chapter 2

   (C) Chapter 3

   D Chapter 4

Tip
Use the table of contents as a guide to help find information in a book.

Lesson 19 ● 79

Use It

Use this section to have students locate information from a sample title page and table of contents.

■ First, direct students to open one of their textbooks.

   Ask *Who is the author of the book?* (Answer will vary based on the book used.)

   Ask *Where was the book published?* (Answer will vary based on the book used.)

   Ask *What is the title of the first chapter?* (Answer will vary based on the book used.)

   Ask *How many chapters does the book have?* (Answer will vary based on the book used.)

Read aloud the *Use It* directions. Work through the first two questions with students, and then have them complete the section independently. Ask volunteers to share their answers.

Practice It

In this section students locate the publisher's name and a chapter number from the sample title page and table of contents.

■ Read the instructions aloud.

■ Ask a volunteer to read the *Tip* aloud.

■ Instruct students to complete questions 1 and 2 independently.

Answers

1. B

2. C

Differentiated Instruction
for kinesthetic, visual, and auditory learners

Investigating Title Pages and Tables of Contents

Students will locate information using a title page and table of contents.

Procedure

● Organize students in pairs: one partner should be the recorder, the other partner the researcher. Give each pair one book from your classroom or from the school library.

● Write these questions on the board: *What is the title of the book? Who is the author of the book? Who published the book? Where was the book published? What kind of information is in Chapter 1?*

● Have each recorder write down and then ask each researcher the questions. The recorder should write down the answers as the researcher finds them.

● Each pair of students should switch roles and repeat the activity, using a second book.

Lesson 20

Objective

Students will use headings and subheadings to locate and organize information.

Words to Know

Headings—tell what information you will be reading

Boldface—words in larger and darker type than other words

Subheadings—headings for small topics

Study It

- Read aloud the opening paragraph. Then look at the passage as a class.

  Say *Notice that some of the words in the passage are written in larger and darker type than others.*

  Ask *Which words in the passage catch your attention first?* (Answer: *Growing Potatoes, Get Ready, Get Started, Plant*)

  Ask *How can you tell the difference between the heading and the sub-headings in the passage?* (Answer: *The heading is in the center above the passage and stands out more than the subheadings do.*)

  Say *Sometimes headings in books will be larger and in capital letters.*

  Ask *What is the paragraph under* Plant *about?* (Answer: *It tells how to put potato plants into pots.*)

- Have volunteers finish reading the page aloud. Use a book from the classroom to point out headings, subheadings, and boldface type.

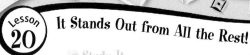

Lesson 20 — It Stands Out from All the Rest!

Study It

Most authors use **headings** to make their writing easier to understand. Headings are like titles. They tell you what information a section or paragraph contains.

Read this passage.

Growing Potatoes

Growing potatoes is easy if you follow these simple rules.

Get Ready
You need several nine-inch pots with holes in the bottom, good soil, and seed potatoes.

Get Started
Put the potatoes in a light, cool place.
Wait for the eyes to send out little green shoots.

Plant
Fill each pot about one-third full with potting soil.

Put the sprouted potatoes in the pots. Cover the potatoes with two to three inches of soil. Add enough water to make the soil damp, but not wet. Wait for green leaves to appear.

This passage has three headings: Get Ready, Get Started, and Plant. They divide the passage into sections and give you a clue to what each section is about.

Headings help you identify the section or paragraph that has the information you need.

Headings are often written in larger, **boldface** type. Sometimes they are underlined. Some the authors use *italics,* or slanted letters. These styles make headings and words stand out on the page.

Authors usually label large topics with headings in a large-size type. Then, under those headings, they label smaller topics with subheadings in a medium-size type. These smaller headings are called subheadings.

Headings and typeface

Curriculum and Assessment Standard

Headings and typeface

Use It

Look at the passage headings on page 80 to answer the questions. Write your answers on the lines. First, look at the example.

Containers for Plants

Pots Plastic pots are inexpensive. They come in many colors and sizes. Wooden containers need care so that the wood will not rot. Many growers prefer clay pots.

Window boxes The best window boxes are made of plastic or clay. They come in many sizes. Think about where you want to use a window box. Then you can decide which size is best.

Containers for plants What is the passage about?

Now you try it.

Pots 1. Which heading says something about the cost of containers?

boldface 2. What kind of type do the headings use?

Practice It

Look at the passage above. Then read the items. Circle the letter of the correct answer.

1. The heading "Containers for Plants" tells you that the passage is about —

   A plastic pots

   B wooden containers

   Ⓒ different kinds of containers

   D clay pots

2. What is the topic of the second paragraph?

   A containers for plants

   B growing plants in pots

   C boxes and barrels

   Ⓓ window boxes

> Tip Use headings to help you locate information in a passage quickly.

Lesson 20 ● 81

Use It

Students will answer questions about headings and subheadings.

■ Show students an article or a page from a children's magazine.

   Ask *What kinds of type do the headings use?* (Possible answers: *boldface, italic, all capital letters*)

   Ask *What is the article or story about? Can you tell from the heading?* (Answers will vary based on the page.)

Read aloud the *Use It* directions. Work through the first question with students, and then have them complete the section independently. Ask volunteers to share their answers.

Practice It

In this section students will have another opportunity to get information from the headings and subheadings in the passage.

■ Read aloud the *Tip.*

■ Have students complete items 1 and 2 independently.

■ Invite volunteers to read their answers aloud.

Answers

1. C

2. D

Differentiated Instruction
for visual, kinesthetic, and tactile learners

Drawing Conclusions

Students will use headings and subheadings in designing a poster.

Procedure

● Organize the class into groups of three to five students each. Give each group a posterboard or large sheet of paper.

● Ask each group to choose a topic and get approval before starting.

● First, students should decide what information they want to show.

● Then, students should think about how they will organize the information under headings and subheadings on a poster they will make.

● Have students display their posters and discuss how the headings and subheadings make the posters easier to read.

Lesson 21

Objective

Students will use indices to locate information in books.

Words to Know

Index—usually found in the back of a book and tells what information is found on which page

Topic—a subject covered in a book

Subtopic—a part of a larger topic

◢ Study It

■ Read aloud the opening paragraph. Then look at the sample index as a class.

Say *Notice that some of the words in the index are written in darker type. These are the topics.*

Ask *Which topics are shown in the sample index?* (Answer: *Drawing board, erasers, paints, paper, pencils*)

Ask *What kinds of paints can you read about in this book?* (Answer: *acrylic paints, oil paints, poster paints, watercolors*)

■ Have volunteers read the last two paragraphs aloud. Then use a book to show students an example of an index.

Lesson 21 — Like a Guide Book

◢ Study It

The **index** appears at the back of the book. An index tells you which pages of the book have the information that you need.

The information in an index is organized into **topics,** or single ideas that are discussed in the book. Topics in the index are written in alphabetical, or *ABC,* order.

Below a topic you might find **subtopics.** Subtopics are ideas that are part of a larger topic. Page numbers follow the topics and subtopics. Numbers separated by a dash, such as 67–73, mean that information begins on page 67 and ends on page 73. Single pages separated by commas, such as 67, 70, 74, mean that information is on each of those pages.

Look at this index from an art book.

> **Drawing board,** 4
>
> **Erasers,** 5
>
> **Paints,** 26–35
>   acrylic paints, 26–29; oil paints, 31–32;
>   poster paints, 30; watercolors, 33–35
>
> **Paper,** 36–38
>   drawing, 36; poster, 36; construction, 37–38
>
> **Pencils,** 7, 39

The topics are sometimes in **boldface,** or darker type. To find out about erasers, turn to page 5. The topic of paints is covered on pages 26–35. Poster paints is a subtopic. To find out about poster paints, look on page 30. You could find information about pencils on two different pages, 7 and 39.

Sometimes you might not find the topic you want in an index. Think of another way to say the topic. For example, suppose that you want to learn how to draw squares. But you cannot find squares in the index. Look under the topic shapes. Squares may be a subtopic there.

82 ● Unit 4   Index

Curriculum and Assessment Standard

Index

Use It

Use the index on page 82 to answer the questions. Look for the topics and subtopics. Write your answers on the lines.

subtopic   Is poster paints a topic or a subtopic?

Now you try it.

pages 33–35   1. Where would you find information about watercolor paints?

drawing and   2. What two subtopics about paper are on
poster   page 36?

Practice It

Read this index. Then read the items. Circle the letter of the correct answer.

> **Chalk,** 7–8
>
> **Circles and cubes,** 9–11
>
> **Colors,** 12–25
> combining, 14–19; mixing of, 20, 22,
> 24; primary, 12, 14, 25

1. **Which page would give you information about combining colors?**

   A page 12

   (B) page 15

   C page 20

   D page 24

2. **On what page would you find information about circles?**

   A page 6

   B page 8

   (C) page 10

   D page 13

> **Tip**
> An index is a quick and easy guide to find the information you need.

Use It

Students will use the sample index on page 82 to answer questions.

- Direct students' attention to the sample index on the previous page.

  Ask *Is the topic* paste *included in the index?* (Answer: *no*) *If it were included, where would you find it?* (Answer: *after* paper *and before* pencils)

  Ask *Where else in the index might you find information about paste?* (Possible answers: *under* glue *or* adhesives)

Read aloud the *Use It* directions. Work through the first item with students, and then have them complete the section independently. Ask volunteers to share their answers.

Practice It

In this section students will answer questions using another sample index.

- Read aloud the *Tip*.
- Have students complete questions 1 and 2 independently.
- Invite volunteers to read their answers aloud.

Answers

1. B
2. C

(D)ifferentiated Instruction
for visual, kinesthetic, and tactile learners

A Topic Hunt

Students will locate information in an index.

Procedure

- Organize students in pairs. Let each student choose a book with an index.
- First, each student should flip through one book, listing topics on a sheet of paper. On another sheet of paper, students should list the topics again, along with the page numbers on which the topics can be found.
- Next, have student partners trade books. Partners should also exchange the sheets of paper on which the topics are written, but not the page numbers.
- Using the index of the book, one partner should try to find the pages on which his or her partner's topics are written.
- Have partners check their answers with each other.

Teach the Strategy

Write on the board:

I'm going home now.

I'm going home now?

I'm going home now!

Ask *How are these three sentences different?* (Answer: *One is a statement, one is a question, and one is an exclamation.*)

Ask *How do you know which sentence is a question?* (Answer: *It has a question mark at the end.*)

Look for the Signals Strategy

Remind students to look for different kinds of signals as they read.

■ Read aloud the bulleted points.

Ask *What do signal words tell you?* (Answer: *time sequence*)

Ask *What do headings tell you?* (Answer: *how a passage is organized*)

Ask *What can these things tell you?* (Possible answers: *that these words are supposed to stand out; that these words can help readers find information in the text*)

Try It Out

Read the directions aloud, and have students complete this section independently. Encourage students to use the *Look for the Signals Strategy* to answer the question.

■ Instruct students to read the passage. Make sure students know that they do not have to write the story ending.

■ Have students select the correct answer (*D*).

■ Have volunteers explain the reasons for their answers.

Ask *How did the* Look for the Signals Strategy *help you find the correct answer?*

Discuss the explanation that follows the question in the student book.

Test-Taking Strategy

Strategy: Look for the Signals

In this unit you learned that writers give signals to help you understand what you read.

- Signal words, such as <u>first</u>, <u>next</u>, <u>last</u>, <u>yesterday</u>, or <u>next month</u>
- Headings
- **Boldface type**
- <u>Underlining</u>
- *Italics*, or slanted letters
- Colored print
- CAPITALIZATION

You also learned that books give you signals, too. The title page and table of contents tell you what the book is about. The index tells you where to find information.

Try It Out

Read the passage. Then answer the question. Circle the letter of the correct answer.

> Think of your favorite fairy tale. How could the ending be different? Start in the middle of the story. Then write a new ending.

Which of these words from the passage is a signal word?

A Think

B How

C Write

(D) Then

<u>Think</u> and <u>write</u> are words that tell you what to do. <u>How</u> is a question word. <u>Then</u> is a signal word that shows time order. So, the correct answer is **D, Then.**

Put It to the Test

Name _____

This test will check what you have learned in this unit.

DIRECTIONS: Read the title page and table of contents. Then read each item. Circle the letter of the correct answer.

FUN
ACTIVITIES
FOR SUMMER DAYS

Tom Claussen and Sue Cook

Illustrated by Mary Long

Summertime Press, New York

Contents

1. Who drew the pictures in the book?

   A Tom Claussen

   B Sue Cook

   C Mary Long

   D Summertime Press

2. In which chapter would you probably find recipes?

   A Paper Projects

   B Using Cans and Jars

   C Good Enough to Eat

   D Materials

3. If you wanted to make something from pine cones, which chapter would you probably read?

   A Painting Fun

   B Games and Puzzles

   C Making Music

   D The Great Outdoors

GO ON

Achieve It! Practice Cards

_____

Put It to the Test • 85

This page may not be reproduced without permission of Steck-Vaughn.

Connect the Test to the Practice Cards (page 85)

Correct Answers	Related Practice Cards	Skill
1. C	69	TOC/title page
2. C	69	TOC/title page
3. D	69	TOC/title page

Put It to the Test

Students will:

- demonstrate what they have learned
- identify skills that require more practice before students achieve proficiency*

* Refer to pages T17–T19 for a complete explanation and directions for using *Achieve It!* Practice Cards.

Administer the Test

Explain that students will now practice the skills from this unit by taking a short test. Tell students that the test has items like those they will find on standardized tests. Explain that you will read the directions aloud. Remind students to pay close attention and follow your directions exactly.

Say *Open your books to page 85. I will read the directions aloud.* Read the directions to students. Then continue.

Say *You will have 10 minutes to finish this test. Read each item and the answer choices carefully. Circle the letter of the correct answer. When you reach the words* GO ON *at the bottom of a page, turn the page and continue working. When you reach the word* STOP *at the bottom of a page, stop working and put down your pencil. Are there any questions?*

If students have no questions,

Say *You may begin.*

At the end of 10 minutes,

Say *Stop. Check to be sure that you have circled the letter of the correct answer choice. Erase any stray pencil marks. Then put down your pencil.*

Assign Practice Cards

After scoring a student's test, note which items the student missed. Match each incorrectly answered item to the related *Achieve It!* Practice Cards listed in the chart on this page.

In the *Achieve It!* Practice Cards space in each student's book, write all of the Practice Cards you want the student to complete.

Additional Practice Cards

The following cards cover additional skills for

Unit 4: Parts and Patterns

Card	Topic
65	Compare and contrast
66	Cause and effect
68	Proposition and support

You may want to assign these cards as practice for students who have done well on the unit test or as extended practice for all students.

DIRECTIONS: Look at the index. Then read each item. Circle the letter of the correct answer.

INDEX

Brushes, types of, 72
Cans, 27–30
Cardboard, 4, 6, 7, 10
Crossword puzzles, 49, 51
Drawing paper, 3, 5, 9
Drums, 65

Foods, 35–46
 breads, 35–37;
 muffins, 38–40;
 snacks, 41; yogurt
 smoothies, 42–46
Jars, 31–34
Jigsaw puzzles, 48
Paints, kinds of, 15–16
Tools, 72–76

4. Which of these topics has subtopics?

   A jars

   B cans

   C foods

   D tools

5. On which of these pages would you look to find out what kind of can to use?

   A page 5

   B page 6

   C page 31

   D page 35

DIRECTIONS: Read this passage. Then read each item. Circle the letter of the correct answer.

What Should I Do Today?

Summer days can seem long and dull. Now you'll never again have to say, "There's nothing to do!" The first things you need are some paper, glue, and a bit of imagination!

6. You can tell that the word imagination is important because it is —

   A slanted

   B in capital letters

   C underlined

   D in dark print

7. The heading tells you that the passage is probably about —

   A painting a poster

   B finding things to do

   C drawing a picture

   D making things with paper

8. Which of these is a signal word in the paragraph?

   A Summer

   B long

   C glue

   D first

STOP

Achieve It! Practice Cards

Connect the Test to the Practice Cards (page 86)

Correct Answers	Related Practice Cards	Skill
4. C	70, 71, 72	Headings/typeface, Index
5. C	72	Index
6. C	70, 71	Headings/typeface
7. B	70, 71	Headings/typeface
8. D	67	Sequential or chronological order

Unit 5 — Kinds of Books

Your Ticket to Read

There are many ways we can travel. Bicycles, cars, buses, trains, ships, and airplanes take us where we want to go. There are many different kinds of books to read, too. There are stories, poems, fables, and plays. They all take us somewhere special. By reading, we can travel to new places. We can learn about ourselves. We can enjoy a good adventure.

In this unit you will learn about different kinds of books. You will discover what makes each one special.

87

Skills

- Distinguishing between fiction and nonfiction texts
- Distinguishing between biographical and autobiographical texts
- Recognizing characteristics of informational texts
- Recognizing fantasy writing
- Distinguishing between fairy tale and fable
- Identifying myths and legends as types of fiction writing
- Identifying parts of a play
- Identifying elements of a poem

Materials to Gather in Advance

- paper ● pencils ● crayons, markers or colored pencils ● scissors ● old magazines

Introducing the Unit

Your Ticket to Read Refer students to the photograph of the bus. Ask whether any students have traveled in a bus across town or to someplace away from their town.

Ask *What new information did you learn, and what new things did you see?*

Ask *Do you know how to see new things and learn new information without traveling?*

- Remind students that books help us to learn about new places and see new things.

- Read the *Your Ticket to Read* paragraph aloud. Discuss books that students have read that helped them see and learn about new places and people.

Research Says

If today's children are not just to survive but thrive in the Information Age, we must immerse them in the literatures of fiction and fact.

—*Moss*

Lesson 22

Objective

Students will learn the differences between fiction and nonfiction.

Words to Know

Fiction—writing based on ideas from the author's imagination, such as stories, plays, poems, fantasies, and fables

Nonfiction—writing based on real people, places, things, events, or ideas, including articles, essays, and biographies

Study It

Read the first paragraph aloud, and then read the directions for the chart aloud.

■ Write the following titles on the board: *James and the Giant Peach; How to Grow Vegetables in Your Backyard; The Legend of Paul Bunyan; The Life of George Washington.* Ask a student to read the titles aloud. In another area of the board, write the column headings *Fiction* and *Nonfiction*.

Ask *Which of these titles do you think go with fiction writing?* (Answer: *James and the Giant Peach; The Legend of Paul Bunyan*)

■ Write the titles in the *Fiction* column.

Ask *What words in these titles are clues that the titles are fiction?* (Answer: *Giant Peach, Legend*)

Say *Now let's look at the two titles that do not look like fiction.*

Ask *Would a book about George Washington probably be based on real people and events?* (Answer: *yes*)

Ask *Would a book about growing vegetables likely give you real facts and information?* (Answer: *yes*)

■ Write the titles in the *Nonfiction* column.

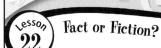

Fact or Fiction?

Study It

Why do you read? Sometimes you read for fun, and sometimes you read to learn.

Most writing fits into two groups, fiction and nonfiction. **Fiction** is writing that comes from an author's imagination. It can be based on facts, or on real people, or even on real experiences. However, if any part of a story is make-believe, it is fiction. **Nonfiction** is writing that is about real people, places, things, or ideas. Everything that you read about in nonfiction is true or has actually happened in real life.

Look at the chart. It shows some types of fiction and nonfiction.

Fiction	Nonfiction
Short story	Autobiography
Historical fiction	Biography
Poem	Informational text
Fantasy	Essay
Legend	
Fairy tale	
Fable	

How can you tell that you are reading fiction?

● The writing comes from the author's imagination.
● Some or all of the characters and places are make-believe.

How can you tell that you are reading nonfiction?

● You are reading about something that really happened.
● The writing contains facts and other information.
● You are reading about a real person or event in a real place and time.

Curriculum and Assessment Standard

Fiction/nonfiction

Read this passage. Then look at the chart. Use the chart to decide whether the passage is fiction or nonfiction.

Animals have different ways of hiding from other animals and people. The color of an animal is one thing that can help it hide. An animal may have a body color that matches the color of its surroundings, or where it lives. For example, the green grasshopper stays well-hidden in the grass. Also, the copperhead snake has bands of orange and brown that help it stay hidden on the ground. The snake looks just like the fallen leaves. Some animals actually change color to match the things around them. The arctic fox is one such animal. In spring the fox's fur is brown, to help the animal blend into its surroundings. But in winter, the fox's fur is white, to match the snow.

Fiction or Nonfiction?	
Fiction	**Nonfiction**
It comes from the author's imagination.	What happens is real.
The characters, actions, or settings are make-believe.	There are facts and other information.
The characters, actions, or settings can be real, but other parts are make-believe.	It is about real people, places, or things.

According to the information in the chart, the passage is nonfiction. It gives facts about real animals. In real life, grasshoppers do blend in with their surroundings. The facts about copperhead snakes are true, too. The arctic fox really is able to survive because of its protective color. Nothing in this passage is make-believe.

■ Ask students to follow along in their books as you read the passage aloud. Then direct students to the chart at the bottom of the page.

Say *This chart will help you decide whether the passage is fiction or nonfiction.*

Ask *Does the passage use details that are make-believe, or does it use facts?* (Answer: *facts*)

Ask *What are some of the facts in the passage?* (Possible answer: *The color of an animal can help it hide. The copperhead snake has bands of orange and brown. The artic fox turns white in winter.*)

■ Write student responses on the board. Explain that a passage that does not contain make-believe characters, actions, or settings is nonfiction.

Encourage students to ask questions about fiction and nonfiction. Help them understand that a passage that contains anything that is make-believe is fiction.

Differentiated Instruction
for ELL and auditory learners

Which Is My Real Life?

Students will practice distinguishing fiction from nonfiction.

Procedure

● Ask students to write three sentences. Two of these sentences will contain facts about their lives, and the other sentence will be make-believe.

● Model by writing one fiction and two nonfiction sentences on the board about your own life. Explain to students that even though the last sentence is something you would like to do, it is only an idea that you made up.

● As students write, remind them not to tell anyone which sentences contain facts. Encourage them to write the sentences in random order.

● Ask students to read their sentences aloud, and have the class guess which sentence is fiction.

Use It

Use this activity to help students determine whether a piece of writing is fiction or nonfiction.

■ Direct students to the passage from the story "Pearl." Read the directions aloud. Then ask a student to read the passage aloud.

■ Direct students to the questions below the passage. Read the directions aloud. Then read question 1 aloud.

Ask *Who are the characters in this passage?* (Answer: *the narrator, the narrator's grandfather, and George Washington*)

Say *Sometimes authors write about make-believe characters, but use real settings and real events in history.*

Ask *Even though we know that George Washington is a real person, is it likely that the author made up the characters of the girl and her grandfather?* (Answer: *yes*)

■ Have the students circle *both* next to question 1. Read question 2 aloud.

Ask *Is it possible that the parade with George Washington was a real event in history?* (Answer: *yes*)

Ask *If the girl and her grandfather are make-believe, can the things they do be real?* (Answer: *no*)

■ Have the students circle *both* next to question 2. Read question 3 aloud.

Ask *Is New York City a real place?* (Answer: *yes*)

■ Have the students circle *real* next to question 3. Then ask them to complete question 4 independently. When they have finished, discuss their answers. Help them understand that because the passage contains some elements of make-believe, it has to be fiction.

Use It

Read this passage from "Pearl" by Debby Atwell. Look for parts that are real and parts that are make-believe.

At night, when the house is quiet, I look out my bedroom window and see only stars above the dark trees. It's then that I remember family events all the way back to when this country began.

My grandfather told me that when he was just a small boy, he rode in a big parade with the first president of the United States. It was down Wall Street, New York City, on Inauguration Day. Grandfather said George Washington scooped him up just like that out of the crowd and carried him on his horse while everybody cheered. He felt that he was the luckiest person alive.

Is this passage nonfiction or fiction? Use this checklist to find out. Circle <u>real</u>, <u>make-believe</u>, or <u>both</u> after each question.

1. What are the characters in this passage?

   real   make-believe   (both)

2. What are the events in this passage?

   real   make-believe   (both)

3. What is the setting in this passage?

   (real)   make-believe   both

Now circle your answer to this question.

4. Is this passage an example of fiction or nonfiction?

   (fiction)   nonfiction

Practice It

Read the passage. Then read the items. Circle the letter of the correct answer.

Many people think that all sharks are large, man-eating creatures. But not all sharks are like the great white shark. Even the largest shark, the whale shark, is not thought to be harmful to people. In fact, there are more than 300 kinds of sharks, and they come in many interesting sizes and shapes. The dwarf shark is only about six to ten inches long. Angel sharks do not look like sharks at all because they are almost flat. The zebra shark has patterns like stripes on its skin. The hammerhead shark may be the strangest-looking shark. Its head looks like a hammer, and it has eyes on each end of the "hammer."

1. **This passage is nonfiction because it —**

   A   tells about make-believe animals

   B   takes place in a make-believe setting

   C   gives facts

   D   comes from the author's imagination

2. **To write this passage, the author would first need to —**

   A   have a good imagination

   B   read a short story about sharks

   C   see a real shark

   D   study sharks

3. **You would probably find this passage in a book called —**

   A   *Ocean Plants*

   B   *Sammy, the Shark*

   C   *All About Sharks*

   D   *What's in the Fish Tank?*

 If any part of the story you are reading is make-believe, you are reading fiction.

QAR Strategy

Strategy	Definition	How It Works
Think and Search	This strategy teaches students that the correct answer may appear in several places in whatever they are reading.	Students *reread* the paragraph and look for the answer choices in the text. They try to find which answers are incorrect so that they can narrow down the correct answer to as few choices as possible.

Refer to pages T22–T23 for a complete chart of QAR Strategies that students may use to achieve greater success on tests of reading comprehension.

Practice It

Use this activity to help students understand the differences between fiction and nonfiction.

Question 1   Read the directions aloud. Then give students time to read the passage silently. When they have finished, have them complete question 1 independently.

To help students understand why *C* is the correct answer, use the *Think and Search Strategy.* (See the *QAR Strategy* below.)

Say   *Read the possible answers to the question. Then reread the passage to see which answer makes the most sense.*

Say   *When you reread the passage, check for animals and places that are make-believe. You see that there is nothing make-believe, so you know* A *and* B *are incorrect.* D *is also incorrect because imagination is how we create things that are make-believe.*

Ask   *What about answer* C*? When you reread, can you find facts in the passage?* (Answer: *yes*)

Say   *You used the* Right There Strategy. *When you reread the facts in the passage, you saw that* C *is the correct answer.*

Questions 2 and 3   Have students complete questions 2 and 3 independently. Discuss the answers to both questions.

Help students understand that a writer needs to learn facts in order to write nonfiction, which is why the correct answer to question 2 is *D.* Help students understand that the correct answer to question 3 is *C* by explaining the incorrect answers.

● *A* is incorrect because the text does not discuss plants.   ● *B* would be the title of a story from an author's imagination.   ● *D* is incorrect because sharks live in the ocean.

Lesson 23

Objective

Students will learn the difference between biographies and autobiographies.

Words to Know

Biography—a true story written about someone else's life

Autobiography—a true story that someone writes about his or her own life

Subject—the person who is written about by the author of the biography

Interview—when one person asks another person questions

◢ Study It

Read the directions for the chart aloud.

■ Copy the titles from the chart onto the board. Ask a student to read the first title.

   Ask *Who is the subject of* If a Bus Could Talk*?* (Answer: *Rosa Parks*)

   Ask *Who is the author?* (Answer: *Faith Ringgold*)

   Ask *What do you call a book written by one person about another person's life?* (Answer: *a biography*)

■ Write *biography* next to the first title. Then ask a volunteer to read the second title.

   Ask *Are the author and the subject the same person?* (Answer: *yes*)

   Ask *Who can tell me what a story that someone writes about his or her own life is called?* (Answer: *an autobiography*)

◢ Study It

Biographies and **autobiographies** are true stories about people's lives. An author writes a biography about someone else's life. An author writes an autobiography about his or her own life.

Look at the chart. It shows examples of the titles of a biography and of an autobiography.

Biography	Autobiography
If a Bus Could Talk: The Story of Rosa Parks, by Faith Ringgold	*Rosa Parks: My Story*, by Rosa Parks

Biographies and autobiographies are alike because both are true stories about a person. That person is called the **subject.** However, if the subject writes the story, it is an autobiography. If someone else writes the story, it is a biography.

Both biographies and autobiographies are usually told in time order, or the order in which events actually happened. But sometimes the author may skip back and forth between the past and the present. This helps the author show how the events are related.

Biographies and autobiographies contain information about real people and events. However, the author of an autobiography has information that the writer of a biography does not. The author of an autobiography can remember feelings or thoughts that he or she had in the past. The author of a biography must use information from things like letters, books, and **interviews.** Interviews are talks with the subject or people who have known the subject.

Curriculum and Assessment Standard

Biography/autobiography

Use It

Use what you have learned to answer each question.
Write biography, autobiography, or both on the lines. Look at these examples.

biography 1. Interviews are a source of information.

both 2. The author tells events in the order in which they happened.

Now you try it.

autobiography 1. The author uses his or her own thoughts and feelings.

both 2. It is a true story of someone's life.

biography 3. The author tells the story of someone else's life.

Practice It

Read each question. Circle the letter of the correct answer.

1. **If you wrote your autobiography, which of the following would make the BEST title?**

   A _My Friend Ralph_

   B _My Grandfather_

   C _My Life As I Remember It_

   D _Memories of Fourth Grade_

2. **The author of a biography would probably find which source useful?**

   A a dictionary

   B the subject's letters

   C a television commercial

   D recipes by the subject

Tip
Autobiographies usually include the author's feelings and thoughts.

Lesson 23 ● 93

Use It

This activity gives students practice recognizing characteristics of biographies and autobiographies.

■ Copy onto the board example questions 1 and 2. Read the directions aloud.

Read question 1 aloud.

Ask _Who can tell me what an interview is?_ (Answer: _An interview is an event in which one person asks another person questions. It is also a written version of their talk._)

Say _An interview would be a good source for a biography, but would not make sense for an autobiography._

■ Write _biography_ next to question 1.

Read question 2 aloud.

Ask _Does it make sense to put events in the right order in both an autobiography and a biography?_ (Answer: _yes_)

■ Write _both_ next to question 2.

Have students complete the rest of the items independently. Ask for volunteers to share answers with the class.

Practice It

In this section students will use what they have learned about biographies and autobiographies to answer questions.

■ Read the _Tip_ aloud.

■ Have students complete questions 1 and 2 independently.

■ Ask volunteers to share their answers.

Answers

1. C

2. B

Differentiated Instruction
for auditory and kinesthetic learners

This is Your Life

Students will interview each other for biographical information.

Procedure

● Have students brainstorm a list of interview questions they might ask biography subjects. Model by writing _Where were you born?_ and _Where do you live?_ on the board. Write students' questions on the board.

● Have students work in pairs, taking turns asking each other questions and writing down the responses.

● Then have students work independently to write at least three sentences with facts about the person they interviewed.

● Encourage students to read the sentences they wrote to the class.

Lesson 24

Objective

Students will recognize characteristics of informational texts.

Words to Know

Informational Texts—texts that give information and facts, such as textbooks, dictionaries, and newspapers

Study It

Remind students that facts are different from opinions or fiction.

■ Copy the three informational text titles onto the board. Ask for a volunteer to read the titles aloud.

Say *All of these titles are informational texts.*

Ask *What do you think these books have in common?* (Answer: *They all teach the reader about something or how to do something.*)

■ Read the directions above the chart. Ask a student to read the types of informational texts aloud.

Ask *What types of texts do you use when you want to learn more about something?*

■ Ask students to tell you the names of specific books, magazines, newspapers, or reference books. Write responses on the board. Discuss how signs and flyers can also provide information.

■ Direct students to the passage at the bottom of the page, and have students follow along as you read aloud.

Ask *What are some of the facts in this informational text?*

Write student responses on the board. Discuss with the class what kind of report one might write using this passage (for example, a report on John Philip Sousa, on famous composers, or on traditional American songs).

Lesson 24 · I Want to Know

Study It

Have you ever wanted to find out more about something? Maybe you needed to learn more about dog care. Maybe you wanted to know why the planet Mars is red. Or maybe you wanted to learn to ride a skateboard safely. If so, you would probably look for information in books such as these:

- *Dogs: How to Care for and Understand Them*
- *Learn More About the Planets*
- *Skateboard Safety*

These books are part of a group called **informational texts.** Informational texts explain and give facts about something. They can be written about almost any subject.

Look at the chart. It shows some of the different types of informational texts.

Types of Informational Texts	
Textbooks	Magazines
Newspapers	Signs
Reference Books	Flyers

In good informational texts, the author—

- uses facts that have been checked for accuracy, with no important facts left out
- writes the information so that the reader can understand it

Read this passage.

John Philip Sousa wrote "The Stars and Stripes Forever" in 1897. Not many people know that Sousa wrote this famous march while on a boat, without the help of a single musical instrument! The tune is now the official march of the United States. In 1997, one hundred years after Sousa completed the piece, a special United States postage stamp was created to honor this march.

You can tell that this passage is an informational text because it gives you facts about John Philip Sousa and explains the history of "The Stars and Stripes Forever."

Informational texts

Curriculum and Assessment Standard

Informational texts

Use It

Use what you have learned about informational texts to decide whether each statement below is true or false. Write your answers on the lines. Look at these examples.

_____true_____ 1. Informational texts explain and give facts.

_____true_____ 2. Informational texts are written so that the reader can understand them.

Now you try it.

_____false_____ 1. Fiction books are a kind of informational text.

_____true_____ 2. The facts in an informational text have been checked for accuracy.

_____false_____ 3. It is all right to leave some important facts out of an informational text.

Practice It

Read each question. Circle the letter of the correct answer.

1. **Which of these is a title of an informational text?**

    A *Beauty and the Beast*

    B *The Lives of Fairies*

    C *How Computers Work*

    D *Fluffy, the Kitten*

2. **If you wanted to learn about whales, which book would probably be the BEST source of information?**

    A *Under the Ocean*

    B *Humphrey, the Lost Whale*

    C *My First Fishing Trip*

    D *Whales: Strange and Wonderful*

Tip Choose an informational text to learn more about a topic.

Lesson 24 • 95

Use It

Use this activity to help students demonstrate what they know about informational texts.

- Copy example questions 1 and 2 onto the board. Read the directions aloud.

Read question 1 aloud.

Ask *Is it true or false that informational texts give the reader facts and explain facts?* (Answer: *true*)

- Write *true* next to question 1 on the board.

Read question 2 aloud.

Ask *Why does an author write an informational text?* (Answer: *to explain facts so that the reader can understand something*)

- Write *true* next to question 2 on the board.

Have students complete the rest of the questions independently. Ask for volunteers to share answers with the class.

Practice It

In this section students use what they have learned about informational texts to answer questions.

- Read the *Tip* aloud.
- Have students complete questions 1 and 2 independently.
- Ask students to share their answers.

Answers

1. C
2. D

Differentiated Instruction
for ELL, auditory, and kinesthetic learners

Teaching New Tricks

Students will direct other students through simple tasks in order to write an informational text that explains how to do something.

Procedure

- Remind students that some informational texts explain how to do something.
- Brainstorm with the class a list of simple tasks done every day in the classroom, such as sharpening a pencil or tying a shoe.
- Organize students into pairs, and have each student pick a task that they will talk their partner through. Tells students to act like the student doing the task has never completed this task before. Encourage the student giving the instructions to be as detailed as possible and to be sure to include all steps.
- When students have finished, have them write out each step of the task.

Lesson 25

Objective

Students will learn about fantasy writing and the differences between types of fantasy writing.

Words to Know

Fantasy—a kind of fiction writing with magical events and unusual make-believe characters

Fairy tale—a type of fantasy that is usually set in make-believe places

Fable—a kind of short fantasy story that tries to teach a lesson with talking animals as the main characters

Study It

Discuss the descriptions of *fantasy, fable,* and *fairy tale.*

- Ask for a volunteer to read the fairy tale passage aloud.

  Ask *What unusual elements does this story have?* (Answer: *Cinderella wears glass slippers; the coach turns into a pumpkin.*)

  Ask *Is a fairy godmother a real-life or make-believe character?* (Answer: *make-believe*)

- Ask for a volunteer to read the fable passage aloud.

  Ask *Are the wolf and the crane like animals you know?* (Answer: *No, they are talking animals.*)

  Ask *What problem is solved in this fable?* (Answer: *The crane gets the bone out of the wolf's throat.*)

  Ask *What happens at the end of the story? What lesson could the author be trying to teach by ending the fable this way?*

Discuss student responses. Ask students to share other fables or fairy tales that they know.

Lesson 25 Imagine That!

Study It

Fantasy is a special kind of fiction. It involves things that never happen in real life. Fantasies contain magical events and unusual characters, such as giants, elves, fairies, and talking animals. **Fairy tales** are a type of fantasy and are sometimes set in make-believe places. A fairy tale often begins with the familiar words, "Once upon a time."

Fables are like fantasy stories. For example, both fantasies and fables may contain talking animals. However, in a fantasy story, animals talk because they are special, or magical. In a fable, the animals think and talk like humans, but they behave like real-life animals.

Fables are usually short. There is a clear problem that is solved in the end. The author of a fable usually ends the story by telling the reader the lesson that he or she should learn from the story. Unlike fantasies, fables are almost always set in the real world.

Read the following examples of a fairy tale and a fable.

Fairy tale

It was getting late and the ball was ending. Cinderella had forgotten the time! She ran out the door in a hurry. As she raced down the steps, one of her glass slippers fell off.

The clock struck twelve. The beautiful coach that her fairy godmother had given her turned back into a pumpkin.

Fable

A wolf had a bone stuck in his throat. He went looking for someone to help him. "I would do anything for you if you would just take it out," he said. But everyone ran away. At last a crane agreed to help. It put its long neck down the wolf's throat and took the bone out. "Will you please give me my reward now?" asked the crane. The wolf said, "You should be happy. You put your head inside a wolf's mouth and took it out again! That reward is good enough."

Fantasies, fairy tales, and fables

Curriculum and Assessment Standard

Fantasies, fairy tales, and fables

Use It

Look at the fairy tale on page 96 and answer the questions. Write your answers on the lines. Look at this example.

What magical event happens in this story?

a coach becomes a pumpkin

Now you try it.

1. Could the events in this story happen in the real world or in an imaginary world?

   in an imaginary world

2. What unusual characters are in this story?

   a fairy godmother

Practice It

Read the fable on page 96. Then read the questions. Circle the letter of the correct answer.

1. **What is the setting of the fable?**

   A a magical planet

   (B) the real world

   C an island that floats on the water

   D a city in the clouds

2. **What is the lesson of this fable?**

   (A) Doing a good deed should be reward enough.

   B Do not chew your food too fast.

   C Do not put your head down a wolf's throat.

   D Do not do favors for wolves.

Tip If the story has animal characters and teaches a lesson, it is probably a fable.

Lesson 25 ● 97

Use It

Use this activity to help students demonstrate what they know about fairy tales.

■ Read the directions for the example aloud. Ask for a volunteer to read the example question aloud.

   Say *Let's look back and reread the passage about Cinderella to find unusual events.*

   Ask *Which event seems magical?* (Answer: *The coach turns into a pumpkin.*)

Have students complete the rest of the items independently. Ask for volunteers to share answers with the class. Help students understand the idea that make-believe events are common in fairy tales.

Practice It

In this section students use what they have learned about fables to answer questions.

■ Read the *Tip* aloud.

■ Have students complete items 1 and 2 independently.

■ Ask students to share their answers.

Answers

1. B
2. A

Differentiated Instruction
for ELL, visual, and tactile learners

Fable Cartoons

Students will write and illustrate a fable.

Procedure

● Have students divide a sheet of paper into four sections by folding it in half two times.

● Ask students to think of a simple fable in which two or more animals talk to each other and solve a problem or conflict.

● Have students illustrate each action or line of dialogue in a different box. Show students how to use speech balloons to write what the characters in each box are saying.

● Ask students to title their fables.

● Ask for volunteers to explain their fables or illustrations to the class.

Unit 5 ■ 97

Lesson 26

Objective

Students will identify myths and legends as types of fiction writing.

Words to Know

Legends—stories in which heroes perform deeds

Myths—stories created to help people understand things they see every day but cannot explain, such as why the sun rises or why the moon shines

Study It

Discuss the descriptions of *legends* and *myths* in the student book.

■ Direct students to the legend about John Henry. Ask for a volunteer to read each paragraph aloud.

Ask *What does John Henry do in this legend?* (Answer: *He drives railroad spikes faster than a machine can.*)

Ask *Does it seem impossible that a man could drive railroad spikes into the ground faster than a machine without getting tired?* (Answer: *yes*)

Ask *Do you know of any other stories where people do things that seem impossible?*

■ Write student responses on the board.

■ Direct students to the myth about the Spokane River. Ask for a volunteer to read each paragraph aloud.

Say *This myth explains the beginning of something that people in Idaho see everyday.*

Ask *What does the myth explain?* (Answer: *how the Spokane River was formed*)

Ask *How was the river formed?* (Answer: *The dragon tore a trench in the ground that reached the lake.*)

Discuss any other myths or legends that the students have heard of.

98 ■ **Unit 5**

It's Hard to Believe

Study It

Some stories about heroes are hard to believe. The heroes do things that seem impossible. These stories are called **legends.** Often, the hero in a legend reminds the reader of himself or herself. Legends teach us valuable lessons about ourselves.

Have you ever seen something you could not explain? Long ago, people did not know why the sun came up. They did not know what caused the seasons to change. **Myths** are stories that were created to explain such things. Myths gave people answers to their questions. They helped people make sense of the world. Myths often include gods as characters.

Read the following examples of a legend and a myth.

Legend

John Henry was a big, strong man. He could drive railroad spikes faster than any man.

One day, his boss wanted to decide whether to use machines or men to drive spikes. He asked John Henry to run a race. John Henry would have to drive spikes faster than a machine, which he did.

Myth

Long ago lived a dragon that could tear down trees. One day a girl from the Native American Spokane tribe was picking berries and saw the creature. It was sleeping on a hill where the Spokane River is today.

The girl ran quietly back to her village and told everyone what she had seen. The chief gathered his warriors and every rope in the village. Then the warriors crept up on the dragon. They tied it to several trees and then attacked it. The dragon woke up and instantly broke free. As he ran away, he tore a deep trench to Lake Coeur d'Alene in Idaho. The lake waters flowed through this trench, all the way to the sea. That is how the Spokane River was formed.

98 ● Unit 5   Myths/legends

Curriculum and Assessment Standard

Myths/legends

Use It

Look at the legend on page 98. Then read the items. Write your answers on the lines. Look at this example.

Who is the hero of this story?

John Henry

Now you try it.

1. What is special about John Henry?

   He can drive railroad spikes faster than any man.

2. What did John Henry do in the race?

   He drove spikes faster than a machine.

Practice It

Look at the myth on page 98. Then read the questions. Circle the letter of the correct answer.

1. **Which part of the story is NOT real?**

   A the Native American warriors

   B the Native American chief

   C the dragon

   D the Spokane River

2. **What does the myth explain?**

   A how the state of Idaho got its name

   B how the Spokane River was formed

   C how dragons came to be

   D how rope was first made

3. **What awoke the dragon?**

   A the girl picking berries

   B a tree falling

   C its own snoring

   D the attack by the warriors

   Tip If the hero of a story does things that seem impossible, the story is probably a legend.

Lesson 26 ● 99

Use It

Use this activity to help students demonstrate what they read in the legend of John Henry.

■ Write the example question on the board. Read the directions aloud. Ask for a volunteer to read the example question aloud.

   Ask *Who remembers the name of the hero who completed the impossible tasks in the legend we read?*

   Say *If you don't remember the name, reread the legend in your book.*

■ Give students a moment to look at the passage, then ask for a volunteer to answer the question. Write *John Henry* on the board below the question.

Have students complete the rest of the items independently. Ask volunteers to share their answers with the class.

Practice It

In this section students use what they have learned about myths to answer questions.

■ Read the *Tip* aloud.

■ Have students complete items 1–3 independently.

■ Ask volunteers to share their answers with the class.

Answers

1. C
2. B
3. D

Differentiated Instruction
for ELL, visual, and tactile learners

Modern Myth

Students will write a short myth about why a modern object has come to be.

Procedure

● Have students look at old magazines to find pictures of everyday items, such as an appliance or a part of nature. Each student should cut out one picture.

● Use the title *Why the Sun Shines* to explain that myths can answer a question. Have students think of something special about the picture they chose and think of a title that suggests a question about it. Model the process with the title *Why the Refrigerator Is Cold*.

● Write on the board: *Long ago, refrigerators were as hot and dry as a desert.* Have students think of a first sentence that explains why the object or scene in the picture was not always like it is today.

● Have students write about how their object came to be as it is today.

Lesson 27

Objective

Students will identify parts of a play.

Words to Know

Characters—people who perform the actions in a play

Setting—where the action happens

Script—a written version of all that must happen in a play

Dialogue—words that characters speak

Stage directions—part of a script that tells the actors what actions to do or how to say dialogue

◢ Study It

Explain to students that a play is a story that is acted out in front of an audience. Help them understand that it is written in a special way so that each actor knows what to say and do.

■ Direct students to the play *How the People Got Fire*. Ask them to look at how the play is written out.

Ask *Who can name the characters in this play?* (Answer: *Narrator, Coyote, Lizard, Lizard's Brother, Mouse, Frog, Animals*)

Ask *How do you know the difference between the names of the characters and the words they are saying?* (Answer: *Names are in all capital letters followed by a colon.*)

Ask *What are the first words of dialogue that Coyote says?* (Answer: *Animals of the World, we have seen smoke!*)

■ Assign students different characters, and guide them through reading the script aloud. Point out that the stage directions are in parentheses and that they tell the character what to do or how to say the lines of dialogue.

◢ Study It

Plays are stories that are acted on a stage. Actors play the parts of the story's **characters**.

How do actors know what to say and do when they are on stage? What is the **setting**, or the place where the action occurs? People who write plays put that information into a **script**.

Scripts tell actors and readers the **dialogue**, or what characters say to one another. Scripts also have **stage directions** that tell what action is taking place and what the stage looks like.

Look at the script from *How the People Got Fire* by L. E. McCullough. The play is set in a forest, and the characters are the animals of the world. Notice the different parts.

> **Tag lines** tell which character is speaking.

> **Stage directions** describe the scene and tell what the characters are doing.

NARRATOR: And in awhile, all the animals of the World came: Frog . . . Fox . . . Snake . . . Wildcat . . . Mouse . . . Deer . . . Dog . . . Chipmunk . . . Skunk.

COYOTE: Animals of the World, we have seen smoke!

LIZARD: And where there is smoke —

LIZARD'S BROTHER: There is fire!

ANIMALS: *(cheer)* Hurrah! They have seen smoke! They have seen fire!

COYOTE: Quiet, please. This smoke and fire belongs to Thunder and Lightning.

ANIMALS: *(moans)* Oh, no . . . not Thunder and Lightning.

MOUSE: We must get this fire and bring it to The People.

FROG: That will not be easy. They say an evil bird, Woswosim, guards the fire at night. He never sleeps.

> **Lines** tell what each character is saying.

Curriculum and Assessment Standard

Plays

Use It

Look at the play on the previous page. Then read the questions. Write your answers on the lines. Look at this example.

_____a forest_____   What is the setting of the play?

Now you try it.

_____the narrator_____ 1. Which character speaks first?

_____They moan._____ 2. What do the characters do after the coyote mentions Thunder and Lighting?

Practice It

Read this scene from *Come Quick! A Play for April Fool's Day* by Sue Alexander. The scene takes place in a boy's room. The characters are a boy and his father. Then read the items. Circle the letter of the correct answer.

BOY: Father! PLEASE come quick! Now there is a seal in my room! And he is saying GWARK! And he is clapping his fins together — like this! (*The boy bounces like a seal and claps his hands.*) GWARK! GWARK!

FATHER: Hmmm. Maybe I had better go and look after all. If those animals ARE in your room, we will have to call the zoo! (*He puts down his book and gets up and goes out.*)

BOY: Ha! Ha! I did it! I made him look! And there's nothing there! What a good April Fool's joke!

1. **What do the stage directions tell you that the boy is doing?**

   A leaving the room

   B reading a book

   C bouncing a ball

   (D) acting like a seal

2. **What does the boy do in this play?**

   A He makes his father angry.

   (B) He tricks his father.

   C He makes his father laugh.

   D He protects his father.

> **Tip** Read the stage directions in a play to understand what the characters are feeling or doing.

Lesson 27 • 101

Use It

Use this activity to let students demonstrate what they know about the parts of a play.

■ Write the example question on the board. Read the directions aloud. Ask for a volunteer to read the example question aloud.

  Ask *Who can tell me what a setting is?* (Answer: *the place where the action in a play is happening*)

  Ask *Who remembers the action that took place in the play we just read? Where were the animals when they were speaking to each other about the smoke and fire?* (Answer: *in a forest*)

■ Write *a forest* on the board below the question.

Have students complete the rest of the items independently. Ask volunteers to share their answers with the class.

Practice It

In this section students use what they have learned about plays to answer questions. Read the directions aloud, and then read the *Tip* aloud.

Question 1 Read question 1 aloud. Have students complete the question independently. Ask students to point to the stage direction in their book where the answer can be found. Check to see that students can locate the stage direction. This will help students understand why *D* is the correct answer.

Question 2 Read question 2 aloud. Have students read both the boy's dialogue and the stage directions so they understand why *B* is the correct answer.

Answers

1. D
2. B

Differentiated Instruction
for ELL, auditory, and visual learners

Writing a Script

Students will write lines of a script based on a conversation.

Procedure

● List vertically on the board: *Speaker 1:, Speaker 2:, Speaker 1:, Speaker 2:.*

● Have students think of the first conversation they had that day or an interesting conversation they have had recently. Have them write their own name and the name of the person they spoke to as you have written it on the board.

● After each name have students add dialogue that is based on the conversation. Tell them to add names as the speaker changes.

● When they have finished, have students work with a partner and take turns reading their scripts aloud.

Lesson 28

Objective

Students will identify elements of a poem.

Words to Know

Poet—a person who writes poems

Rhyme—word endings that sound alike

Rhythm—the beat that the words in a poem create

Study It

Discuss the parts of a poem with students. Use the chart in the student book to point out that poets use rhyme and rhythm to create special sounds. Poets also create special pictures for the reader with the words they choose.

- Write the column headings *Rhyme, Picture,* and *Rhythm* on the board. Direct students to the poem "Deer" at the bottom of the page. Ask students to read along as you read the poem aloud.

  Ask *What rhyming words do you hear?* (Answer: *trips/lips, deer/ disappear, pass/grass*)

- Encourage students to reread the poem to find the rhyming words. Ask for volunteers to write the different rhyming pairs on the board under the heading *Rhyme.*

  Ask *Which words in the poem helped you make a picture in your head?* (Possible answers: *prancing, spotted deer, leafy woods, field of grass, dancing, spotted deer*)

- Write student responses under the heading *Pictures.*

- Read the poem aloud a second time, this time emphasizing the playful rhythm of the prancing deer.

- Help them understand that rhythm can be playful or serious, fast or slow, depending on the ideas in the poem.

102 ■ Unit 5

Lesson 28 — Musical Words

Study It

Poems often describe the world around us or express feelings about a subject. **Poets,** or the writers of poems, usually use very few words and give them a musical sound.

Poetry uses all five senses: sight, sound, smell, taste, and touch. But sound and sight are used most often.

Look at the web to the right to see the ways that poets use these senses.

A poet arranges the sounds of words in a poem like a songwriter arranges notes in music. One type of sound used in poetry is **rhyme.** When the ends of words sound alike, they rhyme. In the line *Uncle Stan dropped the can,* the words Stan and can rhyme.

Like a piece of music, a poem has a beat. This is called **rhythm.** Rhythm helps create a mood. Notice how the words went, store, get, and more feel different than the other words when you read this line aloud: *I went to the store just to get a little more.*

The words in poetry also create **pictures** that you can see in your mind. Your imagination lets you see the valley in this line: *The bright sun cast its rays on the green valley.*

Read the poem "Deer," translated by Sylvia Cassedy and Parvathi Thampi.

> Beneath the harvest moon there trips
> a herd of prancing, spotted deer.
> Through the leafy woods they pass,
> searching for a field of grass;
> As dusk begins to disappear
> there come the dancing, spotted deer,
> with half a smile upon their lips.

The poem paints a playful picture of deer in the woods at night. The rhyming words trips and lips, pass and grass, and disappear and deer help present the scene. The rhythm suggests the movement of deer walking through the fields.

102 ● Unit 5   Poetry

Curriculum and Assessment Standard

Poetry

Use It

Read the poem "The Sun Comes Up" by Carol Diggory Shields. Then answer the questions. Write your answers on the lines. Look at the example.

> The sun comes up, the moon goes down,
> By tick and tock a day goes round.
> The days go dancing, one by one,
> When seven pass, a week is done.
> The moon is counting in the sky,
> As week by week a month goes by.
> Month by month the seasons swing:
> Summer, autumn, winter, spring.
> The moon comes up, the sun goes down,
> And month by month a year goes round.

Which words in the poem rhyme? __down and round;__
__one and done; sky and by; spring and swing__

Now you try it.

1. What senses are used in the poem? __sight, sound__

2. What word picture do you see? __Possible answers:__
__the seasons, a clock, the moon in the sky__

Practice It

Read the poem in the Use It section. Then answer the questions. Circle the letter of the correct answer.

1. **What is the poem about?**

   A a merry-go-round

   B sunshine

   C time

   D the planets

2. **What do the days do?**

   A go down

   B dance

   C come up

   D count

Tip When you read a poem, look at and listen to the ways in which the poet uses words.

Use It

Use this activity to give students practice identifying the different parts of a poem.

- Copy the poem onto the board. Then read the directions aloud. Ask for volunteers to read the poem aloud. Direct students to the example question.

  Ask *How do you know when words rhyme?* (Answer: *word endings sound the same*)

  Ask *Which words rhyme in this poem?* (Answer: *down/round, one/done, sky/by, spring/swing*)

- Ask for volunteers to circle the pairs of rhyming words on the board.

Have students complete the rest of the items independently. Ask for volunteers to share answers with the class.

Practice It

In this section students use what they have learned about poems to answer questions.

- Read the *Practice It* directions aloud, and then read the *Tip* aloud.

- Have students read the poem and then complete items 1 and 2 independently.

- Ask volunteers to share their answers.

Answers

1. C
2. B

Differentiated Instruction
for ELL and auditory learners

Rhyming Teams

Students will work in teams to think of rhyming words.

Procedure

- Divide the class into two teams. Write *Team 1* and *Team 2* on the board.

- Have one person from Team 1 begin by saying a word that he or she thinks the team will be able to rhyme with other words. Give Team 1 time to offer words that rhyme with that word. List the words under the team's heading. Then give Team 2 a chance to think of words that Team 1 has not yet listed, and write those under the Team 2 heading.

- Repeat the process with a student from Team 2, letting Team 2 offer rhyming words first.

- Switch back and forth between teams three to four times. Then determine which team has the most words on the board.

- If possible, keep the rhyming words on display for future poetry instruction.

Teach the Strategy

Write the following question on the board: *How does Arthur remove the sword from the stone?*

Direct students to the reading passage in the student book. Have students read through the story independently and then stop.

Ask *Who are the characters in this story?* (Answer: *Arthur, Sir Kay*)

Ask *What does Arthur do?* (Answer: *pulls the sword out of the stone*)

Say *If you're not sure of the answer, you can read the passage again to find the answer. Use the question on the board as an example.*

Ask a student to read the question aloud.

Ask *Do you think many people are able to remove swords from stones?*

Read It Again Strategy

Explain that rereading a passage to find the answer is a test-taking strategy.

- Write these answers on the board below the question:

  A by tugging on it for hours

  B by breaking the stone

  C by kicking it loose

  D by pulling it out

- Ask students to reread the passage to find the correct answer. (Answer: *D*)

- Read aloud and discuss the strategy section on the student page.

Try It Out

Read aloud the directions and have students complete this section independently. Encourage them to use the *Read It Again Strategy*.

Have volunteers offer their answers.

Ask *When you reread the passage, was it easy to find the answer to the question?*

Ask *What sentence tells you the answer?* (Answer: *He found it easy to pull the sword out of the stone.*)

Discuss the explanation that follows the question in the student book.

Test-Taking Strategy

Strategy: Read It Again

In this unit you learned about different kinds of books. Books can be fiction or nonfiction, poetry or stories. Knowing about different kinds of books will make answering test questions easier.

- Think about the information in the passage. Is the passage real or make-believe? Is it a play or a poem?
- Read the question and the answer choices. Reread the passage if you are not sure about the answer.

Try It Out

Read the story. Then answer the question. Circle the letter of the correct answer.

> Arthur was worried. The knight he served, Sir Kay, had left his sword back at the inn. Arthur had gone back to the inn to get the sword, but the inn was locked. He did not want to return without the sword. Arthur knew of a sword magically encased in a stone. He decided to get that sword. He found it easy to pull the sword out of the stone. He took the sword to Sir Kay.

This passage is an example of —

A an autobiography

B a poem

C a legend

D a play

Look at all of the answer choices. The passage is not an autobiography because Arthur did not write it himself. The passage does not have rhyming words or rhythm, so it is not a poem. Without dialogue or stage directions, the passage is not a play. Arthur was able to pull the sword from the stone, something that seemed to be impossible. Heroes in legends do things that seem impossible, so answer **C** is correct.

Unit 5 • Kinds of Books

Put It to the Test

This test will check what you have learned in this unit.

DIRECTIONS: Read each item. Circle the letter of the correct answer.

1. An interview is a good way to get information for —

   A a fiction book

   B a myth

   (C) a biography

   D an autobiography

2. Which of these has stage directions?

   A a biography

   (B) a play

   C a poem

   D a fable

3. Which of these uses rhythm and rhyme?

   A a biography

   B a myth

   C a fantasy

   (D) a poem

4. In what kind of book do gods often appear?

   (A) myths

   B nonfiction

   C fables

   D plays

5. Which of these has make-believe people or events?

   A autobiography

   B nonfiction

   (C) fiction

   D biography

6. Who is the main character in a legend?

   A an animal

   B a god

   (C) a hero

   D an actor

7. An author would have to know facts about something in order to write —

   A a poem

   B a legend

   C a short story

   (D) an informational text

GO ON

Achieve It! Practice Cards

_____

Connect the Test to the Practice Cards (page 105)

Correct Answers	Related Practice Cards	Skill
1. **C**	75	Biography/autobiography
2. **B**	83	Plays
3. **D**	84	Poetry
4. **A**	81	Myths
5. **C**	73, 74	Fiction/nonfiction
6. **C**	82	Legends
7. **D**	76, 77	Informational text

▬ Put It to the Test

Students will:

- ▪ demonstrate what they have learned
- ▪ identify skills that require more practice before students achieve proficiency*

* Refer to pages T17–T19 for a complete explanation and directions for using *Achieve It!* Practice Cards.

Administer the Test

Explain that students will now practice the skills from this unit by taking a short test. Tell students that the test has items like those they will find on standardized tests. Explain that you will read the directions aloud. Remind students to pay close attention and to follow your directions exactly.

Say *Open your books to page 105. I will read the directions aloud.* Read the directions to students. Then continue.

Say *You will have 10 minutes to finish this test. Read each item and the answer choices carefully. Circle the letter of the correct answer. When you reach the words* GO ON *at the bottom of a page, turn the page and continue working. When you reach the word* STOP *at the bottom of a page, stop working and put down your pencils. Are there any questions?*

If students have no questions,

Say *You may begin.*

At the end of 10 minutes,

Say *Stop. Check to be sure that you have circled the correct answer. Erase any stray pencil marks. Then put down your pencil.*

Assign Practice Cards

After scoring a student's test, note which items the student missed. Match each incorrectly answered item to the related *Achieve It!* Practice Cards listed in the chart on this page.

In the *Achieve It!* Practice Cards space in each student's book, write all of the Practice Cards you want the student to complete.

Additional Practice Cards

The following cards cover additional skills for

Unit 5: Kinds of Books

Card	Topic
85, 86	Historical fiction

You may want to assign these cards as practice for students who have done well on the unit test or as extended practice for all students.

8. Which of these is an example of fiction?

   A a biography

   (B) a fantasy

   C an informational text

   D an autobiography

9. Which of these books is MOST likely to have such characters as elves and giants?

   A a biography

   (B) a fairy tale

   C a legend

   D a myth

10. To learn about tigers, the book that would be the MOST helpful is —

   A *The Big Book of Animals*

   (B) *All About Tigers*

   C *Tiger Finds a Toy*

   D *Jungle Adventures*

11. In which type of story is an author MOST likely to teach a lesson?

   A a myth

   B a legend

   C a fantasy

   (D) a fable

12. In which kind of book does the author write about his or her own life?

   A an informational text

   B a fiction story

   (C) an autobiography

   D a biography

13. Some myths are written to —

   A express feelings

   B teach a lesson

   C get people to do something

   (D) explain something in nature

14. Which of these describes nonfiction?

   A It comes from the writer's imagination.

   B It contains facts, but some things are make-believe.

   (C) It is about real people or things.

   D It has make-believe settings.

15. The lines in a play —

   A tell how the stage looks

   (B) are the words the actors speak

   C are the characters

   D tell the actor what to do

Achieve It! Practice Cards

_____

Connect the Test to the Practice Cards (page 106)

Correct Answers	Related Practice Cards	Skill
8. **B**	78	Fantasy
9. **B**	80	Fairy tales
10. **B**	76, 77	Informational text
11. **D**	79	Fables
12. **C**	75	Biography/autobiography
13. **D**	81	Myths
14. **C**	73, 74	Fiction/nonfiction
15. **B**	83	Plays

Unit 6 Understanding Parts of a Story

Stitching the Pieces

When you look at a quilt, do you look at each patch? The patches in a quilt are different, but when stitched together they make a beautiful pattern. Stories and poems are like quilts. A writer stitches characters, events, and ideas together.

In this unit you will learn about the parts of a story or a poem. Then you will see how they are put together.

107

Skills

■ Analyzing characters including their traits, motivations, conflicts, points of view, relationships, and changes they undergo

■ Using knowledge of a character's traits and motivations to determine the causes for that character's actions

■ Recognizing and analyzing story plot, theme, setting, and mood

■ Defining and identifying figurative language, sense words, rhyme, rhythm, assonance, alliteration, and cultural and historical influences in literary works

Materials to Gather in Advance

● copies of short stories from a children's magazine ● cut-apart comic strips ● glue or paste ● paper ● pencils ● selection of *Aesop's Fables* ● old magazines ● variety of art and craft supplies ● index cards

Introducing the Unit

Stitching the Pieces Refer students to the photograph of the quilt. Ask students to describe the different patches. Ask them to describe the patterns they see. Explain that like a quilt, a writer joins separate elements to create a story or a poem that has textures and patterns.

Read the *Stitching the Pieces* paragraph aloud. Ask students what parts of a story they think they will study in this unit. (Discuss all answers students suggest.) Tell them that they will learn how the parts of a story fit together. Explain that when they pay attention to the different parts of a story, they will understand it better.

Research Says

Knowledge of episodic content (setting, initiating events, internal reactions, goals, attempts, and outcomes) helps the reader understand the who, what, where, when, and why of stories as well as what happened and what was done.

— *National Reading Panel*

Lesson 29

Objectives

Students will analyze a character's traits and motivations to determine the causes for that character's actions.

Words to Know

Character—an imaginary person, animal, or make-believe creature in a story

Narrator—the person telling the story

Study It

Tell students that many stories include pictures or drawings of characters, but this is not always the case.

Ask *How can you learn information about a character when there are no illustrations?*

Read the first paragraph aloud. Ask students to give examples of characters they know from books, movies, and other sources. Write the examples on the board.

Ask *How can you get to know a character?*

- Ask students to follow along as you read the bulleted points aloud. Copy the chart onto the board beside the list of characters. Then refer students to the list of characters on the board.

  Ask *Who can tell me what one of these characters looks like?* (Answers will depend on the character chosen.)

- Write the character's name and description in the left-hand column in the chart.

- As a class, fill in the chart for two or three of the characters on the list.

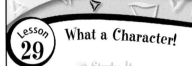

Lesson 29 — What a Character!

Study It

A **character** is an imaginary person, animal, or make-believe creature in a story. Even though characters are imaginary, you often learn about them in the same ways that you learn about real people. As events happen in the story, the writer may tell you what characters look like. You will see what they do and say. Many writers also let you see what a character is thinking and feeling. Most writers make their characters seem like someone we might meet in real life.

How do you learn about a character in a story?

- Look at descriptions of what the character looks like and does. These will give you clues about what has happened to the character in the past and how he or she wants to be seen by other people.

- Look at what the character says, thinks, and feels. In a story, a character's words and thoughts usually appear in quotation marks.

- Figure out what the character needs or wants to help you understand why he or she acts in a certain way.

If a character is the **narrator,** or the person telling the story, that person will use the words I or me to tell the story. The narrator's point of view can also help you get to know him or her.

Look at the chart. It shows questions that you should ask about characters in a story.

What does the character look like and do?	What does the character say, think, or feel?	What does the character need or want?

Character/speaker

Curriculum and Assessment Standard

Character/speaker

Read the story.

Tyler was late for school again. He had forgotten to set his alarm clock. "Rats! I slept late again!" he yelled when he woke up.

Tyler jumped out of bed and pulled on the clothes he wore yesterday. His shirt was inside out, and his jeans had muddy knees. Tyler didn't care. He picked up a pair of smelly socks and ran downstairs.

"Late again! I'm in trouble," thought Tyler as he poured cereal into a bowl. "Dad, I need a ride to school!" Tyler called. Then he saw the note on the table. It said, "Enjoy the first day of summer. Love, Dad." Tyler dropped his spoon in surprise. "Never mind!" he said to himself.

Look at the chart. It shows how the questions about the character can be answered.

What does the character look like and do?	What does the character say, think, or feel?	What does the character need or want?
He wakes up late.	He says, "Rats! I slept late again."	He wants to keep from getting into trouble.
He pulls on dirty clothes, and he looks sloppy.	He thinks, "Late again! I'm in trouble."	He wants a ride to school.
He makes breakfast.	He feels worried, and then surprised and happy.	
He tries to ask his dad for a ride.		
He finds a note.		
He drops his spoon in surprise.		

What kind of person is Tyler? He seems to be forgetful and messy. Notice the sentence "Tyler was late for school again." The word again is a clue that he has slept late before.

- Have a volunteer read the story aloud. Then direct students' attention to the chart.

  Ask *What does Tyler look like and do?* (Accept all answers.) *Why do you think so?* (Encourage students to refer to the text for support.)

- Direct students' attention to the chart.

- Invite volunteers to link information in the chart with information in the story.

  Ask *What does Tyler say, think, and feel?* (Accept all answers.) *Why do you think so?* (Encourage students to refer to the text for support.)

  Ask *What does Tyler need or want?* (Accept all answers.) *Why do you think so?* (Encourage students to refer to the text for support.)

  Ask *What kind of person is Tyler?* (Accept all answers.) *Why do you think so?* (Accept all answers. Encourage students to refer to the text for support.)

  Say *Sometimes the information you need to answer questions about characters is not directly stated in the story. You have to put clues together. For example, in the sentence, "Tyler was late for school again." The word* again *tells you that Tyler has been late before.*

⟮Differentiated Instruction

for ELL, kinesthetic, and visual learners

Acting It Out

Students will create descriptions of characters from a story.

Procedure

- Organize students into groups of three to five students. Give each group copies of a short story from a children's magazine. Ask students to read the story.
- Ask students to imagine that they have been given the job of making the story into a play. Part of this job is deciding what kinds of clothing, characteristics, and personalities each character will have. Students may want to use a chart like the one above to guide their discussion.
- Then have students act out their stories for the class or another group. Encourage students to link their actions to clues in the original story.
- If time does not permit or students do not want to act out their story, you might allow them to translate the story into a play with stage directions, costume information, and so on.

Use It

Use this section to help students find clues about a character in a story.

■ Write the following sentence on the board: *Jonathan blew his nose.*

Ask *What could this sentence tell you about Jonathan?* (Possible answers: *He's sick; he's been crying; he has allergies.*)

Ask *How can we find out why Jonathan blew his nose?* (Possible answers: *by reading the rest of the story and looking for more clues*)

Say *As you read a story, think about how the information ties together.*

Read the *Use It* directions aloud. Give students a moment to read the story independently. Invite volunteers to answer the example question.

Then have students answer the next three questions independently. Ask volunteers to share their answers.

Use It

Read the story. Look for clues that help you answer questions about Nina's character. Then write your answers on the lines. Look at the example.

Nina sat at the piano with her hands in her lap. "I don't want to practice today," she thought.

Nina stared out the window. She could see her sister playing kickball with her friends. "I want to go outside," Nina said to her mother.

Nina's mother closed the curtain. "If you practice for half an hour, then you can go out, okay?" she said.

Nina thought her mother's idea was fair and started to play.

What does Nina look like at the beginning of the story?

She is sitting with her hands on her lap.

Now you try it.

1. What feelings does Nina express in the story?

   She is unhappy about practicing the piano.

2. What does Nina want to do?

   She wants to play outside.

3. What makes you think that Nina is willing to listen to her mother?

   She thinks her mother's idea of practicing for half an hour and then going out to play is fair.

Practice It

Read this passage from the book *Stellaluna* by Janell Cannon. Then read each item. Circle the letter of the correct answer.

As the birds flew among the bats, Flap said, "I feel upside down here."

So the birds hung by their feet.

"Wait until dark," Stellaluna said excitedly. "We will fly at night."

When night came Stellaluna flew away. Pip, Flitter, and Flap leapt from the tree to follow her.

"I can't see a thing!" yelled Pip.

"Neither can I," howled Flitter.

"Aaeee!" shrieked Flap.

"They're going to crash," gasped Stellaluna. "I must rescue them!"

Stellaluna swooped about, grabbing her friends in the air. She lifted them to a tree, and the birds grasped a branch. Stellaluna hung from the limb above them.

1. **Why did Pip, Flitter, and Flap decide to hang by their feet?**

   A Their feathers were dirty, and they wanted to shake them out.

   (B) They wanted to do the same thing as Stellaluna did.

   C Their wings were tired, so they were resting.

   D They wanted to exercise their legs.

2. **How did Stellaluna feel when the birds nearly crashed in the dark?**

   A She did not really care.

   B She was sad because she could not help them.

   (C) She was worried and knew she had to help them.

   D She was happy because it would help them learn to fly at night.

Tip
To better understand characters, look at what they say, do, and feel.

Lesson 29 • 111

Practice It

Work through the page to help students find clues about characters in the story.

Read the directions aloud. Ask students to read the passage from *Stellaluna*.

Question 1 To help students understand why *B* is the best answer, use the *Think and Search Strategy*. (See the *QAR Strategy* below.) Explain that when they use this strategy, they must reread the text and the answers carefully.

Say *First, find the part of the passage where the birds start to hang by their feet.*

Ask *Why does Flap feel upside down?* (Answer: *Flap, a bird, is among bats, who are hanging by their feet.*)

Ask *Which answer choice refers to the birds wanting to be like a bat?* (Answer: *B, They wanted to do the same thing as Stellaluna did.*)

Say *So answer* B *is correct. Answers* A, C, *and* D *are incorrect. These sentences are not supported by the information in the passage.*

Question 2 Read the question aloud. Ask students how Stellaluna felt when the birds almost crashed. (Answer: *C*) Point out that the words *gasped* and "*I must rescue them!*" give clues to the correct answer.

Discuss students' answers. Explain to students that they must sometimes look for clues in a story to find the correct answer.

QAR Strategy

Strategy	Definition	How It Works
Think and Search	This strategy teaches students that they must think about relationships between items in the text and search through the passage to find information that applies.	Students think about the characters as they reread the text. They look for clues that explain characters' actions, words, and feelings in order to find the correct answer.

Refer to pages T22–T23 for a complete chart of QAR Strategies that students may use to achieve greater success on tests of reading comprehension.

Lesson 30

Objectives

Students will recognize and analyze story plot.

Words to Know

Plot—the events or action in a story

Conflict—a problem in a story that must be solved

Resolution/solution—the way the problem is solved

◢ Study It

Read the first paragraph aloud.

Say *Has anyone ever told you what happened in a movie or a book? If so, he or she was telling you the plot. Here are some questions to help you follow the plot of a story.*

■ Read the bulleted questions aloud.

Say *Let's try it.*

■ Copy the chart onto the board. Have a volunteer read the beginning of the story aloud. Ask students to follow along in their books.

Ask *Who are the characters? What is the problem? What happens?*

■ Fill in the chart with students' answers.

Ask *What do you think will happen next?* (Accept all reasonable predictions.)

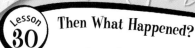

Lesson 30 — Then What Happened?

◢ Study It

A story has a setting, characters, and a **plot.** The plot usually contains a **conflict,** or a problem that must be solved. Sometimes there is more than one conflict. The plot makes the story interesting because we want to continue reading to find out what happens. The plot also contains a **resolution,** or **solution,** or the way that the problem is solved. To understand the plot of a story, ask yourself these questions.

- What problem does the main character have?
- What does the character do to solve the problem?
- What is the result of the character's action?

The author usually identifies a problem near the beginning of the story.

Read the beginning of this story.

> Chris was a very good speller. She always got all the spelling words right. Her best friend Andy thought that she should be in the state spelling contest. But Chris was too shy. So Andy sent her name to the contest without telling Chris.

Look at the chart. It shows the beginning of the story's plot.

Who are the characters?	What is the problem?	What happens?
Chris and Andy	Chris is good at spelling, but she is shy.	Andy enters Chris in a spelling contest without telling her.

In the beginning of the story, you meet the characters, Chris and Andy. You learn that Chris is shy. Then you find out about the first event in the story when Andy enters Chris in a spelling contest but does not tell her.

Can you predict, or guess, what might happen next?

Plot

Curriculum and Assessment Standard

Plot

Read the middle of the story.

Chris felt mad. She said, "I won't do it."

Andy said, "I will help you get ready." They practiced spelling every day.

Chris went to the contest, but she was still afraid. Andy said, "Just pretend you are practicing with me."

Chris did her best. Soon there was only one other speller on the stage. He misspelled a word. Now it was Chris's turn. She closed her eyes, took a deep breath, and spelled the word.

Look at the chart. It shows how the plot continues.

What is the problem?	What solution is offered?	What is the result?
Chris says she will not go to the contest.	Andy helps Chris get ready.	Chris goes to the contest and is one of the two final spellers.

Can you predict what will happen next? Notice how the plot of the story holds the reader's interest. Does Chris spell the word correctly and win the contest?

Read the ending of the story.

Chris opened her eyes. Everyone was cheering. Someone gave her a gold statue. People took her picture. Andy ran up and exclaimed, "You won!"

Look at the chart. It shows how the problem in the plot is solved.

What happens?	What happens next?	What is the final result?
Chris opens her eyes and sees people cheering.	People take her picture and give her a statue.	Chris finds out she has won the contest.

Many stories are longer than this one, but the plot of a story usually follows the same pattern. The main character has one or more problems. The story reaches its high point when the problem is most difficult. The story usually ends when the problem is solved.

Lesson 30 ● 113

Say *Let's see what happens next. We are following the plot of the story.*

- Copy the first chart onto the board. Have a volunteer read the middle of the story aloud. Ask students to follow along in their books.

  Ask *What is the problem? What solution is offered? What is the result?*

- Fill in the chart with students' answers.

  Ask *What do you think will happen next?* (Accept all reasonable predictions.)

  Say *See how the plot is keeping our interest? Let's see what happens next.*

- Copy the second chart onto the board. Have a volunteer read the end of the story aloud. Ask students to follow along in their books.

  Ask *What happens? What happens next? What is the final result?*

- Fill in the chart with students' answers.

Differentiated Instruction
for ELL and visual learners

Following the Plot

Students will use comic-strip frames to create the order of events in a plot.

Procedure

- Organize students into pairs. Give each pair a comic strip that has been cut into individual frames. (You can use the same strip for all pairs, or provide a variety of strips.)
- Have each pair arrange the comic frames in a way that tells a story. Tell students they can draw any missing frames that are needed for their story.
- Have students then paste their frames in order on a piece of paper. Below each frame, students should write the segment of the story shown in the frame.
- Have pairs then trade stories with another pair. Each pair should identify the characters, plot, conflict, and resolution in the story.

Use It

In this section students identify the events, conflict, and resolution in a story's plot.

- Copy the first chart on the board. Read the directions aloud.

  Say *As you read the story, think about what is happening.*

- Have students read the story and fill in the chart independently.

  Ask *What happens first?* (Answer: *Mario's sister makes him go to the hospital.*)

  Ask *What happens next?* (Answer: *Mario stops to tie his shoe.*)

- Have students read the end of the story and complete the rest of the page independently. Ask volunteers to share their answers.

Use It

Read the story. Then fill in the missing information in the chart.

Mario thought hospitals were scary and did not want to visit his grandmother there. But his sister Abby made him go. The hospital had many hallways. Mario stopped to tie his shoe. When he stood up, Abby was gone. Mario was lost!

Problem #1	Problem #2	Problem #3	Problem #4
Mario did not want to go to the hospital because he was scared.	Mario's sister made him go to the hospital.	Mario stopped to tie his shoe.	Mario lost track of his sister, and he got lost.

Now you try it.

Mario saw a nurse at a desk and told her, "I'm lost."
The woman looked up his grandmother's room number and walked Mario to the room. His grandmother and Abby were happy to see Mario.
"What happened to you?" they asked.
"Nothing. I just stopped to talk to one of my friends here at the hospital," Mario said, giving the nurse a secret smile.

What is the problem?	What solution is offered?	What is the result?
Mario is lost.	Mario asks a nurse for help.	The nurse takes Mario to his grandmother's room.

Practice It

Read the passage from "Oh No, It's Robert: Pink Underwear" by Barbara Seuling. Then answer the questions. Circle the letter of the correct answer.

Inventions Day was here at last. Robert was ready. Mrs. Bernthal asked for the first volunteer. Susanne Lee Rodgers waved her hand and then went up to the front of the room. She carried a small lamp. Mrs. Bernthal plugged the lamp into a wall socket.

Susanne Lee wrote THE ELECTRIC LIGHT on the blackboard. She clicked on the lamp.

"We use electric lights every day," she began. Susanne Lee must have read forty books on Thomas Edison and the electric light bulb for her report. By the time she was finished, Robert felt as though he had read forty books, too.

1. **How did Robert probably feel about Inventions Day?**

   A He was unhappy that Inventions Day was here.

   B He was worried about Inventions Day.

   Ⓒ He was looking forward to Inventions Day.

   D He was sad because he wasn't interested in inventions.

2. **How did Robert feel about Susanne Lee's report?**

   A He wished that he had chosen Thomas Edison for his report.

   Ⓑ He thought her report was too long.

   C He was happy that he had not volunteered to give his report.

   D He thought Susanne Lee's report was very interesting.

Tip When you read a story, make a list of the events, problems, or conflicts in the plot.

Lesson 30 ● 115

Practice It

Work through the page with students to help them use the *Think and Search Strategy* to answer questions about plot.

Question 1 Read the directions aloud. Ask students to read the passage and work independently to answer the question.

To help students understand why *C* is the best answer, use the *Think and Search Strategy*. (See the *QAR Strategy* below.)

Say *First, reread the passage. By looking for clues in the passage, you can figure out how Robert probably feels about Inventions Day.*

Ask *What clue tells you how Robert probably feels about Inventions Day?* (Answer: *The first sentence ("Inventions Day was here at last.") implies that Robert has been looking forward to the day.*)

Say *Now look at the answer choices. Compare each answer choice with the clue.*

Ask *Which answer is supported by the clue?* (Answer: *C*)

Say *So* C *is the correct answer. When you think about the answers as you search for information in the text, you are using the* Think and Search Strategy.

Question 2 Ask students to read and answer question 2.

Discuss students' answers. Explain to students that they must look for clues in the passage that tell how Robert feels about the report. The last sentence implies that Susanne Lee's report was long and made Robert tired, so *B* is the correct answer.

QAR Strategy

Strategy	Definition	How It Works
Think and Search	This strategy teaches students that they must think about relationships between items in the text and search through the passage to find information that applies.	Students think about the characters and events as they reread the text. They look for clues that explain characters' actions, words, and feelings in order to find the correct answer.

Refer to pages T22–T23 for a complete chart of QAR Strategies that students may use to achieve greater success on tests of reading comprehension.

Lesson 31

Objective

Students will identify and discuss the theme of a story.

Word to Know

Theme—a lesson about life or human nature that is suggested in a story

Study It

- Read the first two paragraphs aloud. Review the meaning of the word *theme*.

  Say *A story's theme is not the same as its topic.*

  Ask *What is the story of* Beauty and the Beast *about?* (Possible answers: *a beautiful young girl who goes to live with an ugly beast*)

  Ask *Who can tell me the theme of* Beauty and the Beast*?* (Possible answers: *Beauty is skin deep; it's what is inside that counts, and so on.*)

- Ask a volunteer to read the passage aloud while the rest of the class follows along.

  Ask *What is the passage about?* (Answer: *a grandmother who plants and talks to seeds*)

  Ask *What is the theme?* (Answer: *You must believe in things you cannot see.*)

What's the Lesson?

Study It

A **theme** is an idea that a writer wants to share. A story's theme tells you something important about life. It is like a lesson.

The theme of a story is not the topic. The topic of a story might be about a boy who loses a bicycle. The theme might be that losing something can teach us to care more about people than things. A writer does not need to say the theme of a story in the story itself.

To find the theme, use clues from the story.

- Look at what the speaker or narrator says. The theme is sometimes an important idea that the speaker or narrator talks about at the end of a story.
- Look at what the characters say and do. Characters often suggest the theme of the story when they talk to other characters.
- Notice what the characters learn. The theme is often an important idea that a character learns.

Read the passage.

My grandmother filled little pots with dirt and put a seed in each one. Each day she talked to the pots. I asked my grandmother why she talked to the dirt. She said, "Anna, I am not talking to dirt. I am talking to the plants. Even though I can't see them, I know they are growing." Grandmother knows that you must believe in things even if you can't see them.

Look at the chart. It shows how clues can help you find the theme.

What is the passage about?	What is the theme?	What clues told you the theme?
A grandmother who plants seeds	Sometimes you must believe in things even if you can't see them.	Anna's grandmother talks to plants she can't see. Grandmother knows the plants are growing even if she can't see them.

Curriculum and Assessment Standard

Theme

Both characters talk about the important idea that you can believe in something even if you can't see it.

Read the passage.

Nick wanted a basketball for his birthday. He told everyone, "I sure hope I get a basketball." Ten of Nick's friends came to his birthday party. Each one gave him a basketball.

"Gosh! I wanted one basketball, not ten!" said Nick.

His dad said, "You should be careful what you wish for. Your wish might come true."

Look at the chart. It shows how clues can help you find the theme.

What is the passage about?	What is the theme?	What clues told you the theme?
A boy who wants a basketball for his birthday	Wishing for something may not bring you what you want.	Nick was not happy when he got ten basketballs. Nick's dad told him to be careful about his wishes.

To find the theme, look at what the characters say. Then think about what the characters learn at the end of the story.

- Direct students to the passage. Have students follow along as you read the passage aloud.

  Ask *What is this passage about?* (Possible answer: *Nick, who wants a basketball for his birthday*)

  Say *Nick is not happy about receiving 10 basketballs for his birthday. His father states the theme at the end of the paragraph.*

  Ask *What is the theme?* (Answer: *Wishing for something may not bring you what you want.*)

Read aloud the information in the chart. Discuss with students the clues that led them to decide on a theme.

Differentiated Instruction
for auditory and visual learners

Name the Theme

Students will practice recognizing themes from reading selections.

Procedure

- Organize the class into groups of three or four. Give each group a different selection from *Aesop's Fables.*
- Have each group read and discuss their assigned fable. Ask students to determine the theme of the story.
- Encourage students to share their fables and the themes with the class.
- You may substitute fairy tales or children's movies for *Aesop's Fables.*

◢ Use It

In this section students look for clues about the theme of a story.

- ■ Direct students' attention to the story.

  Say *As you read the story, think about what the writer is trying to say.*

- ■ Have students read the story. Then read the example question aloud and allow time for students to answer the question independently.

  Ask *What is this story about?* (Answer: *a girl who is sad because her friend has moved away*)

- ■ Have students complete the rest of the page independently. Ask volunteers to share their answers.

◢ Use It

Read the story. Look for clues that tell you the theme. Then answer the questions. Look at the example.

Jen felt sad because her best friend was moving away. Jen and Sarah had been friends since preschool. They saw each other every day. Sometimes they talked on the phone at night, too.

Jen's mother said, "You can still be friends even when you and Sarah are far away. I still talk to my best friend from when I was your age."

Jen did not believe her mother. She stayed in her room on the day Sarah moved away. At dinner, she said, "I will never talk to my best friend again."

Then the phone rang. It was Sarah. They talked a long time. Later Jen said, "I think maybe you were right, Mom. Sarah and I will stay friends forever."

What is the story about?

a girl who is sad because her friend has moved away

Now you try it.

1. What is the theme of this story?

   Good friends stay friends even when they are far apart.

2. What is one clue that helps tell you the theme of this story?

   Possible answers: Jen's mother says that Jen and Sarah will always be friends. Sarah calls Jen on the telephone. Jen says that her mother was right about friendship. Jen says, "Sarah and I will stay friends forever."

Practice It

Read the story. Then read each question. Circle the letter of the correct answer.

The Harris family gathering was taking place in Janelle's backyard. "This family gathering is great," Janelle said to her Aunt Liz.

"That's nice," Aunt Liz sighed. "I'm glad you are having fun. These gatherings are a lot of work. I never seem to have any fun at them."

Janelle came up with an idea to make the day special for her aunt. She and her cousin Whitney began asking each person in the crowd a question about Aunt Liz.

After lunch, Janelle stood up. "Listen, everyone. Whitney and I put together this book. It's called Why We Love Aunt Liz. The girls took turns reading. When they finished, everyone stood up and cheered.

"Thank you, girls," Aunt Liz said. "I am really glad I came."

1. **What is the story about?**

   A good food to make at a family gathering

   B how to put a book together

   C a girl and her cousin who make a book of nice stories about their aunt

   D a special birthday party

2. **What is the theme of this story?**

   A Family gatherings are a lot of fun.

   B Even if you think your hard work goes unnoticed, people appreciate it.

   C If you work hard, people will write nice things about you.

   D It is hard to make a book.

Tip To find the theme, think about what the characters learn from what happened in the story.

Lesson 31 ● 119

This page may not be reproduced without permission of Steck-Vaughn.

Practice It

In this section students identify the topic and theme of a story.

Question 1 Read the directions aloud. Ask students to read the story and work independently to circle the correct answer, *C.* Point out that question 1 is asking for the topic of the story.

Question 2 Read the *Tip* aloud. Ask students to answer the question independently.

To help students understand why *B* is the best answer, use the *Author and Me Strategy.* (See the *QAR Strategy* below.)

Say *First, reread the story.*

Ask *What sentences in the story might help you figure out the theme?* (Possible answers: *Aunt Liz's thanks and her reflection that this time she had fun at a family gathering.*)

Ask *What lesson do you think the story teaches?* (Answer: *Hard work makes a difference.*)

Say *Now look at the answer choices. Compare each answer choice with your idea about the theme.*

Ask *Which choice is closest to your idea?* (Answer: *B*)

Explain to students that they must sometimes use their background knowledge to find the correct answers.

QAR Strategy

Strategy	Definition	How It Works
Author and Me	This strategy teaches students to use both their prior knowledge and their understanding of a text to answer a question.	Students think about what they already know and about what is in the text. In this example, students determine the theme of a story by reading the story carefully and thinking about what lesson they can learn from it.

Refer to pages T22–T23 for a complete chart of QAR Strategies that students may use to achieve greater success on tests of reading comprehension.

Unit 6 ■ 119

Lesson 32

Objectives

Students will recognize and analyze setting and mood.

Words to Know

Setting—where and when a story takes place

Place—where the story happens

Time—when the story happens

Mood—the feeling a story gives the reader

Study It

Read the first paragraph aloud. Have a volunteer read the bulleted points aloud.

Ask *What is the setting of* Little Red Riding Hood? (Possible answers: *a forest and grandmother's cottage*)

■ Read the paragraph about *mood* aloud.

   Ask *What is the mood of* Little Red Riding Hood? (Possible answers: *cheerful in the beginning and then scary after the wolf enters the story*)

■ Copy the chart onto the board. Have a volunteer read the passage aloud. Ask students to follow along in their books.

   Ask *What is the setting?* (Answer: *a field of snow in winter*) *What clues helped you figure out the setting?*

■ Fill in the chart with students' answers.

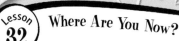

Lesson 32 **Where Are You Now?**

Study It

The **setting** of a story tells you where a story took place and when it happened. Sometimes writers tell you about the setting directly. At other times, they only give you clues. They talk about how the setting looks, sounds, smells, and feels.

A story's setting

● tells you the **place** where the story happens (in a kitchen, on a boat, in the woods, at a bus stop)

● tells you the **time** when the story happens (100 years ago, yesterday morning, in the year 1945)

Details about a setting can help give the story a certain **mood,** or feeling. Two stories with the same setting, but different details, can give you different feelings. Think of a story about walking in the woods. One writer might say that the light shines through the leaves like stars in the sky. Another writer might say that the branches are so tangled that no light can shine through. The mood of the first setting is pleasant. The mood of the second setting is gloomy.

Read the passage.

Robbie walked alone through a field, the snow crunching under his boots. The wind shook the trees. The pond, covered with a thin sheet of ice, was still.

Look at the chart. It answers questions about where the story happened.

Setting	
Where does the story happen?	**What clues help you?**
in a field	Robbie walked through an empty field.
in the snow	The snow crunched.
near trees	The trees shook.
near a pond	A thin sheet of ice covered the pond.

Setting

Curriculum and Assessment Standard

Setting

Read the next passage. Then look at the chart. It answers questions about when the story happened.

> The sky was dark even though it was only 4:30 P.M. Robbie had stayed late at school to practice basketball. As he kicked the snow, he thought, "It never gets this cold before Thanksgiving."

Setting	
When does the story happen?	**What clues help you?**
in late afternoon	It was only 4:30 P.M.
on a school day	Robbie had stayed late at school.
in November	It never gets this cold before Thanksgiving.

Read this passage.

> The houses next to the field were dark. Shadows in the snow made everything seem a little strange. Robbie thought, "Did I take the wrong path by mistake?" He started to walk faster through the snow.

Look at the chart. It will give you clues about the mood of the story.

Mood	
How does the story makes you feel?	**What clues help you?**
a little scared	the dark houses
worried	the snow's strange appearance
	Robbie's fear of being lost

- Copy the first chart onto the board. Have a volunteer read the first passage aloud. Ask students to follow along in their books.

  Ask *What is the setting?* (Answer: *late November afternoon after school, in the school yard or on his way home from school*) *What clues helped you figure out the setting?*

- Fill in the chart with students' answers.

  Say *Let's see what happens next. We are following the plot of the story.*

- Copy the second chart onto the board. Have a volunteer read the second passage aloud. Ask students to follow along in their books.

  Ask *What is the mood?* (Possible answers: *scary, worried, anxious*) *What clues helped you figure out the mood?*

- Fill in the chart with students' answers.

Differentiated Instruction
for ELL and visual learners

Visualizing Setting and Mood

Students have a chance to identify setting and mood by describing what they see in pictures from magazines.

Procedure

- Organize students into pairs.
- Have each pair flip through the old magazines looking for a picture or pictures to be the setting of a story.
- Have students then cut out and paste their picture(s) on a clean sheet of paper. Beneath the picture(s), ask students to write the setting and the mood conveyed by the picture. Remind students that setting should tell both where and when.
- Have each pair display their story picture(s) and discuss with the class the setting and mood.

Use It

In this section students identify a story's setting.

■ Read the directions aloud.

Say *As you read the story, look for clues that tell you where and when the story takes place.*

■ Have students read the story and answer the example question independently.

Ask *Where does this story take place?* (Answer: *in a farmhouse kitchen*)

■ Discuss students' answers and the clues that indicate the correct answer.

■ Have students complete the rest of the page independently. Ask volunteers to share their answers.

 Use It

Read the story. Then answer the questions about the setting. Look at the example.

The kitchen of the farmhouse was large and warm. The morning sun poured through the window onto the wooden floor. A fire was burning in the stove. The smell of the baking bread filled the air.

The clock struck six o'clock. The old woman stopped sewing and put a clean apron over her long skirts. Today was Saturday. She wanted her son to drive the wagon into town and take her to buy some supplies.

Where did the story happen?

in the kitchen of a farmhouse

Now you try it.

1. Which sentence in the story tells you where the story takes place?
   "The kitchen of the old house was large and warm."

2. How did the setting of the story make you feel?
   warm, cozy, sleepy

3. When does the story take place?
   at six o'clock on a Saturday morning, probably a long time ago

4. Which sentences in the story tell you when the story takes place?
   "The clock struck six o'clock." "Today was Saturday." "She wanted her son to drive the wagon into town and buy some supplies." "The morning sun poured through the window onto the wooden floor."

Read the passage. Then read the items. Circle the letter of the correct answer.

The room was small but very clean. It smelled like soap. There were two beds. Each bed had a blue blanket and a white pillow. The orange curtains blocked out the hot summer sun.

I put my bags down on the floor and sat on the bed. We had been driving all day and were tired. Dad said, "Do you want to eat dinner now or go for a swim?" I was hungry, but the hotel pool would close at dark. "We should go swimming first," I said.

1. **Where did the story happen?**

   A in a car

   B in a swimming pool

   C in a hotel room

   D in a hospital room

2. **When did the story take place?**

   A on a summer evening

   B on a winter morning

   C on a spring night

   D on an autumn day

3. **Which words tell you when the story takes place?**

   A small but very clean

   B two beds

   C on the floor and on the bed

   D the hot summer sun

Tip Ask where and when to figure out the setting of a story.

Lesson 32 • 123

Practice It

Work through the page with students to help them answer questions about setting.

Question 1 Read the directions aloud. Ask students to read the passage and work independently to answer the question.

Help students understand why *C* is the best answer. Explain that they must put several clues together to figure out the answer.

Say *The first sentence tells us the story takes place in a room.*

Ask *What clues tell you what kind of room?* (Answer: *the description of the room, the fact that they have been driving all day, and the reference to the hotel pool*)

Say *Now look at the answer choices. Compare each answer choice with the clues. We know that answers* A *and* B *are not correct; they do not refer to rooms.*

Ask *Which answer is supported by the clues?* (Answer: *C, a hotel room.*)

Question 2 Ask students to read and answer question 2. Help students understand why *A* is the best answer.

Ask *What clues tell you that it's summertime?* (Answer: *The curtains block out the hot summer sun, the family plans to go swimming, and so on.*)

Ask *What clues tell you that it's evening?* (Answer: *They have been driving all day, it's time for dinner, and the pool will close soon at dark.*)

Question 3 Ask students to read and answer question 3. Help students understand why *D* is the best answer.

Discuss students' answers. Explain to students that they must look for clue words in the passage that tell when the story takes place.

Lesson 33

Objectives

Students will define and identify figurative language.

Words to Know

Figures of speech—interesting and different ways to describe things

Simile—figure of speech that compares two things using the words *like* or *as*

Metaphor—figure of speech that describes an object as if it were something else

Personification—figure of speech that gives nonhuman things human qualities

Hyperbole—figure of speech that greatly exaggerates a fact or opinion

◢ Study It

Read the first paragraph aloud. Have a volunteer read the bulleted definitions aloud.

■ Direct students' attention to the examples.

Say *Similes use the words* like *or* as.

Ask *Who can think of an example of a simile?* (Accept any comparison that includes the words *like* or *as*.)

■ Write the students' examples on the board.

Say *Metaphors do not use the words* like *or* as. *Metaphors say something is something else.*

Ask *Who can think of an example of a metaphor?* (Accept all reasonable metaphors.)

Say *Personification treats an animal or object as if it were a person.*

Ask *Who can think of an example of personification?* (Accept all reasonable examples of personification.)

Say *Hyperboles are exaggerations.*

Ask *Who can think of an example of hyperbole?* (Accept all reasonable hyperboles.)

124 ■ Unit 6

Lesson 33 What's It Like?

◢ Study It

Figures of speech make writing more lively and interesting. They show new or different ways of describing or comparing things. Many popular sayings are figures of speech.

- A **simile** (sim´-ə-lē´) shows how two unlike things can seem alike. A simile always uses the words <u>as</u> or <u>like</u> to compare.
- A **metaphor** (met´-ə-fôr´) shows how two unlike things can seem alike. A metaphor does not use <u>as</u> or <u>like</u>.
- **Personification** means treating an object or animal like a person.
- **Hyperbole** (hi-pur´-bə-lē) means overstating a fact or opinion. Hyperboles are often meant to be funny.

Look at these figures of speech.

Similes **My pancakes were as tough as tires. They tasted like cardboard.**

The similes above use as and like to show how the pancakes felt and tasted. Pancakes are not really like tires or cardboard. The similes show that the pancakes were hard to chew and tasteless.

Metaphors **The baby was a little doll. She was a perfect picture.**

The metaphors compare the baby to a doll and a picture, without using the words <u>like</u> or <u>as</u>.

Personification **The sun pushed its yellow face through the clouds.**

The sun does not really have a face. The writer is using personification.

Hyperbole **Today was the longest day of Tina's life. It was 100 hours long.**

The hyperbole makes it sound as if this day were longer than other days. In real life, all days are 24 hours long. But this figure of speech makes you feel how the day felt to Tina.

124 ● Unit 6   Figurative language

Curriculum and Assessment Standard

Figurative language

Read the poem.

Ode to a Coconut

In the palm-tree throne,
so close to the sun,
you sit, like king of the tropical nuts.

A whole world in yourself,
covered in tall brown grass,
with your milky ocean protected inside.

In the warm salty breeze
of a forgotten kingdom,
you quietly soak up the view.

Waiting for the moment
when the wind's steady push
knocks you back to earth where you
started.

Your crown on the ground,
Oh hard king,
is now in the hands of whoever comes first.

Maybe an ocean wave
scoops you up in its arms,
and takes you off home.

Or maybe just silence
and sun and time
will let you sit and sprout a new throne.

Held up to the sky,
young ones will grow
and take over your seat in the sun.

Look at the chart. It shows figures of speech from the poem.

Figure of Speech	Example from the Poem
Metaphor	"In the palm-tree throne" compares the tree to a throne, but does not use the words like or as.
Simile	The phrase "like king of the tropical nuts"compares the coconut to a king using the word like.
Personification	The words "you quietly soak up the view" treat the coconut like a human. A coconut cannot have a view because coconuts cannot see.
Hyperbole	"A whole world in yourself" is an exaggeration because a coconut cannot be as large as the whole world.

Lesson 33 ● 125

- Direct students' attention to the poem "Ode to a Coconut."

  Say *As we read this poem, underline examples of figurative language.*

- Read the poem aloud. Have students follow along in their books.

- Invite students to share the examples they underlined. Ask students to tell what kind of figurative language each example is.

  Say *Let's look at the chart.*

- Review the examples in the chart. Compare the examples listed with those students underlined.

Differentiated Instruction
for ELL, visual, and tactile learners

Illustrating Figurative Language

Students will think about an example of figurative language and then create a visual representation of it.

Procedure

- Ask each student to choose an example of figurative language to illustrate. Students can make a drawing or a sculpture using materials of their choice.

- Allow students to write their own example of figurative language or to choose an example from the poem "Ode to a Coconut."

- Have students identify which type of figurative language they are illustrating.

- Display students' illustrations alongside each example of figurative language.

Use It

In this section students identify different kinds of figurative language in a passage.

- Read the directions aloud.

  Say *As you read the passage, pay attention to the underlined sentences.*

- Have students read the story and answer the first example independently.

- Discuss students' answers and the clues that indicate the correct answer.

  Ask *What clues tell you this is a simile?* (Answer: *The word* as *is used.*)

- Have students read the second example and then complete the rest of the page independently. Ask volunteers to share their answers. Discuss the clues students can use to categorize each example of figurative language.

Use It

Look at the passage. Identify each underlined figure of speech. Some figures of speech will be found more than once. Write your answers on the lines. Look at the examples.

David woke up with a cold. He felt awful. His head felt as heavy as a bowling ball. His throat was sore. His nose was a dripping faucet. His mother put her hand on his forehead. She said, "You are on fire! Go back to bed and get some rest." David went back to bed. Sleep soon took him in its arms. He woke up the next morning, looking like a blooming flower. When he walked outside, the sun kissed his cheeks.

simile	metaphor	personification	hyperbole

_____simile_____ 1. His head felt as heavy as a bowling ball.

_____metaphor_____ 2. His nose was a dripping faucet.

Now you try it.

_____hyperbole_____ 1. You are on fire!

_____personification_____ 2. Sleep soon took him in its arms.

_____simile_____ 3. looking like a blooming flower

_____personification_____ 4. the sun kissed his cheeks

126 ● Unit 6

Practice It

Read the poem. Then read the items. Circle the letter of the correct answer.

Look at that!
Look at that!
But when you look
there's no cat.

Without a purr
just a flash of fur
and gone
like a ghost.

The most
you see
are two tiny
green traffic lights
staring at the night.

1. **Which of the following choices is a simile?**

   A just a flash of fur

   (B) like a ghost

   C two tiny green traffic lights

   D without a purr

2. **The "two tiny green traffic lights" in the poem are really —**

   A a porch light

   B the cat's fur

   (C) the cat's eyes

   D a ghost

Tip
To find a simile, look for a comparison using like or as.

Lesson 33 ● 127

Practice It

Work through the page with students to help them answer questions about figurative language.

Question 1 Read the directions aloud. Ask students to read the poem and work independently to answer the question.

Help students understand why *B* is the best answer.

Say *Similes are comparisons that use certain words.*

Ask *What clue tells you that a comparison is a simile?* (Answer: *The words* like *or* as *are used.*)

Say *Now look at the answer choices. Only one is a simile.*

Ask *Which answer contains the word* like*?* (Answer: *B*)

Question 2 Ask students to read and answer question 2.

Ask *What clues tell you the correct answer is* C*?* (Answer: *the words* staring at the night, *the fact that there are two*)

Discuss students' answers. Explain to students that they must look for clues in the poem to figure out what the green traffic lights are.

● *A*, a porch light, is not discussed in the poem.   ● *B*, the cat's fur, is not green or shining, and it does not stare.   ● *D*, a ghost, is a simile for the cat that disappears quickly.

Lesson 34

Objectives

Students will define and identify sense words, rhyme, rhythm, assonance, and alliteration in literary works.

Words to Know

Alliteration—words that start with the same consonant sound

Assonance—words that contain the same vowel sound but do not rhyme

Study It

Read the first paragraph aloud. Have a different volunteer read each bulleted point aloud.

Say *Alliteration refers to words that begin with the same consonant sound.*

Ask *Who can think of an example of alliteration?* (Accept any examples: *Peter Piper picked a peck of peppers.*)

■ Write the examples students generate on the board.

Say *Assonance refers to vowel sounds.*

Ask *Who can think of an example of assonance?* (Accept all examples: *Pat fanned her hand with a plastic fan in the sand.*)

■ Direct students' attention to the poem.

Say *As we read this poem, underline examples of poetic language.*

■ Read the poem aloud. Have students follow along in their books.

■ Invite students to share the examples they underlined. Ask students to tell what kind of poetic language each example is.

---

^{Lesson} **34** How Writing Comes to Life

Study It

Poets and other writers choose words carefully. They use words to fill your mind with pictures, feelings, and thoughts. Storytellers and poets use language to help you share and enjoy the writer's experiences.

• **Words that touch your senses** Sense words make you think about seeing, hearing, touching, tasting, and smelling what the author is writing about. Notice the sense words in these sentences. "The old beach house smelled of salt and fish. The sand crunched under our shoes."

• **Words that rhyme** Words that rhyme end with the same vowel sounds and consonants sounds. <u>How</u>, <u>now</u>, and <u>cow</u> are words that rhyme.

• **Words that have rhythm** Rhythm is the way words are stressed when you read them aloud. Writers place words in certain ways so that they have a beat in much the same way that music does.

• **Words with special sounds** The way words sound also makes them musical. **Alliteration** is similar to rhyme. It happens when writers use words that start with the same letter or consonant sound, such as "<u>P</u>eg <u>p</u>unched the <u>p</u>ink <u>p</u>illow." **Assonance** is another kind of sound similar to rhyme. The words contain similar vowel sounds but do not rhyme. "<u>Sa</u>die w<u>a</u>ved her f<u>a</u>ded d<u>ai</u>sy" is an example of assonance.

Read the poem.

> The rain played in the yard all day.
> It jumped into puddles, and it danced on the grass.
> It drummed against the windows and it pounded
>   on the glass.
> It fell down the drainpipe after running off the roof.
> I think that rain is silly. Now I've got lots of proof.

Poetic language

Curriculum and Assessment Standard

Poetic language

Look at the chart to see how the writer uses language.

Sense words (Seeing, Hearing, Feeling, Tasting, Smelling)	**Seeing:** The rain jumped, danced, fell, and ran. **Hearing:** It drummed against windows and pounded on the glass.
Rhyme	glass and grass roof and proof
Rhythm	The rhythm is quick, like rain falling.
Alliteration	running, roof down the drain pipe
Assonance	rain, played, day jumped, puddles danced, grass

Language is also an important part of stories.

Read the passage.

The summer sunlight slipped silently into Danny's bedroom and sat for a moment on his pillow. Then it wandered lightly across his forehead and along his eyelashes. Danny woke up slowly, his eyes still closed, and stretched lazily. Each of his senses tuned in to the new day. He heard the first chirping of bird songs and breathed in the warm smell of pancakes cooking on the griddle downstairs. Then his eyes popped open. He threw the covers back in one quick move and bounced out of bed. This was the first day of summer vacation! He didn't want to miss a minute of it!

Look at the chart to see how the writer uses language.

Sense words (Seeing, Hearing, Touching, Tasting, Smelling)	**Seeing:** sunlight slips into the room **Touching:** stretching lazily, throwing back the covers **Hearing:** chirping birds **Smelling:** pancakes
Rhyme	The passage does not have rhyme.
Rhythm	slow in the first part of the passage; quick in second part
Alliteration	summer, sunlight; slipped silently
Assonance	woke, slowly, closed

- Direct students' attention to the first chart.
- Review the examples in the chart. Compare the examples listed with those students underlined.
- Direct students' attention to the passage.

  Say *As we read this passage, underline examples of poetic language.*

- Read the passage aloud. Have students follow along in their books.
- Invite students to share the examples they underlined. Ask students to tell what kind of poetic language each example is.
- Review the examples in the second chart. Compare the examples listed with those students underlined.

Differentiated Instruction
for auditory learners

Identifying Poetic Language

Students will listen to examples of poetic language and then identify which type they are.

Procedure

- Give each student five index cards.
- Ask students to write one example of poetic language on each card. Allow students to use examples from literary works as well to create their own examples.
- Collect all of the cards and shuffle them.
- Read each card aloud and have students identify the type of poetic language used.

This page may not be reproduced without permission of Steck-Vaughn.

Use It

In this section students identify different kinds of poetic language in a passage.

- Read the directions aloud.

  Say *As you read the poem, look for examples of poetic language.*

- Have students read the poem and fill in the first row of the chart independently.

- Discuss students' answers.

- Have students complete the rest of the chart independently. Ask volunteers to share their answers.

 Use It

Read the poem. Look at the language the poet uses.

The winter wind blows so fierce and so cold.
It bites like a bear that is cranky and old.
I wear coat and boots. I wear mittens and hat,
But still the wind howls like a mean alley cat.
It turns my nose red and my ten fingers blue.
The cold has us cornered. What can we do?
Except wait for spring when wind becomes nice.
Until then keep warm! And don't slip on the ice!

Fill in the missing information.

Sense words (Seeing, Hearing, Touching Tasting, Smelling)	**Seeing:** red nose, blue fingers **Hearing:** The wind howls; it howls like a cat. **Touching:** The wind blows fierce and cold. It bites like a bear.
Rhyme	cold/old hat/cat blue/do nice/ice
Rhythm	The rhythm is playful, like the poem.
Alliteration	winter wind bites, bear cold, cornered, can what, wait, wind
Assonance	spring, wind

Practice It

Read the passage. Then read the questions. Circle the letter of the correct answer.

"Let's go to the lighthouse," I said to my dad. We walked near the waves and watched the water. The storm had turned the ocean from a bright blue to a dark gray. Now the sea looked like dirty mop water. Each wave hit the beach with a crash. The water roared and hissed as the waves slid back into the sea. The air was full of salt and circling birds. The sand was as flat and cold as a ski trail.

1. **Which words from the passage make you think about how things look?**

   A walked near the waves

   B the sea looked like dirty mop water

   C hit the beach with a crash

   D go to the lighthouse

2. **Which words use alliteration?**

   A hit the beach with a crash

   B full of salt and circling birds

   C flat and cold as a ski trail

   D walked near the waves and watched the water

3. **Which words make you think about how something feels to the touch?**

   A from a bright blue to a dark gray

   B hit the beach with a crash

   C roared and hissed

   D flat and cold as a ski trail

Tip As you read, see how the writer uses words that appeal to your senses.

Practice It

Work through the page with students to help them answer questions about poetic language.

Question 1 Read the directions aloud. Ask students to read the passage and work independently to answer the question.

Help students understand why *B* is the best answer.

Say *Look for words that make a complete picture in your mind.*

Ask *Which answer tells you what the sea looks like?* (Answer: *B, the sea looked like dirty mop water.*)

Say *Now look at the other answer choices. Notice these are all actions, not images.*

Question 2 Ask students to read and answer question 2.

Say *Alliteration refers to the first consonant sound of words. Read each answer choice to yourself.*

Ask *Which answer shows alliteration?* (Answer: *D, walked near the waves and watched the water*)

Question 3 Ask students to read and answer question 3.

Say *Look for the answer that talks about something you can touch.*

Ask *Which answer shows how something feels to the touch?* (Answer: *D, flat and cold as a ski trail*)

Say *Answer* A *refers to something you see. Answers* B *and* C *refer to something you hear.*

Lesson 35

Objectives

Students will identify cultural and historical influences in texts.

Study It

Read the first paragraph aloud. Have a different volunteer read each bulleted question aloud.

Say *When you read, you can learn about different kinds of people and how they live.*

Ask *Who can give an example of a text they read about another culture?* (Accept any reasonable examples.)

■ Direct students' attention to the passage.

   Say *As we read this passage, look for clues about the characters' world and life. Use the bulleted questions to guide you.*

■ Ask a volunteer to read the passage aloud. Have students follow along in their books.

■ Invite students to discuss the clues they noticed in the passage. Write the clues on the board along with students' conclusions about them.

■ Direct students' attention to the chart. Help students find the clues in the passage.

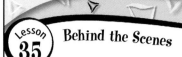

Behind the Scenes

Study It

Stories are like windows that let you look into different places and times. When you read, you can learn about many kinds of people and their ways of living. Writers give you clues about their characters' worlds and themselves. As you read, ask yourself these questions.

- What are the characters' names and what languages do they speak?
- What traditions do they have?
- What do you know about the author's background?
- What ideas are important to the writer?

Read the passage from *Song of the Honda* by Rector Lawrence Lee.

Finally it was completed, and all three were hot and tired. Tomo ran to the end of the patio to get a good look at the finished oven.

"Hola!" he shouted with pride. "You can see it a long way off."

"A little lopsided," his father declared, "but it's not too bad."

"Maybe it will fall down when it gets hot," said Juan. "Then we won't have to poke it with poles."

Look at the chart to find clues about the characters' world.

Clues About the Character's World	Your Conclusions
• The boys' names are Tomo and Juan. • Tomo speaks Spanish and English. • The boys and their father have built an oven.	The story may be about a Spanish-speaking family that lives in the United States. The family may be from long ago, or they may be practicing an old tradition of oven building. The writer may be a Spanish speaker who thinks family activities are important.

You can use the clues to get ideas about the characters and the writer. Writers often write about the world they know or remember.

Cultural/historical influences

Curriculum and Assessment Standard

Cultural/historical influences

Read the passage.

The first thing my sister Nuala and I loved about America was the food. At home in Ireland, my father's potato plants caught a plant disease. We had little to eat, and life was hard. So we moved to America.

Near the place where our boat landed in America, the city streets were filled with people and horses. We did not go far before we saw the shops. Our mouths watered when we saw the baskets of food. Nuala said, "Oh, look! Apples!"

Look at the chart. It shows clues from the passage and the conclusions you can make.

Clues About the Characters' World	Your Conclusions
• The sister's name is Nuala. • The character's home was in Ireland. • The characters took a boat to America. • The city streets are filled with people and horses. • The children are excited to see food.	The characters are new to America from Ireland. The characters must be from long ago because there are horses in the street, and they came to the United States by boat. The writer must know about life for Irish people in the United States. He or she may be writing about a true life event.

To learn about the world of the characters and the writer, look for the characters' names and how they speak, and clues about how and when the characters live. Then look for clues about the writer's life or ideas.

- Direct students' attention to the passage.
  Say *As we read this passage, underline clues about the characters' world.*
- Read the passage aloud. Have students follow along in their books.
- Invite students to share the clues they underlined. Ask students to tell what they can conclude from each clue.
- Review the clues in the chart. Compare the clues listed with those students underlined.

Differentiated Instruction
for ELL and auditory learners

Identifying Cultural and Historical Influences

Listening to descriptions about other time periods or cultures will allow students to practice identifying cultural clues.

Procedure

- Give each student an index card.
- Have students think of another culture or historical period that they know about. Ask students to write one or two sentences describing this place, time, or culture on their index cards.
- Collect all of the cards and shuffle them.
- Read each card aloud and have students identify clues that tell about the culture or history.

◢ Use It

In this section students look for clues in a passage about the characters and about the writer.

- Read the directions aloud.

  Say *As you read the passage, look for clues that tell you about the characters and the writer.*

- Have students read the passage independently.

- Direct students' attention to the first chart. Help students find the clues in the passage. Then ask students to fill in their conclusions.

- Discuss students' answers.

- Have students complete the rest of the page independently. Ask volunteers to share their answers.

◢ Use It

Read the passage. Look for clues that tell you about the characters and the writer.

Four times a week Lilikala went to the halau, or school. There she learned about the hula, the dance that is special to the people of Hawaii. Just like her mother and grandmother, Lilikala was learning the songs and dances of the islands.

At first, Lilikala was not sure she wanted to go to the halau. She would miss playing computer games with her friends. Then her grandmother said, "Lili, the hula is more than a dance. It tells our history as a people. It shows how much we love the land."

What conclusions can you draw about the characters' world? Write your answers in the chart.

Clues About the Characters' World	Your Conclusions
• Lilikala is from Hawaii. • She is going to a special school. • She likes to play computer games. • The hula and the halau are part of Lilikala's family history.	Lilikala is a girl who lives in Hawaii today. She is learning a dance that is important to her family.

What conclusions can you draw about the writer? Write your answers in the chart.

Clues About the Writer	Your Conclusions
• The writer uses special language—halau and hula—in the story. • The writer tells what the hula means.	The writer knows about life in Hawaii today and long ago. The writer thinks the hula is important. The writer also thinks history is important.

Practice It

Read the story. Then read the items. Circle the letter of the correct answer.

Aunt Lula Mae sat in a rocking chair on her front porch. She took a drink of iced tea. She said, "Did you finish your homework?"

"Yes," I said.

"Yes, *ma'am*," she said to correct me. "In my day, young people were polite. And Southern girls did not wear blue jeans. They dressed like ladies."

"Things are different today. I can wear jeans, and I can be anything I want. Like a doctor."

Aunt Lula Mae said, "Fine. Be a woman doctor. But you should still be polite."

"Yes, ma'am," I said.

1. **What would be the BEST conclusion to make about the characters in this story?**

   A The speaker and her aunt both think that girls today should wear blue jeans.

   B The speaker and her aunt both want her to become a doctor.

   C The speaker and her aunt both think girls should wear dresses.

   (D) The speaker and her aunt have different ideas about how young people today should act.

2. **From reading the story, you can tell that the writer probably thinks that it is important to —**

   A become a doctor

   (B) be polite

   C wear blue jeans

   D drink iced tea

   Tip
   When you read, look for clues in the story that tell about the character's life and the writer's ideas.

Practice It

Work through the page with students to help them find clues about culture and history.

Question 1 Read the directions aloud. Ask students to read the story and work independently to find the answer to the question.

Help students understand why *D* is the best answer.

Say *Look for clues that tell you what each character thinks about Southern girls.*

Ask *What can you conclude from the clues in the story?* (Answer: *The speaker and her aunt have different ideas about how girls should act and dress.*)

Say *Now look at the answer choices. Answer* D *is supported by the clues. Answer* A *is incorrect because Aunt Lula Mae does not think polite girls should wear jeans.* B *is incorrect because the story does not tell us whether the aunt wants her niece to become a doctor.* C *is incorrect because the speaker says she can wear jeans.*

Question 2 Ask students to read and answer question 2.

Say *Look again at the clues in the story.*

Ask *What can you conclude about the writer?* (Answer: B, *be polite*)

Say *Answers* A *and* C *refer to examples the aunt and niece discuss. Answer* D *refers to what the aunt is drinking. Only Answer* B *refers to the main point of the story.*

Teach the Strategy

Write *Goldilocks and the Three Bears* on the board. Ask a volunteer to retell the story.

Ask *Who are the characters?* (Answer: *Goldilocks, Mama Bear, Papa Bear, Baby Bear*)

Ask *What is the plot?* (Answer: *Goldilocks enters the bears' home and tries their porridge, chairs, and beds.*)

Ask *What is the setting?* (Answer: *in the bears' home in the forest during the day*)

Ask *What did you learn from the story?* (Possible answer: *What suits one person might not suit another. You should respect other's property.*)

Find the Parts Strategy

Ask *What are some parts of a story?* (Possible answers: *plot, theme, characters, and setting*)

■ Read the first paragraph and the bulleted points aloud.

 Ask *What clues tell you about the characters in a story?* (Possible answers: *dialogue, text about characters' actions, feelings, and thoughts*)

 Ask *What clues tell you about setting?* (Possible answers: *text about time, place, time of day, weather, dress, and so on*)

Try It Out

Read the directions aloud and have students complete this section independently. Encourage students to use the *Find the Parts Strategy* to answer the question.

■ Instruct students to read the passage and select the correct answer (*D*).

■ Have volunteers explain the reasons for their answers.

Discuss the explanation that follows the question in the student book.

Test-Taking Strategy

Strategy: Find the Parts

In this unit you learned that a story has characters, a plot, a setting, and a theme. Finding these parts can help you answer questions about a story on a test.

● As you read, look for clues that help answer these questions.
 Who are the characters?
 What is happening?
 Where and when is the story happening?

● Look for language that helps you picture the story in your mind.

● After you finish reading, ask yourself *What did the character learn?* and *What did I learn as a reader?* These questions help you find the theme of the story.

Try It Out

Read the passage. Then answer the question.

> The cold air bit at Ben's fingers. He unhooked the dogs from the sled. After Ben fed them, the dogs dug holes in the snow for sleeping. Ben sat by the fire and studied the stars in the black sky. They helped guide him on his journey.

Which words tell you that the story probably takes place in Alaska?

A sat by the fire

B cold air bit at Ben's fingers

C studied the stars in the black sky

Ⓓ unhooked the dogs from the sled

The story gives lots of clues that Ben is in a cold place. The air bites at his fingers. Ben sits by a fire. But winter weather happens in many places. The best clue is that Ben unhooks the dogs from the sled. Dog sleds are common in Alaska. So the answer is **D**.

Put It to the Test

Name _____

This test will check what you have learned in this unit.

DIRECTIONS: Read the story. Then read each item. Circle the letter of the correct answer.

Summer Camp Lesson

It was Max's first time at summer camp. He was excited but also a little worried. He was small for his age. He was afraid that he would not make any friends.

A woman named Jenny took Max to his tent. He would share it with two other boys. "Your tent team is called the Yellow Jackets," said Jenny. Max looked at the other boys. They were not wearing jackets. "Where are your yellow jackets?" asked Max.

"Yellow jackets are like bees. They are insects that sting," said Tyler, who was a big kid with freckles. He sounded a little mean.

"Yes, but real yellow jackets do not sting each other," said Alec. Max felt worried. He tried not to show it. "Tyler is okay," Alec whispered to Max. "You just need to get used to him. I did. Trust me."

Max enjoyed life at camp. But he stayed out of Tyler's way. Tyler called him "Shorty" and would say things like "Get out of my way, or I'll step on you."

One day Tyler lost his watch. It had fallen between some rocks by the pond. Tyler's hand was too big to reach it. He said, "Hey, Shorty. Can you get my watch?" Max thought it was a trick. The hot sun pressed down on him. He started to sweat. But he decided to trust Tyler. He reached down and grabbed the watch like a fresh peach from a tree. Tyler said, "Thanks a lot! You're okay, Shorty!"

Max took a deep breath and said, "You're welcome. But could you please call me Max?" Tyler said, "You got it, Max."

Put It to the Test • 137

Put It to the Test

Students will:

- demonstrate what they have learned
- identify skills that require more practice before students achieve proficiency*

* Refer to pages T17–T19 for a complete explanation and directions for using *Achieve It!* Practice Cards.

Administer the Test

Explain that students will now practice the skills from this unit by taking a short test. Tell students that the test has items like those they will find on standardized tests. Explain that you will read the directions aloud. Remind students to pay close attention and to follow your directions exactly.

Say *Open your books to page 137. I will read the directions aloud.* Read the directions to students. Then continue.

Say *You will have 20 minutes to finish this test. Read each item and the answer choices carefully. Circle the letter of the correct answer. When you reach the words* GO ON *at the bottom of a page, turn the page and continue working. When you reach the word* STOP *at the bottom of a page, stop working and put down your pencil. Are there any questions?*

If students have no questions,

Say *You may begin.*

At the end of 20 minutes,

Say *Stop. Check to be sure that you have circled the letter of the correct answer. Erase any stray pencil marks. Then put down your pencil.*

Assign Practice Cards

After scoring a student's test, note which items the student missed. Match each incorrectly answered item to the related *Achieve It!* Practice Cards listed in the chart on this page.

In the *Achieve It!* Practice Cards space in each student's book, write all of the Practice Cards you want the student to complete.

1. **At the start of the story, Max wants to —**

   A stay out of Tyler's way

   B go home

   Ⓒ make friends

   D trust Tyler

2. **Which word best describes the character of Max at the beginning of the story?**

   A brave

   Ⓑ worried

   C silly

   D friendly

3. **What is the first thing that happens to Max?**

   A He meets Tyler and Alec.

   B He stays out of Tyler's way.

   C He picks up Tyler's watch.

   Ⓓ He goes to his tent.

4. **The story takes place —**

   A at summer school

   Ⓑ at summer camp

   C in Max's neighborhood

   D in winter

5. **What idea does Alec talk about with Max?**

   A being afraid

   B feeling different

   Ⓒ trusting others

   D acting brave

6. **What word best describes Max at the end of the story?**

   A sad

   Ⓑ trusting

   C afraid

   D angry

7. **When Tyler asks Max for help, Max decides to —**

   Ⓐ trust Tyler

   B stay out of Tyler's way

   C ask Alec for help

   D share a peach with Tyler

Achieve It! Practice Cards

_____

138 ● Unit 6

Connect the Test to the Practice Cards (page 138)

Correct Answers	Related Practice Cards	Skill
1. C	87, 88, 89, 90, 91, 92, 93	Character, Plot
2. B	87, 88, 89	Character
3. D	90, 91, 92, 93	Plot
4. B	98, 99	Setting
5. C	90, 91, 92, 93	Plot
6. B	87, 88, 89	Character
7. A	90, 91, 92, 93	Plot

8. **What important idea does Max learn in the story?**

   A Summer camp is fun.

   B Tyler is okay.

   C It is good to have small hands.

   (D) It is all right to trust people.

9. **Which words from the story show a thing acting like a person?**

   A insects that sting

   B fallen between some rocks

   (C) hot sun pressed down on him

   D like a fresh peach from a tree

10. **Which words from the story compare unlike things?**

    A small for his age

    B too big to reach it

    (C) like a fresh peach from a tree

    D big kid with freckles

11. **Read this passage.**

> The sun set slowly over the green fields. A light breeze whistled softly through the trees. Soon it would be dark.

    Which group of words all start with the same sound?

    (A) sun, set, slowly

    B green, breeze, trees

    C through, the, trees

    D green, light, dark

12. **Read the poem.**

> We three sisters climbed the tree.
> We felt like birds, and as free.
> We let our imaginations fly
> To sail out over the sea.

    Which words from the poem rhyme?

    (A) tree, free, sea

    B the, sea, let

    C sisters, sail, sea

    D our, out, over

13. **Read the passage.**

> Dear Teddy,
>   This letter may not reach you soon. I sent it by Pony Express. But it takes a long time for the ponies to cross the mountains. Soon the train will come to our town.

    The passage was probably written —

    A by a woman

    (B) a long time ago

    C last week

    D by a young person

GO ON

Achieve It! Practice Cards

_____

Connect the Test to the Practice Cards (page 139)

Correct Answers	Related Practice Cards	Skill
8. **D**	**94, 95, 96, 97**	**Theme**
9. **C**	**101, 102**	**Figurative language**
10. **C**	**101, 102**	**Figurative language**
11. **A**	**104, 105, 106, 107**	**Poetic language**
12. **A**	**104, 105, 106, 107**	**Poetic language**
13. **B**	**109, 110, 111, 112**	**Cultural/historical influences**

Additional Practice Cards

The following cards cover additional skills for

Unit 6: Understanding Parts of a Story

Card	Topic
100	Story variants
103	Symbol and theme
108	Literary terms

You may want to assign these cards as practice for students who have done well on the unit test or as extended practice for all students.

14. Read the passage.

> Back when I was young, we walked to school. We did not have school buses like you kids have today.

The passage was probably written —

A a long time ago

B by a young person

C by an older person

D by a woman

15. Read the passage.

> I learned a lot that summer. Mostly, I learned that Mr. Wiggins was not nearly as rude and grumpy as we boys thought he was. Once I got to know him, I saw how kind he was to the stray animals he cared for. I guess people need to look a little deeper before they make up their minds about someone.

The writer probably wrote this in a story to show —

A plot

B setting

C mood

D theme

16. Read the passage.

> The fog wound around the bare branches of the trees. Shapes appeared and disappeared into the mist. Although everyone had turned on their porch lights, the fog turned them into dim, glowing eyes on this dark night. What a perfect Halloween, I thought.

What is the mood that the writer creates in this passage?

A sad

B funny

C a little scary

D very happy

17. In the passage, the writer compares the porch lights to —

A glowing eyes

B tree branches

C the fog

D shapes

Achieve It! Practice Cards

Connect the Test to the Practice Cards (page 140)

Correct Answers	Related Practice Cards	Skill
14. C	109, 110, 111, 112	Cultural/historical influences
15. D	94, 95, 96, 97	Theme
16. C	98, 99	Setting
17. A	101, 102	Figurative language

Unit 7 — Research and Study Skills

A World of Information

The research to develop the Internet first began in the 1960s. Today, more than 350 million people worldwide have access to the Internet. No wonder our time in history is called the "Information Age."

In this unit you will learn ways to find and arrange information.

Skills

- Choosing a topic and framing questions to direct research
- Selecting and using reference materials and resources for writing
- Taking notes and organizing ideas from different sources
- Organizing ideas into outlines
- Creating bibliographies that are correct in format, punctuation, and order

Materials to Gather in Advance

- timer • set of encyclopedias
- index cards • pencils • various sources (including magazines, books, and newspapers) • paper clips • examples of graphic organizers (timelines, spider maps, Venn diagrams, and so on) • paper
- source cards

Introducing the Unit

A World of Information Refer students to the photograph of the early computers. Ask students whether they have ever used a computer to find information. They may have done a search on the Web, used a CD-ROM, or used a computer at the library to find a book. Ask what steps they followed. Students probably typed a word or words into the computer. Point out that the computer then searched through information to find a "match." Make sure students understand that they do the same thing when they look for information in a phone book, dictionary, encyclopedia, or other reference source.

- Read the *A World of Information* paragraph aloud.

  Ask *Did you ever have trouble looking for an item at store? What happened?*

- Point out that it is easier to find what you are looking for when you know how things are arranged. This is true for finding information, too. Information can be organized in different ways, such as by topic, subject, or author.

Research Says

Notetaking assists students in focusing attention and processing new material . . . summarization training makes students more aware of the structure of ideas within the reading assignment and how the individual ideas relate to each other.

—*Devine*

Lesson 36

Objective

Students will learn strategies for choosing a topic.

Words to Know

Brainstorm—a way to choose a topic by letting your ideas flow

Topic web—a diagram of possible topics with questions you would like to answer about each of them

◣ Study It

- **Say** *Suppose I ask you to write a report about something that interests you. How would you choose a topic?*

- Have each student write the first 10 things that come to mind. Tell students that this is called brainstorming. Encourage volunteers to share their lists with the class.

- Have volunteers read the text aloud.

- Draw a circle on the board. Write the word *storms* inside the circle.

  Ask *What kinds of storms can you think of?* (Possible answers: *thunderstorms, dust storms, tornados*)

- Add all appropriate answers to the topic web on the board. Ask questions about each kind of storm. Add students' questions to the topic web on the board.

- Direct students' attention to the topic web.

- Compare the topic web with the work on the board.

  Say *Different people will make different topic webs. There is no one way to make a topic web.*

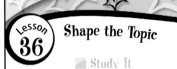
Shape the Topic

◼ Study It

To write a report, you can **brainstorm** to pick a topic. When you brainstorm, make a list of every possible topic that comes to mind. It is not important that the topics on the list go together. Then pick one of the topics.

Sometimes a topic is too broad, or large, and covers too much information. Making a **topic web** can help you narrow your topic.

To make a topic web, ask questions about the topic. If you chose the topic of storms, for example, you could ask *What kinds of storms are there?* Then ask questions about each kind of storm, such as *What do I need to know about hurricanes?* Use a different shape for each level of your topics to keep ideas about each topic together. In the web below, notice that the main topic is in a circle; the subtopics are in rectangles; and the details are in diamonds.

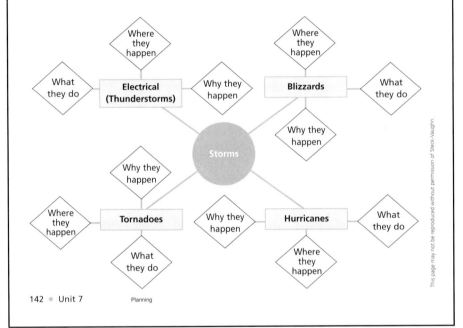

142 ● Unit 7   Planning

Curriculum and Assessment Standard

Planning

Finding subtopics helps you think about what to put in your report. The subtopic you choose will depend on

- your interests
- how easy or hard it is to find information about your subtopic
- the length of the report

A longer report might be about different kinds of storms. A shorter report might only be about one subtopic, such as hurricanes.

After you have narrowed your topic, keep asking questions to find information about the topic.

Look at the questions in the chart for a report on hurricanes.

Question Word	Report Question
Who	Who keeps track of hurricanes?
What	What happens during a hurricane?
When	When is hurricane season?
Where	Where do hurricanes form?
Why	Why do hurricanes have names?
How	How do people stay safe during hurricanes?

Make a list of questions about your topic using the six question words. Look for the answers to the questions as you read. Some questions will lead to more questions. Keep a list of the questions and the answers that you find.

Finally, decide which of the answers you want to put in your report. Remember that some information may be more important and interesting than other information you find.

- Have a volunteer read the text above the chart aloud.
- Read the directions for the chart aloud.

  Ask *Who can think of other questions to go with these words?* (Possible answers: *Who has been in a hurricane? What conditions cause a hurricane?*)

- Read the final two paragraphs. Write the word *Music* on the board and circle it. Have volunteers suggest ways to create a topic web using this word.

- Invite volunteers to choose one of the kinds of music and write possible report questions.

  Say *Each person can come up with his or her own report topics. Everyone is different. So is every report.*

Differentiated Instruction
for auditory and visual learners

Brainstorming Out Loud

Students work in groups to develop topics for a report.

Procedure

- Organize students into groups of four or five.
- Have each group select a person to record ideas.
- Students will set a timer for three or five minutes. During this time, students will quietly call out ideas that might make good topics for a report. The purpose of this step is to generate as many ideas as possible.
- The recorder should continue to write ideas until the timer goes off.
- Have the recorder post the list of ideas. Students can now discuss the ideas as possible report topics. If time permits, students could choose and narrow a subtopic by asking questions the report might answer. Alternatively, students can repeat the activity to generate different ideas.

Use It

Use this activity to help students learn the difference between topics and subtopics.

Say *Sometimes a very broad topic, such as storms, contains too much information for a short report.*

Ask *Which topic is broader—Storms or Hurricane season?* (Answer: *storms*)

Read the *Use It* directions aloud. Have students complete the section independently. Ask volunteers to share their answers. Help students understand how the strategies learned in this lesson can help them choose a topic for a report.

Use It

Look at this topic web. It shows you how to narrow the topic of exploring space. Then answer the questions.

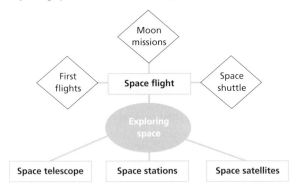

1. Which topic is broader, or larger — Exploring space or Space flight?
   Exploring space is the broader topic. Space flight is a subtopic of Exploring space.

2. Which topic is broader, or larger — Space flight or Space shuttle?
   Space flight is the broader topic. A space shuttle is one kind of vehicle for space flight.

Now read each topic on the chart. Write one more question for each topic. Start the question with a question word—who, what, when, where, why, or how.

Topics		
Chocolate	**Diamonds**	**Jazz Music**
How is chocolate made?	What are diamonds?	When did jazz start?
Where does chocolate come from? Ex: What is the history of chocolate?	Ex: Where are diamonds found?	Ex: Who are some important jazz musicians?

144 • Unit 7

Practice It

Read each item. Circle the letter of the correct answer.

1. You want to write a report on poetry. You could narrow your topic by writing about —

   A newspapers

   (B) rhyme

   C pictures

   D historical fiction

2. Which question will help you write a report about important machines invented in the twentieth century?

   A When did people start riding horses?

   (B) What machines do we use every day?

   C How did people learn about fire?

   D Who discovered the wheel?

3. You are planning to write a report about clocks. You could narrow your topic by writing about —

   A furniture

   B wall calendars

   (C) pocket watches

   D train schedules

Tip

Write questions to help you narrow your topic for your report.

Lesson 36 ● 145

Practice It

In this section students practice narrowing topics. Have students answer the questions independently, then review the correct answers to ensure understanding.

Question 1 Read the question aloud. Point out that *B* is the correct answer because the other choices are not about poetry.

Ask *What does rhyme have to do with poetry?* (Answer: *Rhyme is sometimes found in poetry.*)

Question 2 Read the question aloud.

Say *Only one answer choice is about machines invented in the twentieth century.*

Ask *Why is* D *an incorrect choice?* (Answer: *The wheel was invented long before the twentieth century.*)

Question 3 Read the question aloud.

Ask *Why is* C *the correct answer?* (Answer: *It's the only one about clocks.*)

Discuss students' answers.

Read the *Tip* aloud. Discuss how writing questions can be helpful in narrowing topics.

Lesson 37

Objective

Students will learn to select and use dependable reference materials and resources for writing reports.

Words to Know

Research—finding information

Sources—items that have information, such as encyclopedias and Internet sites

Encyclopedia—set of books that contain information about people, places, things, and events

Volume—one book in a set of books

Entry—a topic, found in alphabetical order within a volume

Guide word—word at the top of a page that helps you find the entry you are looking for

Dewey Decimal System—the order of numbers used to organize and identify books in a library

◢ Study It

- Read the text aloud.
- If possible, show students a set of encyclopedias.

    Ask *How many volumes are there?* (Answers will vary, depending on the set.)

    Ask *Where could I find information about hurricanes?* (Possible answer: *in Volume H*)

    Ask *Where could I find information about tornadoes?* (Possible answer: *in Volume T*)

    Ask *Does every letter of the alphabet have its own volume?* (Answer: *no*)

- Direct students to the sample entries.
- Allow each student to flip through the pages of a volume to see the guide words and entries.

◢ Study It

After you've chosen your topic and written your questions, you need to find the information to answer your questions. Finding information is often called doing **research.** You get your information from **sources.**

Libraries have many kinds of sources. Almanacs, atlases, books, dictionaries, encyclopedias, magazines, and newspapers are sources. Some libraries have computers. Other sources are experts on your topic who can help answer your questions. Make sure you can depend on your sources.

An **encyclopedia** is a good place to start. Most encyclopedias are in a set made up of several **volumes,** or books, in alphabetical order. Each volume has information about people, places, things, and events. **Entries,** or topics, are also in alphabetical order within each volume.

To use an encyclopedia, look for your topic alphabetically by volume. For example, you would look in Volume H for information on hurricanes. You can also look in the encyclopedia's index. The index is either at the end of the entire set of encyclopedias or in a volume by itself.

Look at this entry from an encyclopedia.

Guide words are at the top of each page. They name the topic of the first article on a left-hand page and the topic of the last article on a right-hand page. Your topic will be in alphabetical order between the two guide words.

Entry word
This is the topic you are looking up.

261 Humor

Hurricane Hurricanes are powerful storms. Hurricanes form over oceans when the water temperature is warm. The heat from the water causes the storm to form. A hurricane has strong winds that travel at speeds as high as 150 miles per hour. In the Atlantic Ocean, hurricane season lasts from June through November.

146 ● Unit 7   Locate sources

Curriculum and Assessment Standard

Locate sources use reference materials

When you write a report, you need to use more than one source. To find a book in the library, you need to understand how the books are arranged. The books in the library are classified, or put in an order called the **Dewey Decimal System.** Each book has a number that tells you what kind of information is in it and where it is in the library.

Books about what happens in a town after it is hit by a hurricane would have a number between 300–399.	**Dewey Decimal System** 000–099 General Knowledge 100–199 People's Ideas (Philosophy) 200–299 Religion
Books about the science of how hurricanes happen would have a number between 500–599.	300–399 Social Science 400–499 Language 500–599 Math and Science 600–699 Medicine and Technology 700–799 Art and Entertainment
Books about where hurricanes have happened or famous hurricanes in history would have a number between 900–999.	800–899 Literature 900–999 Geography and History

Find a book's number by looking in the library's card catalog under the topic or the author's last name. The catalog is in alphabetical order. The catalog may be on cards in a set of drawers in the library or stored on a computer. The information about the books is arranged in the same way on cards as it is on the computer.

Author's name   Title of book

Dewey Decimal **call number** 589.7 shows that the book is about math or science.

589.7
Willard, Bill
The Science of Hurricanes
Storm Books, Chapel Home, NM 1982

Notice that the title shows the book is about science.

Publisher and place and date of publication

Lesson 37 ● 147

Ask *How are the books in the library organized?* (Possible answers: *by numbers, topics, author's last name*)

■ Read the first paragraph aloud. Direct students' attention to the Dewey Decimal System.

Say *Almost all libraries use the same system for organizing books.*

Ask *Where will you find books about math?* (Possible answers: *in the 500s*)

Say *You could also use the card catalog. This works well if you are looking for a specific book or author.*

■ Read the second paragraph. Review the parts of the sample catalog card.

Ask *Who has used the card catalog in our school library? Did you use the cards or the computer?*

Differentiated Instruction
for tactile and visual learners

A Trip to the Library
Students will explore reference sources and look for information about a topic.
Procedure

● Have students work in pairs to choose a topic from the list they narrowed in the previous lesson.

● At the library, students should look for information on the topic in the card catalog. If the card catalog is stored in drawers as well as on computers, encourage students to compare the two forms of storage. Students should locate the materials on the library's shelves.

● Encourage students to explore other sources in the library's reference and periodical sections. Students can then compare and contrast the information they found.

Use this activity to help students interpret an entry from an encyclopedia and a card catalog.

Say *It's important to know how information is organized in different sources.*

Ask *How is information organized in an encyclopedia?* (Answer: *alphabetically by topic*)

Ask *How is information organized in a card catalog?* (Answer: *alphabetically by topic, author, and subject*)

Read the *Use It* directions aloud. Have students complete the section independently. Ask volunteers to share their answers. Stress that knowing how information is organized makes doing research easier.

Use It

Look at this entry from an encyclopedia. Then answer the questions. Look at the example.

192   Medicine

Meerkat The meerkat is a small mammal. Its home is the grasslands of Africa. Meerkats live in large groups. A meerkat may stand on its hind legs in a high place. From there it watches for danger. It protects the whole group. In the meerkat community there is more than one family group.

Metric system The metric system is based on the number ten. It is a way of measuring. In the United States, metric measurements are most often used in science. In most other countries, metric measurement is part of everyday life.

What are the entry words? _____ meerkat, metric system

Now you try it.

1. In which volume of an encyclopedia would you find information about the metric system? _____ Volume M

2. What is the guide word on this page? _____ medicine

Look at this card from a card catalog. Then answer the questions. Look at the example.

> 942.3
>
> Rosen, Allen P.
>
> *Jackie Robinson and the 1947 Dodgers*
>
> Smalltown Press, New York, NY 1999

What is the title of the book? _____ Jackie Robinson and the 1947 Dodgers

Now you try it.

1. What is the call number of the book? _____ 942.3

2. This call number is about what topic? _____ geography and history

148 • Unit 7

Practice It

Look at this example page from an encyclopedia. Then read the items. Circle the letter of the correct answer.

321   Goldfish

Golf Golf is a sport. The object of the game is to hit a small, hard ball along a course. The ball has to be hit into certain holes on the course. Players hit the ball with special sticks, or clubs. The winner gets the ball into all the holes with the fewest hits.

Goodall, Jane Jane Goodall's studies about chimpanzees are world-famous. She has worked with chimpanzees for more than 40 years. She does her work in Tanzania, Africa. Goodall's findings about chimpanzees have improved the way people understand these very smart animals.

1. **What is the guide word on this page?**

   A 321

   B Goodall, Jane

   Ⓒ Goldfish

   D Volume G

2. **What are entry words on this sample page?**

   Ⓐ Golf and Goodall, Jane

   B chimpanzees and clubs

   C course and Tanzania, Africa

   D 321 and Golf

3. **When you look at a card from a library card catalog, the call number tells you —**

   A how many pages are in the book

   B the address where the book was published

   Ⓒ the topic of the book and where to find it

   D where to buy the book

Tip
Use the sources in your library to help you find information you need.

Lesson 37 • 149

Practice It

In this section students will practice reading an entry from an encyclopedia. Read the *Tip* aloud. Have students answer the questions independently. Review the correct answers together.

Question 1 Read the question aloud.

Ask *Where can you find guide words?* (Answer: *at the tops of pages*)

Question 2 Read the question aloud.

Ask *How can you recognize entry words?* (Possible answers: *They are in color or boldfaced and appear in alphabetical order.*)

Question 3 Read the question aloud.

Say *Remember why you use a card catalog.*

Ask *Why is* C *the correct answer?* (Answer: *Call numbers organize books by topic.*)

Discuss students' answers.

Answers

1. C
2. A
3. C

Lesson 38

Objective

Students will learn to take notes from sources and then summarize and organize those ideas from different sources.

Words to Know

Taking notes—collecting information from sources in order to write a report

Bibliography—a list of sources used to find information

Note card—card that contains your notes for each research question

Summarize—to record the main idea and other important information found in a source

Study It

This section will introduce students to source cards and note cards. Pass out examples of each type of card.

Ask *What is the difference between these two types of cards?* (Answers: *Source cards tell about the source; note cards tell about the information you've gathered.*)

■ Direct students to the example cards.

Ask *Who is the author of source #1?* (Answer: *Stanley Smith*)

Ask *What year was source #1 published?* (Answer: *2004*)

Ask *What questions are answered on the note cards?* (Answer: *Why are storms named? Why did storms start to be named?*)

Make a Note

Study It

Before you write a report, collect information to answer your questions about the topic. Writing down this information is called **taking notes.**

When you are taking notes, write a **bibliography,** or list of the sources you use to find information. Make a note card for each source you use. Write the title, author, publisher, and year the book was published on each card. Number each source. For example, here is a note card for a source on hurricanes.

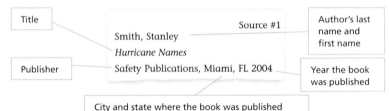

When you take notes, write a note card for each of your questions. You can **summarize,** or briefly say in your own words, the information from the source. Include on the note card the page numbers where you found the information.

Look at this passage from Source #1 above. Then look at the note card.

Since 1978 both men's and women's names have been used to name hurricanes. One reason hurricanes are named is so people can share information about them. During the Atlantic hurricane season, there can be more than one hurricane at the same time. It is important that everyone knows which storm is being talked about.

Source #1, pages 232–233
Why are hurricanes named?
More than one storm can happen at the same time. Names help people know which storm is being talked about.

Curriculum and Assessment Standard

Notes/summarize

Use It

Read this passage. Then look at the sample note cards. Fill in the missing information.

Source #2: Earth is surrounded by layers or zones of gases. These layers make up the atmosphere. The layer closest to Earth is called the troposphere. This layer is where hurricanes form.

Source #2, page 535
What is the atmosphere?
layers of gases around Earth's surface

Source #2, page 535
Where do hurricanes form?
troposphere

Practice It

Read each item. Circle the letter of the correct answer.

1. **What would you write on your note cards for a report?**

   (A) the page numbers where the information was found

   B why you are interested in the topic

   C how many hours you read

   D the title of your favorite novel

2. **When you summarize information, you —**

   A copy a paragraph from a book you used

   B write questions you need to answer

   (C) retell the facts you have read in your own words

   D write a list of all the sources

Tip Use note cards to summarize information that answers your questions.

Use It

In this section students practice taking notes from a source.

Ask *Why is it important to link your notes to your sources?* (Possible answer: *This makes it possible to find the information again.*)

Read the *Use It* directions aloud. Have students complete the rest of the section independently. Ask volunteers to share their answers.

Practice It

In this section students answer questions about taking notes.

- Read the instructions aloud.
- Ask a volunteer to read the *Tip* aloud.
- Instruct students to complete items 1 and 2 independently.

Answers

1. A
2. C

Differentiated Instruction
for tactile, kinesthetic, and visual learners

Note-taking Treasure Hunt

Students practice recording facts and using sources.

Procedure

- Show examples of bibliographic entries for magazines and newspapers.
- Give each student two index cards, and provide a selection of sources, such as magazines and newspapers.
- Have each student find a fact in a source and then use one index card to make a source card.
- On the other index card, students should record the interesting fact in the form of a question and answer.
- Have each student paper clip his or her two cards together. Collect the clipped cards and distribute them to other students.
- Students should look through the sources to locate the fact recorded on the note card using the information on the source card.

Lesson 39

Objective

Students will learn how to write outlines to summarize and organize ideas.

Word to Know

Outline—a written version of the main ideas and supporting details found while doing research; the information in an *outline* appears in an order that makes sense before the writing of the report starts.

Study It

This section will show students how to make an outline.

- Read the first two paragraphs.

  Ask *Why is it a good idea to write an outline?* (Answer: *Outlines help you organize your information before you begin writing.*)

- Direct students to the outline. Read the instructions.

  Say *When you write a report, you want your reader to understand your meaning. Organizing your ideas logically will help your reader.*

  Ask *What do you do after you write the outline?* (Answer: *You write the report.*)

  Ask *Why might an outline change after you start writing?* (Possible answer: *You might think of a better way to organize the ideas.*)

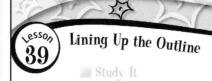

Lesson 39 — Lining Up the Outline

Study It

Sometimes you will be asked to write an **outline** after you have collected the information for your report. An outline helps you put the information in an order that makes sense.

Think about the questions that you asked about your topic. Put the questions in the order that will make sense to the reader. Your questions can become the main topics and subtopics in an outline.

Look at the outline below.

Title: Hurricanes

I. Introduction

> The introduction tells the reader what the report is about. It tells the main idea of the report.

II. What is a hurricane?

> Decide on the main topics of the report. Identify each main topic with a Roman numeral.

    A. Where do hurricanes form?

    B. When is "hurricane season"?

III. What happens during a hurricane?

> You might need to break a subtopic into details. Identify each detail with a number.

    A. Over the ocean

    B. Over land

> Subtopics support the main topics. Identify each subtopic with a capital letter.

      1. Causes damage

      2. Loses power

IV. Conclusion

> The conclusion retells the main idea of the report.

You may need to make changes to your outline. After you finish writing it, you may realize that another order for the information makes more sense, or that you need to add some main topics or details. Then you will need to change the order in the outline. Putting the ideas in another order can help you decide the best way to write your report.

152 ● Unit 7   Outline

Curriculum and Assessment Standard

Outlines

Use It

Look at the outline. Use the items in the box to fill in the blanks in the outline.

Title: Nature in Antarctica

I. Introduction

II. The continent of Antarctica

    A. Southern tip of the world

        1. No daylight for six months

        2. No darkness for six months

    B. Ice caps all year

III. Antarctica's wildlife

    A. Sea birds

    B. Bottlenose dolphins

    C. River otters

IV. Conclusion

Bottlenose dolphins
Antarctica's wildlife
No darkness for six months
River otters
Conclusion

Practice It

Read each item. Circle the letter of the correct answer.

1. Which two parts of an outline go together?

   (A) Roman numeral and main topic

   B Roman numeral and detail

   C capital letter and main topic

   D number and subtopic

2. The purpose of an outline is to —

   A make the report more interesting

   (B) put ideas in order

   C brainstorm to find a topic

   D take notes and collect information

Tip Use an outline to put your ideas in an order that makes sense to the reader.

Lesson 39 ● 153

Use It

Use this activity to help students practice completing an outline.

Ask *What do the Roman numerals and the ABCs mean in an outline?* (Answers: *The Roman numerals indicate main ideas. The letters indicate subtopics that support the main ideas.*)

Ask *What do the numbers under the ABCs give you?* (Answer: *details about the subtopic*)

Read the *Use It* directions aloud. Have students complete the rest of the section independently. Ask volunteers to share their answers.

Practice It

In this section students answer questions about outlines.

- Read the instructions aloud.
- Ask a volunteer to read the *Tip* aloud.
- Instruct students to complete items 1 and 2 independently.

Answers

1. A
2. B

Differentiated Instruction
for ELL and visual learners

Visualizing an Outline

Students use graphic organizers to create an outline for a topic.

Procedure

- Allow students to work independently or in pairs.
- Have each student return to one of the report topics that he or she has already worked on in this unit.
- Provide a selection of blank graphic organizers. Each student should use one of these graphic organizers or one of his or her own design to help draft an outline for a topic.
- If time permits, allow students to explain their graphic outlines to other students. Remind students to focus on constructive criticism.

Lesson 40

Objective

Students will learn to arrange bibliographical information correctly and use the proper format for the entries.

Words to Know

Bibliography—list of sources you used in your report

Study It

This section will show students how to write bibliographical entries for different kinds of sources.

Ask *When you write a report, what do you do with the information on your source cards?* (Answer: *You use it to make a bibliography.*)

- Read the first paragraph.

- Direct students to the examples of bibliography entries. Read the instructions.

Say *The format of a bibliography entry is different for each kind of source.*

Ask *How do the entries for books and encyclopedias differ?* (Possible answers: *The entry for a book begins with an author. The entry for an encyclopedia begins with an article title.*)

Ask *How do the entries for magazines and encyclopedias differ?* (Possible answers: *The entry for a magazine begins with an author; the article title comes second. The entry for an encyclopedia begins with the article title.*)

Ask *Why do you include the date you read a website in its entry?* (Possible answers: *Because websites change from time to time, someone who checks your source may find different information.*)

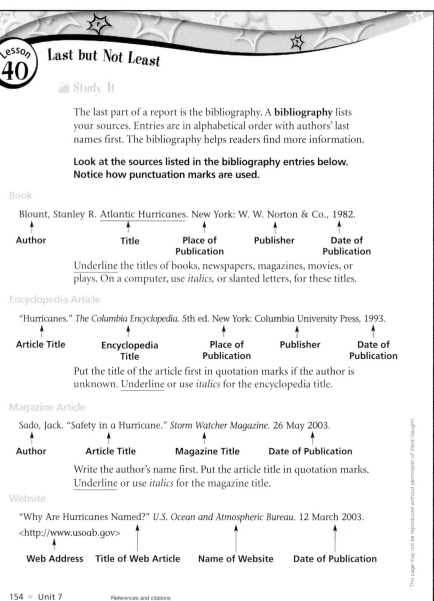

Lesson 40

Last but Not Least

Study It

The last part of a report is the bibliography. A **bibliography** lists your sources. Entries are in alphabetical order with authors' last names first. The bibliography helps readers find more information.

Look at the sources listed in the bibliography entries below. Notice how punctuation marks are used.

Book

Blount, Stanley R. Atlantic Hurricanes. New York: W. W. Norton & Co., 1982.

Author **Title** **Place of Publication** **Publisher** **Date of Publication**

Underline the titles of books, newspapers, magazines, movies, or plays. On a computer, use *italics*, or slanted letters, for these titles.

Encyclopedia Article

"Hurricanes." *The Columbia Encyclopedia*. 5th ed. New York: Columbia University Press, 1993.

Article Title **Encyclopedia Title** **Place of Publication** **Publisher** **Date of Publication**

Put the title of the article first in quotation marks if the author is unknown. Underline or use *italics* for the encyclopedia title.

Magazine Article

Sado, Jack. "Safety in a Hurricane." *Storm Watcher Magazine*. 26 May 2003.

Author **Article Title** **Magazine Title** **Date of Publication**

Write the author's name first. Put the article title in quotation marks. Underline or use *italics* for the magazine title.

Website

"Why Are Hurricanes Named?" *U.S. Ocean and Atmospheric Bureau*. 12 March 2003. <http://www.usoab.gov>

Web Address **Title of Web Article** **Name of Website** **Date of Publication**

References and citations

This page may not be reproduced without permission of Steck-Vaughn.

Curriculum and Assessment Standard

References and citations

Use It

Look at these examples from a bibliography. Find what is wrong with each entry. Write your answer on the line. Look at this example.

Archer, Diane P. Run Like the Wind. Lincoln, NE: Weather Wise, 1997.

The title of the book is not underlined.

Now you try it.

1. Peterson, Marie. How to Make Your Home Safe in a Hurricane. USA Nation, August 22, 1999.

   The article title is not in quotation marks.

2. "Weather." Natural Encyclopedia. 7th Edition. New York: Nature's Press, 2001.

   The name of the encyclopedia is not underlined.

Practice It

Read each question. Circle the letter of the correct answer.

1. **How do you arrange a bibliography?**

   A by date a book or article was published

   B by number of pages

   C by alphabetical order

   D by author's first name

    **Tip** Write the bibliography cards for your sources when you take notes for your report.

2. **Which of the following is a correct entry for a bibliography?**

   A "Cherry Trees." The Baldwin Encyclopedia. 9th Edition. New York: Timbucktu University Press, 1996.

   B Beautiful Beaches. Gardnist, Calvin R. New York: P.G. Lartop & Co., 1978.

   C New York Mirror. Feb. 3, 1981. Flanner, Kim. "Bicycle Helmets."

   D Jill Mandel. New York: Paperback Press, 1990. Great Winds.

Lesson 40 ● 155

Use It

Students will learn to use correct punctuation and format in bibliography entries.

Ask *What parts are underlined or italicized?* (Answer: *titles of books, magazines, and newspapers*)

Read the *Use It* directions aloud. Have students complete the rest of the section independently. Ask volunteers to share their answers.

Practice It

In this section students answer questions about bibliographies.

■ Read the instructions aloud.

■ Ask a volunteer to read the *Tip* aloud.

■ Instruct students to complete items 1 and 2 independently.

Answers

1. C

2. A

Differentiated Instruction
for ELL, tactile, and visual learners

Putting a Bibliography Together

Students practice organizing a bibliography.

Procedure

● Organize students into groups of three.

● Provide each group with several source cards. Try to vary the kinds of sources each group receives.

● Have students check the format and punctuation of each entry.

● Then ask students to arrange the cards in the order in which they would appear in a bibliography.

● Ask each group to write a bibliography on a sheet of paper, using the correct order, format, and punctuation.

Teach the Strategy

Write on the board: *camp* and *canary*.

Ask *Does the topic* cabin *come between these guide words?* (Answer: *no*)

Ask *How about the topic* campfire*?* (Answer: *yes*)

Ask *Where would* cantaloupe *come—before or after this page?* (Answer: *after*)

Say *Guide words can help you find information quickly.*

Use Your ABCs Strategy

Remind students to compare the letters in guide words with those in their topics.

■ Read the bulleted points aloud.

Ask *What do guide words tell you?* (Answer: *that words coming after the first word and before the second word will be found on this page*)

Ask *What kinds of sources use guide words?* (Possible answers: *encyclopedias, dictionaries, and telephone books*)

Try It Out

Read the directions aloud and have students complete this section independently. Encourage students to use the *Use Your ABCs Strategy* to answer the question.

■ Have students select the correct answer, *C*.

■ Have volunteers explain the reasons for their answers.

Ask *How did the* Use Your ABCs Strategy *help you find the correct answer?*

Discuss the explanation that follows the question in the student book.

Test-Taking Strategy

Strategy: Use Your ABCs

In this unit you learned to locate sources. You learned how to use guide words at the top of a page of an encyclopedia. The guide word on the left-hand page tells the first entry on the two pages. The guide word on the right-hand page tells the last entry on the two pages.

To answer questions about whether your topic is between the guide words

● look at the beginning letter or letters of the guide words

● look at the topic you are searching for

● use alphabetical order to determine whether the topic comes between the two guide words

Try It Out

Read the question. Circle the letter of the correct answer.

Which topic comes between the guide words <u>teeth</u> and <u>telescope</u>?

A temperature

B television

Ⓒ telephone

D tea

Look at each of the answer choices. <u>Temperature</u> begins with *tem*. *Tem* comes after *tel* in telescope. <u>Temperature</u> does not come between the two guide words. <u>Television</u> comes after the word <u>telescope</u>. It does not come between the two guide words. <u>Tea</u> comes before the word <u>teeth</u>. It does not come between the two guide words. <u>Telephone</u> comes after the word <u>teeth</u> and before the word <u>telescope</u>. So, **C** is the correct answer.

Put It to the Test

Name _____

This test will check what you have learned in this unit.

DIRECTIONS: Circle the letter of the correct answer.

1. You could narrow the topic <u>sports</u> to —

   A board games

   (B) swimming

   C pizza

   D playing

2. The purpose of a bibliography is to —

   A tell people what your report is about

   (B) show what sources you used for your information

   C show people how you put your information in order

   D have more pages in your report

3. The purpose of an outline is to —

   A think about questions for your topic

   B use the question words

   C put your sources in order

   (D) put your ideas in an order that makes sense

4. On an encyclopedia page, the guide word is the —

   A name of the encyclopedia

   B word that names the topic

   (C) word at the top of the page

   D page number

5. Where would you look in the library to find a book about healthful foods?

   (A) the card catalog

   B an encyclopedia

   C a newspaper

   D a note card

6. When you take notes from a source, it is a good idea to —

   A make up the facts you need

   B use only one source

   (C) write down the information that answers your questions

   D have no clear topic in mind

GO ON

Achieve It! Practice Cards

_____

This page may not be reproduced without permission of Steck-Vaughn

Connect the Test to the Practice Cards (page 157)

Correct Answers	Related Practice Cards	Skill
1. B	114	Selecting a topic
2. B	126, 127	Cite references
3. D	121	Outlines
4. C	116, 117	Locate sources
5. A	116, 117	Locate sources
6. C	118, 119	Take notes, Summarize notes

Put It to the Test

Students will:

- demonstrate what they have learned

- identify skills that require more practice before students achieve proficiency*

* Refer to pages T17–T19 for a complete explanation and directions for using *Achieve It!* Practice Cards.

Administer the Test

Explain that students will now practice the skills from this unit by taking a short test. Tell students that the test has items like those they will find on standardized tests. Explain that you will read the directions aloud. Remind students to pay close attention and to follow your directions exactly.

Say *Open your books to page 157. I will read the directions aloud.* Read the directions to students. Then continue.

Say *You will have 10 minutes to finish this test. Read each item and the answer choices carefully. Circle the letter next to the correct answer. When you reach the words* GO ON *at the bottom of a page, turn the page and continue working. When you reach the word* STOP *at the bottom of a page, stop working and put down your pencil. Are there any questions?*

If students have no questions,

Say *You may begin.*

At the end of 10 minutes,

Say *Stop. Check to be sure that you have circled the letter of the correct answer. Erase any stray pencil marks. Then put down your pencil.*

Assign Practice Cards

After scoring a student's test, note which items the student missed. Match each incorrectly answered item to the related *Achieve It!* Practice Cards listed in the chart on this page.

In the *Achieve It!* Practice Cards space in each student's book, write all of the Practice Cards you want the student to complete.

Additional Practice Cards

The following cards cover additional skills for

Unit 7: Research and Study Skills

Card	Topic
120	Logs
125	Evaluate relevance of information

You may want to assign these cards as practice for students who have done well on the unit test or as extended practice for all students.

7. **What important question could you ask before you write a report about the human eye?**

   Ⓐ How does the eye work?

   B Why do people have eyes?

   C How many eyes do people have?

   D Where are people's eyes?

   p   148634.6

   Pawdeer, Devorah
   Helpful Home Pets: from friend to helper
   Crows Branch, N.S.W.: Smith & Jones, 2012.

8. **The call number 634.6 tells you —**

   A how many pages are in the book

   B where to buy the book

   Ⓒ the topic of the book and where to find it in a library

   D the publisher's address

9. **The first item you write for your source in a bibliography is the —**

   A date it was published

   Ⓑ author's last name

   C publisher

   D illustrator's name

10. **When you take notes, you should —**

    A copy exactly what you read

    B write down all the information

    Ⓒ summarize what you read in your own words

    D write down anything that is interesting

11. **Which topic belongs in a topic web about health?**

    Ⓐ exercise

    B driving

    C movies

    D books

12. **Which part of an outline starts with a Roman numeral?**

    A a subtopic

    B a fact

    C a detail

    Ⓓ a main topic

Achieve It! Practice Cards

Connect the Test to the Practice Cards (page 158)

Correct Answers	Related Practice Cards	Skill
7. **A**	**115**	**Developing questions**
8. **C**	**116, 117**	**Locate sources**
9. **B**	**126, 127**	**Cite references**
10. **C**	**118, 119**	**Take notes, Summarize notes**
11. **A**	**113, 122, 123, 124**	**Planning, Graphic organizers**
12. **D**	**121**	**Outlines**

Unit 8 Writing Skills

Amazing Writing

Have you ever tried to make your way through a maze? The confusion is part of the fun, isn't it? In some ways writing is like leading your readers through a maze. When you write, you invite your readers to follow you through a maze of ideas. However, as a writer, you do not want your readers to be confused.

In this unit you will learn to write so that your readers can follow your lead and easily find their way from one idea to the next.

Skills

- Identifying purpose and audience
- Organizing writing into a beginning, middle, and end
- Demonstrating understanding of the terms *introduction, body,* and *conclusion*
- Stating the main idea of a passage
- Finding facts and details in a passage to support the main idea
- Revising to improve coherence by adding, deleting, and combining sentences

Materials to Gather in Advance

- various reading materials
- paper
- pencil
- photocopies of paragraphs from textbooks or children's magazines
- scissors
- paste
- photocopies of short text passages

Introducing the Unit

Amazing Writing Refer students to the photograph of the hedge maze. Ask students if they have ever gone through a maze like this one. Perhaps they have used their pencils to try to reach the end of a maze on paper. Ask what steps they followed. Students probably tried different paths and turned around when they ran into a dead end. Point out that writing can be the same way. Just as you do not always reach the end of a maze on your first try, you also do not usually write a perfect paragraph the first time.

- Read the *Amazing Writing* paragraph aloud.
- Point out that when writing is unclear, a reader can get lost, too. When this happens the reader does not understand what the writer is trying to say. This is why it is important to make writing as clear and easy to follow as possible. You do not want your writing to be a maze!

Research Says

. . . (R)esearch suggests that almost any approach to teaching the structure of informational text improves both comprehension and recall of key text information.

—*Duke and Pearson*

Lesson 41

Objective

Students will learn that writing varies according to its purpose and audience.

Words to Know

Audience—people who read your writing

Purpose—your reason for writing something

Entertain—to amuse with something lively or funny

Express—to write about personal feelings

Persuade—to convince your audience to do something or to believe something

Inform—to give information about something

Study It

Introduce students to the concepts of *audience* and *purpose*.

■ Ask volunteers to read the first two paragraphs aloud.

Ask *Who can give me an example of something you wrote recently?* (Possible answers: *homework assignment, letter, journal entry*)

■ Write each example on the board.

Ask *Who is the audience for each of these?* (Possible answers: *a teacher, a friend, your family, yourself*)

Ask *What is the purpose of each of these writings?* (Possible answers: *to show the teacher that I learned the material, to keep in touch with a friend, and to tell about my personal experiences*)

■ Read the third paragraph aloud.

■ Review each question in the chart and why each question is important.

Lesson 41 — Who's Out There?

Study It

Whenever you write, there is always someone who will read your writing. Your friend may read a letter about your visit with your aunt and uncle. Other students may read your story in the school newspaper about cleaning up the playground. If you keep a diary or a journal, you are writing for yourself.

Your readers are your **audience.** Good writers think about their audience and make writing choices based on what they know about their audience.

Good writers also think about their **purpose,** or reason, for writing. You may write a story to **entertain** your little sister. You may write to **express** your feelings, such as in a journal or a personal letter. You may express your opinion in an essay to **persuade** other students to join a school club. You may create a flyer to **inform,** or give information, to community members about an event. Each writing task is special. Each audience is special, too.

Before you write, think about these questions.

Question	Why the Question Is Important
Who are my readers?	Different readers have different needs. You write one way for your little brother and another way for your teacher.
What do my readers know about my topic?	You want to build on what your readers already know.
What do my readers need to learn about my topic?	You want to give your readers the information they need.
What is the best way to give my readers information?	Some information can be written. Other information is easier to understand if it appears in charts or pictures.
Why am I writing?	Sometimes you write to entertain. At other times you write to express, to persuade, or to give information.

Curriculum and Assessment Standard

Audience/purpose

Use It

Read these items. Write what or who would probably be the BEST purpose or audience for each writing task.

teacher or
another student
   1. a report about rain forests (audience)

to express
feelings
   2. I love my grandmother's garden. It smells like summer. The tomato vines are drooping from the weight of the plump red and yellow tomatoes. (purpose)

Now you try it.

to give
information
   1. The fourth graders will present their class play next Thursday at 7:00 P.M. in the cafeteria. (purpose)

friend or
family member
   2. a letter about what you did during the summer (audience)

to entertain
   3. Long ago a little elf lived under a rose bush. (purpose)

to persuade
   4. Vote for Amy for class president because she has a lot of experience. (purpose)

Practice It

Read this question. Circle the letter of the correct answer.

People in our community should help with the park cleanup!

What is the purpose for writing this sentence?

A   to express

B   to give information

C   to entertain

D   to persuade

Tip
Before you begin writing, think about your audience and your purpose for writing.

Lesson 41 • 161

Use It

Use this activity to have students practice identifying audience and purpose.

■ Show students a thank-you note.

  Ask *Who is the writer's audience?* (Answer: *the recipient*) *What is the writer's purpose?* (Answer: *to thank the recipient*)

Read the *Use It* directions aloud. Refer students back to the four purposes stated on page 160: *entertain, express feelings, persuade,* and *inform.* Complete the example question with students. Then have students answer questions 1–4 by matching each sentence with one of the purposes. Ask volunteers to share their answers.

Practice It

In this section students answer a question about purpose.

■ Read the instructions aloud.

■ Ask a volunteer to read the *Tip* aloud.

■ Instruct students to complete the item independently.

Answer:

D

Differentiated Instruction
for kinesthetic, visual, and auditory learners

Identifying Who and Why

Students will practice identifying audience and purpose by reading different types of texts.

Procedure

● Organize students into groups of four.

● Give each group a different set of five reading materials. (Examples: a toy catalog, copies of the school newspaper, textbooks, dictionary, and so on.)

● Have each group choose one piece of writing from each of the five materials.

● Ask each group to discuss the audience and purpose for each of the five pieces of writing.

● If time permits, ask each group to present a short summary and to name the audience and purpose for each piece of writing.

Lesson 42

Objective

Students will learn that writing is organized into sections—the introduction (beginning), body (middle), and conclusion (ending).

Words to Know

Introduction—the beginning part of a piece of writing, where readers learn what the topic will be

Body—the middle of a piece of writing, where readers learn more about the topic or main idea

Conclusion—the end of a piece of writing, where readers are reminded of the main ideas they have learned

Study It

Read the first two paragraphs aloud. Then have students look at the chart.

■ Have a volunteer read the heading and bulleted points in the first column aloud.

Ask *What should the introduction do when you write?* (Answer: *get a reader's attention, introduce a topic, and show a purpose*)

■ Have a volunteer read the heading and bulleted points in the second column aloud.

Ask *What should the body do in a piece of writing?* (Answer: *state, explain, and support each main idea*)

■ Have a volunteer read the heading and bulleted points in the third column aloud.

Ask *What should the conclusion do?* (Answer: *restate the most important ideas and leave readers with thoughts*)

Ask *Of these three parts, which do you think is usually the longest?* (Answer: *the body*) *Why?* (Possible answers: *It contains all the main ideas and the information that supports them.*)

162 ■ Unit 8

Lesson 42

Begin, Explain, End

Study It

You want your audience to understand what you are writing. A very important part of writing is how you organize, or arrange, your ideas. The **introduction**, or beginning, will introduce the topic. The **body**, or middle, will state and explain your main ideas. The **conclusion**, or end, will complete your writing and remind your reader of the main ideas.

Much of the writing you are doing now has an introduction in the first paragraph and a conclusion in the last paragraph. The body of the writing usually has one or more paragraphs.

Look at this chart. It will help you understand how to organize your writing.

How to Organize Your Writing		
Introduction (Beginning)	**Body (Middle)**	**Conclusion (End)**
· Gets the reader's attention and makes him or her want to read the writing · Introduces the subject or topic of the writing · Shows the writer's purpose	· Explains each main idea in its own paragraph · States each main idea in a topic sentence · Supports each main idea with facts and details	· Finishes the writing · States the most important ideas and details again in different words · Leaves the reader with an interesting thought

There are generally three ways to introduce your topic. You can start with someone doing something, saying something, or thinking something, often by asking a question. Then write at least one paragraph for each main idea in the body. Be sure to support each main idea with facts and details. Decide what ideas and details you want your reader thinking about as he or she finishes reading your writing. Use these ideas and details to write your conclusion.

Curriculum and Assessment Standard

Introduction/body/conclusion

Read this passage. Circle the paragraph with the introduction. Put a box around the body paragraphs. Underline the paragraph with the conclusion.

Hopscotch

1　Have you ever played hopscotch? It has been around for hundreds of years. It is older than basketball. The game may have first been played in Rome.

2　Hopscotch is played on a hard surface. The board is made of numbered squares. Players hop across the squares to move back and forth on the board. Sometimes players use a stone to mark where they cannot hop. A turn ends when a player steps on a line. A turn can also end if a player falls or if his or her raised foot touches the ground.

3　The name hopscotch comes from two old words. You know that <u>hop</u> means "jump." The meaning of <u>scotch</u> comes from <u>scratch</u>, a word that once meant "line." In other words, players hop over a line. That is a good description, isn't it?

4　So the next time you play hopscotch, remember two things. You are playing a very old game. And remember to hop the scotch to keep your turn!

Look at this chart to see how the beginning, middle, and end of the passage work together.

Hopscotch		
Introduction	**Body**	**Conclusion**
Paragraph 1 asks a question to make readers want to continue reading.	Paragraph 2 explains the game. Paragraph 3 tells how the game got its name.	Paragraph 4 retells the two main points in different words.

Readers of this passage will be able to understand the writing because of the way it is organized. Paragraph 1 gets the reader's attention. Paragraphs 2 and 3 state and support the main ideas. Paragraph 4 restates the most important ideas and leaves the reader with an interesting thought.

■ Have a student volunteer read the directions aloud. Then ask students to wait to mark the passage until you have read the passage aloud. Direct students to the chart at the bottom of the page.

Say *This chart shows how the paragraphs in the passage are organized.*

Ask *What are some clues that paragraph 1 is the introduction?* (Possible answers: *It introduces hopscotch; it comes first.*)

Ask *What are some clues that paragraph 4 is the conclusion?* (Possible answers: *It retells the main ideas; it comes last.*)

Ask *What do paragraphs 2 and 3 do?* (Possible answer: *These body paragraphs tell the main ideas.*)

Encourage students to ask questions about how paragraphs are organized. Help them understand the functions of the three parts and the differences between them.

Differentiated Instruction
for visual and tactile learners

Putting a Puzzle Together

Students will practice identifying an introduction, the body, and the conclusion.

Procedure

● Organize students into pairs.

● Give each pair a copy of a short passage cut into three parts (introduction, body, and conclusion) and paper-clipped together.

● Ask students to assemble the passage segments into an introduction, body, and conclusion.

● Still working in pairs, ask students to read their assembled passage aloud.

● Have the pairs exchange passages and repeat the activity.

● Working as a whole class, ask students to discuss how they determined the order of each passage.

Use this activity to help students identify the introduction, body, and conclusion of a passage.

Say *Passages are often organized into an introduction, a body, and a conclusion.*

- Direct students to the passage. Read the directions aloud. Then, ask a student to read the passage aloud.

  Ask *Which paragraph is likely to be the introduction?* (Answer: *the first one*)

  Ask *Which paragraph is likely to be the conclusion?* (Answer: *the last one*)

- Direct students to the chart below the passage and read the directions aloud.

- Have students complete the rest of the section independently. Ask volunteers to share their answers.

■ Use It

Read this passage. Circle the paragraph with the introduction. Put a box around the body paragraphs. Underline the paragraph with the conclusion.

1 Not many people know John Muir's name. But we should be thankful to him. He worked hard to preserve a great treasure of the United States, the wilderness.

2 Muir, an immigrant, was born in Scotland in 1838. He moved to the United States in 1849. He lived on a farm in Wisconsin. He loved the outdoors.

3 Muir thought people should take better care of the wilderness. Famous people like President Theodore Roosevelt were interested in his ideas.

4 Because of Muir's work, the areas around Sequoia and Yosemite were set aside as national parks in 1890. Soon afterward, a national parks program began.

5 We may not have heard of John Muir, but every person who enjoys our national parks benefits from his work.

Look at this chart. Fill in what each paragraph does.

John Muir		
Introduction	**Body**	**Conclusion**
Paragraph 1 tells about someone the reader probably does not know.	Paragraph 2 tells about Muir's background and interests. Paragraph 3 tells about Muir's thoughts and ideas. Paragraph 4 tells about Muir's influence on national parks.	Paragraph 5 tells that every person who enjoys our national parks benefits from Muir's work even if his name is unknown.

Read this passage. Then read the questions. Circle the letter of the correct answer.

1   What did people do before there was money? They had to trade goods. This trading was called bartering.

2   This is how bartering worked. Suppose I had some meat that you wanted. You would offer to give me a shirt for the meat. If I agreed, we would trade, or barter.

3   But what if I did not want your shirt? I could be left with lots of meat that I might not need. Perhaps other people would join our barter circle. This could become hard to keep track of, couldn't it?

4   Money was invented to solve the problems with bartering. Money helps people get what they need without having to trade things. It is a good idea, isn't it?

1. **Which paragraph in the body of the passage explains the problem with bartering?**

    A paragraph 1

    B paragraph 2

    C paragraph 3

    D paragraph 4

2. **Which paragraph is the conclusion?**

    A paragraph 1

    B paragraph 2

    C paragraph 3

    D paragraph 4

Tip   Organize your ideas in your writing so that you have an introduction, a body, and a conclusion.

Practice It

Use this activity to help students understand how passages are organized into an introduction, a body, and a conclusion.

■ Read the directions aloud. Then, give students time to read the passage silently.

Question 1 Have students complete question 1 independently.

Help students understand why *C* is the correct answer. Explain that students should look for key information by rereading the passage.

Say *Reread the passage to see which paragraph explains the problem with bartering.*

Say *When you reread the passage, you see that bartering is introduced in paragraph 1. How bartering works is explained in paragraph 2. So answers* A *and* B *are incorrect. Paragraph 4 tells how the problems with bartering are solved, so answer* D *is also incorrect.*

Ask *What about answer* C? *Does paragraph 3 explain the problem with bartering?* (Answer: *yes*)

Say *When you reread the passage, you saw that* C *is the correct answer. Sometimes you may have to reread more than once to be certain you have the correct information.*

Question 2 Have students complete question 2 independently.

Help students understand the correct answer (*D*) by explaining why the other answers are incorrect.

■ *A* is incorrect because it is the introduction.

■ *B* and *C* refer to body paragraphs.

Ask a volunteer to read the *Tip* aloud.

Lesson 43

Objective

Students will learn about main ideas, topic sentences, and details.

Words to Know

Topic sentence—a sentence that contains the main idea of a paragraph, usually the first or last sentence

Support—information in a paragraph that offers facts and details that help explain the main idea

◼ Study It

Have a volunteer read the first paragraph aloud. Review the terms *topic sentence* and *support* with the class.

◼ Ask students to follow along as you read the passage about the dictionary aloud.

Say *The first sentence is the topic sentence. It contains the main idea that the dictionary is a useful book.*

Ask *What details does the writer give to support the main idea?* (Answer: *We use it to find information about spelling, pronunciation, and word origins.*)

Say *The topic sentence is usually the first or last sentence in a paragraph.*

Ask *How can you tell if a sentence is the topic sentence?* (Answer: *The other sentences in the paragraph support the topic sentence.*)

Go over the remaining information with students.

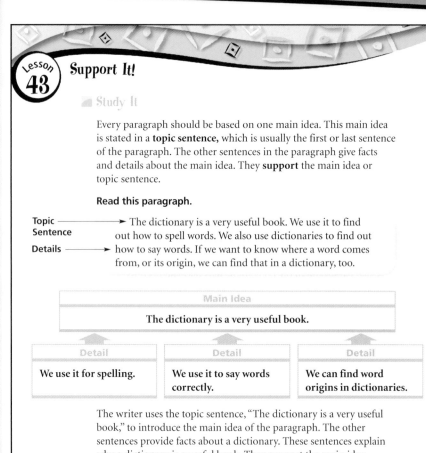

Curriculum and Assessment Standard

Main idea/supporting details

Read this passage.

The setting of this book is an old farm. The author's descriptions made me feel as though I were there. The characters seem very real, especially the ten-year-old twins. Like me, they get into trouble. The action in the book is also very real. The twins have a map and go looking for their grandfather's treasure. All in all, this is an excellent adventure book.

Look at this chart. Notice how the details are used to support the main idea.

Main Idea
This is an excellent adventure book.

Detail	Detail	Detail
The descriptions make the reader feel as though he or she is there.	The twins get into trouble, just as real people do.	The twins use a map to find their grandfather's treasure.

Where is the topic sentence in this paragraph? This writer put it at the end of the paragraph. The writer chose to discuss the details of the book before giving an opinion about the book as a whole.

■ Read the passage aloud. Then direct students' attention to the chart.

Say *Some details support the main idea of the paragraph.*

Ask *What is the main idea?* (Answer: *This is an excellent adventure book.*)

Ask *Where is the topic sentence?* (Answer: *It is the last sentence in the passage.*)

Ask *Why might a writer choose to put the topic sentence at the end of a paragraph?* (Possible answers: *to keep the reader reading; to save his or her opinion until the end*)

Ask *Can you find more details in the paragraph that support the main idea?* (Possible answers: *the characters and the action are real*)

Differentiated Instruction
for ELL, tactile, and visual learners

Supporting a Main Idea

Students will look at a paragraph and identify the topic sentence and the main idea.

Procedure

● Organize students into pairs.

● Give each pair a photocopy of a paragraph from a textbook or children's magazine. Ask students to identify the topic sentence and the supporting details in the paragraph.

● Ask students to carefully cut the sentences apart from one another. Using the chart on this page as a model, they should paste the topic sentence at the top of a piece of paper, clearly marking it "Main Idea." Sentences that contain details should be pasted below, each clearly marked "Detail."

● When students have finished, have them show their work to the class.

Use It

Use this section to help students identify a topic sentence and support.

- Ask a volunteer to give a sentence that states an opinion about a sport he or she likes to play or watch. Then ask students to give two or three reasons to support the opinion. For example, *I enjoy running track. It challenges my body. It keeps me in shape. I like the way running makes me feel.*

  Ask *Which of these sentences could be a topic sentence?* (Possible answer: *I enjoy running track.*)

- Give students time to read the passage about packages independently. Have them underline any important facts and details.

  Say *As you read the passage, think about how the sentences tie together.*

- On the board, draw this chart. Write in the main idea.

  Ask *What information can you find in the text to support the main idea that packages play a big part in our life?*

- Write the supporting details on the board and have students fill in the chart.

Have students answer the two items independently. Ask volunteers to share their answers.

Use It

Read this paragraph.

You may not think about it, but packages play a big part in your life. Think about a trip to the grocery store. Colorful cardboard packages help you find your favorite cereal. Honey, a liquid, is easier to handle because it is in a jar. Milk is kept clean and fresh because of its container. Soap and other cleaning products are wrapped in packages that keep their scents away from food items.

Fill in the chart with details that support the main idea.

Main Idea
Packages play a big part in your life.

Detail	Detail	Detail	Detail
They help you find your favorite cereal.	They make honey easier to handle.	They keep milk clean and fresh.	They keep the scent of cleaning products away from food.

Read each question. Write your answer on the line.

1. Where is the topic sentence in this paragraph?

   the first sentence of the paragraph

2. Why do you think the writer chose to put the topic sentence in this place?

   The purpose of this paragraph is to persuade the reader to see the writer's point of view. In this case it is best to write the topic sentence first so that the reader knows what to expect.

Read this paragraph. Then read each item. Circle the letter of the correct answer.

Cotton is one of the world's most useful plants. In many countries people have jobs growing cotton or working with it. A lot of clothing is made from cotton. Other cotton products we use include rugs, curtains, and towels. Cotton even provides cottonseed oil, which is used in cooking!

1. **What is the topic sentence of this paragraph?**

   (A) Cotton is one of the world's most useful plants.

   B In many countries people have jobs growing cotton or working with it.

   C Clothing is made from cotton.

   D Cotton even provides cottonseed oil, which is used in cooking!

2. **Look at this chart.**

Main Idea
Cotton is one of the world's most useful plants.

Detail	Detail	Detail	Detail
Cotton provides jobs.	Clothes are made from cotton.		Cooking oil is made from cotton.

   Which detail from the paragraph should be added to the chart?

   A Cotton is grown on plants.

   B Socks and shirts are made from cotton.

   (C) Rugs, curtains, and towels are made from cotton.

   D Cotton is a good fabric for summer.

   Tip Put the topic sentence of each paragraph where it will help a reader understand your ideas.

Lesson 43 • 169

Practice It

Help students identify the topic sentence and supporting details.

Read the directions aloud. Ask students to read the passage.

Question 1 Ask students to answer question 1 independently.

To help students understand why *A* is the best answer, discuss the importance of searching for key words.

Say *A correct answer has important words called* key words. *Sometimes the key words appear multiple times in the paragraph. At other times, the key words are found in other forms in the paragraph.*

Ask *Does the word* work *come up over and over in the paragraph?* (Answer: *no*)

Ask *Does* clothes *seem to be a key word in the paragraph?* (Answer: *no*)

Ask *Do the other sentences in the paragraph talk about* cottonseed oil *or* cooking? (Answer: *no*)

Ask *Do the other sentences in the paragraph talk about how cotton is a useful plant?* (Answer: *yes*)

Say *Useful is a key word because all the other sentences help explain the ways cotton is used, or state that people have jobs because of cotton. So answer* A *is correct. Answers* B, C, *and* D *are incorrect.*

Question 2 Read the directions for question 2 aloud. Ask students to identify the missing detail and circle the correct answer. (Answer: *C*)

Discuss students' answers. Explain to students that they must sometimes think about relationships between pieces of information to find the correct answer.

Lesson 44

Objective

Students will learn techniques for making writing more clear, such as adding, deleting, combining, and rearranging text.

Study It

Say *Sometimes we can make our writing better by making connections between our ideas. Let's look at some ways to improve first drafts.*

- Direct students' attention to the chart. Ask a student to read the directions for the chart aloud. Then, ask one student to read each row aloud.

- Read the paragraph aloud. Ask students to follow along in their books.

  Say *Look at the underlined words. These words tell the order in which Ramon followed steps to get ready for his camping trip.*

- Ask a volunteer to read the passage aloud, skipping the underlined words.

  Ask *Do the underlined words improve the writing? How?* (Possible answers: *Yes; the words help the reader follow the steps Ramon took in getting ready for his trip.*)

Tell It Well

Study It

Good writers connect ideas well. Readers should be able to follow one idea to the next easily, without a lot of questions or confusion.

Look at this chart. It shows three ways to improve your writing.

Add	Look for places to add main ideas, facts, or details that will make your writing clearer to the reader. You can also add sequence, or time order, words to help the reader move from one idea to the next. Some sequence words include <u>once</u>, <u>before</u>, <u>first</u>, <u>next</u>, <u>then</u>, <u>after</u>, <u>last</u>, and <u>finally</u>.
Remove	Take out words, sentences, or paragraphs that are not related to the topic or that simply repeat information.
Combine	Rewrite short, choppy sentences into one longer sentence. Also combine repeated information into one clear sentence or paragraph.

Read this paragraph.

> <u>First</u>, Ramon got his backpack out of the closet. He threw three pairs of socks into it. <u>Then</u>, he put in pajamas and some t-shirts. <u>Next</u>, he folded jeans and added them to the pack. <u>Finally</u>, he threw in his favorite book and a toothbrush. He ran downstairs and called, "I'm ready to go camping!"

This paragraph is about how Ramon gets ready for his camping trip. The writer added sequence words to help you move from one event to the next.

Coherence

Curriculum and Assessment Standard

Coherence

Read this paragraph.

(1) Tyrone liked riding the bus to school. (2) He was at the bus stop on time every morning. (3) Buses are a very popular way for students to get to school. (4) He waited with his friends Jimmy and Kezia. (5) They would tell jokes and talk about their homework. (6) On the bus Tyrone usually sat with Ben. (7) They studied together for tests. (8) All in all, it was a good way to start the day.

This paragraph is about Tyrone and his experiences on the school bus. Most of the sentences support this topic. However, sentence 3 is about buses in general and not about Tyrone's school bus. It is not related to the topic and needs to be removed from the paragraph.

Read this paragraph.

(1) Moths and butterflies are very much alike. (2) Moths are insects. (3) Butterflies are insects.(4) Moths have four wings. (5) Butterflies have four wings. (6) Moths collect nectar from flowers. (7) Butterflies collect nectar from flowers. (8) Moths take pollen from flower to flower. (9) Butterflies take pollen from flower to flower.

This paragraph is about the similarities between moths and butterflies. This passage is hard to read because many words are repeated. Also, the sentences are short and choppy. The writing improves when you combine some of the sentences and remove the words that are repeated. For example, sentences 2 through 5 could be combined into the sentence <u>Both moths and butterflies are insects with four wings.</u>

Lesson 44 ● 171

■ Direct students to the first paragraph. Have students follow along as you read the passage aloud.

Ask *What is this passage about?* (Answer: *Tyrone and his experiences riding the school bus*)

Say *Read sentence 3 again.*

Ask *What is sentence 3 about?* (Answer: *school buses*) *Is it about Tyrone or his experiences riding the school bus?* (Answer: *no*) *Does sentence 3 fit in this paragraph?* (Answer: *no.*)

Say *Removing sentence 3 makes the paragraph easier to follow.*

■ Direct students to the second paragraph. Have students follow along as you read it aloud.

Ask *What is this paragraph about?* (Answer: *how butterflies and moths are alike*) *How could we improve this paragraph? Look at the chart on page 170.* (Consider all student suggestions.)

■ Show students how sentences 2–5 can be combined into one sentence.

Say *Now look at sentences 6–9.*

Ask *How could these sentences be combined into one sentence that is easier for the reader to follow?* (Answer: *They both collect nectar from flowers and take pollen from flower to flower.*)

(Differentiated Instruction
for auditory and visual learners

Revising a Story

Students will practice rewriting a paragraph to make the writing more clear.

Procedure

● On the board write: "On my way home from school yesterday, I saw . . ."

● Invite a volunteer to finish the sentence, recording it on the board. Ask for another volunteer to contribute the next sentence to the story. Add three more volunteered sentences to the board to form a paragraph.

● Organize students into pairs.

● Have each pair rewrite the paragraph. Ask them to use the chart on page 170 to guide them. Tell them you would like to see sentences added, removed, and combined, if doing so will help the writing become more clear.

● Encourage students to explain the changes they made as part of class discussion. Point out that there is more than one good way to revise a paragraph.

Use It

In this section students will add, remove, and combine sentences to improve a piece of writing.

- Direct students to the first passage.

  Say *As you read the passage, think about what the writer is trying to say.*

- Have students read the passage.

  Question 1 Read the first question aloud. Allow time for students to answer the question independently.

  Ask *What is this passage about?* (Answer: *spaghetti with tomato sauce and macaroni and cheese*)

  Say *The writer describes spaghetti with tomato sauce as* spicy.

  Ask *Does the writer describe macaroni and cheese in detail?* (Answer: *no*) *What could the writer add about macaroni and cheese?* (Possible answers: *It is made with a creamy cheese sauce. It is mild and filling.*)

- Have students complete the rest of the section independently. Ask volunteers to share their answers.

Use It

Read this passage.

Two favorite dishes, spaghetti with tomato sauce and macaroni and cheese, are very similar foods. The sauce for spaghetti is usually made with tomatoes. This makes a spicy dish. Both meals are very good.

1. What information should be added to this passage?

   information about macaroni and cheese

Read this passage.

(1) Benjamin Franklin left a special mark on the city of Philadelphia. (2) He started the first public library in America. (3) He began a firefighting company. (4) He also lived in France for a while.

2. Which sentence should be removed from this passage?

   sentence 4

3. Why should this sentence be removed?

   It is not about what Benjamin Franklin did in Philadelphia.

Read this passage.

Macaroni is a noodle. To make macaroni and cheese, first add cheese to the cooked noodles. Then add butter and milk.

4. Identify the sequence words used in this passage.

   first, then

5. Combine the sentences in this passage to make one sentence.

   To make macaroni and cheese, add cheese, butter, and milk to cooked macaroni noodles.

Practice It

Read this paragraph. Then read each item. Circle the letter of the correct answer.

(1) The milk that you buy from a store has taken quite a journey. (2) Then it is cooled and taken to a dairy to be prepared. (3) At the dairy the milk is heated to kill any bacteria in it. (4) Next, the cream is removed from the milk. (5) The cream is packaged separately. (6) This keeps any fat in the milk from rising to the top. (7) The milk is then sent through a machine with many tiny holes. (8) Finally, the milk is packaged and sent to the store. (9) You should drink three glasses of milk each day.

1. **Which sentence does NOT belong in this paragraph?**

   (A) sentence 9

   B sentence 2

   C sentence 7

   D sentence 8

2. **Which of these is the BEST way to combine sentences 4 and 5?**

   A The cream is packaged after the milk is removed.

   B First, remove the milk. Then, package the cream.

   (C) Next, the cream is removed from the milk and packaged separately.

   D The cream and the milk are packaged together.

3. **Which sentence could BEST be added after sentence 1?**

   (A) The milk is collected on a farm.

   B Most people buy milk at a grocery store.

   C Trucks are used to take milk from one state to another.

   D Milk is a good source of calcium.

Tip Look for ways to combine ideas in your writing to make them clear to the reader.

Lesson 44 • 173

Practice It

In this section students will practice revising a paragraph. Complete the section with students to help them use the *Think and Search Strategy.*

Question 1 Read the directions aloud. Ask students to read the passage and work independently to find the sentence that does not belong.

To help students understand why *A* is the best answer, use the *Think and Search Strategy.* (See the *QAR Strategy* below.) Explain that when students use this strategy, they must reread the text and the answers carefully. By thinking about the main idea of the passage, students can determine which sentence does not belong.

■ Ask students to reread the passage.

Ask *What is the main idea?* (Answer: *Milk takes a long journey from its source to the store.*)

Say *Now look at the answer choices. Compare each sentence with the paragraph's main idea.*

Ask *Does* A *support the main idea?* (Answer: *No. It is about drinking milk.*)

Say *Read* B, C, *and* D.

Ask *Do these sentences support the main idea?* (Answer: *Yes, they are all steps in the journey.*)

Say *So* A *is the correct answer. When you think about the answers as you search for information in the text, you are using the* Think and Search Strategy.

Question 2 Read the *Tip* aloud. Ask students to identify the best way to combine sentences 4 and 5. Circle the correct answer, *C.*

Question 3 Ask students to identify the best sentence that could be added after sentence 1. Circle the correct answer, *A.*

Discuss students' answers. Explain to students that they must sometimes use their background knowledge to find the correct answers.

QAR Strategy

Strategy	Definition	How It Works
Think and Search	This strategy teaches students that information may be found in multiple places in a passage in order to answer a question.	In this example students determine how sentences relate to others in a paragraph and then use their background knowledge to fill in a missing step in a process.

Refer to pages T22–T23 for a complete chart of QAR Strategies that students may use to achieve greater success on tests of reading comprehension.

Teach the Strategy

Write the following on the board:
Why did the teacher wear sunglasses?
Because her class was so bright!

Ask *What is the purpose of this piece of writing?* (Answer: *to entertain*)

Ask *Who is the audience?* (Answer: *students and teachers*)

Determine Purpose and Audience Strategy

Remind students to think about audience and purpose when they write.

■ Read the first bulleted point aloud.

Ask *How might your purpose affect your writing?* (Possible answer: *Purpose helps you decide how and what to write. For example, when you inform, you need facts. When you write to persuade, you need to be convincing.*)

■ Read the second bulleted point aloud.

Ask *How might your audience affect your writing?* (Possible answers: *I might use slang when writing a letter to a friend. I might use formal language if I am writing a report.*)

Try It Out

Read the directions aloud and have students complete this section independently. Encourage students to use the *Determine Purpose and Audience Strategy* to answer the questions.

■ Ask a student to read the directions aloud. Then ask students to read the passage. Make sure they know that they do not have to do the writing task described.

■ Have students select the correct answers.

1. C
2. D

■ Have volunteers explain the reasons for their answers.

Ask *How did the* Strategy *help you find the correct answers?*

Discuss the explanation that follows each question in the student book.

174 ■ **Unit 8**

Unit 8
Test-Taking Strategy

Strategy: Determine Purpose and Audience

In this unit you learned to identify different purposes for writing and different kinds of audiences. When you are asked about writing tasks on a test, ask yourself

● What is the purpose of this piece of writing? Is it to entertain, to express, to persuade, or to inform?

● Who will read this piece of writing? Is it for friends, for a teacher, or for someone else?

Try It Out

Read these questions. Circle the letter of the correct answer.

> Explain how to make something. Include enough information so that your reader will understand how to make the thing.

1. **What is the purpose of this writing task?**

    A to entertain

    B to persuade

    C to inform

    D to express

The purpose is to inform someone about making something, so **C** is the best answer.

2. **Who would probably be the audience for this piece of writing?**

    A a newspaper editor

    B a teacher

    C a baby brother

    D a student

The writing would explain to a student how to do something, so **D** is the best answer.

174 ● Unit 8

This page may not be reproduced without permission of Steck-Vaughn.

Put It to the Test

Name _____

This test will check what you have learned in this unit.

DIRECTIONS: Read this passage. Then read each item.
Circle the letter of the correct answer.

Two Heroes

(1) Pecos Bill was a legendary cowboy. (2) As a baby he was raised by coyotes. (3) When he grew up, his strength was well known. (4) Instead of a horse, he rode a mountain lion. (5) He also used a rattlesnake for a whip. (6) Once, during a dry spell, Pecos Bill drained a river to water his ranch. (7) It has been said that cowboys told stories about him each evening as they gathered at the campfire. (8) These stories always talked about Bill's quick thinking and courage. (9) Bill's wife, Slue-foot Sue, was also part of the stories.

(10) Paul Bunyan was a legend, too. (11) However, he was famous in the American forests. (12) He was a lumberjack. (13) Paul could cut down two trees at once. (14) The Great Lakes were formed from his footprints. (15) His companion was Babe, a big blue ox. (16) Babe could pull entire forests to the lumber mill in one trip. (17) Lumberjacks traded Paul Bunyan stories in their camps at night. (18) Stories about Paul Bunyan told of his power and speed.

1. What is the passage MAINLY about?

A Coyotes are smart and make good parents.

B Cowboys are clever and courageous.

C Heroes in legends have qualities that people admire.

D Large oxen once lived in America.

2. In the second paragraph, sentence 10 is —

A an important detail in the paragraph

B the main idea of the paragraph

C a definition in the paragraph

D the purpose of the paragraph

Achieve It! Practice Cards

_____

Connect the Test to the Practice Cards (page 175)

Correct Answers	Related Practice Cards	Skill
1. C	139, 140, 141	Paragraphs with main idea/supporting details, Topic sentences
2. B	139, 140, 141	Paragraphs with main idea/supporting details, Topic sentences

Put It to the Test

Students will:

- demonstrate what they have learned
- identify skills that require more practice before students achieve proficiency*

* Refer to pages T17–T19 for a complete explanation and directions for using *Achieve It!* Practice Cards.

Administer the Test

Explain that students will now practice the skills from this unit by taking a short test. Tell students that the test has items like those they will find on standardized tests. Explain that you will read the directions aloud. Remind students to pay close attention and to follow your directions exactly.

Say *Open your books to page 175. I will read the directions aloud.* Read the directions to students. Then continue.

Say *You will have 10 minutes to finish this test. Read each item and the answer choices carefully. Circle the letter of the correct answer. When you reach the words* GO ON *at the bottom of a page, turn the page and continue working. When you reach the word* STOP *at the bottom of a page, stop working and put down your pencil. Are there any questions?*

If students have no questions,

Say *You may begin.*

At the end of 10 minutes,

Say *Stop. Check to be sure that you have circled the letter of the correct answer. Erase any stray pencil marks. Then, put down your pencil.*

Assign Practice Cards

After scoring a student's test, note which items the student missed. Match each incorrectly answered item to the related *Achieve It!* Practice Cards listed in the chart on this page.

In the *Achieve It!* Practice Cards space in each student's book, write the numbers of all of the Practice Cards you want the student to complete.

Additional Practice Cards

The following cards cover additional skills for

Unit 8: Writing Skills

Card	Topic
128	Prewriting
131	Point of view
132	Voice
133	Drafting
143	Word choice

You may want to assign these cards as practice for students who have done well on the unit test or as extended practice for all students.

3. The writer uses the words <u>once</u>, <u>too</u>, and <u>when</u> in the passage. What are these words called?

Ⓐ sequence words

B cause and effect words

C comparison and contrast words

D descriptive words

4. What is the purpose of "Two Heroes"?

A to describe ranches

Ⓑ to give information about folk legends

C to entertain people around a campfire

D to persuade people to become lumberjacks

5. This passage is from the middle of a report on legends. What is the middle of a report called?

A the title

B the introduction

C the conclusion

Ⓓ the body

6. Who would probably be the audience for this report about two heroes?

A the mayor and city council

Ⓑ your teacher and other students

C your baby brother and sister

D your aunt and uncle

7. Which sentence does NOT belong in the first paragraph?

A sentence 2

B sentence 5

C sentence 7

Ⓓ sentence 9

8. Sentences that are not related to the topic should be —

Ⓐ removed from the paragraph

B moved to another paragraph

C combined with other sentences

D added to another paragraph

9. What should you do with short, choppy sentences in a paragraph?

A remove them

B move them

C add to them

Ⓓ combine them

Achieve It! Practice Cards

176 ● Unit 8

Connect the Test to the Practice Cards (page 176)

Correct Answers	Related Practice Cards	Skill
3. **A**	**145, 146, 147**	**Transition words and sentences, Coherence**
4. **B**	**130**	**Write with a purpose**
5. **D**	**134, 135, 136, 137, 138**	**Introduction, body, and conclusion**
6. **B**	**129**	**Audience**
7. **D**	**142, 144, 146, 147, 148**	**Sentence variety, Coherence, Revising, Editing**
8. **A**	**142, 144, 146, 147, 148**	**Sentence variety, Coherence, Revising, Editing**
9. **D**	**142, 144, 146, 147, 148**	**Sentence variety, Coherence, Revising, Editing**

Unit 9 — Kinds of Writing

Unit 9

The "Write" Way

You read stories, poems, and articles in the newspaper or magazines all the time. They are written by other people. But you can write your own real or imaginary story. You can describe something that happened to you in a personal narrative. In a persuasive piece, you can try to change someone's opinion. Or maybe you need to give someone else directions for how to make or do something.

In this unit you will learn about different kinds of writing and the elements of each of them. There are so many ways to write!

177

Skills

- Recognizing elements of a narrative, including character, plot, setting, and order of events
- Writing creative, personal responses to texts
- Recognizing types of expository writing
- Recognizing elements of persuasive writing

Materials to Gather in Advance

- paper
- pencils
- crayons, markers, or colored pencils

Introducing the Unit

The "Write" Way Direct students to the photograph of the pen and the journal. Ask students what kind of information someone would put in a journal.

Ask *What kind of writing do you do at home?*

Ask *Do you ever write poems or stories just for yourself or someone you love? Do you ever write in a diary so that you remember what happened to you each day? Do you ever write letters?*

Ask students to think about why they write and to name some differences between writing about personal experiences and writing a report. Ask them whether things they write always have to be true.

Read the *The "Write" Way* paragraph aloud. Ask students to think about what kinds of books they like to read and why. Ask students to explain their opinions. Discuss why it is important to know about all kinds of writing.

Research Says

Because writing processes are closely tied to cognitive processes, a natural link exists between writing and thinking.

—*Dahl and Farnan*

Lesson 45

Objective

Students will recognize elements of a narrative, including character, plot, setting, and order of events.

Words to Know

Narrative—a story that describes events over a period of time

Order of events—the way events in a story happen over time

Elements—parts of a story

Characters—who a narrative is about

Plot—what a narrative is about

Setting—the time and place in which the events of a narrative happen

Personal narrative—a narrative in which the author writes about his or her own experiences

---

Study It

Discuss the elements of a *narrative* with the class. Read the opening paragraph to the class.

■ Direct students to the passage about Samantha. Ask the students to think about the elements of the story as you read it aloud.

Ask *What is the name of the main character in this narrative?* (Answer: *Samantha*)

Ask *What is the setting of this narrative?* (Answer: *Samantha's house, Saturday morning*)

Ask *What is this story about? What is the plot of the story?* (Answer: *Samantha has to get ready for her track meet.*)

Lesson 45 — What Happens Next?

Study It

Are you a fan of science fiction, adventures, mysteries, or true stories? **Narratives** come in many forms. Some narratives are made up. Other narratives, such as a newspaper article or another kind of true story have facts. You can write a narrative that describes events as you remember them, such as what happened on a trip you took. You can also make up a narrative that comes from your imagination. But no matter where the narrative comes from or what type of narrative it is, a narrative needs to have an **order of events.** The narrative should have a beginning, a middle, and an end.

- What happens first?
- What happens next?
- What happens after that?
- How does the story end?

If your narrative is a fictional story, it will usually have other parts, or **elements.** A fictional story has **characters.** It also has a **plot,** or problem, and a conclusion that solves the problem. Fictional stories also have **settings,** or a time and place where the story's events happen.

Read the story. Think about elements in the story and the order of events.

On Saturday Samantha woke up with a start. Why, she wondered, was she awake so early?

Then she remembered. Today was the day of the big track meet. She had been training for this for weeks.

Jumping out of bed, she put on her running clothes and grabbed her sneakers. She ran downstairs to find her father putting breakfast on the table.

"Thanks, Dad," Samantha said. She ate breakfast and brushed her teeth before pulling on her sneakers and tying them. "I'm ready to run!"

Samantha is the main character of the story. The events that happen to her are the action in the story. Her problem is solved because she knows she is prepared for the track meet. The order of events keeps the story moving in a way that makes sense.

178 • Unit 9   Narratives/stories

This page may not be reproduced without permission of Steck-Vaughn.

Curriculum and Assessment Standard

Narratives/stories

One kind of narrative is called a **personal narrative.** A personal narrative is a true story about something that happened to the person writing the story. The story often tells about an event and the author's ideas or thoughts about it. Usually an author describes his or her feelings in a personal narrative.

Read this personal narrative. Look for the parts of the story. Think about who is telling the story.

It was the last weekend of summer. Mario and I had been planning to camp out for weeks. Mario's backyard was the perfect place. There were so many trees that the yard seemed like a forest. A small creek even ran through it.

For days I had been feeling a little nervous about just the two of us sleeping outdoors all night. I was afraid that Mario would make fun of me if I said I was scared.

On Saturday morning Mario said, "Hey Daniel, is it OK if my dad camps out with us?"

"What a great idea!" I told him.

This story is a personal narrative because it is based on an event that happened to the author. The author, Daniel, is telling about his experience. He uses the word I to signal a personal story. Sometimes an author uses I in an imagined story, too.

Lesson 45 ● 179

- On the board draw a time line with a dot on the left end and an arrow on the right end. Write *Beginning* to the left of the time line, *Middle* above the time line, and *End* to the right of the end arrow.

  Ask *What are the events that happen in this narrative about Samantha?*

- Write student answers on the board until you have a list of at least five actions that happen in the story.

  Ask *What is the order of the events in the story?*

- Have students help you number the events in the order in which they occur. Then ask volunteers to plot the events on the time line.

- Direct students to the personal narrative and read the directions aloud. Ask a volunteer to read the passage aloud.

  Ask *What are the names of the two characters in this story?* (Answer: *Mario and Daniel*)

  Say *This story is told in a different way than the story you just read about Samantha.*

  Ask *How is it different? Who is telling the story in this narrative? How does the person telling the story talk about himself?* (Answer: *The story is told by Daniel, who refers to himself as "I" and talks about his feelings*)

Remind students that narratives can be true stories or they can be invented by the author. Help students understand that the story about Daniel and Mario could be a true story written by Daniel.

Differentiated Instruction
for ELL and auditory learners

A Collective Narrative

Students think of story elements to help create a group story.

Procedure

- Explain to students that in some parts of the world, telling a story in a group is an important part of life. Explain that sometimes people work together to tell stories.

- Organize the class into three groups, *Characters, Setting,* and *Events.*

- Ask the *Setting* group to think of a time and place for a story. Ask the *Characters* group to think of who will be in the story. Ask the *Events* group to think of events, or a problem for the characters to solve. Model a general problem by saying: *Two people are trying to get across a river.*

- Write the sentence *There once was a _____ named _____* on the board. Ask one student to start by completing the sentence. Then give each student a chance to add a sentence until the story's problem has a solution.

This page may not be reproduced without permission of Steck-Vaughn.

◢ Use It

Use this activity to help students think about the elements of a narrative.

■ Write the heading *Before Bed* on the board. Below the title, list the words *First, Next, Then,* and *Last.* Ask students to think of what they do to get ready for bed at night.

Ask *What is the first thing you do?*

■ Have one student respond to the question in a complete sentence. Write the sentence on the board, beginning with the word *First.*

Ask *What would you do next?*

■ Have another student complete the second sentence and write the sentence on the board. Continue until you have at least four sentences. Then read the sentences together.

Ask *If you were reading these sentences as a narrative, what would be the setting? Where and when would it take place?* (Answer: *at night, in my house*)

■ Direct students to the story and read the directions aloud. Copy the example question onto the board and read it aloud. Ask for a volunteer to read the first two sentences of the story aloud.

Ask *Does the first sentence tell you the first event?* (Answer: *No; it tells the setting.*)

Ask *Does the second sentence tell you the first event? What is the first event?* (Answer: *Yes; Roland pulls things out of his closet.*)

Have students read the rest of the story silently and complete items 1–4 independently. When they have finished, discuss their answers.

 Use It

Read this story. Look at the example. Then read the questions. Write the answers on the lines.

On Saturday morning Roland was in his room. He was wildly pulling things out of his closet. He had already checked under his bed. His library book was due today. He wanted to take it back so that he could get another book.

Roland was getting more and more worried that he would never find the book. He had searched everywhere. As he was looking through the books on his shelves, he heard his bedroom door open. When he turned around, he saw his dog Champ. Champ was gently carrying Roland's library book in his mouth.

"You're a great pal," Roland told Champ.

What is the first event in the story?
Roland wildly pulls things out of his closet.

Now you try it.

1. What would make the story a personal narrative?
   If Roland were to tell the story himself, using the pronoun I

2. What is the setting of the story?
   The story takes place in Roland's room on Saturday morning.

3. In the conclusion how is the problem solved?
   Champ brings in Roland's library book.

4. What happens right after Roland has searched everywhere?
   Roland looks through his books and hears his door open.

Practice It

Read the story. Then read the items. Circle the letter of the correct answer.

Olga lived in Chicago, Illinois. Her family lived close to the museum. One morning her friend Liza called to ask her to ride over to the museum. There was a new teddy bear exhibit that they both wanted to see.

After asking permission, Olga grabbed her bicycle helmet and ran outside. Then she saw it. The back tire of her bicycle was completely flat. Olga rushed into the house. Her mother was just leaving for the store.

"Could you please take me to the museum?" Olga asked.

"Hop in!" said her mother, opening the car door.

1. What is the first event in the story?

   A Olga lived in Chicago, Illinois.

   B Her family lived close to the museum.

   C Liza called Olga to ask her to ride over to the museum.

   D They both wanted to see the new teddy bear exhibit.

2. How is Olga's problem solved?

   A Liza invited her to the teddy bear exhibit.

   B Olga grabbed her bicycle helmet.

   C Olga's bicycle tire was flat.

   D Olga's mother agreed to give her a ride.

3. Which is the BEST clue that this story takes place in present time?

   A Chicago, Illinois

   B the museum

   C the teddy bear exhibit

   D the car door

Tip
When you write a narrative, be sure to tell the events in an order that makes sense.

Lesson 45 • 181

QAR Strategy

Strategy	Definition	How It Works
Right There	This strategy teaches students that the correct answer appears in one place in whatever they are reading.	Students look for the *key words* in the answer choices that match the words in the text. The match is sometimes, but not always, exact.

Refer to pages T22–T23 for a complete chart of QAR Strategies that students may use to achieve greater success on tests of reading comprehension.

Practice It

Work through the page to help students understand how the elements of a narrative work together to tell a story.

Question 1 Read the directions aloud. Then read question 1 and the *Tip* aloud. Have students complete question 1 independently and then stop.

To help students understand why *C* is the best answer, use the *Right There Strategy*. (See the *QAR Strategy* below.) Explain that this strategy uses *key words* to find the correct answer to a question.

Say *The correct answer has important words called* key words. *Sometimes the same key words are also in the passage. Other times, the key words in a correct answer mean the same thing as key words in the paragraph.*

Ask *Who can name the key words in the correct answer,* Liza called Olga to ask her to ride over to the museum? (Answer: *Liza, called, ride, museum*)

Say *Underline these keys words in answer* C.

Ask *Who can find these words in the passage?*

Say *Underline these words in the passage.*

Say *You have used the* Right There Strategy *to find the correct answer to question 1. The answer you needed was "right there."*

Questions 2 and 3 Ask students to complete questions 2 and 3 independently. When they have finished, discuss student answers.

This page may not be reproduced without permission of Steck-Vaughn.

Lesson 46

Objective

Students will write creative, personal responses to texts.

Words to Know

Respond—to explain opinions about a story

Study It

Discuss with students the idea of responding to a story.

- Write on the board the name of a story that most students are familiar with.

  Ask *If you were going to tell some-one about this story, would you repeat the story back to them word for word? If you did, would it help them under-stand how you feel about the story?* (Answers: *no; no*)

  Say *If you are writing about a story, the person reading your response might not have read the story. That is why you have to include important details from the story.*

- Write on the board: *The things that happened to her in the story were not good.* Read the sentence aloud.

  Ask *If this sentence were a response to a story, what seems to be missing? What questions would you want to ask so that you could understand this response?* (Answers: *Who is "she"? What things happened in the story? Why were they "not good"?*)

- Write the words *Introduction, Body,* and *Conclusion* on the board. Review the definitions of the words with the class.

- Direct students to the passage "The Secret Unicorn." Ask volunteers to real the story aloud.

Study It

When you read, you bring your own experiences and thoughts to the story to help you understand it.

You and a friend may have completely different views of a story that both of you have read. For example, you may think that the main character is brave. Your friend may think the character is foolish for taking too many chances.

After you read a story, you may want to **respond,** or write about it, to help others understand your point of view. First, write the story's title and the author's name. If there are pictures with the story, write the name of the person who drew them, too.

When you write your thoughts about the story itself, include examples from the story to support your ideas. Like any good essay, a written response should have an introduction, a body, and a conclusion. The introduction should state the main idea of your response. The body should give details from the story about the setting, the main character, and events from the plot that support your main idea. The conclusion should restate the main idea.

Read the following passage from "The Secret Unicorn" by Lloydene Cook. Look for story elements to use for writing a response.

> Tiffany reached out slowly and petted the goat's head. "What's your name?" she asked. "Where did you come from?"
>
> "BAAA. BAAAA," the goat answered, backing into the corner.
>
> "Don't be afraid. I won't hurt you," Tiffany said.
>
> Tiffany closed the shed door and went inside to tell her mother about the goat. "Let's go for a drive," said her mother. "Maybe we can find out who's missing a goat."
>
> A few miles down the road they saw a farmhouse and— another goat eating grass in the pasture.
>
> Tiffany and her mother knocked on the door of the house.

Response to literature

Curriculum and Assessment Standard

Response to literature

A chart can help you organize the important parts of the story.

Title: "The Secret Unicorn"

Author: Lloydene Cook

Parts of a Story	Examples from Story
Main Characters: Tiffany: kind and caring Mother: helpful and supportive	She is worried about the lost goat. She drives Tiffany to find the goat's owner.
Setting: Tiffany's house	Tiffany goes into her house to find her mother.
Problem: Lost goat	Tiffany asks the goat, "Where did you come from?"
Solution: Looks for the owner	The characters find a house that has another goat.

Your written response should include these important parts of the story, supported by details or examples.

Look at one reader's response to the story.

In "The Secret Unicorn," Tiffany lives in the country with her mother. Tiffany is a kind and caring person. I know this because she finds a lost goat and wants to help it find its home. She talks very nicely to the goat. She probably likes animals because she isn't afraid to pet the goat. She asks her mother to help her find the goat's home.

They find a house that has another goat in the yard. They think that the lost goat might live there. Tiffany and her mother knock on the door to ask.

Differentiated Instruction
for ELL, auditory, and visual learners

Responding with Pictures

Students will respond to texts with drawings and then write about their drawings.

Procedure

- Choose a story from the class library and read it aloud to the students.
- When you have finished, ask students to draw pictures that show how the story made them feel or that illustrate an event in the story.
- When they have finished, ask students to explain their pictures to the class and encourage other students to ask questions about the picture.
- Have students write three sentences that explain their drawings and how they relate to the story.

- Copy the headings from the chart to the board. Then copy the subheadings in the left column: Main Characters, Setting, Problem, Solution. For each story part, ask students to identify that part of the story.

  Ask *Who are the main characters in this story and what are they like?*

- Write each response on the board, and then ask the students to find an example from the text that proves their answer.

- Help students find the examples if necessary and model the process for them.

  Say *We know that Tiffany and her mother are caring because they try to return the goat safely to its home.*

- Continue to fill in the chart on the board with examples from the passage.

- Remind students that key information can be found in the introduction, body, and conclusion of a story that can help them respond to the story.

  Ask *What kind of information could you include in a response to help a reader who has not read the story?* (Answers: *title of the story, author, names of characters, setting, what happens in the story*)

- List answers on the board.

  Say *Once you have explained these elements, you can explain specific details and events in the story and how those events made you feel.*

Read the sample response aloud.

Use It

Use this section to let students identify elements of a passage.

- Read the *Use It* directions aloud. Then ask students to follow along as you read the passage aloud.

- Direct students to the chart below the passage. Copy the chart onto the board. Ask the following questions, and fill in the chart with the answers.

  Ask *What is the title of the story?* (Answer: *The BFG*)

  Ask *Are there any other characters in the story besides the Giant?* (Answer: *Sophie, the Goochey children*)

  Say *The chart says that the story takes place at night. What clue in the story tells the reader that it is nighttime?* (Answer: *The Goochey children are sleeping.*)

- Read the example of the story's "Problem" aloud.

  Ask *After reading this part, what do you think the plot, or problem, in this story is?*

Have students fill in the chart. When they have finished, ask for volunteers to share their answers. (Answer: *There is a giant outside the house at night doing strange things.*) Remind students that it is always important to use examples in the text to support their ideas.

Read the following passage from *The BFG* by Roald Dahl. Circle the main characters. Underline words that tell about the setting.

She saw the (Giant) step back a pace and put the suitcase down on the pavement. He bent over and opened the suitcase. He took something out of it. It looked like a glass jar, one of those square ones with a screw top. He unscrewed the top of the jar and poured what was in it into the end of the long trumpet thing.

(Sophie) watched, trembling.

She saw the Giant straighten up again and she saw him poke the trumpet in through the open upstairs window of the room where the Goochey children were sleeping. She saw the Giant take a deep breath and *whoof*, he blew through the trumpet.

Look at the chart. Fill in the missing information.

Title: The BFG

Author: Roald Dahl

Parts of a Story	Examples from Story
Main Characters: Giant, Sophie	Sophie watches the Giant.
Setting: nighttime	The children are asleep.
Problem: Giant outside the house, doing strange things	Sophie sees the Giant blow stuff into the Goochey children's window.

184 ● Unit 9

184 ■ Unit 9

Practice It

Read the story. Then read the questions. Circle the letter of the correct answer.

For the past two nights, Roberta had heard giggles and other sounds coming from the shed. She asked her mom about it, but her mom hadn't heard anything.

Roberta decided to wait near the shed one evening to find out what was making the sounds. When she heard the giggling, she peeked around the door. Two raccoons ran around on top of the garbage cans. They sounded as though they were giggling. Roberta crept away to get her mom.

1. **A written response should include —**

   (A) an introduction

   B all of the details from the story

   C a picture from the story

   D facts about the author

   Tip When you write a response to a story, be sure to include details from the story to support your ideas.

2. **Look at the chart.**

Parts of a Story	Examples from Story
Main Characters: Roberta	Roberta hears sounds.
Setting: nighttime	She hears sounds at night.
Problem: Roberta hears sounds in the shed.	
Solution: Raccoons make the noise.	Roberta sees raccoons playing on the garbage cans.

What detail is missing from the chart?

A Roberta knows that her brothers make the sounds.

(B) Roberta hides and watches to see what makes the sounds.

C Roberta is dreaming.

D Roberta's mother is cleaning the shed.

Lesson 46 ● 185

QAR Strategy

Strategy	Definition	How It Works
Right There	This strategy teaches students that the correct answer appears in one place in the passage they are reading.	Students *reread* the paragraph and look for the answer choices in the text. The match is sometimes, but not always, exact.

Refer to pages T22–T23 for a complete chart of QAR Strategies that students may use to achieve greater success on tests of reading comprehension.

Practice It

Work through the page to help students understand what the important elements of a good written response are.

Question 1 Ask students to complete question 1 independently. When they have finished, discuss student answers.

Help students recognize that only *A, an introduction* is something needed in a written response.

Question 2 Read question 2 and the *Tip* aloud. Have students work independently to find the missing example from the chart, circle the answer to complete question 2, and then stop. (Answer: *B, Roberta hides and watches to see what makes the sounds.*)

To help students understand why *B* is the best answer, use the *Right There Strategy.* (See the *QAR Strategy* below.) Explain that with this strategy, students can reread the passage to find the correct answer to a question.

Say *The correct answer is in the text, but not always in the same exact words. Sometimes you just need to reread the passage to see which of the answers are in the text.*

Say *First read the chart and the description of the plot problem. Then read all of the answers.*

Ask *Which answer do you see when you reread the text?* (Answer: *B*)

Say *You have used the* Right There Strategy *to find the correct answer to question 2. The answer you needed was "right there."*

Lesson 47

Objective

Students will recognize types of expository writing.

Word to Know

Expository—writing that explains something or gives information

◢ Study It

Discuss the definition of *expository* writing. Review the different examples of expository texts.

- Write the following paragraph on the board: *Many animals live in the sea. Some animals, like fish, swim in the water. Other animals crawl on the ocean floor. Some animals attach themselves to rocks.* Read the paragraph aloud.

  Ask *What kind of information is the author giving you?* (Answer: *information about sea animals*)

  Ask *What does the author say is similar about these animals?* (Answer: *they live in the sea*)

  Ask *What does the author say is different?* (Answer: *where the animals go and how they move*)

- Direct students to the chart.

  Say *Look at this chart that the author used to plan the passage.*

- Ask a student to read the topic sentence aloud.

  Ask *What is the author planning to write about?* (Answer: *how to make a sandwich*)

  Ask *What does the author write on the left side of the chart?* (Answer: *the things you need to make a peanut butter and jelly sandwich*)

  Ask *What does the author write on the right side of the chart?* (Answer: *the steps for making the sandwich*)

- Read through the steps in making a sandwich with the class.

Lesson 47 — Tell Me About It

◢ Study It

Suppose that you want to explain why a volcano erupts, or blows up. Maybe you want to give directions to explain how to make a model volcano.

Expository writing explains something or gives information to the reader. You can organize the information in different ways.

- Compare and contrast—You can explain how two things are alike and how they are different.
- "How to" do or make something—You can describe, step by step, how to make a snack or build a birdhouse, for example.
- Explain a cause and its effect—You can explain how something works or why something happens.
- Give directions on how to get somewhere—You can give simple directions in a list, or you can describe directions in more detail.

Before you write, plan how you want to show your information.

Look at this plan to explain how to make a peanut butter and jelly sandwich.

Plan for Writing Directions	
Topic Sentence: You can make a delicious peanut butter and jelly sandwich in minutes!	
Things Needed	**Steps to Follow**
• two slices of bread	1. First, put the slices of bread on a napkin or plate.
• peanut butter	2. Next, carefully spread peanut butter on one slice.
• jelly	3. Then, spoon some jelly onto the other slice of bread. Spread it around.
• dull knife to spread peanut butter	4. Pick up the slice of bread with peanut butter and place it, peanut-butter-side down, on top of the other slice.
• spoon for jelly	5. Finally, eat the sandwich!

186 ● Unit 9 — Expository writing

Curriculum and Assessment Standard

Expository writing

You can also use expository writing to explain a cause and effect. In this kind of writing, the author gives only the facts. The author's opinion or feelings about the topic are usually not in the passage.

The author begins with a topic. Then he or she gives details that explain how something happens. The author explains what happens and what causes that effect to happen. This kind of writing usually answers Who?, What?, When?, Where?, How?, and Why?

Read this passage. Think about how the author has organized the information.

> It starts with a tickle. Your eyes water. Your mouth opens. Ah . . . Ah . . . Ah-choo!
>
> You know how a sneeze feels, but do you know why we sneeze?
>
> Sneezing is the body's way of getting rid of something that is bothering the nose. When something starts to bother the inside of the nose, a message is sent to the brain. The brain tells the body to get rid of the bothersome thing. Then air is forced out of the nose and mouth at great speed.
>
> A sneeze is a reflex, or an action that happens automatically. You cannot control the action. Dust and pepper are some things that can cause you to sneeze. Some people sneeze when they go out into the sunlight or look at a bright light!

This passage answers the question "Why do we sneeze?"

Cause	Effect
Something starts to bother the inside of the nose.	A message is sent to the brain.
The brain tells the body to get rid of the bothersome thing.	Air is forced out of the nose and mouth at great speed.
Dust, pepper, sunlight, bright light	You may sneeze.

This page may not be reproduced without permission of Steck-Vaughn.

- Read the first two paragraphs to the class. Remind them what *cause* and *effect* mean. Ask them for examples so that you can check their understanding of cause and effect.

- Direct students to the passage. Remind students that some expository writing tells the reader the cause and effect of things. Ask the students to follow along as you read the passage aloud. Then give students a few minutes to underline the cause and effect relationships in the text.

- Have a student read the text in the first *Cause* box aloud.

  Ask *What happens when something starts to tickle the inside of your nose? What is the effect?* (Answer: *A message is sent to your brain.*)

- Have a student read the text in the second *Effect* box aloud.

  Ask *Why is air forced out of the nose and mouth at a great speed? What is the cause of this action?* (Answer: *The brain tells the body to get rid of it.*)

- Have student close their student books. Read the text in the last *Cause* box aloud.

  Ask *According to this author, what do dust, pepper, and sunlight or bright light sometimes cause?* (Answer: *sneezing*)

Differentiated Instruction
for ELL, auditory, and kinesthetic learners

How Do I Get There?

Students will give directions to other students.

Procedure

- Choose one place in the room and mark it as the starting point.
- Let students choose another place in the room (far from the starting point), and ask them to write directions for how to get there from the starting point.
- Stand at the starting point and ask a student to read his or her directions aloud. Follow the directions to try to get to the student's destination. If you cannot, ask other students how the directions could be changed.
- Let volunteers stand at the starting point while other students read their directions.

Use It

Use this section to let students find important details in an expository passage.

- Read the directions aloud. Ask for volunteers to read the passage aloud.

- Draw two overlapping circles on the board. Label one circle "Bikes" and label the other circle "Scooters." Label the overlapping area "Both."

- Have students read the passage again. Ask students to underline the words that compare and contrast, circle the facts that are only about bikes, and draw a box around the information that is only about scooters.

  Ask *Which words are clues that the author is comparing and contrasting bikes and scooters?* (Answer: *different, alike, both, but, both, However*)

  Ask *What is common to both bikes and scooters?* (Answer: *Children ride them, they have been around for many years, and both take balance.*)

- Write answers on the board in the *Both* area.

  Ask *What are some details about scooters only?* (Answer: *became popular recently, need one foot to push, easier to ride than bicycles*)

- Write answers on the board in the *Scooters* circle.

  Ask *If the author says that scooters are "easier to learn to ride," what is he or she saying about bikes?* (Answer: *that they are harder to learn to ride*)

  Ask *What else does the passage tell us about bikes?* (Answer: *You need two feet to pedal.*)

- Write the answer on the board in the *Bikes* circle.

Ask students to look at the Venn diagram in their book and compare it to the diagram on the board to find the details that are missing in the book.

Use It

Read this passage. Underline the words used to compare and contrast.

Children have <u>different</u> ways to get around today. Two of these ways are bikes and scooters. These are <u>alike</u> in many ways. <u>Both</u> have been around for many years, <u>but</u> scooters have become more popular recently. You need to pedal with two feet to ride a bike. On a scooter you just push with one foot. It takes good balance to ride <u>both</u> bikes and scooters. <u>However</u>, a scooter may be a little easier to learn to ride.

Look at the chart.

Bikes
1. hard to learn
2. _____

Both
1. ride them
2. _____
3. need to balance

Scooters
1. _____
2. push with one foot
3. recently became popular

1. What information is missing under "Bikes"?
   <u>pedal with two feet</u>

2. What information is missing under "Both"?
   <u>been around for many years</u>

3. What information is missing under "Scooters"?
   <u>a little easier to learn to ride</u>

This page may not be reproduced without permission of Steck-Vaughn.

Practice It

Read this passage from *Breathing* by John Gaskin. Then read each item. Circle the letter of the correct answer.

The air is made up of lots of different gases mixed together. There's only one that your body needs. It's called oxygen.

Each time you breathe in, your body takes the useful oxygen from the air. It sends the oxygen to all parts of your body.

As your body uses up the oxygen, it makes a waste gas. It is called carbon dioxide. Your body doesn't need this gas, so you get rid of it by breathing out.

Your body needs oxygen all the time. It takes just the right amount from the air you breathe.

1. **This passage is expository because it —**

   A describes a place

   B gives an opinion

   C gives information

   D tells a story

2. **What method did the writer use to organize the information in this passage?**

   A comparison and contrast

   B "how to" do something

   C description of the writer's opinion

   D cause and effect

> **Tip**
> If the purpose of a piece of writing is to give information, you know that the piece is an example of expository writing.

Lesson 47 • 189

QAR Strategy

Strategy	Definition	How It Works
Think and Search	This strategy teaches students that they have to put together different parts of the text to find the correct answer.	Students think about the main idea of the passage as they are searching for the answer. They remember that they may need to gather information from several places in the passage rather than find it in just one place.

Refer to pages T22–T23 for a complete chart of QAR Strategies that students may use to achieve greater success on tests of reading comprehension.

Practice It

Work through the page to help students identify the important parts of an expository text.

Question 1 Read the directions aloud. Then read question 1 and the *Tip* aloud. Have students read the passage silently. Ask them to circle the answer that best explains why this passage is expository writing.

To help student understand why *C* is the correct answer, explain the *Think and Search Strategy*. (See the *QAR Strategy* below.) Explain that with this strategy, it is important to reread the passage carefully with the question and answer choices in mind.

Say *First, read all of the answer choices. Then reread the passage.*

Say *Think about what the passage is about and summarize it.* For example, The author is explaining why we breathe and what gases our bodies use. *Now read the answer choices to find the best choice.*

Ask *Is the author describing a place?* (Answer: *no*)

Ask *Is the author giving an opinion or telling a story?* (Answer: *no*)

Say *Your summary should tell you that the passage is trying to give information. Your summary has helped you remember what you read and helped you find the best answer.*

Question 2 Read question 2 aloud, then have students complete it independently. Discuss students' answers.

Help students understand why *D* is the best answer.

Lesson 48

Objective

Students will recognize elements of persuasive writing.

Words to Know

Persuade—when a writer tries to get the reader to do or believe something

Study It

Discuss the definition of *persuasive* writing with the class.

- Ask students if they have ever tried to get someone to do something.

  Ask *Who did you try to convince? Your parents? A friend?*

  Ask *What did you say to try to persuade them? Did you point out the reasons why doing it would be good? Did you point out the reasons why not doing it would be bad?*

  Ask *Did you persuade the person to change his or her mind?*

- Work through the opening paragraphs with students. Allow volunteers to read aloud. Go over the bulleted items and ask students for examples to illustrate each item.

- Direct students to the passage about getting a dog. Have students follow along as you read the passage aloud.

  Ask *Who is the author writing this passage for? Who is the reader?* (Answer: *his or her family*)

  Ask *What is the author trying to convince the family to do?* (Answer: *get a dog*)

  Ask *What reasons does the author give for getting a dog?* (Answer: *protection, exercise*)

Lesson 48 — Change Your Mind

Study It

People try to get others to do things all the time. Ads in the newspaper and on TV are meant to persuade you to buy something or to go somewhere. You may try to talk a friend into letting you borrow her bike.

When you have a strong opinion or belief that you want someone else to share, you try to **persuade.** When you write to persuade, you give your opinion about something. Then you give evidence or reasons for your reader to agree with your opinion and take action. You want the reader to agree with you and act in a certain way.

When you write to persuade, you should

- clearly state your opinion in the first paragraph
- give reasons and details about why the reader should agree with your opinion
- retell your opinion and let the reader know what action you want taken and when you want it done

Read this persuasive passage.

> I think it is important for our family to have a dog. We have never had a dog before. Dogs make great pets because they are friendly.
>
> Many of my friends have dogs, and I think I am old enough to take care of one, too. I can get exercise while I walk it every day. Exercise is good for me, and the dog would help me get it. If we got a big dog, it could protect our house.
>
> A family dog would be a great thing to have. I would like to have a family meeting right away to talk about getting one.

Curriculum and Assessment Standard

Persuasive writing

Notice how the writer follows the steps in writing to persuade.

1. The writer clearly states an opinion in the first paragraph.

   I think it is important for our family to have a dog.

2. The writer gives reasons for getting a dog.

   Dogs make great pets.

   He or she would get exercise when walking the dog.

   A dog could protect the family's home.

3. The writer retells the opinion and states the action that he or she wants to have happen.

   A family dog would be a great thing to have.

   I would like to have a family meeting right away.

Read this persuasive passage.

Most schools offer P. E., or physical education, as an important part of learning. P. E. classes help us stay healthy. Yet our school does not offer one of the best physical activities, swimming, because we don't have a pool. Our school needs a pool for a number of reasons.

Swimming exercises every muscle in the body. Swimming is also a skill that could save a life someday. During the summer the entire city could use the pool for exercise and for classes that teach swimming.

At the next school board meeting, I urge the members to discuss building a pool at our school.

Opinion	Reasons	Action
Our school needs a pool.	1. good exercise 2. swimming lessons 3. used by the whole town	School board should discuss building a pool.

In this passage the writer's opinion is clear. There are reasons and details to support the opinion. The last sentence tells what action the writer would like to have happen.

Lesson 48 ● 191

- Point out to students that there are three steps to writing a good persuasive piece. Discuss the steps:

  Step 1—State an opinion.

  Step 2—Give reasons for your opinion.

  Step 3—Retell the opinion and explain what action the reader should take next.

- List the three steps on the board.

- Direct students to the passage. Ask for volunteers to read the passage aloud.

  Ask *What is the author's opinion?* (Answer: *The school needs a pool.*) Write the answer on the board next to Step 1.

  Ask *What reasons does the author give for wanting a pool?* (Answer: *Swimming exercises every muscle, students could learn lifesaving skills, and the whole pool could be used by town.*) List the answers on the board next to Step 2.

  Ask *What is the last thing the author does?* (Answer: *states the action that the reader should do*)

  Ask *What does the author want the reader to do?* (Answer: *discuss the pool at the next meeting*) Write the answer on the board next to Step 3.

Point out the chart with the three steps. Help students understand how these three steps work together. Discuss the explanation of the passage below the chart.

Differentiated **I**nstruction
for ELL and auditory learners

Power of Persuasion

Students will persuade other students to do or not do something.

Procedure

- Ask a volunteer to name one thing that he or she does not like to do. Write that activity on the board.

- Divide the class into two groups, one *To Do* group and one *Not to Do* group.

- Ask the *To Do* group to come up with reasons why the volunteer should do the activity.

- Ask the *Not to Do* group to come up with reasons why the volunteer should not do the activity.

- Have groups take turns reading their reasons.

- Ask the volunteer to tell which reasons were more convincing and why.

Use It

Use this section to let students demonstrate what they have learned about persuasive writing.

■ Draw three boxes on the board with arrows connecting the boxes using the chart as a model. Copy the headings from all three boxes and the numbers from the second box.

■ Read the directions aloud. Then have a volunteer read the first paragraph of the passage aloud.

Ask *What does the writer state in this paragraph: an opinion, reasons, or an action to take?* (Answer: *an opinion*)

Ask *What is the author's opinion?* (Answer: *Everyone should get a library card.*)

■ Have a student write the answer in the first box on the board. Then ask for a volunteer to read the second paragraph aloud.

Ask *What does the writer state in this paragraph: an opinion, reasons, or an action to take?* (Answer: *reasons*)

Say *Underline the reasons.*

Ask *What are the reasons the author gives?* (See chart for the answers.)

■ Have students write the answers in the second box on the board as they respond. Help students compare the chart on the board to the chart in their book and have them fill in the missing reasons. Then ask a student to read the last paragraph aloud.

Ask *What does the writer state in this paragraph: an opinion, reasons, or an action to take?* (Answer: *an action*)

Say *Circle the action.*

Ask *What is the action the author wants the reader to take?* (Answer: *Get a library card.*)

Have a student fill in the last box on the board and ask students to add the missing information to the chart in their book.

Use It

Read this persuasive passage. Put a box around the writer's opinion. Underline the reasons for the opinion. Circle the action that the writer hopes will happen.

Going to the public library is a lot of fun. The library has many exciting books. Everyone should get a library card.

If you have a library card, you can check out books, tapes, and movies. Some libraries have reading programs during the summer. If you read a lot of books, you might get a prize. Libraries have story time and visits from authors. You might find computers in the library, too. The library is a great place to learn how to use a computer.

Books are exciting and libraries are the place to find them. If I were you, I would get a library card right away!

Fill in the blanks with the missing reasons and action.

Opinion	Reasons	Action
Everyone should get a library card.	1. check out books, tapes, movies 2. reading programs 3. a prize 4. story time 5. author visits 6. computers	get library card

Practice It

Read this persuasive passage. Then read the questions. Circle the letter of the correct answer.

All students should belong to an after-school club. No matter what you are interested in, there is something fun you can do after school.

Being part of a club is exciting. You can share the same interests with other students. If you like to play chess, you can join the chess club. Students who like to be active can join the dance group.

No matter what you like to do, there is a club for you. Sign up today and become part of an after-school club.

1. **A persuasive passage should always have —**

   A main characters

   B reasons for the opinion

   C descriptive words

   D a setting

2. **What is the writer's opinion in this passage?**

   A Students like to have fun.

   B Students have many different interests.

   C You should be part of the chess club.

   D Every student should join an after-school club.

Tip
When you write to persuade, be sure to give reasons for your opinion.

Practice It

Work through the page to help students understand how authors express their opinions in persuasive writing.

Question 1 Read the directions aloud. Then read question 1 and the *Tip* aloud. Have students read the passage silently. Ask them to circle the answer that best explains why this passage is considered persuasive writing.

To help students understand why *B* is the correct answer, discuss the incorrect answers.

Question 2 Read question 2 aloud, then have students complete question 2 independently. Discuss student answers.

To help students understand why *D* is the best answer, use the *Think and Search Strategy.* (See the *QAR Strategy* below.) Explain that with this strategy, students reread the passage to find the best answer.

Say *First, think about what you know about persuasive writing.*

Ask *Where in the passage does the author usually state his or her opinion?* (Answer: *in the first paragraph*)

Say *Then, reread the first paragraph of the passage to find the writer's opinion. Underline the sentence with the writer's opinion.*

Ask *Which sentence in the first paragraph best states the author's opinion?* (Answer: *the first sentence—"All students should belong to an after-school club."*)

Ask *Which answer best matches this sentence?* (Answer: *D, Every student should join an after-school club.*)

Say *You have reread the passage and found the answer in several different places. That is how to use the* Think and Search Strategy.

QAR Strategy

Strategy	Definition	How It Works
Think and Search	This strategy teaches students that they have to put together information from different parts of the text to find the correct answer.	Students think about the answer they are looking for as they reread the text. They remember that they may need to find key information throughout the text rather than in just one place.

Refer to pages T22–T23 for a complete chart of QAR Strategies that students may use to achieve greater success on tests of reading comprehension.

▬ Teach the Strategy

Write on the board: *It was a stormy night. Julia could not sleep. She got out of bed and walked to the kitchen.*

Ask *Where does this story take place? What is the setting?* (Answer: *nighttime; Julia's house*)

Ask *What is the name of the character in this story?* (Answer: *Julia*)

Ask *What is the problem in this story?* (Answer: *Julia cannot sleep.*)

Ask *What would be a logical solution for this story?*

Look for Story Elements Strategy

Explain that noticing the elements of the story is a test-taking strategy called the *Look for Story Elements Strategy.*

- Write these answers under the paragraph on the board:

  A Julia wakes up.

  B Julia goes back to bed.

  C Julia makes some tea so she can fall asleep.

  D Julia goes outside to sit in the sun.

- Ask students to use the strategy to find the correct answer. (Answer: *C*)

- Discuss the strategy page in the student book.

Try It Out

Read the directions aloud and have students complete this section independently. Encourage them to use the *Look for Story Elements Strategy* to find the answer.

Have volunteers explain their answers.

Ask *How did knowing the elements of the story help you find the answer?*

Discuss the explanation that follows the question in the student book.

Test-Taking Strategy

Strategy: Look for Story Elements

In this unit you learned that narratives have certain elements.

- characters
- setting
- problem or plot
- solution

When you read questions on a test about a story, ask yourself *Who is this story mostly about? Where does the story take place? What is the problem or the plot? How is the problem solved?*

Try It Out

Read the story. Look for the story elements. Then read the item. Circle the letter of the correct answer.

> Gabriella, Erica, and Aaron had gone to the park to play baseball. Erica was at bat. She hit the ball hard. Then there was a loud crash that sounded like breaking glass.
> Just then Ms. Givens drove up to the park. A window in her car was broken. "Which one of you hit that ball?" she asked.
> "I did," said Erica. "I'm really sorry. I don't have money to pay for a new car window."
> "That's OK," said Ms. Givens. "Maybe you can come by my house tomorrow and help paint my fence instead."
> "I'll be there," said Erica.

What is the problem in this story?

(A) Erica has broken Ms. Givens's window.

B There is no place to play baseball.

C Ms. Givens needs help painting her fence.

D Gabriella has lost her baseball mitt.

Think about what happens in the story. The friends heard a crash after Erica hit the ball. The ball had hit Ms. Givens's car window and broken it. So, **A** is the correct answer.

194 ● Unit 9

Put It to the Test

Name _____

This test will check what you have learned in this unit.

DIRECTIONS: Read the passage. Circle the letter of the correct answer.

Sign Up Now

This year will be the best ever at summer camp. At Camp ChiChiWa, we will be having lots of fun. Campers will learn to canoe and fish. If you like cooking, there will be a special class for young chefs. For those campers who like to hike, our trails promise lots of exercise and wildlife. Our new cabins have bunk beds and showers. No more hiking across camp to get clean!

Our counselors have planned many craft classes from papermaking to painting. They have lots of hikes planned. Our counselors are full of energy and tell good stories. Plus, they are all trained in CPR and water safety.

So if you don't have plans for this summer, ask your parents to sign you up for a week of fun at Camp ChiChiWa. See you there!

1. **The purpose of this passage is to —**

   A give facts about craft classes

   B give directions to the camp

   C persuade you to go to camp

   D tell a story about camp

2. **What action does the writer want you to take?**

   A learn to canoe

   B take a chef's class

   C have a fun summer

   D talk to your parents

3. **This passage gives information about —**

   A a summer camp

   B water safety

   C exercise

   D hiking

GO ON

Achieve It! Practice Cards

_____

Put It to the Test • 195

Connect the Test to the Practice Cards (page 195)

Correct Answers	Related Practice Cards	Skill
1. **C**	159, 160, 161	Persuasive
2. **D**	159, 160, 161	Persuasive
3. **A**	159, 160, 161	Persuasive

▬ Put It to the Test

Students will:

■ demonstrate what they have learned

■ identify skills that require more practice before students achieve proficiency*

*Refer to pages T17–T19 for a complete explanation and directions for using *Achieve It!* Practice Cards.

Administer the Test

Explain that students will now practice the skills from this unit by taking a short test. Tell students that the test has items like those they will find on standardized tests. Explain that you will read the directions aloud. Remind students to pay close attention and to follow your directions exactly.

Say *Open your books to page 195. I will read the directions aloud.* Read the directions to students. Then continue.

Say *You will have 20 minutes to finish this test. Read each item and the answer choices carefully. Circle the letter of the correct answer. When you reach the words* GO ON *at the bottom of a page, turn the page and continue working. When you reach the word* STOP *at the bottom of a page, stop working and put down your pencil. Are there any questions?*

If students have no questions,

Say *You may begin.*

At the end of 20 minutes,

Say *Stop. Check to be sure that you have circled the letter of the correct answer. Erase any stray pencil marks. Then put down your pencil.*

Assign Practice Cards

After scoring a student's test, note which items the student missed. Match each incorrectly answered item to the related *Achieve It!* Practice Cards listed in the chart on this page.

In the *Achieve It!* Practice Cards space in each student's book, write all of the Practice Cards you want the student to complete.

4. **Which sentence tells you the writer's opinion about the camp?**

   A Campers will learn to canoe and fish.

   B No more hiking across camp to get clean!

   C Plus, they are all trained in CPR and water safety.

   D This year will be the best ever at summer camp.

5. **What is the main idea of this passage?**

   A This summer will be the best ever at Camp ChiChiWa.

   B Camp ChiChiWa offers all kinds of classes.

   C Children should ask parents to sign them up for camp.

   D The counselors are trained in CPR and water safety.

6. **What is one of the details in this passage?**

   A Campers will learn to canoe and fish.

   B All campers need sunscreen.

   C Campers must know how to swim.

   D Campers will hike two miles every day.

7. **What sentence might be included in a written response to this passage?**

   A Most children do not like camp.

   B This camp is too far away.

   C I think this camp sounds like a lot of fun.

   D Camp is for younger children.

8. **Who would be the best audience for this passage?**

   A children who like to stay at home

   B parents who want to go to camp

   C teachers who want to be counselors

   D children who like camp

9. **The conclusion in an expository passage should —**

   A include an introduction

   B restate the main idea

   C have a lot of details

   D state an opinion

Achieve It! Practice Cards

_____

Connect the Test to the Practice Cards (page 196)

Correct Answers	Related Practice Cards	Skill
4. D	159, 160, 161	Persuasive
5. C	159, 160, 161	Persuasive
6. A	159, 160, 161	Persuasive
7. C	155, 156, 157	Response to literature
8. D	155, 156, 157	Response to literature
9. B	158, 163	Expository

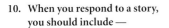

10. **When you respond to a story, you should include —**

    A a lengthy conclusion

    B the author's picture

    C an introduction and setting

    (D) details about the characters, the setting, and the plot

11. **The conclusion of a story usually —**

    A gives the author's name

    B tells the problem of the story

    (C) tells the solution to the problem

    D describes the main characters

12. **You would use expository writing to —**

    A tell a story

    (B) give information about a topic

    C write a thank-you note

    D write a poem

13. **If you wanted to explain how dogs and cats are alike and different as pets, you could organize the information using —**

    A cause and effect

    (B) comparison and contrast

    C directions

    D persuasion

14. **When you respond to a story, you want the reader to understand —**

    A who your favorite author is

    B how many books you read this year

    C your favorite kind of poetry

    (D) your point of view about the story

15. **A passage that gives directions would probably use the words —**

    A both, unlike, like

    B because, if, why

    (C) first, next, then

    D who, when, how

Achieve It! Practice Cards

Connect the Test to the Practice Cards (page 197)

Correct Answers	Related Practice Cards	Skill
10. **D**	**155, 156, 157**	**Response to literature**
11. **C**	**149, 150, 151, 152**	**Narratives**
12. **B**	**158, 163**	**Expository**
13. **B**	**158, 163**	**Expository**
14. **D**	**155, 156, 157**	**Response to literature**
15. **C**	**163**	**Write directions**

Additional Practice Cards

The following cards cover additional skills for

Unit 9: Kinds of Writing

Card	Topic
153	Poems
162	Write summaries
164	Formal letters
165	Informal letters

You may want to assign these cards as practice for students who have done well on the unit test or as extended practice for all students.

No Soup for Me!

One day I said to my grandmother, "Let's help out at the soup kitchen downtown." We walked to the kitchen on Saturday morning.

I thought I would just hand out bowls of soup. Everybody would thank me and think I was so helpful. Was I surprised!

Instead of serving soup, I wound up washing and peeling a mountain of potatoes. It took hours. My hands got sore and wrinkly. I kept dropping potatoes. People yelled, "Hurry up! We need potatoes for the soup!"

I never got to serve a bowl of soup. At the end of the day, my grandmother said, "Lisa, I'm hungry. What should we eat?" I cried, "Anything but soup or potatoes!"

16. **This story is a —**
   A reader's response
   (B) personal narrative
   C set of directions
   D persuasive passage

17. **"Saturday morning" tells you about the story's —**
   A plot
   B characters
   (C) setting
   D problem

18. **The first thing Lisa and her grandmother do in this story is —**
   (A) decide to help at the soup kitchen
   B wash and peel potatoes
   C hand out bowls of soup
   D eat soup and potatoes for dinner

19. **Which words from the story BEST tell time order?**
   A One day
   B Hurry up
   C Instead
   (D) At the end of the day

STOP

Achieve It! Practice Cards

Connect the Test to the Practice Cards (page 198)

Correct Answers	Related Practice Cards	Skill
16. **B**	149, 150, 151, 152, 154	Narratives, Dialogue
17. **C**	149, 150, 151, 152, 154	Narratives, Dialogue
18. **A**	149, 150, 151, 152, 154	Narratives, Dialogue
19. **D**	149, 150, 151, 152, 154	Narratives, Dialogue

Unit 10 Language Rules

The Writing Game

The first chess game was probably played in the sixth century. By the nineteenth century, the rules of chess were still changing. When people play chess, everyone has to follow the same rules. If someone breaks the rules in chess, the game will not be enjoyable. It is the same with writing. If you do not follow the rules of language when you are writing, readers will not like or understand what you have written.

In this unit you will learn several language rules. These rules will help you write clear sentences so that people will understand your ideas and enjoy reading what you write.

199

Research Says

Researchers suggest that integrating grammar study with reading and writing produces the best results.

— *Noyce and Christie*

Skills

- Identifying different parts of speech in sentences
- Using subjects and verbs that agree with each other
- Distinguishing between different sentence types
- Recognizing sentences in which commas are necessary and using commas correctly
- Understanding when to use uppercase letters
- Using what is learned about grammar and spelling to become stronger and more competent writers

Materials to Gather in Advance

- index cards
- scissors
- masking tape (or any tape that can easily be peeled off paper)
- slips of paper for each student
- pencils

Introducing the Unit

The Writing Game Have students look at the photograph of the chess board. Explain to students that there are rules for many activities, including games. The rules are in place so the game is played correctly. Without the rules, it would be difficult to play, and players would not understand one another's moves.

Explain that language has its own rules, just like the game of chess. Ask students to think about a time when they said something to someone and were not understood.

Say *Sometimes I might know what I meant to say, but another person doesn't understand me and doesn't know what I meant to say.*

Ask *How can we avoid being misunderstood?* (Answer: *by using the same grammar and punctuation rules*)

Read *The Writing Game* paragraph aloud. Explain that this unit will give students a set of rules to work with when they are writing.

Lesson 49

Objective

Students will identify and correctly use parts of speech.

Words to Know

Part of speech—a word, such as a noun or verb, that is part of a sentence

Noun—a word that names a person, place, or thing

Pronoun—a word that takes the place of a noun

Verb—a word that shows action or a state of being

Tense—tells when an action takes place

Adjective—a word that describes a noun or pronoun

Adverb—a word that describes an adjective, verb, or another adverb

Preposition—a word that shows how parts of a sentence are connected

Conjunction—a word that joins other words, phrases, or clauses

Study It

■ Review the different parts of speech. List examples on the board as students name them.

Ask *What part of speech is* Susan*?* (Answer: *noun*)

Ask *Can you tell me some other nouns?* (Answers will vary.)

Ask *Can you name some verbs?* (Answers will vary.)

Have students correctly identify parts of speech in a sentence.

Step 1—Write the following sentence on the board: *Jonas and his friends played ball at the park with their dogs.*

Step 2—Ask students to underline the nouns in the sentence. (Answer: *Jonas, friends, ball, park, dogs*)

Step 3—Direct students to rewrite the sentence substituting different nouns for the ones they identified.

200 ■ Unit 10

Lesson 49 · Word Work

Study It

Each word in a sentence is a **part of speech**. Each part of speech does a different job in a sentence. Understanding a word's job will help you use words correctly.

The main parts of speech are **nouns, pronouns, adjectives, verbs, adverbs, prepositions,** and **conjunctions.**

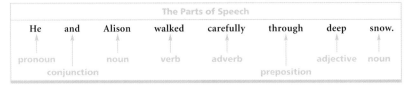

The Parts of Speech							
He	and	Alison	walked	carefully	through	deep	snow.
pronoun		noun	verb	adverb		adjective	noun
	conjunction				preposition		

Noun: A **noun** is a person, place, or thing.

Alison used her **snowboard** in Vermont when she visited Matt.

Pronoun: A **pronoun** also names people or things. A pronoun takes the place of a noun.

Three forms of pronouns are subject pronouns, object pronouns, and possessive pronouns.

● Subject pronouns take the place of the subject. I, you, he, she, it, we, they, and who are subject pronouns.

When Alison was in Vermont, **she** tried the new snowboard.

● Object pronouns take the place of a noun that follows an action verb. Object pronouns include me, you, him, her, it, us, them, and whom.

Matt tried the snowboard, too. He liked **it**.

● Possessive pronouns show ownership. My, your, his, her, its, our, and their are possessive pronouns that tell to whom or what something belongs.

Matt said, "I like the way **your** snowboard feels under **my** feet."

Mine, yours, his, hers, ours, and theirs are possessive pronouns that stand alone.

"I wish I had a snowboard like **yours**," Matt told Alison.

200 ● Unit 10   Parts of speech

Curriculum and Assessment Standard

Parts of speech

Verb: A **verb** shows an action or a state of being in a sentence. To help you decide whether a word is a verb, ask *Does it show what happens (action)?* or *Does it show what is (state of being)?*

Matt **said,** "You always **wear** that hat." Alison **answered,** "Yes, it **is** my favorite, but I **will wear** my other hat tomorrow."

Verbs also have **tenses.** Tenses tell when the action takes place.

- Past tense shows that the action has already happened. **Regular** verbs form the past tense by adding *–ed.* **Irregular** verbs form the past tense differently. The chart shows some irregular verbs.
- Present tense shows that the action happens often or is happening now.
- Future tense shows that the action will happen. In the sentence above, <u>will wear</u> is in the future tense.

Irregular Verbs	
Present	**Past**
break	broke
go	went
know	knew
say	said
think	thought
write	wrote

Adjective: An **adjective** tells how a noun or pronoun looks, acts, sounds, smells, tastes, or feels. To help you decide whether a word is an adjective, ask *What kind?, Which one?,* or *How many?*

Matt wore his **old brown** jacket.

The words <u>a</u>, <u>an</u>, and <u>the</u> are special adjectives called **articles.**

Adverb: An **adverb** tells about a verb, an adjective, or another adverb. To help you decide whether a word is an adverb, ask *When?, Where?, How?,* or *How much?*

Matt skied **quickly** down the hill.
The mountain was **very** beautiful.

Preposition: A **preposition** shows how two parts of a sentence are related, or tied to one another. Some prepositions are <u>to</u>, <u>with</u>, <u>out</u>, <u>over</u>, <u>near</u>, <u>across</u>, <u>in</u>, <u>of</u>, <u>under</u>, <u>before</u>, and <u>along</u>. Nouns or pronouns follow prepositions. The combination of a preposition, a noun or a pronoun, and the words between them is called a **prepositional phrase.**

He came **from** the market. She climbed **over** the mountain.

Conjunction: A **conjunction** joins words or ideas. Common conjunctions are <u>and</u>, <u>or</u>, <u>but</u>, and <u>so</u>.

Alison **and** Matt skied all day, **but** they never fell.

Lesson 49 ● 201

Continue having students write sentences and focusing on using different parts of speech.

- Ask students to change the verb tense in the previous sentence about Jonas and his friends. Direct students to make the sentence take place in the present or future.
- Challenge students to add three adjectives to the sentence about Jonas.
- Have students add one adverb to the sentence. Ask volunteers to share versions of their sentences.

If students need more practice, have them continue writing sentences. Ask them to include certain parts of speech in each sentence. For example: *Write a sentence that contains three adjectives about your favorite book.*

Differentiated Instruction
for ELL, visual, and tactile learners

Mix and Match
Students will make cards to represent each part of speech and will trade cards with each other to form complete sentences.

Procedure
- Organize the class into seven groups. Give each group a pair of scissors and 21 index cards.
- Assign a different part of speech to each group.
- Each group member will make three cards. Each card should have one word written on it. For instance, a student from the *verbs* group could write *run, walk,* and *swim.*
- Give students 5–10 minutes to exchange cards with other groups until each group can put together at least one complete sentence that includes at least a noun, a verb, an adjective or adverb, and a pronoun.

Use It

Use this activity to have students identify parts of speech.

- Write on the board: *The brown, spotted cat quickly ran behind the old car and sat down.*

- Create a chart on the board like this one, and have students fill it in by using words from the sentence.

   Ask *What part of speech is the word* spotted *in this sentence? What does it describe?* (Answer: *An adjective; It describes the noun,* cat.)

   Ask *What part of speech is the word* behind *in this sentence?* (Answer: *a preposition*)

   Ask *Are there any adverbs in the sentence?* (Answer: *yes—quickly, down*)

Complete the chart with students, making sure to identify the part of speech for each word in the sentence. Then read the *Use It* directions aloud. Have students complete the page independently. Ask volunteers to share their answers.

Use It

Read the passage. Decide what part of speech each word is.

Yesterday was a warm spring day. Martin and I drank raindrops. He jumped high in deep puddles. He got his shoes muddy. We ran quickly and skipped through his large garden on the wet path.

Look at the chart. Fill in the blanks with words from the passage. Write each word next to its correct part of speech.

Part of Speech	Words
Noun	day, Martin, __raindrops__, __puddles__, __shoes__, garden, __path__
Pronoun	I, He, He, __his__, __We__, __his__
Verb	was, drank, jumped, __got__, __ran__, __skipped__
Adjective	a, warm, spring, deep, __muddy__, __large__, the, __wet__
Adverb	Yesterday, high, __quickly__
Preposition	in, __through__, __on__
Conjunction	__and__, __and__

Read the passage. Look at the underlined verbs. Then fill in the chart below.

Verb	Tense
is	present
clean	present
said	past
looked	past
thought	past
will clean	future

"Abby, your room is a mess. Please clean it up," said Abby's mother.

Abby looked at the toys and clothes on the floor. "Maybe my mother is right," Abby thought. "I will clean this up tonight."

Read each item. Circle the letter of the correct answer.

1. | John wrote a long letter to Lia and <u>me</u>. |

   The <u>underlined</u> word is a —

   A noun

   Ⓑ pronoun

   C adjective

   D verb

2. | He hid <u>under</u> his bed during the game of hide and seek. |

   The <u>underlined</u> word is a —

   A pronoun

   B adjective

   C verb

   Ⓓ preposition

3. Which word below is an irregular verb?

   A jumped

   B talked

   C guessed

   Ⓓ brought

4. Which word below is a preposition?

   A she

   B talk

   Ⓒ in

   D quickly

Tip
Ask questions to help you find a word's part of speech.

Practice It

Work through the page with students to be sure they understand the different parts of speech.

Question 1 Read the directions aloud. Ask students to complete question 1 independently and then stop. Then help students recognize why *B* is the correct answer.

Question 2 Read the sentence aloud. Ask students to identify the underlined word and to circle the letter of the correct answer. (Answer: *D, preposition*)

Discuss students' answers. Help students recognize that *under* is an example of a preposition. To help students understand the correct answer, explain the incorrect answers.

● *A* is a pronoun that takes the place of a noun. ● *B* is an adjective that describes a noun or a pronoun. ● *C* is a verb that shows an action or state of being.

Questions 3 and 4 Repeat the process used with question 1, and help students understand the difference between regular and irregular verbs. For question 4 be sure that students go over each incorrect choice to make sure that students understand why it was not the right answer.

Lesson 50

Objective

Students will correctly use subjects and verbs that agree in number.

Words to Know

Singular subject—one person, place, or thing

Plural subject—more than one person, place, or thing

Compound subject—two or more subjects joined by *and*

■ Study It

Read about *singular, plural,* and *compound* subjects with students.

■ Review singular and plural subjects and the correct verb forms to use in each case.

Ask *What kind of subject is* she? *What form of* to go *would* she *take in a sentence?* (Answer: *singular; she goes*)

Ask *What about* you? (Answer: *Be sure students understand that* you *can be both singular and plural.*)

Ask *If your subject were* Monica and Steve, *what form of* eat *would you use in a sentence and why?* (Answer: *plural—eat; Compound subjects take plural form.*)

Continue to have students use subjects and verbs that agree.

Subjects and Verbs Agree

■ Study It

How do you know which verb to use in a sentence? It depends on the subject of the sentence. The subject tells <u>who</u> or <u>what</u> the sentence is about. Subjects are usually nouns or pronouns.

The subject and verb must always agree in number.

- A singular subject is one person, place, or thing. A singular subject takes a singular verb. The pronouns <u>he</u>, <u>she</u>, and <u>it</u> are also singular subjects.

  Jonathan likes his new sweater. It looks comfortable.

  Are you going swimming?

<u>You</u> can be singular or plural. Sometimes <u>you</u> is a group of people. At other times, <u>you</u> is one person.

- A plural subject is more than one person, place, or thing. A plural subject takes a plural verb. The pronouns <u>we</u>, <u>you</u>, and <u>they</u> are also plural subjects.

  The **boys paddle** the canoe. **They prepare** the meals.

Subjects and verbs agree even when other words come between them. Watch for **compound subjects,** two or more subjects joined by a conjunction. Compound subjects joined by <u>and</u> need a plural verb.

  Jonathan and Keesha like lemonade.

  Greg and his sisters sing in the play.

<u>Jonathan and Keesha</u> is a compound subject. The verb <u>like</u> is a plural verb. The subject of the second sentence is <u>Greg and his sisters</u>. This is also a compound subject, so the verb <u>sing</u> is plural.

Subjects and verbs must also agree when the verb comes before the subject.

  On the desk are two pencils.

The verb <u>are</u> comes before the subject <u>pencils</u>. The subject is plural, so the verb <u>are</u> agrees with the subject.

204 ● Unit 10   Subject-verb agreement

Curriculum and Assessment Standard

Subject-verb agreement

Use It

The subject and the verb in each sentence are <u>underlined</u>. If the subject and verb agree, write **agree** in the blank. If they do not agree, write the correct verb in the blank. Look at these examples.

_____agree_____ 1. The <u>firefighter</u> <u>hooks</u> the ladder to the fire truck.

_____are_____ 2. A <u>whale</u> and a <u>seal</u> <u>is</u> two animals that swim.

Now you try it.

_____wants_____ 1. <u>Greg</u>, like his sisters, <u>want</u> to see the movie.

_____are_____ 2. <u>Is</u> <u>Nina</u> and <u>Isa</u> ready to go?

_____agree_____ 3. <u>She</u> <u>has</u> a green notebook.

Practice It

Read each sentence. Choose the answer that will correct the underlined words. Circle the letter of the correct answer.

1. | The <u>train</u> <u>pull</u> into the station early in the morning. |

   A trains pulls

   (B) train pulls

   C train are pulling

   D correct as is

2. | The <u>flag</u> <u>flap</u> in the breeze. |

   A flag are flapping

   B flags flaps

   (C) flags flap

   D correct as is

Tip
Before you choose a verb, ask yourself whether the subject is singular or plural.

Lesson 50 • 205

Differentiated Instruction
for tactile and visual learners

Choose the Right Words

Filling in missing verbs will give students another opportunity to practice using subjects and verbs that agree with each other in number.

Procedure

- Tell students to write a short story about a loud noise. Have them tell where the noise was heard, who heard the noise, and what caused it. Students' stories should be 5–7 sentences long. Remind them to be sure that their subjects and verbs agree.

- After students have completed their stories, have students place a strip of tape over all the verbs in their stories.

- Have students exchange papers with partners. Students will then read the other student's story and write in verbs that they think would make sense.

- Students can peel back the tape to see whether they selected the same verbs.

Use It

Use this activity to practice finding and correcting subject and verb agreement mistakes.

- Write on the board: *Even though we goes to the same school, Luis and I does not know each other.*

  Ask *Who can underline the verbs in this sentence?* (Answer: *goes, does not know*)

  Ask *Can someone underline the subjects that go with each verb?* (Answer: *we, Luis and I*)

  Say *Come to the board and circle anything you think is incorrect.* (Answer: *we goes, Luis and I does not know*)

- Have a volunteer rewrite the sentence using the correct verbs for each subject.

Read the *Use It* directions aloud. Have students read the example items and then complete the section independently. Ask volunteers to share their answers.

Practice It

In this section students will have another opportunity to correct sentences with subject and verb agreement errors.

- Remind students to decide whether the subjects in each sentence are singular or plural.

- Read the directions aloud. Read the *Tip* aloud.

- Have students complete items 1 and 2 independently. Invite volunteers to share their answers with the class.

Answers

1. B
2. C

Lesson 51

Objective

Students will learn to write complex sentences that will make their writing more interesting.

Words to Know

Independent clause—a group of words that is a complete thought and that has a subject and a predicate

Dependent clause—a group of words that has a subject and a predicate but is not a complete sentence

Simple sentence—an independent clause

Compound sentence—a sentence with two or more independent clauses

Complex sentence—a sentence with one independent clause and at least one dependent clause

◼ Study It

Read through the page with students, and discuss different types of sentences.

◼ Talk about the difference between *independent* and *dependent* clauses and the difference between *simple* and *compound* sentences.

Ask *Can a dependent clause be a complete sentence?* (Answer: *no*)

Ask *Can a simple sentence be a complete sentence? Could* I walk *be a complete sentence?* (Answers: *yes; yes*)

Ask *Name one difference between a compound sentence and a complex sentence.* (Answer: *A compound sentence has two or more independent clauses. A complex sentence has only one independent clause.*)

Have students practice creating complex and compound sentences.

Lesson 51 — Different Ways to Say It

▦ Study It

Using different types of sentences keeps readers interested. Careful use of punctuation and language helps readers understand how ideas in a sentence work together.

Look at the chart. It shows three different kinds of sentences.

Sentence Type	Example
Simple	Antoine's dog is friendly.
Compound	Antoine's dog is friendly, and he likes to play.
Complex	Antoine's friendly dog wags his tail when I visit.

Basic Sentence Parts

An **independent clause** is a group of words that is a complete thought. It has a subject and a predicate. An independent clause is a sentence.

Jane learned about elephants.

A **dependent clause** is a group of words that has a subject and predicate, but it is not a sentence. A dependent clause may also be called a **subordinate clause.**

After they swam in the lake, Frederick and Jamal were tired.

Types of Sentences

Simple Sentence

A simple sentence is an independent clause.

Baseball is a game.   Birds flew across the sky.

Compound Sentence

A compound sentence is a sentence made up of two or more independent clauses joined by a comma and a conjunction such as <u>and</u>, <u>or</u>, <u>but</u>, and <u>so</u>.

My aunt fixed lunch, and I set the table.

Complex Sentence

A complex sentence has one independent clause and at least one dependent clause.

When Mary reached the corner, she turned left.

OR Mary turned left when she reached the corner.

Curriculum and Assessment Standard

Sentence types

Use It

Read the sentences. Write compound or complex on the line. Look at these examples.

complex   1. After I ate my lunch, I took a nap.

compound   2. It was raining, but the sun shone brightly.

Now you try it.

complex   1. When I dropped my pencil, the tip broke.

compound   2. Ana left the birthday party, but I stayed to help clean up.

compound   3. We can walk, or we can ride the bus.

complex   4. I always wash my hands before I eat.

Practice It

Read the items. Circle the letter of the correct answer.

1. **Which of the following is a dependent clause?**

   Ⓐ When the summer season ends.

   B We sailed and landed on a tiny island.

   C He had a snack after lunch.

   D She painted the name on the boat.

2. **Which sentence is a complex sentence?**

   A Gil brushed the horse's mane, and Betsy cleaned the stable.

   Ⓑ Sal loved picking blueberries when she came to visit.

   C Isabella mowed the lawn last week.

   D They pulled the red wagon behind them.

> **Tip**
> To find the sentence type, look for independent and dependent clauses.

Lesson 51 ● 207

Use It

Use this activity to give students an opportunity to use what they have learned about different sentence types.

■ Write on the board: *I sleep.*

Ask *What kind of sentence is this?* (Answer: *a simple sentence*)

Ask *How could we make this into a compound sentence?* (Answer: *add another independent clause*)

Say *Tell me an example of an independent clause that could make this sentence more interesting.* (Answers will vary.)

Have students make the original sentence into a complex sentence, and ask volunteers to share their sentences with the class.

Read the *Use It* directions aloud. Have students read the example items and then complete the section independently. Ask volunteers to share their answers.

Practice It

In this section students have another opportunity to practice distinguishing between different types of sentences.

■ Read the directions aloud. Remind students to look for both independent and dependent clauses when they are finding sentence types.

■ Have students complete questions 1 and 2 independently.

■ Invite volunteers to share their answers with the rest of the class.

Answers

1. A
2. B

Differentiated Instruction
for ELL, visual, and auditory learners

Changing Sentences

Students will start with a list of subjects and verbs and will create stories containing complex and compound sentences.

Procedure

● Have volunteers call out subjects (names, animals, places). Write at least five subjects on the board. Then write the following verbs on the board: *be, know, go, make, feel, laugh,* and *hear.*

● Instruct students to write stories that use at least two of the subjects on the board and at least four of the verbs listed. Tell students that they must include examples of compound and complex sentences in their stories.

● Invite volunteers to come to the front of the class, share their stories, and to write an example of each type of sentence on the board.

Lesson 52

Objective

Students will understand how and when to use commas appropriately.

Words to Know

Appositive phrase—a noun or group of nouns that explains or renames another noun

Study It

Read through the information on the page, and review correct comma usage with students.

- Give students examples of sentences that need commas and have students tell you where the commas should go. Write the following sentences on the board with the commas omitted.

    Ask *I went to Maine(,) and Tom went to Texas.*

    Ask *Jack brought tuna(,) salmon(,) catfish(,) and trout(,) but we weren't hungry until later that afternoon.*

Continue having students practice using commas correctly.

- Have students write down their birth dates. Check to be sure they include a comma between the day and the year.

- Ask students to write down the city and the state they live in. Remind them to separate the two with a comma.

Help students make lists of different uses for commas. Write the different uses on the board as well. Remind students that using commas correctly can make their sentences easier to understand.

The Busy Comma

Study It

Commas set apart words or phrases within a sentence. They also separate parts of dates and addresses.

Here are some common uses for the comma.

- Use a comma to separate two independent clauses in a compound sentence.

    Mike took the bus, but Isabel drove her car.

- Use a comma to set off a dependent clause when it is the first part of a complex sentence.

    When Ali came up to bat, she hit a home run.

- Use a comma to set off an **appositive phrase.** An appositive phrase is a noun or phrase that explains another noun. Appositives are not necessary to the meaning of the sentence.
    Sentence with appositive: George, **my cousin**, is moving.

- Use a comma in a list of three or more items.

    We saw **bears, tigers,** and **monkeys** at the zoo last week.

    He **cleared the table, washed the dishes,** and **swept the floor.**

- Use a comma to set off the name of a person being spoken to.

    Dwayne, can you come here? I don't think so, **Stephanie.**

- Use a comma to set off words such as <u>yes</u>, <u>no</u>, and <u>well</u> at the beginning of a sentence.

    No, I can't go to the meeting. **Yes,** I'll call you later.

- Use a comma to separate the day of the month from the year. Place a comma after the year when other words follow in the sentence.

    Maria was born **April 2, 1998,** in New York.

- Use a comma to separate the name of a city from the name of a state or country. Place a comma after a state or country when other words follow in the sentence.

    Didn't he move here from **Nome, Alaska,** last fall?

Commas

Curriculum and Assessment Standard

Comma punctuation

Use It

Read each sentence. Rewrite each sentence on the line, with commas in the correct places. Look at these examples.

1. He was born in Springfield Vermont in 1864.
   He was born in Springfield, Vermont, in 1864.

2. Yes I will be glad to take her with me.
   Yes, I will be glad to take her with me.

Now you try it.

1. Vicente washed the car raked the leaves and took a nap.
   Vicente washed the car, raked the leaves, and took a nap.

2. Mrs. Ruiz our neighbor baked a cake for us.
   Mrs. Ruiz, our neighbor, baked a cake for us.

Practice It

Read each sentence. Choose the answer that will correct the underlined part of the sentence. Circle the letter of the correct answer.

1. My <u>cat a tabby</u> is just six months old.

   A cat a tabby,

   B cat, a tabby

   C cat, a tabby,

   D correct as is

Tip: Commas make sentences easier to understand.

2. Mattie <u>cleaned the bathroom swept the rug and folded the clothes.</u>

   A ,cleaned the bathroom, swept the rug and folded the clothes

   B cleaned the bathroom, swept the rug, and folded the clothes

   C cleaned the bathroom swept the rug, and folded the clothes

   D correct as is

Lesson 52 ● 209

This page may not be reproduced without permission of Steck-Vaughn.

Use It

Use this activity to continue practicing correct comma usage with students.

■ Write on the board: *No I haven't seen your glasses.* Read the sentence aloud.

  Say *When I read this sentence aloud, I pause for a moment after saying* no. *The comma also shows you where to pause when you are reading.*

  Ask *What are some other punctuation marks that tell you how to read sentences?* (Answer: *question marks, exclamation marks, periods*)

■ Write the first two example sentences on the board. Have volunteers point out where the commas should appear and why.

Read the *Use It* directions aloud. Have students complete the section independently. Ask volunteers to share their answers.

Practice It

In this section students can practice using commas correctly.

■ Read the directions aloud. Be sure students understand that they are to correct the part of the sentence that has been underlined. Remind students that if they think the sentence is correct, they should choose *correct as is.*

■ Have students complete items 1 and 2 independently and then stop.

■ Invite volunteers to share their answers with the rest of the class.

Answers

1. C

2. B

Differentiated Instruction
for kinesthetic, tactile, and auditory learners

Interviews

Students will interview each other and present the information to the class.

Procedure

● Assign each student a partner. Partners will have a chance to interview one another.

● Write the following questions on the board: *Where and when were you born? Where do you live? What are the names of the people in your immediate family? What are three things you like to do for fun? What are the last three movies you saw? What are three books you have read this year?*

● Have students take turns asking and answering these questions in their interviews. Remind students to use commas correctly in their answers.

● Invite students to present what they have learned about their partners to the rest of the class. Check students' papers for correct comma usage.

Lesson 53

Objective

Students will become stronger writers by learning to use punctuation properly.

Words to Know

Parentheses—marks that set apart words that explain

Direct quotation—a person's exact words

Quotation marks—marks that set off a direct quotation

Apostrophe—a mark that takes the place of a letter in a contraction and that can be used in nouns to show ownership

Contraction—a word made up of two different words

Possession—a way of showing ownership

Study It

Read through the page with students. Show students how punctuation marks can change the meaning of a sentence.

■ Write on the board: *Gwen left.*

Ask *If this sentence had a question mark at the end of it, what would it mean?* (Answer: *Someone is asking whether or not Gwen left.*)

Ask *What would you understand about this sentence if it ended with an exclamation mark?* (Answer: *Gwen's leaving was a surprise.*)

Ask *What would I mean if I wrote on the board:* Gwen's left? (Answer: *to the left of Gwen, or Gwen has left*)

Focus on how punctuation can change the meanings of sentences. Have students repeat the exercise above with a phrase they create themselves.

Lesson 53 — Signs and Rules

Study It

Using punctuation marks correctly makes sentences easier to understand. Parentheses, quotation marks, and apostrophes are all types of punctuation. It is also important to use underlining correctly.

To add an explanation to a sentence, use **parentheses ( )**.

> The school play will be held next Thursday (the second Thursday of the month).

To tell readers that you are using a **direct quotation**, use **quotation marks (" ")**. A direct quotation is someone's exact words. Use a comma before the quotation marks of a direct quotation. At the end of the quotation, add a comma if the sentence does not end with the quotation. Add a final punctuation mark if the sentence does end with the quotation. Then close the quotation marks.

> Father said, "Everyone needs to get in the car."
> "When will you go," asked Chris, "and when will you come back?"

To help the reader understand titles, use **underlining** (italics if you are using a computer) or quotation marks. Underline the titles of books, plays, magazines, films, and works of art. Use quotation marks for the titles of stories, songs, and poems.

> Wilbur is a character in Charlotte's Web.
> **OR** Wilbur is a character in *Charlotte's Web*.
> The song "The Circle of Life" is from the movie *The Lion King*.

In a **contraction,** a word made from two words, an **apostrophe (')** takes the place of letters that have been left out.

> Norma **can't** come to the party.

Apostrophes also show ownership or **possession.** To make a singular noun possessive, add *'s*. To make most plural nouns possessive, add only an apostrophe after the *s*. If a plural does not end in *s*, add *'s*.

> **Singular noun:** Lisa's dog is friendly.
> **Plural noun:** The boys' team won.
> **Plural noun:** The men's hats are black.

Curriculum and Assessment Standard

Punctuation

Use It

Rewrite each sentence on the line, using correct punctuation. Look at these examples.

1. Jan asked How many people are coming to the cookout?
   Jan asked, "How many people are coming to the cookout?"

2. We sang Row, Row, Row Your Boat at the cookout.
   We sang "Row, Row, Row Your Boat" at the cookout.

Now you try it.

1. Did you fill Sparkys water dish?
   Did you fill Sparky's water dish?

2. Rita cant find her spelling book.
   Rita can't find her spelling book.

3. That paper is mine Carlos said.
   "That paper is mine," Carlos said.

Practice It

Read each sentence. Choose the answer that shows the correct punctuation. Circle the letter of the correct answer.

1. I dont see how we can all fit in that car said Rick.

   A I dont see how we can all fit in that car, said Rick

   B "I don't see how we can all fit in that car said Rick."

   C "I don't see how we can all fit in that car," said Rick.

   D correct as is

2. Robert Jones is the author of ten childrens books.

   A "Robert Jones" is the author of ten children's books.

   B Robert Jones is the author of ten children's books.

   C Robert Jones is the author of ten children's books.

   D correct as is

> **Tip** When using quotation marks, find the exact words of the speaker.

Use It

Use this activity to help students apply correct punctuation.

- Write on the board: *The book Marlo read last summer is Gone With the Wind.*

  Ask *When you are writing about a book, how do you indicate its title?* (Answer: *underline it*)

  Say *In the sentence on the board, we don't know if Marlo's book blew away on a windy day, or if its title is* Gone With the Wind.

- Work with students to add the correct punctuation in the first two example items.

Read the *Use It* directions aloud. Have students complete the section independently. Invite volunteers to share their answers.

Practice It

In this section students have another opportunity to show what they have learned about correct punctuation.

- Read the directions aloud. Tell students to think about using correct punctuation. Remind students to decide who the speaker is when they are using quotation marks.

- Have students complete items 1 and 2 independently and then stop.

- Invite volunteers to share their answers with the class.

Answers

1. C
2. B

Differentiated Instruction
for kinesthetic and auditory learners

Writing a Dialogue

Writing dialogue will give students an opportunity to use the appropriate punctuation marks and rules correctly. Afterwards, volunteers will act out their stories in front of the class.

Procedure

- Ask students to think about conversations they have had recently with friends or relatives.

- Then have each student write a short story (about one page) based on his or her conversation. Tell students that their stories should be mostly dialogue. Students can describe the setting and the characters briefly, but should focus on the dialogue and punctuating it correctly.

- Invite volunteers to perform their conversations for the rest of the class.

Lesson 54

Objective

Students will learn to differentiate between common nouns and proper nouns and will learn when to use capital letters in their writing.

Words to Know

Capital—an uppercase letter that begins the first word in a sentence, a direct quotation, and a proper noun

Common noun—a word that names a person, place, or thing

Proper noun—a word that names a particular person, place, or thing

Study It

Read through the information on the page and discuss it with students.

■ Talk about the difference between *common nouns* and *proper nouns*.

  Ask *Which do we always capitalize: common nouns or proper nouns?* (Answer: *proper nouns*)

  Ask *What are some examples of proper nouns?* (Answers will vary.)

  Ask *Can you think of any nouns that could be both proper and common?* (Answer: *Aunt/aunt, Grandmother/grandmother*)

Review the capitalization rules for titles.

■ Write on the board (in all capital letters): A WRINKLE IN TIME, RAMONA THE PEST, THE HOBBIT, THE NAMING OF CATS, GOLDILOCKS AND THE THREE BEARS, THE ANT AND THE DOVE.

■ Ask students to rewrite these titles using uppercase letters where needed.

Standing Tall

Study It

Capital letters, or uppercase letters, always begin the first word in a sentence and the first word of a direct quotation.

Nouns that name a person, place, or thing, such as <u>city</u>, are called **common nouns.** Nouns that name a particular person, place, or thing, such as <u>Dallas</u>, are called **proper nouns.** Each word of a proper noun begins with a capital letter.

Look at these examples of common and proper nouns.

Type of Noun	Common Nouns	Proper (or special) Nouns
Person	aunt	Aunt Sally
	boy	Jim
	teacher	Mr. Simms
Place	city, state	Tampa, Florida
	country	the United States of America
	mountain	Mount Washington
Thing	month	May
	holiday	Thanksgiving
	club	Girl Scouts
	building	the Sears Tower

Here are three rules for capitalizing the **titles** of books, magazines, organizations (groups), works of art, music, and movies.

● Capitalize the first word of the title.
● Capitalize all important words.
● Capitalize forms of the verb <u>be</u>.

Do not capitalize these words unless they begin a title.

● the articles <u>a</u>, <u>an</u>, and <u>the</u>
● conjunctions, such as <u>and</u>, <u>but</u>, <u>or</u>, and <u>so</u>
● prepositions that have fewer than five letters, such as <u>with</u> and <u>for</u>

Curriculum and Assessment Standard

Capitalization

Use It

Rewrite each sentence on the line, using correct capitalization. Look at this example.

She wanted to know whether hector had read a Book called *The Mouse Went To the City.*

She wanted to know whether Hector had read a book called *The Mouse Went to the City.*

Now you try it.

1. During thanksgiving vacation, I traveled with my family to new york.
   During Thanksgiving vacation, I traveled with my family to New York.

2. My sister saw the empire state building for the first time. She said, "it is taller than I thought it would be."
   My sister saw the Empire State Building for the first time. She said, "It is taller than I thought it would be."

Practice It

Read each sentence. Choose the answer that shows correct capitalization. Circle the letter of the correct answer.

1. **He asked, "are we going to Lake Louise?"**

   A He asked, "are we going to lake louise?"

   B He asked, "are we going to lake Louise?"

   C He asked, "Are we going to Lake Louise?"

   D correct as is

2. **We saw the painting *sunflowers* at the museum.**

   A We saw the painting *Sunflowers* at the museum.

   B We saw the painting *sunflowers* at the Museum.

   C We saw the Painting *sunflowers* at the museum.

   D correct as is

Tip Make sure that each proper noun begins with a capital letter.

Lesson 54 • 213

Use It

This activity will give students an opportunity to practice using uppercase letters.

- Write on the board: *My Grandfather and I went camping at a state park in ohio. At night, grandfather read to me from One of his favorite books. It's called* The old man and The Sea.

   Ask *Do you see mistakes in these sentences, or are they correct the way they are?* (Answer: *There are mistakes.*)

   Ask *Which words in the first sentence have capitalization errors?* (Answer: Grandfather *should not be capitalized;* Ohio *should be capitalized.*)

- Review the errors in each sentence and ask volunteers to come to the board and show the changes they made.

Read the *Use It* directions aloud. Ask students to read the example item and then complete the section independently. Invite volunteers to share their answers.

Practice It

This section will give students another opportunity to practice using uppercase letters.

- Read the directions aloud. Remind students that they have the option of deciding that the sentence is correct the way it is.

- Have students complete items 1 and 2 independently. Remind students to check the capitalization of proper nouns.

- Invite volunteers to share their answers with the rest of the class.

Answers

1. C
2. A

Differentiated Instruction
for visual, auditory, and tactile learners

Capital Story

Writing about a special place will remind students to think about proper nouns and when to use capital letters.

Procedure

- Students will write a short story about a place that they would like to visit. Ask students to describe the place, telling where the place is located and why the place is important. Students should include at least six examples of proper nouns: two each of a person, place, and thing.

- Take students to the library to research their stories if necessary.

- Invite students to present their stories to the rest of the class. As they read, have the class identify words from each student's story that require a capital letter.

Teach the Strategy

Write on the board: *My aunt Luisa is from Houston Texas.*

Ask a volunteer to read the sentence aloud.

Ask *When you hear the sentence aloud, does it sound correct?* (Answer: *yes*)

Ask *When you look at the sentence, do you see anything wrong with it?* (Answer: *yes*)

Ask *What kinds of mistakes are you looking for?* (Answer: *incorrect use of uppercase and lowercase letters and commas*)

Toss and Match Strategy

Explain that tossing out incorrect choices can help students find the correct answer.

- Write these choices on the board:

  A My Aunt Luisa is from Houston Texas.

  B My aunt Luisa, is from Houston Texas.

  C My Aunt Luisa is from Houston, Texas.

  D My aunt Luisa is from Houston, Texas.

- Ask students to toss out any answers they recognize as incorrect. Then have students rewrite the sentence themselves. Ask them to see if it matches any of the choices on the board. (Answer: *C*)

Try It Out

Read the directions aloud and have students complete this section independently. Encourage them to use the *Toss and Match Strategy* to answer the question.

Discuss the explanation that follows the question in the student book.

Unit 10
Test-Taking Strategy

Strategy: Toss and Match

In this unit you learned that language follows rules. Use these steps to answer test items that ask you to correct sentences.

- Read the sentence. Then read each answer choice carefully. Think about the language rules. Toss out the answers that you know break the language rules.
- If you are not sure which of the remaining answers is the correct one, think about how you would rewrite the sentence.
- Look for the answer choice that matches your rewrite.

Try It Out

Read the item. Circle the letter of the correct answer.

> Ellie Anna and Trevor are in the big show.

Which sentence uses commas correctly?

A Ellie, Anna, and Trevor, are in the big show.

B Ellie, Anna, and, Trevor are in the big show.

C Ellie, Anna, and Trevor are in the big show.

D correct as is

Read the sentence. Then read the answer choices. Which ones have mistakes? Toss them out. In this item, the sentence is hard to understand without commas. Toss out answer choice **D** because the answer is not correct as is. Answer choice **A** is incorrect. No rule says to put a comma before the verb. Answer choice **B** is incorrect. No rule says to put a comma after the conjunction <u>and</u>. Answer choice **C** uses commas in a list of three or more people. Answer choice **C** is correct.

214 • Unit 10

This page may not be reproduced without permission of Steck-Vaughn.

Put It to the Test

Name _____

This test will check what you have learned in this unit.

DIRECTIONS: Circle the letter of the correct answer.

1. | Pack your gloves hat and sweater |

   What is the correct punctuation for this sentence?

   A Pack your gloves, hat and, sweater.

   (B) Pack your gloves, hat, and sweater.

   C Pack your gloves hat, and sweater

   D correct as is

2. | The child rode her scooter. |

   The nouns in this sentence are —

   (A) child, scooter

   B child, rode

   C rode, her

   D her, scooter

3. **What is the correct way to write the title of a book?**

   A the Dragon nanny

   B "The Dragon nanny"

   (C) *The Dragon Nanny*

   D (The Dragon Nanny)

4. | The students talked over their plan. |

   The pronoun in this sentence is —

   A students

   B talked

   (C) their

   D plan

5. **Which sentence is in the past tense?**

   A The trumpets announce the king.

   B The trumpets are announcing the king.

   C The trumpets will announce the king.

   (D) The trumpets announced the king.

6. | Mr. Wilson was at the wrong house. |

   The verb in this sentence is —

   A wrong

   (B) was

   C at

   D house

GO ON

Achieve It! Practice Cards
_____
_____

Put It to the Test • 215

Connect the Test to the Practice Cards (page 215)

Correct Answers	Related Practice Cards	Skill
1. **B**	**183, 184**	**Comma punctuation**
2. **A**	**166**	**Nouns**
3. **C**	**187, 188**	**Punctuation**
4. **C**	**171**	**Pronouns**
5. **D**	**167, 168, 169**	**Verbs**
6. **B**	**167, 168, 169**	**Verbs**

Put It to the Test

Students will:

- demonstrate what they have learned
- identify skills that require more practice before students achieve proficiency*

* Refer to pages T17–T19 for a complete explanation and directions for using *Achieve It!* Practice Cards.

Administer the Test

Explain that students will now practice the skills from this unit by taking a short test. Tell students that the test has items like those they will find on standardized tests. Explain that you will read the directions aloud. Remind students to pay close attention and follow your directions exactly.

Say *Open your books to page 215. I will read the directions aloud.* Read the directions to students. Then continue.

Say *You will have 10 minutes to finish this test. Read each item and the answer choices carefully. Circle the letter of the correct answer. When you reach the words* GO ON *at the bottom of a page, turn the page and continue working. When you reach the word* STOP *at the bottom of a page, stop working and put down your pencil. Are there any questions?*

If students have no questions,

Say *You may begin.*

At the end of 10 minutes,

Say *Stop. Check to be sure that you have circled the letter of the correct answer. Erase any stray pencil marks. Then put down your pencil.*

Assign Practice Cards

After scoring a student's test, note which items the student missed. Match each incorrectly answered item to the related *Achieve It!* Practice Cards listed in the chart on this page.

In the *Achieve It!* Practice Cards space in each student's book, write all of the Practice Cards you want the student to complete.

Additional Practice Cards

The following cards cover additional skills for

Unit 10: Language Rules

Card	Topic
170	Double negatives
172	Pronoun referents
173	Adjectives
174	Adverbs
175	Conjunctions and compound sentences
176	Prepositions and prepositional phrases
177, 178	Subject-verb agreement
181	Fragments
182	Run-on sentences

You may want to assign these cards as practice for students who have done well on the unit test or as extended practice for all students.

7. After we started the fire, we cooked the fish.

This is an example of a —

A   simple sentence

B   compound sentence

C   complex sentence

D   sentence with an appositive

8. Which sentence is correct?

A   He and I is leaving now.

B   He and I are leaving now.

C   He and I am leaving now.

D   He and I was leaving now.

9. She bringed the parrot to Lisa's house.

The correct verb is —

A   bringing

B   brought

C   branged

D   correct as is

10. Which sentence is correct?

A   "Which way, asked Monica, is the shoe repair shop"

B   Which way, asked Monica, is the shoe repair shop?

C   "Which way," asked Monica, "is the shoe repair shop?"

D   "Which way?" asked Monica, "is the shoe repair shop."

11. Jan was born on July 7 1996.

What is the correct punctuation for this sentence?

A   Jan was born on July, 7 1996.

B   Jan was born on, July 7, 1996.

C   Jan was born on July 7, 1996.

D   correct as is

12. On friday they played in Settlers' park.

What is the correct capitalization for this sentence?

A   On Friday they played in Settlers' Park.

B   On friday they played in Settlers' Park.

C   On Friday they played in settlers' park.

D   correct as is

13. Dr. Ree my doctor is busy now.

What is the correct way to write this sentence?

A   Dr. Ree my doctor is, busy, now.

B   Dr. Ree my doctor, is busy now.

C   Dr. Ree, my doctor, is busy now.

D   correct as is

STOP

Achieve It! Practice Cards

Connect the Test to the Practice Cards (page 216)

Correct Answers	Related Practice Cards	Skill
7. C	179, 180	Complex sentences
8. B	171	Pronouns
9. B	167, 168, 169	Verbs
10. C	185, 186	Sentence punctuation, Quotation marks
11. C	183, 184	Comma punctuation
12. A	189, 190	Capitalization
13. C	183, 184	Comma punctuation

Unit
11 Spelling

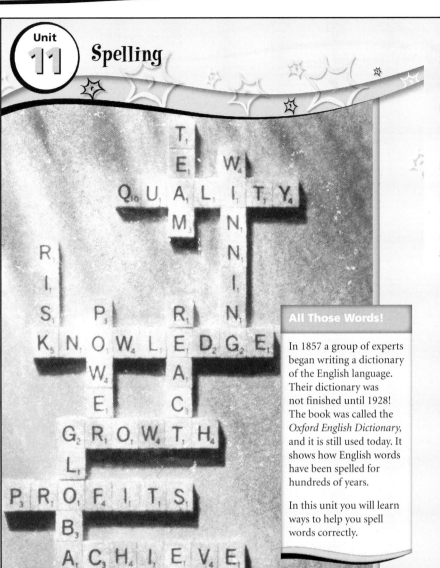

All Those Words!

In 1857 a group of experts began writing a dictionary of the English language. Their dictionary was not finished until 1928! The book was called the *Oxford English Dictionary,* and it is still used today. It shows how English words have been spelled for hundreds of years.

In this unit you will learn ways to help you spell words correctly.

217

Skills

- Identifying misspelled words
- Spelling frequently used words correctly
- Using word roots and spelling rules to spell words correctly
- Dividing words into syllables

Materials to Gather in Advance

- magnetic, rubber, or paper letters
- dictionary   • index cards or slips of paper   • pencils

Introducing the Unit

All Those Words! Refer students to the photograph of the word game. Do they recognize any of these words? If so, are the words spelled correctly? Have students imagine what it would be like if people spelled words any way that they liked. Would people be able to understand one another? Ask students why it might be important that the words we use every day be spelled correctly. Then ask them where they can look to find the correct spelling of a word.

- Read the *All Those Words!* paragraph aloud.

    Ask *Did you ever try to spell a word that you had heard for the first time? What strategies did you use?*

Research Says

The more a reader knows about words . . . about their spelling . . . the more fluent and efficient a reader she or he will be.

—Templeton

Lesson 55

Objective

Students will learn how to spell frequently used words correctly.

◢ Study It

- Read the opening paragraph aloud. Have volunteers read the words in the first chart.

- Read aloud the directions for the second chart. Discuss the chart with students.

- Copy the chart on the board. Then have each student create a similar chart on a separate sheet of paper. Write *here* in Column 1 on the board and have students complete the first row.

  Ask *Who wants to share an example from his or her chart?* (Possible answer: *here; Let's sit here.*)

Read steps 1–5 aloud. Have students make a list of words and use them to fill in their charts.

Everyday Words

◢ Study It

It is important to know how to spell the words that you write.

Look at this chart. It shows some words that are used often. Notice the spelling of each word.

Words You Use Often		
· when	· since	· clothes
· here	· there	· might
· which	· their	· whole
· been	· write	· many

Now look at this chart. It shows a way you can practice spelling words correctly.

Column 1 WORD	Column 2 WRITE	Column 3 SENTENCE
when	when	When can we meet to practice our spelling?

Make a list of words that you use often. You can spell words more easily if you study them in this way.

1. On a sheet of paper, draw a three-column chart like the one above.

2. Copy a word that you want to learn to spell in Column 1.

3. Use a separate sheet of paper to cover Column 1. Think about the word you copied. Write it in Column 2.

4. To check your spelling, compare the word you wrote in Column 2 with the word in Column 1. The two spellings should match.

5. Use the word in a sentence in Column 3.

218 ● Unit 11   High frequency words

Curriculum and Assessment Standard

High frequency words

Use It

Fill in the empty spaces in the chart below. Use a sheet of paper to hide the word in Column 1 when you write in Columns 2 and 3.

Column 1	Column 2	Column 3
WORD	WRITE	SENTENCE
maybe	maybe	Maybe we can feed the goldfish today.
been	been	We have been to the state fair!

Now you try it.

Column 1	Column 2	Column 3
WORD	WRITE	SENTENCE
which	which	Sentences will vary.
their	their	Sentences will vary.

Practice It

Choose the correct spelling for each missing word. Circle the letter of the correct answer.

1. We bought _____ to make toast.

   A bredd

   B bread

   C brid

   D brede

2. The pieces fit _____.

   A toogethr

   B twogether

   C together

   D togeter

Tip When you spell a word incorrectly, add the correct spelling of that word to your spelling chart.

Use It

In this section students will use the strategy from the previous page to practice spelling four common words.

■ First, direct students to return to their own word charts.

   Ask *Give me an example of a word in your chart.* (Possible answer: *you're; You're my friend and I'm yours.*)

Allow several students to share words from their charts.

Read the *Use It* directions aloud. Have students complete the section independently. Ask volunteers to share their answers for Column 3.

Practice It

In this section students choose the correct spellings of two common words.

■ Read the instructions aloud.

■ Instruct students to complete items 1 and 2 independently.

Answers

1. B

2. C

■ Ask a volunteer to read the *Tip* aloud. Encourage students who missed one or both of the questions to add the word(s) to their chart.

Differentiated Instruction
for ELL, visual, and auditory learners

Spell Checking

Students will practice spelling words they use often.

Procedure

● Organize students into pairs. Give each student pair a set of letters.

● Have one student say a word aloud. The word can come from either the charts in the lesson or from the partner's personal chart or word list.

● Have the other student use the letters to spell the word out on the desk. If students are uncertain about the spelling of any word, they should use the chart, word list, or dictionary to check the spelling.

● Each pair of students should switch roles and repeat the activity. Students should practice spelling as many words as time permits.

Lesson 56

Objective

Students will use word roots and spelling rules to practice spelling words correctly.

Words to Know

Root—the main part of a word before prefixes and suffixes are added

Study It

Read the opening paragraph aloud.

- Direct students' attention to the four rules. Have a volunteer read the final *e* rule.

  Ask *What other words fit this rule?* (Possible answers: *ride, write, slide*)

- Have a volunteer read the doubling rule.

  Ask *What other words fit this rule?* (Possible answers: *sit, drag, cut*)

- Have a volunteer read the plural rule.

  Ask *What are the plural forms of these words: bench, box, boy?* (Answers: *benches, boxes, boys*)

- Have a volunteer read the *y* to *i* rule.

  Ask *What other words fit this rule?* (Possible answers: *baby, belly, body, dry, marry*)

Looking at Word Parts

Study It

The **root** of a word is the main part of the word. Sometimes you will need to change the spelling of a root word to add an ending. These rules can help you remember how to add parts to root words.

Final *e* Rule When a word ends in a silent *e*, drop the *e* before adding -*ing* or -*ed*.

fade fad~~e~~ + ed = faded   **glide** glid~~e~~ + ing = gliding

Doubling Rule When a one-syllable word ends in a consonant-vowel-consonant pattern (CVC), such as <u>trap</u>, double the final consonant before adding -*ing* or -*ed*.

tip tip + p + ed = tipped   **fit** fit + t + ing = fitting

Other words have more than one syllable, such as <u>admit</u>. When a word with two or more syllables ends in a CVC pattern, double the last consonant only if the final syllable is stressed.

In the word <u>admit</u>, the final syllable *mit* is stressed, so the last consonant is doubled.

admit admit + t + ed = admitted

In the word <u>quiver</u>, the final syllable *er* is not stressed, so the last consonant is not doubled.

quiver quiver + ing = quivering

Plural Rule To make most nouns plural, add an *s*. For words ending in *s*, *x*, *ch*, or *sh*, add *es*.

<u>table</u> + s = tables   <u>fox</u> + es = foxes

<u>success</u> + es = successes   <u>crash</u> + es = crashes

y to i Rule To make a noun plural when the final two letters are a consonant and *y*, change the *y* to *i* and add *es*.

butterfly butterfl~~y~~ + i + es = butterflies

220 • Unit 11   Structural analysis

Curriculum and Assessment Standard

Structural analysis

Use It

Spell each <u>underlined</u> word correctly. Look at these examples.

<u>swimming</u>   1. I was <u>swiming</u> in the pool.

<u>shivered</u>   2. The dog <u>shiverred</u> in the cold.

Now you try it.

<u>paddling</u>   1. They were <u>paddleing</u> down the river.

<u>bunches</u>   2. We bought three <u>bunchs</u> of grapes.

<u>cherries</u>   3. We saw ripe <u>cherrys</u> on the tree.

<u>clapping</u>   4. They were <u>claping</u> about the ending.

Practice It

Choose the correct spelling for each missing word. Circle the letter of the correct answer.

1. We _____ through the gate.

  A enteried

  B enterred

  Ⓒ entered

  D enterd

2. Three students gave _____ .

  Ⓐ speeches

  B speshes

  C speechs

  D spechs

3. The _____ of the story was very interesting.

  A begining

  Ⓑ beginning

  C begininng

  D beginiing

Tip Spell out long words one syllable at a time, and look at each word part.

Lesson 56 ● 221

This page may not be reproduced without permission of Steck-Vaughn.

Use It

Students will correct misspelled words.

■ Write the following on the board:
The <u>flys</u> <u>tryed</u> to land on the <u>dishs</u>.

  Say *Some of the words in this sentence break the spelling rules we just learned about.*

  Ask *Who can spell each underlined word correctly?* (Answers: *flies, tried, dishes*)

Read the *Use It* directions aloud. Have students complete the section independently. Ask volunteers to share their answers.

Practice It

In this section students will choose the correct spelling of words that follow this lesson's rules.

■ Read the *Tip* aloud.

■ Have students complete items 1–3 independently.

■ Invite volunteers to read their answers aloud.

Answers

1. C
2. A
3. B

Differentiated Instruction
for ELL, visual, and tactile learners

Practicing Spelling Rules

Students will match root words and word endings using correct spelling rules.

Procedure

● Prepare a set of index cards for every pair of students in the class. The card set should include the endings *-ing, -ed, s,* and *-es* and root words *give, bike, slide, cut, sit, begin, study, buy,* and *walk.*

● Organize the class into student pairs. Give each pair a set of index cards.

● Ask students to use the cards to practice matching the root words with the endings. Encourage students to identify which rules are demonstrated with each match.

● Students should use the blank index cards for extra letters, such as those needed to practice the doubling rule. Students can also use the blank cards to list root words of their choosing.

Unit 11 ■ 221

Lesson 57

Objective

Students will use syllables to spell words correctly.

Words to Know

Syllable—contains only one vowel sound as in *ba* and *by* in *baby*

◢ Study It

Read the opening paragraph aloud.

- ■ Direct students' attention to the three rules for dividing words into syllables. Have a volunteer read the *-le* rule.

  Ask *What other words fit this rule?* (Possible answers: *settle, goggle*)

- ■ Have a volunteer read the open syllable rule.

  Ask *What other words fit this rule?* (Possible answers: *final, locate, baby, pilot*)

- ■ Have a volunteer read the closed syllable rule.

  Ask *What other words fit this rule?* (Possible answers: *basket, kitten, puppy*)

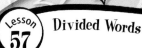

Lesson 57 — Divided Words

◢ Study It

Syllables

A **syllable** is a word or part of a word that can be pronounced by itself, such as <u>fa</u> in <u>father</u>. A syllable contains only one vowel sound.

Learning to spell a word one syllable at a time can help you spell the whole word correctly. Here are some rules to help you divide words into syllables.

-le **Rule** If a word ends in a consonant and *-le*, it is divided before the consonant that comes before *-le*.

jun • gle	rid • dle	han • dle

Open Syllable Rule An **open syllable** is one that ends in a vowel. The vowel usually has a long sound and says its name. Divide the word after the first vowel. For example, the syllable <u>ba</u> in <u>bacon</u> is an open syllable. It has a long ā sound.

ba • con	o • pen	cra • zy	pi • rate

Closed Syllable Rule A **closed syllable** follows the pattern of consonant-vowel-consonant (CVC). In a closed syllable, the vowel has a short sound. Divide the word after the closed syllable.

six • teen	blos • som	res • cue
cos • tume	gal • lop	lum • ber

You can divide a word into syllables to make spelling the word easier. Use the same rules to divide a long word that you use to divide a short one. Check your work by looking up the words in a dictionary. The dictionary shows you the correct spelling and how the word is divided into syllables.

Syllabic rules

Curriculum and Assessment Standard

Syllabic rules

Use It

Divide these words into syllables. Then write which rule you are using. Look at these examples.

1. paddle   _pad • dle; -le rule_
2. problem   _prob • lem; closed syllable rule_

Now you try it.

1. protect   _pro • tect; open syllable rule_
2. mention   _men • tion; closed syllable rule_
3. preserve   _pre • serve; open syllable rule_
4. giggle   _gig • gle; -le rule_

Practice It

Choose the correct spelling for each missing word. Circle the letter of the correct answer.

1. Which is the correct way to divide the word <u>marble</u> into syllables?

   A ma • rble

   B marb • le

   Ⓒ mar • ble

   D marbl • e

2. Which is the correct way to divide the word <u>nature</u> into syllables?

   A nat • ure

   Ⓑ na • ture

   C natu • re

   D nature

Tip Each syllable has one "beat." Count syllables by clapping your hands as you say a word.

Lesson 57 ● 223

Use It

Students will divide words into syllables and identify the rules they follow.

- Write the words *pencil* and *paper* on the board.

  Ask *Who can divide these words into syllables?* (Answers: *pen-cil, pa-per*)

  Ask *Which rules do you use to divide these words into syllables?* (Answers: *pencil*—closed syllable rule; *paper*—open syllable rule)

Read the *Use It* directions aloud. Have students complete this section independently. Ask volunteers to share their answers.

Practice It

In this section students will have another opportunity to choose correct spellings.

- Read the *Tip* aloud.
- Have students complete items 1 and 2 independently.
- Invite volunteers to read their answers aloud.

Answers

1. C
2. B

Differentiated Instruction
for auditory, kinesthetic, and tactile learners

Get the Beat

Students will learn to feel the beat of syllables in a word.

Procedure

- Write the following words on the board: *train, window, album, hidden, oven, balloon, closet, poster, closest, player, telephone, information, elephant, computer.*
- Organize students into pairs.
- As pairs read each word on the list, they should gently tap the table top with one finger for each syllable.
- Then, students should determine how to divide each word into syllables. Have students write each word in syllables.
- Finally, students should check their work using a dictionary.

Teach the Strategy

Write on the board: *We used a _____ to learn the positions of the states on a United States map.*

Say *The missing word is* puzzle.

Ask *How many syllables does this word have?* (Answer: *two*)

Ask *How can you divide the word into syllables?* (Answer: *puz-zle*) *What is this rule called?* (Answer: *the* -le *rule*)

Ask *How do you spell* puzzle? (Answer: *p-u-z-z-l-e*)

Ask *How do you make this word plural?* (Answer: *add* s)

Ask *How does the spelling change if you add* -ing? (Answer: *The silent* e *disappears.*)

Be Prepared Strategy

Tell students that spelling correctly takes practice.

■ Read the bulleted points aloud. Discuss each with students.

Try It Out

Read the directions aloud and have students complete this section independently.

■ Instruct students to read the sentence.

■ Have students select the correct answer (*C*).

■ Have volunteers explain the reasons for their answers.

  Ask *How did the* Be Prepared Strategy *help you find the correct answer?*

Discuss the explanation that follows the question in the student book.

Test-Taking Strategy

Strategy: Be Prepared

In this unit you have learned spelling rules. Here are some tips to help you spell words correctly.

• Make a list of words you use often, and learn their spellings.

• Know that different letters make different sounds.

• Look closely at the differences between homophones, such as their and there, which sound the same but are spelled differently.

• Look at word parts, such as syllables and endings.

• Remember the rules for adding endings to words.

• Remember the rules for dividing words into syllables.

Try It Out

Read this sentence carefully. Think about the spelling rules you have learned.

Choose the word that is spelled correctly. Circle the letter of the correct answer.

Our class is cleaning up the park. Our _____ are painting and sweeping.

A dutys

B dutyies

C duties

D dutties

The word duty ends in a consonant and *y*. You must follow the *y* to *i* rule to make this word plural. Change the *y* to *i* and add *es*. The correct answer is **C**.

Put It to the Test

Name _____

This test will check what you have learned in this unit.

DIRECTIONS: Circle the letter of the correct answer.

1. The weather is _____ cold.

   A geting

   Ⓑ getting

   C gedding

   D getinng

2. The horses are _____ in the parade.

   Ⓐ prancing

   B pranceing

   C pranccing

   D prancceing

3. Add two _____ of salt to the vegetables.

   A pinchs

   B pinchess

   C pinchz

   Ⓓ pinches

4. Which is the correct way to divide the word demand into syllables?

   Ⓐ de • mand

   B dem • and

   C dema • nd

   D deman • d

5. We went to a farm to pick _____ last week.

   A berrys

   B berryes

   Ⓒ berries

   D berrees

6. The boy ate the _____ apple.

   A houl

   Ⓑ whole

   C hole

   D whol

7. They _____ the lights as the movie began.

   A dimed

   Ⓑ dimmed

   C dimd

   D dimmied

Achieve It! Practice Cards

_____

Put It to the Test • 225

This page may not be reproduced without permission of Steck-Vaughn.

Connect the Test to the Practice Cards (page 225)

Correct Answers	Related Practice Cards	Skill
1. **B**	194	Inflectional endings—other
2. **A**	194	Inflectional endings—other
3. **D**	193	Inflectional endings—plural
4. **A**	199, 200	Syllabic rules
5. **C**	194	Inflectional endings—plural
6. **B**	197, 198	High frequency words
7. **B**	194	Inflectional endings—other

Put It to the Test

Students will:

- demonstrate what they have learned
- identify skills that require more practice before students achieve proficiency*

* Refer to pages T17–T19 for a complete explanation and directions for using *Achieve It!* Practice Cards.

Administer the Test

Explain that students will now practice the skills from this unit by taking a short test. Tell students that the test has items like those they will find on standardized tests. Explain that you will read the directions aloud. Remind students to pay close attention and to follow your directions exactly.

Say *Open your books to page 225. I will read the directions aloud.* Read the directions to students. Then continue.

Say *You will have 10 minutes to finish this test. Read each item and the answer choices carefully. Circle the letter of the correct answer. When you reach the words* GO ON *at the bottom of a page, turn the page and continue working. When you reach the word* STOP *at the bottom of a page, stop working and put down your pencil. Are there any questions?*

If students have no questions,

Say *You may begin.*

At the end of 10 minutes,

Say *Stop. Check to be sure that you have circled the letter of the correct answer. Erase any stray pencil marks. Then put down your pencil.*

Assign Practice Cards

After scoring a student's test, note which items the student missed. Match each incorrectly answered item to the related *Achieve It!* Practice Cards listed in the chart on this page.

In the *Achieve It!* Practice Cards space in each student's book, write all of the Practice Cards you want the student to complete.

Additional Practice Cards

The following cards cover additional skills for

Unit 11: Spelling

Card	Topic
191	Structural analysis
192	Structural analysis
195	Homonyms
196	Homonyms

You may want to assign these cards as practice for students who have done well on the unit test or as extended practice for all students.

8. Which is the correct way to divide the word <u>control</u> into syllables?

  A co • ntrol

  B cont • rol

  Ⓒ con • trol

  D contr • ol

9. The girls _____ about the cat in the tree until it was rescued.

  Ⓐ worried

  B woried

  C worryed

  D woryed

10. His mother's _____ gave prizes at our school carnival.

  A busness

  Ⓑ business

  C bisness

  D busines

11. We _____ to help the team win the game.

  A tryed

  B tryyed

  C triad

  Ⓓ tried

12. Which is the correct way to divide the word <u>twenty</u> into syllables?

  Ⓐ twen • ty

  B twent • y

  C twe • nty

  D tw • enty

13. Do not fall and _____ yourself.

  A hurte

  B heart

  C hert

  Ⓓ hurt

14. The new _____ are hiring workers next week.

  A factoryies

  Ⓑ factories

  C factorys

  D factorries

15. Which is the correct way to divide the word <u>person</u> into syllables?

  A pe • rson

  Ⓑ per • son

  C pers • on

  D perso • n

STOP

Achieve It! Practice Cards

Connect the Test to the Practice Cards (page 226)

Correct Answers	Related Practice Cards	Skill
8. C	199, 200	Syllabic rules
9. A	194	Inflectional endings—other
10. B	197, 198	High frequency words
11. D	194	Inflectional endings—other
12. A	199, 200	Syllabic rules
13. D	197, 198	High frequency words
14. B	193	Inflectional endings—plural
15. B	199, 200	Syllabic rules

Name _____

Practice Test A

Here are a few tips to keep in mind when you take a test:

- Read all directions and test items carefully.
- Read each answer choice carefully.
- Choose the best answer.

Complete this sample to help you get ready to take this practice test.

SAMPLE

DIRECTIONS: Read the item. Circle the letter of the correct answer.

> **Vincent got a running start before he <u>bounded</u> across the puddle.**

What does the word <u>bounded</u> mean in this sentence?

A strolled

B swam

Ⓒ jumped

D crawled

The correct answer is **C.** The word <u>bounded</u> means "jumped." Circle the letter **C.**

Some parts of this test will have passages for you to read. Read each passage carefully. Then answer the questions about the passage.

Practice Test A

Explain to students that they will now take a test to help identify the reading and language arts skills that they may need to work on in the *Achieve It!* program. Tell students that you will go over the directions with them. Remind students to pay close attention and to follow your directions exactly.

Say *Open your books to page 227. I will read the directions aloud.* Read the tips to students. Then ask students to look at the Sample question. Read the directions aloud. Ask students to circle the correct answer. Allow students time to find and mark their answer.

Say *You should have circled C.* Check to see that all students have circled the correct answer.

Read the directions following the Sample question.

At this point, have students mark their answers on copies of *Achieve It!* Practice Test Answer Sheet (Blackline Master 3) to simulate a standardized test-taking experience. Directions for using the *Achieve It!* Practice Test Answer Sheet begin on the next page.

Another option is to have students continue marking their answers in their books. If you choose this option, look for this symbol ⑤. It tells you where to begin the instructions.

Give each student a copy of the *Achieve It!* Practice Test Answer Sheet (Blackline Master 3.) Have students write their name at the top of the page. Have them circle the *A* for Practice Test A.

Say *Print your name at the top of the answer sheet. Circle the* A *for Practice Test A. All of your answers must be marked on this answer sheet. Do not write your answers in the book. You may, however, make notes or underline in the book as you read.*

Encourage students to attempt every question. Assist students in test-taking procedures during the test, but be careful not to give clues or hints about answers to questions.

Say *You will have an hour and twenty-five minutes* to finish this test. Read the directions in the test carefully. Read the questions and the stories carefully. Try to answer every question. Then mark your answers on your Practice Test Answer Sheet. When you see the words* GO ON *at the bottom of a page, turn the page and continue working. When you see the word* STOP *at the bottom of a page, stop working and put down your pencil. Are there any questions?*

If students have no questions, write the starting and ending times for the test on the board.*

Say *You will have from _____ to _____ to complete the test. * Turn to page 228. You may begin.*

* Alternate Procedure: You may want to give students the test in two or three separate testing sessions if time and conditions do not allow you to administer the test in one session. The following times in the chart are suggested for the three sections of the test.

DIRECTIONS: Read each item. Circle the letter of the correct answer on your *Achieve It!* Practice Test Answer Sheet.

1. | Keep your answers as short as possible, and do not add any <u>unnecessary</u> words. |

   If <u>necessary</u> means "needed," what does <u>unnecessary</u> mean?

   A   less needed

   B   needed a bit

   Ⓒ   not needed

   D   needed more

2. | We tried to <u>observe</u> the game carefully so we would know how to play it. |

   What does the word <u>observe</u> mean in this sentence?

   Ⓐ   watch

   B   count

   C   photograph

   D   list

3. | After dinner I have several <u>chores</u>, such as clearing the table and washing the dishes. |

   Which word means the SAME as <u>chores</u>?

   A   experiments

   B   loads

   C   objects

   Ⓓ   duties

4. | We got to school late because we were caught in a huge traffic <u>jam</u>. |

   jam (jam) *n.* **1** a sweet food made from fruit and sugar **2** people or cars crowded and unable to move *v.* **3** to get stuck and not work **4** to squeeze things into a small place

   Which meaning BEST fits the way <u>jam</u> is used in this sentence?

   A   meaning 1

   Ⓑ   meaning 2

   C   meaning 3

   D   meaning 4

5. | I looked at the map, but I could not <u>locate</u> your street. |

   Which word means the SAME as <u>locate</u>?

   Ⓐ   find

   B   walk

   C   admire

   D   spell

228 • Practice Test A

Alternate Procedure

Sessions	Time	Practice Test A
Vocabulary	15 minutes	pages 228–229
Comprehension	45 minutes	pages 230–246
Language	25 minutes	pages 247–251

Since the GO ON icon appears on each page of the test except the last one, you will need to tell students to stop on the last page of each section, as shown above.

You may also want to give students a short break after one or more sections of the test if you administer the complete test at one time. If so, use the chart above to tell students on which page to stop.

6. The farmers are expecting a big corn crop this year.

crop (krop) *n.* **1** the amount of a food that is picked at one harvest **2** part of a bird's body where food is stored **3** things that appear at the same time, as in "a crop of problems" *v.* **4** to cut off

Which meaning BEST fits the way crop is used in this sentence?

Ⓐ meaning 1

B meaning 2

C meaning 3

D meaning 4

7. When I saw an elephant at the zoo, I was surprised at how enormous it looked next to a zebra.

Which word means the OPPOSITE of enormous?

A useful

B lively

C eager

Ⓓ small

8. We gave the author a pen so that she could autograph her picture in our books.

What does the word autograph mean in this sentence?

Ⓐ sign

B approve

C buy

D deliver

9. When the ant farm fell to the floor, it took me several hours to recapture the ants.

If capture means "catch," what does recapture mean?

A catch inside

Ⓑ catch again

C catch later

D catch before

10. The teacher will demonstrate the correct way to turn on the computer so we can do it on our own.

What does the word demonstrate mean in this sentence?

A examine

B watch

Ⓒ show

D understand

DIRECTIONS: Read each passage. Then read each item and circle the letter of the correct answer on your *Achieve It!* Practice Test Answer Sheet.

Kira's Stuff

"Kiirrraaa! What is THIS?" Kira's mother, standing next to the washing machine, held up a pair of tattered jeans. "You haven't worn these since you were seven!"

Kira sighed and reached for the jeans. "I know. I didn't want to throw them out. I wore them at the family picnic where I met Susie."

On that day Kira had bumped into Susie as she was getting cold drinks. As the girls said they were sorry to each other, Kira's Aunt Margo hurried up and reached for a diet soda.

"Hi, Kira, I'm glad you're here. Have you two met?" Without waiting for an answer, she continued, "It's too bad you live so far apart. Susie is so sweet. Do you know what her first spoken sentence was?"

Susie rolled her eyes as Aunt Margo continued. "She said, 'I have a collection.' Isn't that cute? Do you collect anything, Kira?" Before Kira could answer, Aunt Margo hurried off, shouting, "You girls go talk!" over her shoulder.

The girls moved over to a picnic bench far away from the smoking barbecue grill. Carefully, Susie placed her basket on the table.

"Is that your lunch?" Kira asked.

"Nope. It's one of those collections Aunt Margo mentioned." Susie reached into the basket and pulled out a tan rock with sharp edges. "See the little bits that shine in the sunlight like diamonds? I found this one day when I was walking home from school. Mom was with me, and I'd had a bad day. I looked down and saw this rock. Mom said it was like life—rough, sharp, but full of diamonds if you just looked. I thought that was kind of neat."

One by one, Susie took out the rocks from her basket. Each rock had a special story.

"Kira," her mother said sharply, bringing her back to the present, "I asked you about these jeans."

"I want to keep them," Kira said firmly, carefully folding the jeans into a small square. "They got in the wash by mistake."

Kira's mother shook her head, picked up the laundry basket, and headed into the kitchen. "I don't even WANT to know what else you've squirreled away," she added.

Kira groaned quietly and went into her room. She pulled an old suitcase out from the back of her closet and lifted it onto the bed. Inside was a jumble of objects. Carefully, she began to arrange the objects so that she could tuck the jeans in among them.

"Kiirrrraaa!" Kira hurried out of her room and down the hall.

Mrs. Cortinez and her daughter Christina were standing in the hallway. "Your Mom and I are working on things for the craft fair," she said to Kira. "Why don't you girls go study?"

Kira sighed and led the way to her room. "I suppose we could clear off the bed. . . ." Horrified, she realized that she had left her suitcase out—and open! Christina would tell everyone at school, and they'd never stop laughing!

"What's this?" Christina headed for the bed like a homing pigeon.

"Nothing." Kira tried to move between Christina and the suitcase, but she wasn't fast enough.

"Oooh, this is a cool necklace." Christina held up a string of purple plastic beads. "Where'd you get it?"

"Please, let me put that away, and we'll study."

Christina reached into the suitcase again and pulled out a soft piece of pink fabric. "What's this? It's really pretty."

"It's part of my baby blanket. My aunt made it for me before I was born."

"You're lucky to have this stuff," Christina said.

One by one, Christina took things out of the suitcase, and Kira told her the story about each object. Soon, bits and pieces of fabric, ribbons, beads, photographs, pictures, and dried flowers littered Kira's bed.

"Kiiirrrraa!"

"Quick, get this stuff into the suitcase!" Kira began grabbing things and stuffing them quickly into the suitcase.

But not quite fast enough. Kira's mother stood in the doorway, staring at the room in dismay. Mrs. Cortinez peered over her shoulder.

"Look!" Christina held out a scrap of purple silk. "This is from an old dress Kira's grandma wore, and this. . . ."

"Kira! What IS all this?" her mother demanded.

Kira hung her head sadly. "Just stuff," she mumbled. "I'll get rid of it."

"No!" Christina protested. "This stuff is important to you."

Mrs. Cortinez nodded. "You must keep what's important where you can see it."

"Betty," Kira's mother said sternly to Mrs. Cortinez, "she can't leave them all out in her room. Look at the mess."

"Oh, I think she CAN leave them out. I have an idea. Christina, help carry Kira's things into the kitchen."

They spent the next few hours sewing and gluing Kira's stuff to a big piece of cloth. Kira's baby blanket was sewn onto the upper right corner and was covered partway by the purple fabric. Across that, the beads were glued in place as well as an old veil taken from a favorite hat of Kira's great grandmother. Kira's "stuff" completely covered the fabric.

"Now," Mrs. Cortinez announced, "we'll put a broom handle through the top, tie ribbons onto the ends of the handle, and hang this on the wall. You'll have all your stuff, Kira, and your wall will be beautiful."

Kira's mother looked at their work and nodded. "That works. That actually works!" She smiled.

Mrs. Corintez added, "Your stuff is full of memories, Kira. Those memories are stories that should be told and remembered!"

11. How does meeting Susie change Kira?

A She becomes interested in collecting rocks.

B She wants to go to more craft fairs.

C She recognizes that she should not keep her old jeans.

(D) She realizes how important it is to remember special stories.

12. Mrs. Cortinez is DIFFERENT from Kira's mother because —

A Mrs. Cortinez likes working at the craft fair

(B) Mrs. Cortinez thinks Kira's stuff is important

C Mrs. Cortinez wants Kira to be neat

D Mrs. Cortinez thinks Kira is unkind

13. What happens AFTER Christina finds the suitcase?

A The girls pull out the old clothes and dress up.

B The girls begin to study for a test.

(C) Kira's stuff gets scattered across her bed.

D Kira hides the suitcase in the closet.

14. What is the MAIN problem in the story?

A Kira's mother thinks Kira does not study enough.

B Kira's mother is unhappy because Kira hides things in the basement.

C Kira's mother thinks Kira's room is not neat and tidy.

(D) Kira's mother thinks Kira's special things make a mess.

15. Kira keeps her stuff in a suitcase because —

(A) it is special and she doesn't want to throw it away

B that is where Susie kept her special things

C she is planning on visiting Susie very soon

D it helps her carry her things around with her

16. What is the MAIN message of the story?

A Everyone should collect something.

B A messy room will always get you in trouble.

(C) Memories of special things are important.

D Save everything from your childhood.

17. Where do Kira and Susie meet?

A at a fair

B at school

(C) at a picnic

D at a house

18. Which phrase from the story is a simile?

A away from the smoking barbecue grill

(B) shine in the sunlight like diamonds

C sharp, but full of diamonds

D those memories are stories

19. Why does Kira want to hide the suitcase before Christina sees it?

(A) She is afraid that Christina will make fun of her.

B She thinks Christina will take her stuff.

C She does not like to share her special memories.

D She wants to study, not play with the suitcase.

20. When the author says that Christina "headed for the bed like a homing pigeon," she means that Christina —

A flapped her arms

B looked like a bird

(C) could not be stopped

D made cooing noises

A Summer Job

Tom looked out the window. The rain streaming down from the dark sky made it hard to see across the street. He sighed heavily and turned away. He took two steps and flopped down on the couch with a groan. "I hate summer," he announced to no one in particular.

"What's the problem?" his mom asked as she came into the room carrying a stack of magazines.

"There's nothing to do," Tom said sadly, as if the gray, rainy weather reflected how he felt.

"Have you read those library books?" his mom asked brightly. "We checked out quite a few last week."

Tom simply nodded unhappily. "I read every one of them twice. They aren't very interesting the third time around."

"You should have gone with Linda to the animal shelter," his mom said. Tom's sister Linda loved animals and spent every spare hour at the shelter.

"Ugh! Walking dogs in this downpour would be a wet, nasty, smelly job."

"Why don't you call Ted? Maybe he could come over, and you could work on that big puzzle we've been trying to finish," his mom suggested.

Tom rolled over and faced the back of the couch. "He's gone to see his uncle in Ohio."

"Well then," his mom said, "I guess it's up to me to find something for you to do." She put the magazines on the table and walked upstairs. Tom stayed on the couch, staring glumly at nothing in particular.

Within a few minutes she returned. This time she was carrying a pile of thin books. Tom's little brother Joe trailed behind her looking disgusted. Four years younger than Tom, he had just finished first grade.

"Here," Tom's mom handed him the books. "Joe needs to work on his reading this summer, and you're going to help him."

Before Tom could protest, she left the room.

"Not going to do it," Joe muttered angrily. "I hate reading."

Tom opened one of Joe's little books. It was the story of a puppy. The book was simple and dull. As if the day wasn't bad enough, Tom thought, I have to read this!

Joe closed his eyes and refused to even look at the book. "NO!" he said loudly.

Suddenly Tom had an idea. "Listen," he said, "how would you like to have your very own book about something you like? Would you read it?"

Joe opened one eye. "Could it be about chickens?" he asked.

"It can be about whatever you want," Tom said firmly.

With Mom's permission, they cut out pictures from the magazines. Then they glued them to sheets of paper. Joe decided what he wanted each page to say, and Tom carefully wrote the sentences. When they finished, Tom stapled the pages together.

When Linda got home, Joe could hardly wait to read to her from his new book.

"Can we make another book tomorrow even if it's not raining?" Joe asked hopefully.

"We can make as many as you want," Tom told him, smiling.

This chicken lives on a farm.

21. Why is Tom unhappy when the story begins?

A He does not like rainy weather.

(B) He has nothing interesting to do.

C His friend is out of town.

D His brother is bothering him.

22. Tom does not want to help Linda because —

A the shelter is far away

B he does not like dogs

(C) the job would be unpleasant

D he does not like Linda

23. At the end of the story, Tom probably feels —

A calm
B lonely
C pleased
D nervous

24. Why does Joe close his eyes?

A He does not want to look at his mom.
B He is tired and wants to sleep.
C He does not want to read the book.
D He does not like his brother.

25. Which word BEST describes Tom?

A thankful
B playful
C curious
D clever

26. How are Joe and Tom ALIKE?

A Both like interesting books.
B Both like to spend time with their sister.
C Both work on big puzzles.
D Both enjoy library visits.

27. What do Tom and Joe do LAST when they are making the book?

A cut pictures from magazines
B staple the pages together
C glue pictures to the pages
D wrote sentences on the pages

28. The author MOST LIKELY believes that —

A it is a mistake to tell your mom you have nothing to do
B everyone should read library books as often as possible
C when you help someone else, you help yourself as well
D learning to read can be difficult

29. Where does this story take place?

A in the library
B at Tom's school
C in a bookstore
D at Tom and Joe's houses

Soccer: You Can Do It

by Kirk Bizley

One way of getting used to a soccer ball is to practice catching and throwing it. Start by rolling the ball along the ground. Practice with a partner. Roll the ball to each other. Try picking the ball up in two hands as it comes to you.

Goalkeepers are the only players who are allowed to use their hands in a soccer game while the ball is in play. Now try a throw-in. Use two hands. Snap your body forward as you throw the ball from above your head. You can practice throw-ins with a partner. You can even practice goalkeepers' catches when the ball is thrown.

You can make the throws a bit different by throwing down. This makes the ball bounce before it gets to your partner.

Learn to kick the ball correctly so you don't hurt your foot. For short kicks and passes, kick with the inside of your foot. Never kick with your toes!

Begin by putting the ball next to your foot. Make sure the ball is not moving before you kick it. Try kicking the ball with your left foot and your right foot.

For fun, try kicking at targets. Cones make good targets. See if you can hit them with the ball. Have a partner roll the ball to you. Try using your foot to stop the ball. Make sure you are lined up with the ball as it comes to you.

When you can stop the ball, you have learned to trap the ball. Trapping the ball makes the ball easier to kick away.

Passing means kicking the ball to someone else. In a game, you pass the ball to your teammates.

To pass, you need to practice controlling the ball. You need to be able to kick it just where you want. Practice passing with a partner. Start close to each other. Don't move further apart until you can trap and pass the ball every time.

---

30. Which of these sentences from the passage is an OPINION?

A Start by rolling the ball along the ground.
B Practice with a partner.
C You can practice throw-ins with a partner.
D Cones make good targets.

31. The author thinks that a good way to control the ball when you kick is to —

A trap the ball
B use your toes
C throw down the ball
D snap your body forward

32. What is the FIRST thing the author says to do to get used to a soccer ball?

A practice catching and throwing a soccer ball
B put the ball by your foot and trap it
C kick the soccer ball when it is moving
D kick the soccer ball with your right foot

33. According to the author, why should you learn to kick correctly?

A so you can win the game
B so you don't hurt your foot
C so you won't miss the ball
D so you can throw the ball

34. What is the BEST summary of the last paragraph?

A Learn to control the ball by passing it to a partner.
B Kicking the ball to someone else is a helpful skill.
C Pass the ball to a partner when you can.
D Kicking at targets is a good way to practice.

35. Goalkeepers are DIFFERENT from other soccer players because they can —

A use their right foot
B pass the ball
C kick the ball
D use their hands

Blowing Bubbles

1 Children may have played with bubbles since soap was invented. Several hundred years ago, they used leftover washing soap. This soap was the only way they had to make bubbles. In 1940 a person in a company that made cleaning supplies had an idea. The company sold bottles of something that looked like water. In fact, the mixture made bubbles. Now this mixture is the best selling toy in the world. Today grown-ups and children alike blow bubbles.

2 Bubbles can be made in many sizes. The small bottles sold at the store make little bubbles. Some bubble experts can make bubbles big enough to hold two people. The people can stand four to eight feet apart. They are still in the middle of a bubble. The longest bubble on record was fifty feet. How do you make these super bubbles?

3 First, make your own bubble liquid. Use dish soap, water, and sugar. Let the mixture sit overnight. Now the fun begins! Almost anything can be used to make bubbles. You can bend a hanger or use a funnel, a straw, or even a string formed into a loop. Get your hands wet with bubble mixture, and you can hold bubbles. Remember, this mixture is very slippery. Be careful not to spill it.

4 A paper cone makes good bubbles. Roll two sheets of paper tightly into a cone. The opening at the large end should be $1\frac{1}{2}$ inches. Tape the cone with masking tape. Put the tape closer to the narrow end. You do not want the tape to get wet. Cut the narrow end of the cone. This will be a mouth piece. It should be small. Then cut the wide end of the cone. Make it as smooth and round as you can. Stand the cone up on this end. If it does not stand up, trim it until it does. You can use this cone many times. Let it dry out after each use.

5 The first time you use it, dip the cone into the mixture for a few seconds. Tap it lightly on the side of the dish to get rid of extra liquid. Then slowly blow your bubble. Hold the cone pointing down at first. Then as the bubble gets bigger, you can lift it up. When you have the size bubble you

want, rapidly flip the cone down or up. Your bubble will float away. Bubbles are not very strong. You will make better bubbles on days where there is very little wind.

6   You can play bubble games with your friends. Have a bubble race and see who can keep a bubble in the air longest. See who can guide a bubble to the finish line. You can even freeze a bubble. Wet a plate and blow a bubble onto the plate. Carefully put the plate in a freezer away from the door. In about two minutes, slowly open the door. Your bubble is frozen.

7   Bubbles can be fun for people of all ages!

36. According to the diagram, what is the FIRST step when you make bubbles?

A   Flip the bubble off the cone.

B   Tap the cone lightly.

C   Dip the cone into the mixture.

D   Slowly blow a bubble.

37. Which sentence describes what is happening in step 5 of the diagram?

A   The bubble is getting bigger.

B   The bubble is being blown upward.

C   The bubble is being flipped off the cone.

D   The bubble is being formed.

38. According to the passage, when were bubbles first sold as a toy?

A   1910

B   1920

C   1930

D   1940

39. Which sentence tells the main idea of paragraph 2?

A   A big bubble can hold two people inside.

B   Super bubbles are easy to make.

C   Someone made a very long bubble.

D   Bubbles range in size from small to very large.

40. The author wrote this passage to —

A   explain ways to make and play with bubbles

B   persuade people to buy more bubble mixture

C   tell stories about different kinds of bubbles

D   explain what a bubble expert does

41. Why should you tape the cone close to the narrow end?

A   so the tape will stick better

B   so the cone will stand up

C   so the tape will stay dry

D   so the cone will be smooth

42. Why is it better to make bubbles on days that are not very windy?

A   The bubble mixture will last longer.

B   The wind will make the bubbles get too big.

C   The wind will quickly break the bubbles.

D   The bubbles will not float very far.

43. How long does it take to freeze a bubble?

A   overnight

B   two minutes

C   one day

D   one and a half minutes

44. What is paragraph 1 MOSTLY about?

A   how to make bubbles with dish soap

B   the history of bubbles

C   how to blow bubbles with a funnel

D   the games children play with bubbles

The Paper Crane

by Molly Bang

A man once owned a restaurant on a busy road. He loved to cook good food and he loved to serve it. He worked from morning until night, and he was happy.

But a new highway was built close by. Travelers drove straight from one place to another and no longer stopped at the restaurant. Many days went by when no guests came at all. The man became very poor, and had nothing to do but dust and polish his empty plates and tables.

One evening a stranger came into the restaurant. His clothes were old and worn, but he had an unusual, gentle manner.

Though he said he had no money to pay for food, the owner invited him to sit down. He cooked the best meal he could make and served him like a king. When the stranger had finished, he said to his host, "I cannot pay you with money, but I would like to thank you in my own way."

He picked up a paper napkin from the table and folded it into the shape of a crane. "You have only to clap your hands," he said, "and this bird will come to life and dance for you. Take it, and enjoy it while it is with you." With these words the stranger left.

It happened just as the stranger had said. The owner had only to clap his hands and the paper crane became a living bird, flew down to the floor, and danced.

Soon word of the dancing crane spread, and people came from far and near to see the magic bird perform. The owner was happy again, for his restaurant was always full of guests. He cooked and served and had company from morning until night.

The weeks passed. And the months.

One evening a man came into the restaurant. His clothes were old and worn, but he had an unusual, gentle manner. The owner knew him at once and was overjoyed. The stranger, however, said nothing. He took a flute from his pocket, raised it to his lips, and began to play.

The crane flew down from its place on the shelf and danced as it had never danced before.

The stranger finished playing, lowered the flute from his lips, and returned it to his pocket. He climbed on the back of the crane, and they flew out of the door and away.

The restaurant still stands by the side of the road, and guests still come to eat the good food and hear the story of the gentle stranger and the magic crane made from a paper napkin. But neither the stranger nor the dancing crane has ever been seen again.

45. Where does the story take place?

A   in an inn

B   in a dream

C   in a restaurant

D   in a house

46. What is the MAIN message of the story?

A   Paper can be magical.

B   Kindness is often rewarded.

C   People like unusual things.

D   Bad luck cannot be avoided.

47. What happens when the stranger returns to the restaurant?

A   He plays a flute.

B   He eats a large meal.

C   He pays for his food.

D   He dances with the crane.

48. How is the stranger different on his second visit?

A   He has on a shabby hat.

B   He wears different clothes.

C   He does not speak.

D   He smiles a lot.

Origami

1 Have you ever made a paper airplane? If so, you are doing some basic paper folding. Over the years, people have turned this simple work into an art form. It is called origami. It was developed in Asia long ago. Origami means "folding paper" in Japanese.

2 Paper was first developed in China in A.D. 105. People in Japan learned about paper in the early seventh century. They developed a special kind of paper. It was strong, yet soft, and did not tear easily. This is the paper they used for origami. They began folding paper about 1,200 years ago.

3 At first, folded paper was used as a kind of gift wrap for food. Later, people made different animals. Beginning about 1600, special "bases" were made. These are starting folds. They were used to make birds and frogs. From about 1688 to 1704, people even used paper cranes and boats as designs on their clothes. Legend says that if someone folds 1,000 cranes, he or she will have good luck. Many people began folding paper. The designs were passed down from mother to daughter. Nothing was written down at first. As time went on, new designs were developed. Many were very hard to make.

4 Anyone can make an easy origami design. You can use plain writing paper. You can even use dollar bills or business cards. The easiest designs begin with a square piece of paper. It is helpful to work on a smooth, hard surface. A table top or desk is a good place to start. A hard surface means that your folds can be made carefully. The best way to learn is to practice folding. Different designs and directions can be found on the Internet. You must follow each step carefully. Do not skip a step. Most people do not like to cut or glue the paper. They use one sheet for each design.

5 Today, paper folding is done in nearly every country. You can find examples in pop-up books, cards, and crafts. A new approach is to use printed cloth instead of paper. Owls, frogs, boxes, even small purses can be made. Whether you are folding paper or cloth, you can make many different objects. Imagine making a pecking bird or a frog on a lily pad out of paper! Do you think you could fold 1,000 cranes?

 GO ON

---

49. **Which of these statements from the passage is an OPINION?**

   A Paper was first developed in China in A.D. 105.

   B Later, people made different animals.

   C Nothing was written down at first.

   (D) Many were very hard to make.

50. **Paper made in Japan was ideal for origami because it was —**

   (A) strong and soft

   B black and white

   C small and round

   D used for food

51. **What is the BEST summary of paragraph 4?**

   (A) Origami is easy if you follow the steps.

   B Paper must be folded on a hard surface.

   C Many people use glue and scissors.

   D Origami needs several sheets of paper.

52. **When did people in Japan first start folding paper?**

   A before A.D. 105

   (B) 1,200 years ago

   C around A.D. 1600

   D in modern times

---

53. **Why did the author write this passage?**

   A to tell a story about origami

   B to persuade people to learn origami

   (C) to give some information about origami

   D to explain why people like origami

Use "Origami" and "The Paper Crane" to answer questions 54 and 55.

54. **The essay and the story both tell about —**

   A a magical paper crane

   (B) unusual paper animals

   C people from Asia

   D different ways to fold paper

55. **The stranger probably made a crane instead of a frog because —**

   (A) cranes were thought to be lucky

   B cranes were easier to make

   C people would not like a frog

   D he could fold only one design

Mai is in fourth grade. She wrote this report about her summer for English class. She wants you to help her revise and edit the report. Read it and think about the changes she should make.

A Great Summer Day

(1) This summer we had a fun event in our neighborhood called "Night Out." (2) A big red, white, and blue banner was strung across the street. (3) It said: "United We Stand!" and meant that everybody should stick together and help each other out.

(4) Everyone in our neighborhood got together and brought food. (5) The streets were blocked off, and we brought our lawn chairs to sit on. (6) I do not like those green lawn chairs. (7) We had tacos, beans fresh carrots from the community garden, and sandwiches.

(8) I met Ryan, who just moved into one of the apartment buildings on our street. (9) I found out that he would be going to my school and would be in the same grade.

(10) People from the centerville police and fire departments were there and handed out safety information. (11) The power company handed out some knew pencils, and we got free cardboard fans from the water company,

too. (12) We played games like ring toss and basketball free throws. (13) We each won a little prize even if we didn't win the game. (14) That was the best night of the whole summer!

 GO ON

---

56. **Which sentence could BEST be added before sentence 8?**

   A Mrs. Alvarez made a huge chocolate cake for dessert.

   B I thought the banner should be left up all year.

   C The games that we got to play were a lot of fun.

   (D) We talked to our neighbors and got to know new people.

57. **Which sentence does NOT belong in the report?**

   A sentence 2

   (B) sentence 6

   C sentence 10

   D sentence 12

58. **The purpose of this report is to —**

   A persuade readers to join a special event

   (B) tell about something that happened

   C explain how to have a "Night Out"

   D entertain readers with a funny story

---

59. **What change should be made to sentence 7?**

   A change had to has

   (B) add a comma after beans

   C change sandwiches to sandwichs

   D make no change

60. **What change should be made to sentence 11?**

   (A) change knew to new

   B change pencils to penciles

   C change too to two

   D make no change

61. **Which word from sentence 13 is a noun?**

   A little

   (B) prize

   C we

   D won

62. **What change should be made to sentence 10?**

   A change there to they're

   B change safety to safty

   (C) change centerville to Centerville

   D make no change

 GO ON

Gilbert is in fourth grade. He wrote this essay about fourth grade at the end of the school year. He wants you to help him revise and edit the essay. Read it and think about the changes he should make.

The Best Year Ever

(1) Fourth grade were the most fun in school so far. (2) I learned about fractions and measuring in math and I made paper masks for art. (3) I read about the American colonys and wrote about them.

(4) Best of all, the class had special study units. (5) For example, each of us had to study a state and learn all about it. (6) I studied Texas because that's where my cousins live. (7) I made a map of texas and drew a picture of the Alamo and some oil wells.

(8) I also liked the games we played, such as volleyball and soccer. (9) Our volleyball team did not win many games, but we had a lot of fun.

(10) The greatest thing about fourth grade was our teacher, Mr. Swinnon. (11) He showed us science experiments. (12) We always liked that because Mr. Swinnon sometimes had a hard time making an experiment come out the way it should. (13) He laughed the loudest when that happened.

(14) I hope fifth grade at lincoln School will be as much fun.

63. What change should be made to sentence 3?

A change American to american

(B) change colonys to colonies

C change them to it

D make no change

64. Which sentence could BEST be added after sentence 9?

A After school some of us play softball in my yard.

B Our coach always tells us the rules of each game.

C Playing different games is a lot of fun, but I really like to play baseball.

(D) Our soccer team had a great year, though, and almost won the championship.

65. Which sentence could BEST be added after sentence 14?

A I really like school, but I think those reports are hard to write.

B I have a friend who is in fifth grade now.

(C) Fourth grade was a great year, and I'm sorry to see it end.

D Mr. Swinnon does not teach fifth grade.

66. What change should be made to sentence 6?

(A) change studied to studied

B change that's to thats

C change where to wear

D make no change

67. What change should be made to sentence 2?

A change learned to lerned

(B) add a comma after math

C change the period to a question mark

D make no change

68. Which word from sentence 12 is a pronoun?

A liked

B because

C an

(D) it

69. What change should be made to sentence 1?

A change Fourth to fourth

(B) change were to was

C change school to School

D make no change

70. What change should be made to sentence 14?

A change fifth to Fifth

(B) change lincoln to Lincoln

C change hope to hopes

D make no change

Allison is in fourth grade. She wrote this report about the state of Illinois. She wants you to help her revise and edit the report. Read it and think about the changes she should make.

The State of Illinois

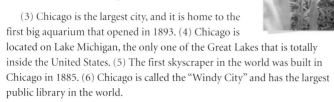

(1) I chose Illinois as my state because I like reading about Abraham Lincoln. (2) He lived in Illinois, and so did President Ronald Reagan.

(3) Chicago is the largest city, and it is home to the first big aquarium that opened in 1893. (4) Chicago is located on Lake Michigan, the only one of the Great Lakes that is totally inside the United States. (5) The first skyscraper in the world was built in Chicago in 1885. (6) Chicago is called the "Windy City" and has the largest public library in the world.

(7) Two important zoos in Illinois is the Lincoln Park Zoo and the Brookfield Zoo. (8) The first animal in the Lincoln Park Zoo was a bear.

(9) Illinois is famous because barbed wire, the round silo for storing grain, and the tasty ice-cream sundae were invented there.

(10) The state bird is the cardinal, and the state flower is the purple violet. (11) The biggest crop is corn. (12) The most interesting thing I learned about Illinois is that it is home to the largest cookie and cracker factory in the world.

71. What change should be made to sentence 7?

A change Two to Too

B change zoos to zooes

C change is to are

D make no change

72. What is the purpose of this report?

A to inform readers about the state of Illinois

B to persuade people to visit Illinois

C to tell a story about the Lincoln Park Zoo

D to tell about the history of Chicago

STOP

At the end of the testing session,

Say *Stop. The testing session is over. Check to be sure that you have circled the correct answers completely. Erase any stray pencil marks. Then put down your pencil.*

If using the Practice Test Answer Sheet, ask students to make sure they have written their name and circled the *A* on the Practice Test Answer Sheet. Then collect all answer sheets from students. Have students put their books away. If students marked their answers in their books, ask them to turn in their books or remove and turn in the test pages.

After scoring all student tests, refer to the Correlation Charts on pages T32–T33. Identify the reading and language arts skills that individual students or most of the students in the class had difficulty with on the test. Use this information to make individual or class assignments in the *Achieve It!* student book.

Practice Test B

Explain to students that they will now take a test to see how well they have done on the reading and language arts skills in the *Achieve It!* program. Tell students that you will go over the directions with them. Remind students to pay close attention and to follow your directions exactly.

Say *Open your books to page 252. I will read the directions aloud.* Read the tips to students. Then ask students to look at the Sample question. Read the directions aloud. Ask students to circle the correct answer. Allow students time to find and mark their answer.

Say *You should have circled C.* Check to see that all students have circled the correct answer.

Read the directions following the Sample question.

At this point, have students mark their answers on copies of *Achieve It!* Practice Test Answer Sheet (Blackline Master 3) to simulate a standardized test-taking experience. Directions for using the *Achieve It!* Practice Test Answer Sheet begin on the next page.

Another option is to have students continue marking their answers in their books. If you choose this option, look for this symbol ◎. It tells you where to begin the instructions.

Practice Test B

Here are a few tips to keep in mind when you take a test:

- Read all directions and test items carefully.
- Read each answer choice carefully.
- Choose the best answer.

Complete this sample to help you get ready to take this practice test.

SAMPLE

DIRECTIONS: Read the item. Circle the letter of the correct answer.

> **Vincent got a running start before he <u>bounded</u> across the puddle.**

What does the word <u>bounded</u> mean in this sentence?

A   strolled

B   swam

Ⓒ   jumped

D   crawled

The correct answer is **C**. The word <u>bounded</u> means "jumped." Circle the letter **C**.

Some parts of this test will have passages for you to read. Read each passage carefully. Then answer the questions about the passage.

DIRECTIONS: Read each item. Circle the letter of the correct answer on your *Achieve It!* Practice Test Answer Sheet.

1. | She did not smile when I gave her the book, so I thought she was **ungrateful**.

If **grateful** means "thankful," what does **ungrateful** mean?

A   thankful after

(B) not thankful

C   less thankful

D   thankful about

2. | The frightened deer quickly **vanished** into the forest.

Which word means the SAME as **vanished**?

A   fell

B   crawled

(C) disappeared

D   arrived

3. | When the woman saw the mouse, she was frightened and **shrieked** loudly.

Which word means the OPPOSITE of **shrieked**?

A   grunted

(B) whispered

C   screamed

D   growled

4. | The print in that book is so small that it is **difficult** to read.

What word means the OPPOSITE of **difficult**?

A   mean

(B) easy

C   costly

D   mysterious

5. | When the actors practiced, we got to **preview** the play.

If **view** means "to look at," what does **preview** mean?

A   view later

(B) view before

C   view again

D   view across

GO ON

Practice Test B • 253

Give each student a copy of the *Achieve It!* Practice Test Answer Sheet (Blackline Master 3.) Have students write their name at the top of the page. Have them circle the **B** for Practice Test B.

Say *Print your name at the top of the answer sheet. Circle the* B *for Practice Test B. All of your answers must be marked on this answer sheet. Do not write your answers in the book. You may, however, make notes or underline in the book as you read.*

Encourage students to attempt every question. Assist students in test-taking procedures during the test, but be careful not to give clues or hints about answers to questions.

Say *You will have an hour and twenty-five minutes* to finish this test. Read the directions in the test carefully. Read the questions and the stories carefully. Try to answer every question. Then mark your answers on your Practice Test Answer Sheet. When you see the words* GO ON *at the bottom of a page, turn the page and continue working. When you see the word* STOP *at the bottom of a page, stop working and put down your pencil. Are there any questions?*

If students have no questions, write the starting and ending times for the test on the board.*

Say *You will have from _____ to _____ to complete the test. * Turn to page 253. You may begin.*

* Alternate Procedure: You may want to give students the test in two or three separate testing sessions if time and conditions do not allow you to administer the test in one session. The following times in the chart are suggested for the three sections of the test.

Alternate Procedure

Sessions	Time	Practice Test B
Vocabulary	15 minutes	pages 253–254
Comprehension	45 minutes	pages 255–271
Language	25 minutes	pages 272–276

Since the GO ON icon appears on each page of the test except the last one, you will need to tell students to stop on the last page of each section, as shown above.

You may also want to give students a short break after one or more sections of the test if you administer the complete test at one time. If so, use the chart above to tell students on which page to stop.

This page may not be reproduced without permission of Steck-Vaughn.

6. We watched the woman <u>cast</u> her fishing net into the water.

cast (käst) **n. 1** the actors in a play **2** a hard plaster covering on a broken arm or leg **v. 3** to vote **4** to throw

Which meaning BEST fits the way <u>cast</u> is used in this sentence?

A meaning 1

B meaning 2

C meaning 3

(D) meaning 4

7. The food had a very <u>peculiar</u> smell, so we decided not to eat it.

What does the word <u>peculiar</u> mean in this sentence?

(A) strange

B amazing

C special

D interesting

8. The speaker was very <u>solemn</u> as he read the sad poem.

What does the word <u>solemn</u> mean in this sentence?

A eager

B astonished

(C) serious

D tired

9. The cat moved slowly and <u>cautiously</u> as she neared the dog because she didn't want it to chase her.

What does the word <u>cautiously</u> mean in this sentence?

(A) carefully

B dangerously

C foolishly

D curiously

10. The <u>beam</u> of the car headlights startled the cat sitting in the driveway.

beam (beem) **n. 1** a long, thick piece of wood or metal used to support a building **2** a ray of light **v. 3** to have a big smile **4** to shine brightly

Which meaning BEST fits the way <u>beam</u> is used in this sentence?

A meaning 1

(B) meaning 2

C meaning 3

D meaning 4

DIRECTIONS: Read each passage. Then read each item and circle the letter of the correct answer on your *Achieve It!* Practice Test Answer Sheet.

Jean [John] James Audubon moved to the United States from France in 1803. He became the most famous wildlife artist of his day. Even now, bird artists measure their work against his. This passage is historical fiction about Audubon's childhood.

Audubon: The Man Who Painted Birds

by Norah Smaridge

Jean grew into a handsome and clever boy. By the time he was fourteen, he could play the violin and the flute. But he did not work hard at his lessons. He wanted only to draw birds.

He was happiest in summer. Then Madame took them all to La Gerbetière, a country house not far from Nantes. There were woods and fields all around it. Every day Jean took pad and pencil and hunted for little creatures to draw. He drew a nest of field mice. He drew a woodchuck.

Mostly he drew birds—a coot, a magpie, and a green woodpecker.

When Captain Audubon came home, Jean had hundreds of pictures to show him. "But they are all bad, Papa," he said. "Very, very *bad*. The claws and bills are wrong. And the tails look as if they would fall off!"

"It is not easy to draw something which is alive," said Captain Audubon. He put the drawings aside. "Now show me your lesson books."

Jean went red with shame. His arithmetic and history were very poor. His geography was not much better.

Captain Audubon frowned. "This will not do, Jean," he said. "It is high time you went to school. When I leave, I will take you to Rochefort with me. I will put you in the naval academy there."

A few weeks later, Jean left with his father. "Don't let them be too hard on him," Madame begged her husband. "I hear it is a very strict school."

In four days they were at Rochefort, a town on a rocky hillside. Captain Audubon showed Jean the seawall, the docks, and the battleships. There were officers and sailors everywhere.

Jean started school, and it was even worse than he feared. The rooms were as bare as a prison. The lessons were hard and long, and there were no drawing lessons at all. When Jean saw a sea gull through the window, he thought, "I wish I could fly like that. I would escape!"

He could not fly, but he could jump. One day he jumped out of a window and began to run, but he did not get far. A sailor spotted him and brought him back. Captain Audubon was sent for, and Jean was scared. But the Captain did not scold him. "Maman is right. You are not meant to be a seaman," he said. "But if you want to spend your life drawing, you must learn to do it properly. I shall take you to Paris, to the best teacher in France. His name is Jacques Louis David, and he is a famous artist."

Once again Jean and his father set out on a journey, this time to Paris. They came to a tall house and climbed up to a studio under the roof.

Jean looked around the big studio in surprise. There were no paintings, no drawings. Only great statues of men and women. They were cold and white, with empty eyes.

A man in a smock came to greet them. "So this is young Jean Audubon, who wants to learn to draw," he said.

"Will you teach me to draw birds properly, sir?" Jean asked. "I want them to be alive. I want them to fly on the paper! I want—"

"You are in too much of a hurry, young man!" David said, laughing. "First you must learn to draw these plaster casts. This—and this—and this." He pointed to the great white statues.

Jean's heart sank. He wanted to beg his father to take him home, but he did not dare.

He was not happy in David's studio. He wanted to draw tiny creatures but the painter would not let him. He made Jean copy all the big white casts in the studio. Day after day passed, and Jean was not allowed to draw a bird.

Jean hated the studio. He did not like to draw men and women with dead eyes. He often left his work and went to look out of the window. He longed to draw the sparrows in the street. They were so alive. They moved so quickly.

One day he packed his bag and climbed into a coach for home. As it bowled along, he began to feel happy. When it reached Nantes, he jumped out and ran all the way to the house. "Maman!" he shouted. "It is I, Jean. I am home for good!"

Madame Audubon came running. So did Rosa. Captain Audubon followed them, looking grave. "I am sorry, Papa, but I cannot work with David," Jean said. "I cannot paint plaster casts. I want to paint living things. Please let me stay home!"

Captain Audubon looked at his wife. "Oh, please!" she said. He nodded. "Very well, you may stay home and study—until I can think of a plan for you," he said.

Jean was happy again. All day long he sat on the riverbank, reading and drawing. Slowly, the birds began to look right. Their little claws seemed to clutch at the branches. Their tails looked real.

11. Why does Jean run away from the naval academy?

(A) There are no drawing lessons.

B He fails his classes.

C He gets in trouble for drawing.

D His mother is sick and needs him.

12. What does Captain Audubon do when Jean returns home from David's studio?

A He punishes Jean.

(B) He allows Jean to study at home.

C He forces Jean to return to the studio.

D He apologizes to David.

13. Jean dislikes David's studio because it is —

A cold and dark

B dirty and smells bad

(C) filled with lifeless statues

D located far from where Jean lives

14. What event happens FIRST in the story?

A Jean goes to Paris to study drawing.

B Jean goes to the naval academy.

C Jean learns to draw birds very well.

(D) Jean does poorly in his school lessons.

15. **What can you tell about Maman from reading the story?**

   A She wants Jean to be a seaman.

   (B) She understands how Jean feels.

   C She wants to help Jean run away.

   D She worries that Jean will learn to draw.

16. **Jean goes to the naval academy because —**

   A his father wants him to learn how to draw boats

   B his father wants him to stop running away

   C he wants to be a sailor

   (D) he is not doing well with his lessons

17. **How are David's studio and the naval academy ALIKE?**

   (A) The work is dull and not what Jean wants to do.

   B The walls are filled with drawings of birds.

   C Jean's teachers are bad tempered.

   D There are statues that are difficult to draw.

18. **Where is Jean happiest during his childhood?**

   A in David's studio

   (B) at the family's country home

   C at the naval academy

   D on the seawall and the docks

19. **Which word BEST describes Jean at the end of the story?**

   A lively

   B careless

   (C) happy

   D amused

20. **The author wrote this story to —**

   (A) entertain readers with a story about an artist

   B give information about a famous art school

   C persuade readers to study wildlife drawings

   D explain how to draw animals that look real

21. **What is the MAIN problem in the story?**

   A Jean likes his classes but not his teachers.

   B Jean's father is angry with him about his poor lessons.

   (C) Jean and his father do not agree about plans for Jean's education.

   D Jean loves to play music, but his father wants him to be a sailor.

The Candlewick Book of Fairy Tales: Rapunzel

Retold by Sarah Hayes

There was once a poor peasant who lived next door to a witch. He and his wife longed for a child, and eventually their wish was granted. As the day drew near for the baby to be born, the peasant's wife began to spend all her time gazing at the vegetables in the witch's garden. At last she could stand it no longer.

"Husband!" she cried. "You must fetch me some of the rampion that grows in the witch's garden, or I shall die." The peasant looked at his wife and saw how pale she had become, and he knew she spoke the truth. When it was dark, he climbed over the high wall and dropped into the witch's garden. He quickly dug up a few rampion roots, which he took back for his wife. She ate the rampion greedily, and by morning she was asking for more. This time the witch was waiting in her garden when the peasant climbed over the wall.

"He who steals my rampion will pay for it with his life!" shrieked the witch.

"It is f-for my w-wife," stammered the peasant. "She will die without it, and the baby too."

The witch thought for a moment. "Give me your baby and I shall spare your life." The peasant was so terrified that he agreed, and as soon as the baby was born, the witch came and took it away. She called the baby Rapunzel after the rampion the peasant had stolen from her garden.

Rapunzel grew up to be a beautiful girl with very long golden hair. On the day of her twelfth birthday, she was taken into the forest by the witch and shut up in a high tower that had neither a door nor stairs. Whenever the witch wanted to go to Rapunzel's room, she stood at the foot of the

tower and said, "Rapunzel, Rapunzel, let down your hair." Then Rapunzel let her hair hang down from the window, and the witch grabbed hold of it and clambered up the wall.

Rapunzel was often lonely in her room, and sometimes she would gaze out across the forest and sing sad songs. One day a king's son was out hunting when he heard the beautiful sad singing and rode toward it. He looked up at the tower, but he could not see Rapunzel's face, for the window was too high. He searched in vain for a door or a stairway and vowed he would return the following day.

True to his word, he came the next day, and the next. On the third day the king's son saw the witch arrive at the tower, and he quickly hid behind a tree. He heard the witch call for Rapunzel, and watched the golden hair come tumbling down and the witch go climbing up. He waited until the witch had gone, and then he came to the foot of the tower.

"Rapunzel, Rapunzel, let down your hair!" he cried, and the golden hair came tumbling down. In a moment he had climbed up the tower and entered Rapunzel's room.

Rapunzel was very frightened at first, for she had never seen a man before. But the king's son visited her every day, and soon she fell in love with him. Every time he came, the king's son brought a skein of silk. And while the witch was away, Rapunzel sewed the silk to make a ladder so that she could escape from the tower and marry the king's son. Soon the ladder was nearly finished, and Rapunzel could think of nothing but her escape. One day she said to the witch without thinking, "Why is it that you take so long to climb the tower? The king's son is with me in an instant."

Then the witch knew that the king's son had been to visit Rapunzel, and she was furious. She took a pair of scissors and cut off all Rapunzel's golden hair.

Then she sent her away to wander in the desert. She fastened the hair to the windowsill and sat down to wait. Toward evening the king's son arrived and cried out, "Rapunzel, Rapunzel, let down your hair!" The witch threw the golden hair out of the window and in an instant the king's son was up

the tower. When he reached the window, there, to his horror, was the witch, who shrieked out, "Your singing bird has flown the nest. Cat got her first; your eyes are next!"

The king's son was so overcome with grief that he threw himself out of the window. He fell onto a thornbush, which scratched his eyes and blinded him. For a year he wandered sorrowfully about the world until one day he came to a desert and heard the sweet sad voice of Rapunzel, whom he thought was dead. When she saw his poor blind eyes, Rapunzel began to weep. And as her tears fell on his eyes, the king's son began to see again.

Rapunzel and he were soon married, and they lived happily ever after.

[Rampion is a vegetable grown in Europe. It is rather like a radish, but the roots taste sweeter. The roots are either boiled or eaten raw.]

22. **How does the witch get up to the tower?**

   A She asks Rapunzel to open the door.

   B She flies up on a broom.

   C She climbs up on a ladder.

   (D) She uses Rapunzel's hair as a rope.

23. **What happens AFTER Rapunzel turns twelve?**

   (A) She is taken into the forest.

   B She returns to her parents.

   C She lives with the witch.

   D She suddenly becomes pretty.

24. **This story was written to —**

   (A) entertain readers with a make-believe story

   B persuade readers to eat rampion

   C warn readers about witches

   D inform readers about eating vegetables

25. **Why does the king's son bring Rapunzel a skein of silk?**

   A to make pretty hair ribbons

   B to weave into a lovely dress

   C to knit into a warm blanket

   (D) to sew a ladder to escape

Left page (262)

26. **Why does the witch send Rapunzel to the desert?**

    (A) to keep her away from the prince

    B to give her a better place to live

    C to let the people hear her sing

    D to set her free from the tower

27. **Why does the peasant agree to give up his child?**

    A He wants to save his wife's life.

    B He hopes the witch will like him.

    (C) He fears the witch will kill him.

    D He wants her to become a princess.

28. **Why did the witch cut off Rapunzel's hair?**

    A to weave it into a wig

    (B) to trick the prince

    C to bring it to Rapunzel's father

    D to make Rapunzel ugly

29. **This story takes place —**

    A in a large city

    B on a dairy farm

    C on a desert island

    (D) in a make-believe kingdom

30. **The tower stands for Rapunzel's —**

    A anger

    B fear

    (C) loneliness

    D joy

31. | Rapunzel is a singing bird that has flown the nest. |

    This sentence is an example of —

    A simile

    (B) metaphor

    C alliteration

    D hyperbole

This page may not be reproduced without permission of Steck-Vaughn

Right page (263)

Japan
by David F. Marx

1. Japan is a country in Asia. It is made up of many islands, large and small. People who live in Japan are called "Japanese." That is also the name of the language spoken in Japan.

2. Japan has four large islands where most people live. Their names are Hokkaido, Honshu, Shikoku, and Kyushu. Not many people live on the hundreds of smaller islands that are also part of Japan. Some are too tiny to build a house on!

3. Japan is surrounded by water. To the west is the Sea of Japan. To the east is the big Pacific Ocean. If you sail east across the Pacific Ocean, you'll reach California in the United States. To the west, across the Sea of Japan, are Japan's neighbor countries: South Korea, North Korea, China, and Russia.

4. Tokyo, the capital of Japan, is on the island of Honshu. It is home to more than eight million people. Tokyo is an exciting, crowded city. From Tokyo, you can see the Pacific Ocean to the east and Mount Fuji to the west. Mount Fuji is the tallest of Japan's many mountains. Its peak, or top, is 12,338 feet above the sea.

5. Most of Japan's 123 million people live in Tokyo and other big cities. These include Yokohama, Osaka, and Nagoya. Many people who live in these cities work in businesses such as stores, banks, and factories. Cars, computers, and televisions made in Japan are used by people all over the world.

6. Japanese people earn a living in other ways, too. Living on the seacoast, many people catch and sell fish and seaweed. These are important foods in Japan. Living along rivers, farmers grow rice in soggy rice paddies. In Japan, rice is eaten with almost every meal. Living near mountains, some people work in mines. These people dig useful rocks out of the ground. Japanese people have learned to live in a place where the land meets the water, and where the mountains reach to the sky.

This page may not be reproduced without permission of Steck-Vaughn

Lower left page (264)

Look at the map of Japan. Use it to answer questions 32 and 33.

32. **Which country is closest to the island of Kyushu?**

    A North Korea

    (B) South Korea

    C China

    D Russia

33. **If you were traveling from Mt. Fuji to Nagoya, what direction would you travel?**

    A north

    B south

    C east

    (D) west

34. **Which of these sentences from the passage is an OPINION?**

    A To the east is the big Pacific Ocean.

    B Tokyo, the capital of Japan, is on the island of Honshu.

    (C) Tokyo is an exciting, crowded city.

    D Japanese people earn a living in other ways, too.

35. **Which foods are eaten the most in Japan?**

    A meat and cheese

    B vegetables and fruits

    (C) fish and rice

    D beans and corn

36. **What is the main idea of paragraph 5?**

    (A) Most Japanese live and work in large cities.

    B Japan has a population of 123 million people.

    C The largest cities in Japan are Tokyo and Yokohama.

    D People who live in big cities have many different jobs.

37. **What is the BEST summary of the passage?**

    A Many people live in Japan, a group of islands located near China, North Korea, South Korea, and Russia. Japan has mountains.

    B Japan has many people. The capital of Japan is Tokyo, and 8 million people live there.

    C Many people in Japan work in factories or catch and sell fish. Other people live on islands.

    (D) Japan is an Asian country made up of four islands. Most people live and work in the big cities, but some earn a living in other ways.

This page may not be reproduced without permission of Steck-Vaughn

Lower right page (265)

The Big Play

"I am so sick of that play I could scream!" Josie said through gritted teeth. Leon nodded in agreement. "I know the part better than she does." They were talking about their friend Sarah.

"All we do now is help Sarah practice," Rob complained.

The three friends were sitting in the school lunch room waiting for Sarah. She had asked them to come to play practice.

"There you guys are!" Sarah said as she dashed in. "Well, come on!" She turned and hurried out without waiting for a reply.

The three friends stood slowly and trudged into the school auditorium. They took seats in the back. As the actors started saying their lines, Rob, Josie, and Leon mouthed the words along with them.

"Marie," Clint said to Sarah, "there's a big storm brewing. It looks bad!"

"Oh, dear," Sarah answered, using her most frightened voice, "listen to the wind!"

Suddenly a man shouted, "STOP! This is TERRIBLE!!!" Mr. Biggs, the director, stomped onto the stage.

Sarah looked as if she were going to burst into tears. "What's wrong?" she asked in a trembling voice.

"Do you hear a storm?" he yelled. "Does it sound like rain and thunder? NO, it does not! I have no idea why I agreed to direct this mess."

"Mr. Biggs?" Clint raised his hand as if he were in class. "You can get different sounds from the Internet. Then we can play them, and it will sound stormy."

"HOW are we going to play them?" Mr. Biggs demanded angrily. "We don't have the money for that fancy equipment. I should never have agreed to direct this play. I quit! I will not do this because it can't be done." He turned to walk off the stage, and Sarah did, in fact, start to cry.

"Wait a minute!" Josie leaped from her seat and ran down the aisle. "Mr. Biggs, wait a minute. Can you put a microphone backstage?"

The director stopped and looked at Josie. "I suppose so. Why?"

"Please, keep practicing now. And give me until tomorrow. Have that mike backstage for me then."

Mr. Biggs looked at her suspiciously. "What are you up to, young lady?" His words were nearly drowned out by the actors, pleading with him to continue. "All right! All right! We will continue today, but just for today."

Josie hurried back up the aisle and motioned for her friends to follow. Once outside the auditorium, she explained her plan.

The next day, after school, Josie's grandpa arrived at the auditorium carrying a big box. The three friends were waiting for him.

"Josie," Grandpa said, "fill this watering can with water. You boys help me unpack this stuff. Where's the microphone?"

In a few minutes they had everything set up.

"Well?" Mr. Biggs's voice boomed from the front of the curtains. "Are we having a play or are we not?"

"We are, sir," Josie said into the microphone. "Start the action."

Just as Clint said his lines, Rob blew gently into the microphone. The sound of wind filled the stage. After Sarah's line, Leon hit a tin cookie sheet with a spoon and shook it while Josie poured water from the watering can onto another cookie sheet. Thunder and rain echoed across the stage.

Quickly Rob picked up a piece of wood and, holding it by the microphone, knocked on it twice. Right on cue, Sarah said her next line, "There's someone at the door! Quick! Come in!" Josh walked on stage and began his lines.

"STOP!" Mr. Biggs shouted. "Everybody on stage, including the people by the mike."

With long faces, fearing the worst, the actors, Josie, Rob, and Leon came on stage, and so did Josie's grandpa.

When Mr. Biggs saw him, he started to grin. "Ed, I might have known this was your work." Mr. Biggs explained that he and Josie's grandpa had acted in the town's Little Theater group for several years. "So how did you get roped into this?" he asked Josie's grandpa.

"I used to work in radio, remember? I'm just helping the kids get started with the sounds. Then they're on their own."

"They'll need to practice some more before opening night," Mr. Biggs said. "The play must go on!"

The actors cheered and Sarah gave Josie, Rob, and Leon big hugs.

The night of the play, the three friends stood expectantly backstage waiting for the curtain to go up. As Sarah said her lines, they made the sound of rain and thunder. She paused, waiting for the sound of knocking. As Rob reached for the piece of wood, he stopped. Josh was not waiting behind the door. He was late! Quickly Rob blew more heavily into the

microphone. Leon bashed the cookie tray harder. Josie poured more water onto the cookie sheet. They could not see what was happening onstage. Then they heard Sarah making up lines. "It sounds like it might be a tornado, Frank! The storm is getting worse! My garden will be washed away!" At that moment, Josh scooted to the set door. Rob grabbed the wood and knocked. "Quick! Come in!" Sarah said, her voice full of relief.

The rest of the play went smoothly. As the curtain went down, Sarah dashed back to her friends. "Come on," she insisted, "you're taking the curtain call with me. You saved the play TWICE!"

38. Which word BEST describes Josie?

A grateful

B playful

C curious

(D) clever

39. What is one lesson the characters learn in this story?

A It is good to take one step at a time.

(B) Friends can work together to solve a problem.

C It is important to be the best actor.

D People should learn to act in plays.

40. What is another lesson the characters learn in this story?

A Sound effects can ruin a play.

(B) An older person's experience can be helpful.

C Radio is better than the Internet.

D It is difficult to be the director of a play.

41. Which of these could BEST be added at the end of the last paragraph?

A Josie decided to try out for the next play to see if she could get a starring role.

B Mr. Biggs was pleased because the play went very well.

(C) Sarah led her friends onstage, and they bowed as the crowd clapped loudly.

D The friends worked hard learning to make new sounds.

42. Why is Mr. Biggs so angry at the beginning of the story?

(A) He thinks the play will be bad.

B He wishes he had better actors.

C He is tired of directing the play.

D He wants more time to practice.

43. Why is it helpful that Josie, Leon, and Rob know all the play's lines?

A They help Sarah learn her lines.

B They might want to be in the play.

C They can take the place of any actor who is sick.

(D) They know when to make all the different sounds.

44. MOST of the action in the story takes place in —

A a classroom

(B) a school auditorium

C a house

D a lunch room

45. What happens AFTER Mr. Biggs stops the play for the second time?

(A) He recognizes Josie's grandpa.

B He refuses to direct the play.

C Josie fills a watering can with water.

D Josie asks him to keep practicing.

46. How are Sarah and Josie ALIKE?

(A) Both girls think quickly to solve a problem.

B Both girls get angry very quickly.

C Both girls are very impatient.

D Both girls want to be popular.

Sound Effects

1 Would you like to hear a train whistle? The wind whistling in the trees? Almost any sound can be found on the Internet. But sounds were not found there first. Sound effects began on the radio. At first, in the 1920s, radio programs did not need special sounds. Air time was filled with music. Sometimes there were speeches. By the 1930s, people were listening to "soap operas." These stories were on the radio every week. There were many other drama shows as well. All these stories needed special sounds.

2 At first, people who made the sounds were not very good. Often, programs used just music. Usually someone played an organ. That was the least expensive way to get music. Many kids' adventure shows used organ music to show changes of scene or mood. Organists were not given sheet music. They had a sheet of paper with words like "danger" or "countryside" written on it. They made up music that went with the action. Making up music was a difficult task. The shows needed other sounds, too. Sounds helped move the story along. If a person walked down a path to get somewhere, listeners wanted to hear footsteps. These had to seem real.

3 Some sounds were recorded. These were sounds that were too large to bring into a radio station. Car engines or the "walla-walla" sounds of large crowds were recorded. Other sounds, such as those made by animals, were also recorded. It would be hard to get a cricket to chirp exactly when needed.

4 Many simple sounds were made during the program. People used ordinary objects to make the sounds. Any water noise was made with a bucket and some water. Twisting cellophane made the sound of a crackling fire. To make footsteps in snow, someone squeezed a box of corn starch. The sound of a pen on paper was made by scratching sandpaper with a paper clip. Thunder was made by shaking a metal sheet. Two coconut shell halves hit

together made the sound of horses' hooves. The sound of wind was made by blowing into a glass jar or simply by blowing softly into a microphone.

5 Many radio stations had a "crash box." This was used to make sounds like breaking dishes. A metal can filled with nails, broken coffee cups, pennies, and gravel can make any sort of crashing noise. A "gravel box" was made of wood and filled with a layer of garden gravel. Blocks of wood "walked" across the gravel to make the sound of boots.

6 Sounds were important to radio stories. They made the stories seem more real. Sound effects make the difference between a good show and a great show.

47. Which of these sentences BEST summarizes paragraph 3?

A   The sound of a car engine could not be made easily.

B   Sometimes a cricket chirp or animal sound was recorded.

C   Some sounds were made during the program.

(D)   Sounds that were difficult to make were often recorded.

48. According to the article, which of these would you MOST LIKELY hear on radio in the 1920s?

A   a drama

B   an adventure show

(C)   music

D   a "soap opera"

49. What is the main idea of paragraph 4?

(A)   Many sounds were made with simple objects.

B   Anyone can make a water noise with a bucket and some water.

C   The sound of a crackling fire can be made with cellophane.

D   Radio programs had many different sounds.

50. Which of these sentences is an OPINION?

A   People used ordinary objects to make the sounds.

B   The sound of a pen on paper was made by scratching sandpaper with a paper clip.

C   Thunder was made by shaking a metal sheet.

(D)   Sound effects make the difference between a good show and a great show.

51. From the passage, you can tell that —

A   making different sound effects is fun

B   there were a lot of programs on the radio

(C)   radio organists were very skilled musicians

D   many people used to listen to the radio

52. Why did the author write this passage?

A   to entertain readers with an old story

(B)   to tell readers about the history of sound effects

C   to describe how different sounds are recorded

D   to show what is used to make sound effects today

53. Recorded sound effects are DIFFERENT from the sound effects made during a radio program because the recorded sound effects —

A   are made using a microphone

B   can sound like the noise of a storm

(C)   provide sounds made by animals

D   can sound like the footsteps of someone walking

Use "The Big Play" and "Sound Effects" to answer questions 54 and 55.

54. Both authors would PROBABLY agree that —

A   there are many ways to make the sound of a storm

(B)   sounds make a drama more interesting

C   putting on a play is very hard work

D   radio is more interesting than a play on the stage

55. Both passages tell about —

A   making crash sounds with a gravel box

B   how the sound of a crackling fire is made

C   how sounds are recorded

(D)   people making sound effects with ordinary objects

Eduardo is in fourth grade. He wrote this report about a special week in school. He wants you to help him revise and edit the report. Read it and think about the changes he should make.

Job Week

(1) When our class had Job Week, we got to hear many speakers. (2) We had a visit from dr. Thomas, who works at the hospital, and we also heard about Mrs. Edward's job at the zoo. (3) I liked the field trips best of all.

(4) First we went to the Oriole Shipping Company. (5) We saw how big trucks were loaded with boxes from different companys. (6) We saw the way the drivers had to keep track of everything on the truck and know where it was supposed to be dropped off.

(7) Then we went to the public library. (8) When I first heard we were going there, I thought it would not be interesting. (9) Last year we visited a restaurant and saw how meals were prepared. (10) We met the librarian, and he showed us all the different ways to find information. (11) One special area was called the "reference section." (12) We saw all kinds of books about every subject we could imagine. (13) For example, there were books on explorers, animals, art, music, and plants. (14) Then we had a treasure hunt. (15) We were put into teams, and each team was given a list of questions to answer. (16) Our team had to find out the height of the Statue of Liberty, and who Henry Hudson was. (17) We had a fun time answering our questions, and now I know where to find things in the library.

56. What change should be made to sentence 2?

(A)   change dr. to Dr.

B   change hospital to Hospital

C   change zoo to Zoo

D   make no change

57. Which sentence does NOT belong in this report?

A   sentence 3

B   sentence 6

(C)   sentence 9

D   sentence 12

58. What change should be made to sentence 5?

A   change boxes to boxs

B   change different to diferent

(C)   change companys to companies

D   make no change

59. Which sentence could BEST be added after sentence 17?

A   The shipping company was fun, too.

(B)   I think this visit was the best part of Job Week.

C   The school library is not nearly as big as the public library.

D   I found an interesting book about dogs.

60. What is the purpose of this report?

A   to persuade classes to go on field trips

B   to invite a speaker to talk about jobs

C   to explain how to have a Job Week

(D)   to tell what students did during Job Week

Russell is in fourth grade. He wrote this report about the parrot fish. He wants you to help him revise and edit the report. Read it and think about the changes he should make.

Parrot Fish

(1) Some of the most interesting creatures in the ocean are parrot fish. (2) They have beaks just like birds. (3) Parrot fish eat mostly plants and they use their beaks to take a bite of coral every now and then.

(4) They have two sets of teeth. (5) The first set is the one you see at the end of there mouths. (6) They use these teeth to bite off plants and coral. (7) Then they uses their second set of teeth to grind the food into tiny pieces.

(8) Parrot fish swim all the time and do not rest. (9) They often travel in groups, so they're sometimes called the "cattle of the sea."

(10) When a parrot fish wants to sleep, it made a thick slime. (11) It takes about half an hour for the slime to cover the parrot fish's body. (12) It is like a sleeping bag. (13) In the morning, the parrot fish takes about thirty minutes to get out of the sack.

(14) Parrot fish are about twelve inches in length and live in the coral reefs by australia. (15) They are very colorful and strange!

61. Which word from sentence 3 is a pronoun?

A mostly

B plants

Ⓒ they

D then

62. What change should be made to sentence 7?

A change teeth to tooths

Ⓑ change uses to use

C change pieces to peaces

D make no change

63. What change should be made to sentence 10?

A change wants to want

B change it to they

Ⓒ change made to makes

D make no change

64. What change should be made to sentence 3?

Ⓐ add a comma after plants

B change beaks to beak's

C change the period to a question mark

D make no change

65. The author wrote this report to —

A entertain readers with a story about fish

B persuade readers to buy fish as pets

Ⓒ inform readers about an unusual fish

D describe several saltwater fish for readers

66. Which sentence is the main idea of the second paragraph?

Ⓐ sentence 4

B sentence 5

C sentence 6

D sentence 7

67. What change should be made to sentence 14?

A change inches to inchs

B add a comma after length

Ⓒ change australia to Australia

D make no change

68. Which sentence could BEST be added after sentence 9?

A They help coral reefs by eating algae that should not be growing there.

B Some people think they look like cows.

C Cattle usually go together in a herd.

Ⓓ They head toward certain feeding places together as the tide goes in or out.

69. What change should be made to sentence 5?

A change first to furst

Ⓑ change there to their

C change mouths to mouthes

D make no change

At the end of the testing session,

Say *Stop. The testing session is over. Check to be sure that you have circled the correct answers completely. Erase any stray pencil marks. Then put down your pencil.*

If using the Practice Test Answer Sheet, ask students to make sure they have written their name and circled the *B* on the Practice Test Answer Sheet. Then collect all answer sheets from students. Have students put their books away. If students marked their answers in their books, ask them to turn in their books or remove and turn in the test pages.

After scoring all student tests, refer to the Correlation Charts on pages T32–T33. Identify the reading and language arts skills that individual students or most of the students in the class had difficulty with on the test. Use this information to plan additional work on these skills.

Lena is in fourth grade. She wrote this journal entry about making a class newspaper. She wants you to help her revise and edit the entry. Read it and think about the changes she should make.

Our Newspaper

(1) Our class made a newspaper. (2) We called it *Super News,* and we had to write news stories about our school.

(3) Each of us got to be a reporter and ask questions about things that were happening? (4) I reported on the fall festival that was going to be held in the gym. (5) I talked to Principal Edwards about it. (6) In my article I explained what each booth was about, who was helping out, when and where the festival would be held, and why we were having the festival. (7) I did not get to go to the festival last year.

(8) After we had written our stories, we found pictures on the computer that went with each story. (9) Then we put all the stories together and numbered the pages. (10) We checked to make sure each word was spelled correctly. (11) Finally, we printed copys of the paper and handed them out. (12) We even put our stories and pictures on Mrs. Barrow's website. (13) Now almost anyone in the world can read about our school.

70. **Which word from sentence 4 is a verb?**

   Ⓐ reported

   B fall

   C in

   D gym

71. **What change should be made to sentence 3?**

   A add a comma after <u>reporter</u>

   B change <u>questions</u> to <u>questions'</u>

   Ⓒ change the question mark to a period

   D make no change

72. **What change should be made to sentence 11?**

   A change <u>Finally</u> to <u>Finaly</u>

   Ⓑ change <u>copys</u> to <u>copies</u>

   C change <u>handed</u> to <u>handded</u>

   D make no change

STOP

Achieve It! Class Progress Sheet

Student Name	Practice Test A Score	Practice Test B Score
1.		
2.		
3.		
4.		
5.		
6.		
7.		
8.		
9.		
10.		
11.		
12.		
13.		
14.		
15.		
16.		
17.		
18.		
19.		
20.		
21.		
22.		
23.		
24.		
25.		

Blackline Master 2

Achieve It! Practice Cards Student Record

Unit Number	*Put It to the Test* Score	Practice Cards Assigned	Date of Completion
	_____ out of _____		
	_____ out of _____		
	_____ out of _____		
	_____ out of _____		
	_____ out of _____		
	_____ out of _____		
	_____ out of _____		
	_____ out of _____		
	_____ out of _____		
	_____ out of _____		
	_____ out of _____		

Name _____ Date _____

Achieve It! Practice Test Answer Sheet

Practice Test A or B (Circle one.)

Read each item on the *Achieve It!* Practice Test. Circle the letter of the correct answer.

Sample			
A	B	Ⓒ	D

1. A   B   C   D
2. A   B   C   D
3. A   B   C   D
4. A   B   C   D
5. A   B   C   D
6. A   B   C   D
7. A   B   C   D
8. A   B   C   D
9. A   B   C   D
10. A   B   C   D
11. A   B   C   D
12. A   B   C   D
13. A   B   C   D
14. A   B   C   D
15. A   B   C   D
16. A   B   C   D
17. A   B   C   D
18. A   B   C   D
19. A   B   C   D
20. A   B   C   D
21. A   B   C   D
22. A   B   C   D

23. A   B   C   D
24. A   B   C   D
25. A   B   C   D
26. A   B   C   D
27. A   B   C   D
28. A   B   C   D
29. A   B   C   D
30. A   B   C   D
31. A   B   C   D
32. A   B   C   D
33. A   B   C   D
34. A   B   C   D
35. A   B   C   D
36. A   B   C   D
37. A   B   C   D
38. A   B   C   D
39. A   B   C   D
40. A   B   C   D
41. A   B   C   D
42. A   B   C   D
43. A   B   C   D
44. A   B   C   D
45. A   B   C   D
46. A   B   C   D
47. A   B   C   D

48. A   B   C   D
49. A   B   C   D
50. A   B   C   D
51. A   B   C   D
52. A   B   C   D
53. A   B   C   D
54. A   B   C   D
55. A   B   C   D
56. A   B   C   D
57. A   B   C   D
58. A   B   C   D
59. A   B   C   D
60. A   B   C   D
61. A   B   C   D
62. A   B   C   D
63. A   B   C   D
64. A   B   C   D
65. A   B   C   D
66. A   B   C   D
67. A   B   C   D
68. A   B   C   D
69. A   B   C   D
70. A   B   C   D
71. A   B   C   D
72. A   B   C   D

Achieve It! Practice Card Answer Sheet

Read the items on the *Achieve It!* Practice Card. Mark your answers on this sheet. Circle the letter for each correct answer.

Practice Card Number _____

1. A	2. A	3. A	4. A	5. A
B	B	B	B	B
C	C	C	C	C
D	D	D	D	D

6. A	7. A	8. A	9. A	10. A
B	B	B	B	B
C	C	C	C	C
D	D	D	D	D

Practice Card Number _____

1. A	2. A	3. A	4. A	5. A
B	B	B	B	B
C	C	C	C	C
D	D	D	D	D

6. A	7. A	8. A	9. A	10. A
B	B	B	B	B
C	C	C	C	C
D	D	D	D	D

Blackline Master

5

Venn Diagram

Complete the Venn Diagram. Show the ways you and your partner are alike, different, and the same.

Support from Text

Write your conclusion. Then write your supporting details.

Conclusion

Detail

Detail

Detail